hn Rawls

Philosophy Now

Series Editor: John Shand

This is a fresh and vital series of new introductions to today's most read, discussed and important philosophers. Combining rigorous analysis with authoritative exposition, each book gives a clear, comprehensive and enthralling access to the ideas of those philosophers who have made a truly fundamental and original contribution to the subject. Together the volumes comprise a remarkable gallery of the thinkers who have been at the forefront of philosophical ideas.

Published

Forthcoming

John Rawls

Catherine Audard

ACUMEN

In memory of John Rawls

First published in 2007 by Acumen

Acumen Publishing Limited
Stocksfield Hall
Stocksfield
NE43 7TN
www.acumenpublishing.co.uk

ISBN-10 1-84465-050-2 (hardcover)
ISBN-13 978-1-84465-050-7
ISBN-10 1-84465-051-0 (paperback)
ISBN-13 978-1-84465-051-4

British Library Cataloguing-in-Publication Data

A Catalogue record for this book is available from
the British Library.

Typeset in Century Schoolbook by
Newgen Imaging Systems (P) Ltd, Chennai, India.
Printed and bound by Cromwell Press, Trowbridge.

Contents

Acknowledgements

This book is dedicated to the memory of John Rawls, with whom I had the privilege of working during my French translations of *A Theory of Justice*, of *Political Liberalism* and of a collection of his recent papers. He was always extremely approachable and a wonderful person, as well as the great mind we all admire. He fundamentally changed the way in which so many others and I envisaged political philosophy as a normative analysis, even if I may differ on some issues in view of my own "continental" background.

I would like to thank my students and colleagues at the London School of Economics, as well as at the École Normale Supérieure in Paris, for helpful discussions, suggestions and criticisms. I would also like particularly to thank John Gray, Jürgen Habermas, Cécile Laborde, Tom Nagel, Onora O'Neill, Thomas Pogge and Joseph Raz for conversations about their own appraisal of Rawls' philosophy. Kok-Chor Tan, Rex Martin and John Tasioulas discussed my interpretation of *The Law of Peoples* in a very helpful way. My particular thanks go to Nick Bunnin, who read the first drafts. Lastly, my thanks go to my husband, Alan Montefiore, for his endless patience and support throughout the writing of this book.

Abbreviations

CP   *Collected Papers*, S. Freeman (ed.) (Cambridge, MA: Harvard University Press, 1999)

CPrR   Kant, I. *Critique of Practical Reason* [1788], tr. Lewis White Beck (Indianapolis, IN: Bobbs-Merrill, 1976)

IO   Habermas, J. *The Inclusion of the Other* (Cambridge: Polity, 1999)

IPRR   "The Idea of Public Reason Revisited" in *LOP* 1999: 131–80

JAFR   *Justice as Fairness: A Restatement*, Erin Kelly (ed.) (Cambridge, MA: Harvard University Press, 2001)

LHMP   *Lectures on the History of Moral Philosophy*, Barbara Harman (ed.) (Cambridge, MA: Harvard University Press, 2000)

LOP   *The Law of Peoples* (Cambridge, MA: Harvard University Press, 1999)

ME   Sidgwick, H. *Methods of Ethics* [1874], 7th edn with a preface by John Rawls (Indianapolis, IN: Hackett, 1981)

PL   *Political Liberalism*, rev. edn (New York: Columbia University Press, 1996)

RH   "Reply to Habermas" in *PL* IX: 372–434

TJ   *A Theory of Justice*, rev. edn (Oxford: Oxford University Press, 1999)

Introduction

No book of political philosophy since I read the great classics of
the subject has stirred my thoughts as deeply as John Rawls' *A
Theory of Justice*.   (H. L. A. Hart, 1975: 230)

There is a wide consensus that John Rawls is one of the major thinkers
of the twentieth century in the Anglophone world. His work covers
and has reshaped most of the major issues of contemporary political philosophy, from constitutional law to distributive justice, from
citizenship to economic efficiency, from global ethics to religious toleration, from cultural pluralism to forms of democratic consensus, etc.
Moreover, most of these topics derive from his own analysis of the relation between ethics and politics: they did not exist as such before. Most
of contemporary political philosophy has been nurtured by his seminal
ideas and can be understood either as a follow-up or a criticism and a
reaction against them. Thus, no student or scholar of the discipline can
ignore them. Still, for most of his life, Rawls lived the life of a university professor at Harvard. "An exceptionally modest and retiring man",
in the words of Ben Rogers,[1] "he consistently refused the honours he
was offered, and declined to pursue the career as public commentator
opened to him by his achievements. He never wrote about himself,
and virtually never gave interviews.[2] Nevertheless, his most important
book, *A Theory of Justice* – written during the Vietnam war – became
required reading for students of philosophy, politics, economics and
law all over the world, and, in that way, Rawls has influenced several
generations".[3] Indeed, the book, which sold more than 300,000 copies

in the US alone and has been translated into every available language, transformed the study of political philosophy.[4] Single-handedly, Rawls reclaimed the field of political philosophy and social justice after decades of neglect.

How and why did that happen?

It is difficult, now that Rawls is an established and well-recognized figure, to recapture the novelty and the controversial nature of his theory when it was first known through his early papers and, then, through the systematic account of *A Theory of Justice*. Many commentators have insisted on "the new departure" that his work represented. They have emphasized quite rightly that political philosophy at that time had practically ceased to exist and how Rawls' substantive conception and method, when it was first formulated in his 1958 paper "Justice as Fairness", changed the situation beyond recognition.

The first point to notice is how remarkable Rawls was among most professional philosophers of the time in showing a deep understanding of the new moral sensitivity, that marked the post-World War II period. The second point is to realize how isolated he was on the philosophical scene at the time, distancing himself from the main currents of utilitarianism and linguistic philosophy. One thing philosophers can do, if they cannot change the world, is to try to understand it. This means, following Hegel's expression, to try to capture the *Zeitgeist*, leading us to a better understanding of the world we live in. Thus it is important to understand the cultural and political context that constitutes the subtext of Rawls' theory of justice, even if it is certainly not easy to contextualize such an abstract and "ideal" conception. Nevertheless, without an appreciation of its historical surroundings and of the formative experiences of its author, it would be very easy to misunderstand the reasons behind Rawls' main thesis, *the priority of justice*.

The new political normativity

A new world order and normativity were emerging after World War II and Rawls, as a young soldier in the Pacific, New Guinea, the Philippines and Japan,[5] and, then, as an academic during the students' protests of the late 1960s, was a witness to all of this. He sought to translate into first principles of political morality the new sensitivity to moral issues and to questions of justice expressed after the horrors of the Jewish Holocaust[6] and the Nuremberg trials and, then, the anti-Vietnam war demonstrations, the civil rights movement,[7] the rise of humanitarian concerns and of NGOs such as Oxfam, Amnesty International, Human Rights Watch, or the dissident movements in the Soviet bloc. We should not forget that he was a contemporary of the first Universal Declaration of Human Rights of 1948 and of the creation of the major international institutions as well as of the Helsinki Declaration of 1975. One should understand Rawls' forceful defence of the priority of equal basic liberties as stemming from these historical experiences of the human rights revolution as do his defences of civil disobedience and of conscientious objection. At the same time, he saw consumerism and the instrumentalization of politics on the rise in Western societies, even if young readers of Herbert Marcuse on campuses all over the world fiercely rejected them in 1968. A controversial transformation of Western democracy into some sort of "market democracy" was taking place. He saw the increasing decline and devaluation of political liberties and participation. He notes, for instance, that, "in a modern democratic society, taking a continuing and active part in public life generally has, and may indeed reasonably have, a lesser place in the conceptions of the (complete) good of most citizens" (*Justice as Fairness: A Restatement*, hereafter *JAFR*: 143).[8] Reacting against such devaluation of politics, he sought to revive the ethical core of democratic citizenship. One should note here that Rawls' understanding of the democratic ideal is very broad. It includes both its political and social aspects, as it did for Tocqueville. Rawls is as much interested in mentalities and in the background culture as in the institutions specific to constitutional democracies. Democracy includes the ideal not only of self-government and political autonomy, but also of a society of equals and of equal respect for persons as ends in themselves, not simply as means, ideals that had been destroyed both by totalitarian and fascist regimes and the rise of consumerism. Giving back its dignity to a quasi-republican conception of citizenship is one of the results of Rawls' conception of justice, as is clear from his 1995 "Reply to Habermas", even if he himself distinguishes his views from the classical neo-Roman republicanism of Machiavelli or Rousseau. Indeed, one important thesis that I want to advance in this book, and which I present in Chapter 4, is that Rawls' conception of justice is aimed at *empowering citizens* through a better understanding of the deep moral and political values that should regulate their social and political institutions. However, such an endeavour was going to meet with fierce resistance from a deeply entrenched ideology in the American psyche: utilitarianism and market democracy, which dominated welfare economics, moral philosophy, philosophy of law, indeed the whole realm of democratic thought at the time.

Rawls was indeed alerting his readers to the dangers of a political system where

> The nature of the decision made by the ideal legislator is not ... materially different from that of an entrepreneur deciding how to maximize his profit by producing this or that commodity, or that of a consumer deciding how to maximize his satisfaction by the purchase of this or that collection of goods.[9]

In a paper given in Paris on the occasion of the publication of the French translation of *A Theory of Justice*, Ronald Dworkin describes the state of democratic thought at the time and the reasons for Rawls' impact: "the dominant opinion (among judges) is that some kind of *market democracy* should decide, that is, that the most popular point of view shared by the majority of the people at one moment or another should be the one judges should adopt".[10] This is precisely the conception of democracy that was fiercely rejected by principled citizens during the demonstrations and protests that were taking place in the name of justice and equality at the end of the 1960s. Some of the more extreme were also anti-capitalist, rejecting consumerism, economic growth and the search for material prosperity as being the causes of the decadence of the democratic ideal and were in favour of socialism even at the cost of individual freedom. The name of Marx[11] is hardly mentioned in *A Theory of Justice*, but we should not forget that, at the time, it was everywhere, beside the names of Mao and Herbert Marcuse! Indeed, this is somewhat reflected in one important argument of the theory of justice, where a central role is given to defending the "worth" of basic political liberties against mere "formal" equality,[12] in an echo of Marx's criticism of "bourgeois" formal rights. The genius of Rawls has been to try to capture the meaning of the dilemma and to show that, in the end, it is possible to reconcile democratic rights and freedoms with social justice – human rights and respect for persons with economic efficiency. According to *A Theory of Justice*, this reconciliation was based on the priority of justice as a *moral* requirement over the values of economic growth and prosperity. Such a controversial claim was bound to be rejected both by socialists, as it did not sufficiently denounce as unjust unequal distributions as such,[13] and by libertarians, as it meant regulating the market through a public conception of justice.[14] Politically, Rawls appears to be both an expression of his time, as he typically expresses the concerns of the liberal left of the 1960s, and a precursor of a "third way" between libertarianism and social democracy. His advocacy of a new conception of social justice that would, beyond the limitations of the capitalist welfare state, take as its benchmark for justice the needs and aspirations of fully participating citizens in a modern constitutional "property-owning" democracy has certainly influenced most progressive parties in Europe (*JAFR*: 135).[15] It would also be very interesting to assess how influential his views have become beyond the limits of the liberal Anglophone world.

Not only was Rawls deeply influenced by the human rights revolution that took place in the 1960s, but he has also been very much aware of the new social movements of the 1970s and 1980s, which brought about the *feminization* and *ethnicization* of injustice, the demands for public recognition of identities and of the cultural, religious and moral diversity that characterizes contemporary pluralist democracies, a fact that he describes as the "fact of reasonable pluralism" in his later work. Coming from a fairly classical liberal background, he has tried to accommodate new moral concerns, such as the communitarian anxiety most ably articulated by Charles Taylor, that no democratic society can survive over time without affirming a common conception of the good. The challenge, for him, in spite of numerous criticisms, has been to show how and why, in spite of new political and social developments, justice as fairness is still the best approximation we can find of principles fit for a democratic context.

The main idea of justice as fairness

Philosophically, too, Rawls' theory of justice as fairness was groundbreaking. At the time, it did not square well with the dominant trends. Its main thesis, the priority of justice, was inspired by Kant and in direct opposition to the dominant ways of theoretical thinking such as utilitarianism, on the one hand, and linguistic moral philosophy, on the other. Such a thesis was grounded in a long tradition of moral and political philosophers, which Rawls knew exceptionally well and valued, even if, at the time, political philosophy as modelled on the likes of Plato, Aristotle, Rousseau, Kant and Hegel was nearly extinct.

Against these two trends of utilitarianism and linguistic philosophy, Rawls was affirming, first, the priority of justice over welfare in the self-understanding of a well-ordered democracy, and secondly, the legitimacy of philosophically discussing substantive issues even when conceptual tools were not yet fully satisfactory or even available. There is a *sense of urgency* running through *A Theory of Justice* that should be stressed and kept in mind, because we tend to read it now as an "official" view of what liberal democratic values should be. But this was not the case then and it took courage for him to turn his back on utilitarianism, "a view that has long dominated our philosophical tradition and continues to do so" (*TJ*: 46), and on linguistic philosophy. He claims instead that "it is obviously impossible to develop a substantive theory of justice founded solely on truths of logic and definition" (*ibid.*: 44), or "deduced from self-evident premises" (*ibid.*: 19), which was, after all, the ambition of most linguistic philosophers at the time. From the beginning, Rawls wanted to contribute to the *practical* justification of principles and his theory "in no way concerns itself with the sense of ethical expressions or their linguistic meaning" (1951, *CP*: 8). This was absolutely new.

I now turn to the main questions that Rawls addresses in his major book and to the conclusions that he reaches. One is obviously aware by now that justice for him does not mean the institution of civil and criminal justice, but the *virtue* of justice applied to institutions, though not to individual actions, and that his aim is to define more sharply the ideal of a just and well-ordered society in terms that fully express its basic values: freedom and equality. Moreover, one should note that for that purpose he adopts a limited point of view, that of an "ideal conception" of justice or of what he calls an ideal of "strict compliance" in a well-ordered society where everyone is expected to act justly and to uphold just institutions (*TJ*: 8). This can be puzzling, as injustice seems to be more obvious a topic for political philosophy. However, he hopes to establish in this way firm guidelines that can then be adapted to deal with injustice, such as the theory of punishment, the doctrine of just war, the principles of international law, or forms of opposition to unjust regimes such as civil disobedience, conscientious objection and even militant resistance and revolution, and forms of institutional injustice. Of these pressing empirical topics, only a few are addressed in *A Theory of Justice*, some will appear in the later work, but it is clear that one should not expect a full theory of justice in the usual institutional sense. Instead, the conceptual foundations are the main concern of the analysis.

Justice as fairness is the new philosophical interpretation of the democratic ideal of justice that he is advancing in *A Theory of Justice* as an alternative to utilitarianism, perfectionism and intuitionism and as an answer to the major controversies in democratic thought over the correct balance between freedom and equality. It is important to note that Rawls is not discussing justice in the void, but with respect to a specific historical context: contemporary constitutional democracies.

Part I of *A Theory of Justice* presents the main ideas of the theory and offers both a set of first principles and a method of justifying them as the desirable or preferable conception of justice, given our fundamental considered convictions. If the principles advanced by Rawls are far from new, the *justification method* is the most innovative part of the book and demands careful examination as it is open to contradictory interpretations. One rapidly notices that the principles of justice are not derived from any specific moral doctrine such as the Kantian notion of respect for persons and of their inherent worth and dignity, which would ground the main democratic values in a straightforward way. As Charles Larmore notes, "Why, we may ask, should there be such a reluctance to admit these assumptions?" (Larmore, 1999: 623). Rawls apparently fails to bring out as clearly as he should have done the moral assumptions of his conception. This may be seen as a fault. He appears unable to make the moral basis of his doctrine fully explicit.[16]

I argue instead that this is not the case, and that such a moral basis is precisely the issue for Rawls as it is problematic and calls for interpretation. It is the result, not the starting point, of the enquiry. It is true that this point is only clearly argued for in his later work, *Political Liberalism* (*PL* hereafter). Still, my interpretation of the unity of Rawls' project is that it aims to generate the justification of justice, not to impose it from the start. This is a central point. No moral doctrine can play such a *foundational* role as this would contradict the very autonomy of the persons concerned and impose on them values that are possibly not fully theirs. *Political morality is not straightforward applied moral philosophy.* The genius of Rawls is to switch the onus on to the justification process itself so that the moral doctrine of equal respect for persons can be adopted as a *result* for political purposes, not as a starting point. Citizens can then autonomously and reflectively begin the process of finding accommodation between their personal morality and the public ethics of a functioning democracy.

> The principles of justice are not derived from the notion of respect for persons, from a recognition of their inherent worth and dignity ... this is not a suitable basis for arriving at these principles. It is precisely these ideas that call for interpretation ... the theory

> of justice provides a rendering of these ideas but we cannot start
> out from them. (*TJ*: 513)

This is, of course, especially important in the case of new citizens
with no or very little familiarity with democratic political values. To
answer this central difficulty, Rawls has developed a new method that
he describes later as *doctrinal autonomy* (*PL*: 98) and that has not
always been fully understood, as I claim in Chapter 1. By that he
means a doctrine that is itself autonomous in its *practice of justification* and expresses its respect for persons not as a value or a foundation
for its principles, but as a method. In that sense, instead of departing from the search for universal principles, he seeks to anchor them
more effectively in citizens' autonomy. The gap between ethics and
politics, in the sense of the discrepancy between personal and political
values, is to be overcome by citizens themselves, not by submission
to one single dominant conception of the good. Rawls' political philosophy is new in that it places respect for autonomy *practically*, not
theoretically, at the heart of his doctrine in the method of justification itself. The best way to respect democracy's main values – citizens'
autonomy and fairness to all concerned – is to embody them in a
fair practice of justification that leaves them free to decide. The justification process itself has to be fair, hence the expression "justice
as fairness", meaning that justice is not a formal treatment of persons, but takes into account and recognizes their specific situations
and needs too.[17] However, such an interpretation of the theory of
justice in *practical terms* and of the unity of Rawls' work is not obvious, and Rawls' method has been widely misunderstood, as I argue in
Chapter 3.

Part II, *Institutions*, deals with institutional justice, the way the principles can be applied to institutions to properly protect equal liberty
for all and fair distributive justice. Part III, *Ends*, is the more controversial part of the book as it deals with questions of feasibility and
stability, and argues that the public conception of justice as fairness
is not only *desirable* but also *reasonable* and *realistic*. It may generate a widespread moral consensus and a common sense of justice. This
aspect of the book has been heavily criticized, as it seems to assume the
possibility of unanimous agreement on principles of justice and does
not fully recognize the plurality of ends that characterizes a democratic society. Rawls' second book, *Political Liberalism*, has been read
as seeking to advance a more realistic answer to the problem of stability and consensus. One should now understand Rawls' work as having

two distinct parts. In the first one, basically in the first part of *A Theory of Justice*, he seeks the best public principles of justice that are true to our deepest moral intuitions as regards political and economic justice. In the second part, in *Political Liberalism* and in his later work, he argues that such principles that have proved to be attractive and fully justified in the first stage are also realistic, not out of "an unwarranted accommodation to power" or "a willingness to compromise justice in the face of the course of the world" (J. Cohen, 1993: 281 and 285), but because they may be supported by a plurality of genuine moral reasons, and by the free exercise of "public reason".

Rawls' first principle of justice addresses the issue of constitutional rights and liberties and says that each person is to have an equal right to a scheme of equal basic liberties compatible with a similar scheme for others. Stringent protections for basic liberties are granted; in particular the *fair value of political liberties* is to be guaranteed, ensuring citizens' full participation in the political process.

The second principle addresses the issue of socioeconomic inequalities and of distributive justice. It states that only inequalities that meet the following two conditions can be justified: *fair equality of opportunity* must obtain, guaranteeing that all equally talented people have equal access to desirable positions, and inequalities attached to such desirable positions must benefit the least advantaged, according to the *difference principle*.

Rules of lexical priority apply: as in a lexicon, the first principle must be fully applied before the second can be implemented. In other words, what is striking about Rawls' conception is that the two aspects of justice – citizens' civil and political rights, on the one hand, and socioeconomic rights, on the other – are strongly united in a concept of *democratic equality*. Rawls' aim is indeed to overcome the tension between liberty and equality that has marred democratic thought for so long, and to offer an argument that makes them inseparable.

As I mentioned earlier, the innovative justification process is equally meant to embody an ideal of fairness and respect for persons that is missing in utilitarianism. Principles of justice are not imposed upon citizens and derived from a superior authority, but are shown to be the result of their generalized agreement as free and equal persons willing to cooperate on a fair basis. This agreement is modelled on a reworking of the traditional idea of a *social contract*, transposed to the choice, not of the best political regime, as for Locke, Hobbes or Rousseau, but of first principles of justice. Such a justificatory process should express respect for citizens' autonomy and moral powers: it is fitting for a democratic society of equals. It should respect their equal dignity and fundamental interests, not simply their rational advantage as in the case of a traditional social contract. Rawls' main idea that justice is prior to considerations of welfare is embodied in the justification process too.

Ethics and politics

Such a bold construction claimed to offer the possibility of a normative critique of politics that had almost disappeared since Rousseau, Kant and Hegel. In contrast, the reaction of mainstream analytical philosophers such as Richard Hare was predictable: philosophy has not much to contribute to normative politics and should keep away from it for fear of subjectivism. In his damaging review of *A Theory of Justice*, Hare writes: "What he [Rawls] says about [normative political questions], however popular it may prove, is unsupported by any firm arguments" (Hare in Daniels, 1975: 82). Hare goes on to say that Rawls is advocating "a kind of subjectivism ... making the answer to the question 'Am I right in what I say about moral questions?' depend on the answer to the question 'Do you, the reader, and I agree in what we say?' " (*ibid.*).

In fact, Hare is inadvertently pointing to a central issue, that effectively the *reader* is at the centre of Rawls' preoccupations, especially the reader as representative of fellow citizens and of their most urgent concerns and considered judgements. The distinctive character of justice as fairness is that it is an analysis that starts, as Sidgwick did, with common-sense views that constitute the "traditions" or the background public culture of contemporary democracies.

> There are questions which we feel sure must be answered in a certain way. For example, we are confident that religious intolerance and racial discrimination are unjust. We think that we have examined these things with care and have reached what we believe is an impartial judgement not likely to be distorted by an excessive attention to our own interests. These convictions are provisional *fixed points* which we presume any conception of justice must fit.
> (*TJ*: 17–18, emphasis added)

These "fixed points" provide the context and the starting point for philosophical analysis. Rawls has in effect changed the nature and role of political philosophy beyond recognition, making it the self-reflection of informed citizens of a well-ordered democracy, not the discourse of a philosopher–king. In a later work, his "Reply to Habermas" (1995), Rawls writes:

> In justice as fairness, there are no philosophical experts. Heaven forbid! But citizens must, after all, have some ideas of right and justice in their thoughts and some basis for their reasoning. And students of philosophy take part in formulating these ideas but always *as citizens among others.*   (*RH*: 426–7, emphasis added)

Legitimate anxieties naturally remain over the value of these "given" moral intuitions and their fitness as starting points. Are they not biased or prejudiced? Is there a way of overcoming their epistemic and moral limitations? In what sense is Rawls right to claim that he is not an intuitionist, relying on first intuitions that cannot be justified or ranked satisfactorily?[18] Why trust common sense and our considered intuitions in the first place? This is obviously a major objection that will have to be addressed in the course of our discussion.

However, one may agree with Rawls that these intuitions are distinct from beliefs informed within an authoritarian or totalitarian social and political system. Rawls believes that, in some important ways, democratic institutions provide the necessary tools and protections that allow ordinary citizens to develop their "moral powers", their sense of justice and their conception of the good, as well as the corresponding cognitive powers of judgement and reasoning. There is a connection in Rawls, well analysed by Richard Rorty,[19] between philosophy and democracy, even a priority of democracy over philosophy, that has changed the nature and scope of the philosophical exercise. This is revolutionary in that it affirms that citizens in free societies are now the "experts". They have access to the means of information, communication, deliberation and reflection that are necessary for an informed sense of justice as well as a rational sense of their own good and the good of others. Their sense of justice is informed, not prejudiced, because they live in a free society where information, comparison, reflection and free discussion on issues of justice as well as full political participation (*TJ*: 205) are permitted. In that sense, the philosopher is the translator of a conception of justice that is already there and the theory only spells out more clearly and explicitly our considered judgements in order to constitute a valid and shared point of view for assessing justice among reflective and free individuals. The main point is to give a voice to what it means to be citizens of a well-ordered democracy.

> Rather than seeing Rawls's work as adopting the authority of philosophy or theory, as a kind of scientist addressing reality or fellow experts, we are more apt to see him as adopting the position of a citizen of a democratic regime, addressing his fellow citizens.
>
> (Laden, 2003: 384–5)

In the end, the question of what constitutes the *well-ordered society* should be re-examined through what Rawls calls "a constitution of discussion out of which would come reasonable principles of justice" (*Harvard Review of Philosophy*: 39). This is where philosophical analysis may be valuable for the stability of democracy. Addressing the concerns of the citizenry, not only of government, is for him the main aim of political philosophy.

This is even clearer in his second book, *Political Liberalism*. There, Rawls redefines the relation between ethics and politics, limiting his ambition to a critique of politics from the point of view not of a comprehensive doctrine of the good, but from a political conception of justice that assumes a separation between the public and the non-public spheres. The domain of the "political" is the realm of public debates, of citizens and representatives defending laws and policies by reference to reasons drawn from their shared conception of justice: a widely idealized view of politics that seems to undervalue the strategic and competitive side of politics (J. Cohen, 2003: 103). I examine in more detail the meaning of this move toward a political conception of justice in Chapter 4 and discuss the many criticisms and misunderstandings it has given rise to. The interpretation I suggest is that political liberalism is in effect a welcome correction of the theoretical dimensions of *A Theory of Justice*, most visible in Part III, and a return both to the *practical* role of political philosophy and to the ideal of doctrinal autonomy: respect for citizens' freedom to choose how to relate their personal morality to public ethics.

Another new concern has been international justice, a topic that was briefly addressed in *A Theory of Justice*, and has been developed more fully in *The Law of Peoples* (1993, 1999, hereafter *LOP*). In it, Rawls examines the way ethics can apply to international relations in a realistic way, not in the idealized manner of cosmopolitanism for which justice applies to individuals, beyond the system of sovereign nation-states. In his attempt to balance realism and utopia, he seeks to show how it would be possible to extend a moral critique of political institutions to justice beyond borders.

However, one could object that in justice as fairness, the balance between justice and democratic politics tilts in favour of abstract analysis and that Rawls' views verge on utopia. Philosophical and political concepts have not much in common and, as Michael Freeden notes, "many of the versions of political philosophy today display a flight from the political, the crowding out of diversity and the shrinking of the political to an area of constructed consensus guided by a vision of the good life".[20] As Joshua Cohen notes, for a political scientist, Rawls' conception of democracy is fairly disappointing and abstract. "It does not tell us much about the politics of a just society: the processes of public argument, political mobilization, electoral competition, organized movements, legislative decision making or administration" (J. Cohen, 2003: 86). A major criticism of Rawls' theory is that it is unable to address "real politics", that it "subordinates democracy to a conception of justice that is defended through philosophical reasoning and is to be implemented by judges and administrators insulated from politics" (*ibid.*). Rawls has been accused, in particular in a recent debate with Jürgen Habermas,[21] of taking the place of citizens in dictating which principles should be suitable for them. Another similar criticism would be to interpret Rawls as an advocate of the rising role of *judges* and of the judiciary against the legitimate power of elected representatives. Such an interpretation insists on Rawls being too "American", too embedded in an American political culture, in a Republic of judges that may be seen as a threat to democratic decision-making.[22]

The question of the balance between ethics and politics in Rawls' conception of political philosophy is obviously open to discussion. We will certainly need to assess how satisfying his answers are as they are so important for the understanding of the discipline of political philosophy itself. I offer a summary of the debate in Chapter 4 on the occasion of the exchange between Rawls and Habermas on the nature of political philosophy. Rawls himself has often defined the role of political philosophy relative to real politics, albeit in fairly vague and abstract terms.[23] My understanding is that the practical task remains the most important for him. As he writes, "Profound and long-lasting controversies set the stage for the idea of reasonable justification as a *practical* and not as an epistemological or metaphysical problem" (*PL*: 44, emphasis added). The philosopher should articulate normative guidelines, which are already present within the public discourse and the political culture of a modern democracy, and are therefore familiar to citizens, but which are still embroiled in confusions, controversies and obscurities. The task is to think through what we normally take for granted in order to provide a firmer basis for criticism. It is a quasi-Socratic self-revelatory process achieved through a very public conversation among fellow citizens.

Rawls describes *reflective equilibrium* or the mutual adjustment of particular judgements and general principles as the result of such a process of examination and as the real aim of political philosophy (*TJ*: 18 and 42–5). Equipped with more solid convictions and perspicuous principles, citizens, especially new ones, are in a better position to decide and choose for themselves, to elucidate issues crucial for the survival and stability of democratic institutions and practices. Philosophy is not political activism, but participating as an academic in this process of reflective equilibrium certainly has political consequences. In his understated and modest way, Rawls is genuinely a *philosophe engagé*.

The democratic impulse

What is distinctive about Rawls' endeavour is his will to give theoretical structure and systematicity to the moral critique of political power and institutions. However, this is not motivated by a dream of theoretical purity, immune from the complexities of politics. On the contrary, it is inspired by the *democratic principle of legitimacy*: citizens, not God or a superior Legislator, produce the political norms by which they abide. The *democratic impulse* is the key to understanding Rawls' conception of ethics and politics. The ambition of the philosopher is neither simply to observe nor to intervene and to dictate new norms, but methodically to clarify and reconstruct the main normative ideas present in the democratic political culture: justice, equality, freedom and fairness. Political philosophy in the democratic age is thus both modest and empowering. Its aim is to transform common-sense intuitions and beliefs into a working set of empowering principles. *A Theory of Justice* is a theory of empowerment, of justice as the result of the capacity to generate rules for one's own collective life without referring to an external pre-given authority. Normative theory is not only about contents: contents of the law, of the rules and principles, but about processes of communication and justification, of legitimization and obligation. This is the deep meaning of "justice as fairness": that the doctrine itself is fair to all or most citizens and respects their autonomy.

In that sense, Rawls is very much a contemporary of postmodern conceptions of decentred communication networks where the origin of norms is to be found not so much in political authority as in personal critical judgement and public exchanges and discussions. Appeal to judgement, says Rawls, is always necessary because principles only go so far and justification always needs judgement formed through debates and discussions as well as first principles. As Anthony Laden claims, "the search for something like the basis for public justification spans Rawls's career".[24]

The consequence of this understanding of the nature of political philosophy leads to a deep tension that marks all of Rawls' work: the tension between substantive justice and justification procedures. Justice as a constitutive requirement of democratic regimes is not simply the result of treating similar cases similarly or of giving to everyone their due; it is not simply formal. The Nazi regime was formally "just" in the sense that it had laws; it was nevertheless deeply unjust. Justice requires more. However, in a democratic context, there is no obvious agreement on what is required except for some vague humanitarian concerns. Rawls' claim is that only the justification procedure gives validity to certain substantive norms over others. In effect, he is appealing to universal suffrage, to consent and agreement to give content to the claims of justice: that which is just is what is publicly agreed upon by citizens who consider themselves as free and equal, as rational and reasonable and who seek to nullify the inequitable effects of social and natural contingencies. Justice is the outcome of their agreement: it does not rely on an independent and prior criterion.

Looking at the question in this manner leads Rawls to the familiar problems of consensus and the dangers of demagogy. What if all citizens prefer a situation where minorities are discriminated against? What if they all prefer injustice to justice? Appealing to *vox populi* has never been a wise move, especially for philosophers who usually warn against the popular *doxa* that condemned Socrates to death! Are we not bound to ask again for an independent criterion to escape such dreadful results? The genius of Rawls is to have stuck against the odds to this conception of political philosophy as essentially democratic self-understanding in spite of its obvious difficulties and challenges, and to have forged a new idiom for it, a new method, the famous device of the Original Position, that seeks to include democratic representation in the legitimating process itself. His answers, as we shall see, are on the whole extremely complex and sophisticated, sometimes disappointing, sometimes obscure, as they try, not always successfully, to avoid naivety and illusions about the *demos*. However, what is remarkable is that they always appear as "work in progress", as necessitating further debates and explanations. Most readers of Rawls want to participate and add their contribution, because he is simply reconstructing ideas that are familiar, albeit puzzling on reflection. One is often amazed by the huge secondary literature his work has generated on a scale unparalleled in the case of even more important philosophers. One reason is that his style and his *democratic impulse*, not simply his ideas, are responsible for such an outcome. His work has created a huge community of discussion among philosophers, economists, sociologists, politicians, technocrats and even the wider public, as if every citizen had some comment to make and some contribution to add to the whole endeavour. In that sense, Rawls' work is certainly unique.

The democratic impulse goes even deeper. It expresses a profound *moral* commitment to treat persons, readers, colleagues, fellow citizens, etc. with respect as autonomous beings or "ends in themselves", in Kant's language.[25] Rawls believed, following Kant, that from the moral point of view, the most distinctive feature of human nature is our ability freely to choose our own ends and to be responsible for them. It follows, on his account, that the state's first duty to its citizens is to respect their capacity for autonomy – to let them live their lives according to their own lights, and to treat them, in Kant's phrase, "never merely as a means, but always at the same time as an end". Many commentators, most prominently Ronald Dworkin and Charles Larmore,[26] have noted that there is a deep moral inspiration beneath the political and social concerns of *A Theory of Justice*. One interpretation is that respect is the core value on which the whole theory rests, even if it is never expressed as such. This is the approach that this book will seek to develop. One has to recognize this deep moral strand in Rawls' style and his manner of reasoning as well as in his conclusions to fully understand his political philosophy. At each step of the demonstration, Rawls asks whether his views could be justified for someone from a different background, cultural outlook or social class. This is why the question of public justification is so prominent. As Charles Larmore writes:

> Respect is a value on which that theory rests. Respect for persons plays two roles in his conception of justice. It shapes the two principles themselves with their emphasis on the inviolability of the individual – the role, which Dworkin was concerned to lay bare.

It also figures in the demand that persons be treated in ways that they can see to be justified. That is the role of respect underlying the ideal of publicity.   (Larmore, in Freeman, 2003: 374–5)

The main argument developed in this book is that autonomy and respect for persons constitute the deep moral core of Rawls' political philosophy. This explains the continuity and strong unity of his work that, on the whole, have been overlooked or even dismissed.[27] However, the tension between moral and political philosophy, while implicit, is not always properly addressed by Rawls. Autonomy is a moral concept that has difficulties finding its expression in political practices and institutions. One can never claim that real politics is about making citizens conscious that they share in the political power; it is rather the reverse, as Joseph Schumpeter famously argued. Kant himself never claimed that politics could be reconciled with moral imperatives.[28] There is a constant danger, here, of normative theory losing contact with political realities. Free and equal citizens may prove impossible to govern: they cannot easily submit to political power or coercion. Fully rational and reasonable citizens do not need politics as they can manage very well on their own, without the apparatus of the state. How can we make sure that normative political philosophy does not degenerate into sheer utopia?

Interestingly, Rawls refers to his endeavour as "a realist utopia".[29] Justice does not exist, but we need guidelines to fight injustice, to prevent states from treating unjustly their own people and from harming other nations, as well as to punish and sanction them if they seek to do so. For Rawls, it is crucial to show how politics and morality might be reconciled, and to demonstrate how a constitutional regime precisely manages that. "The success of liberal constitutionalism came as a discovery of new social possibility: the possibility of a reasonably harmonious and stable pluralist society" (*PL*: xxvii). Autonomy is not simply a moral value that one pursues, but a condition of legitimacy in the use of political power. This is why the mediation of a public conception of justice between citizens' conflicting claims and arguments is so important for democracies. However, such a public conception of justice must reflect the equal dignity of human beings as ends in themselves and never impose a comprehensive moral argument on the people concerned. It must be "*doctrinally* autonomous" (*ibid.*: 98–9, emphasis added). Equal dignity is at the core of the ideal conception of democracy for Rawls, both politically and epistemically. A theory of justice fit for democracy should aspire to full doctrinal autonomy and prioritize the personal and political autonomy of the people concerned.

Such a strong moral core inevitably collides with Rawls' other ambition to be fair to the plurality of other valuable conceptions of justice that exist in a democratic political culture, such as utilitarianism, meritocracy or perfectionism. One of the major difficulties for the reader is the constant conflict between, on the one hand, Rawls' attempt at understanding people's own considered and deeply held conceptions and ideas of justice, and, on the other hand, the will to push forward his own view of justice as fairness as *the* best interpretation of these very ideas. One obscurity of his major book is probably that he did not succeed in making these two moves sufficiently distinct for the reader. Here, my suggestion is that we should proceed as if we did not know what the preferred solution is and follow all the steps indicated by Rawls in a process of self-discovery. This is only partly successful as such a method is slightly artificial: we learn very rapidly what *the* principles of justice are for Rawls whereas we, the readers, are meant to discover and test them by ourselves. This is the price to be paid for remaining true to what I call the "democratic impulse".

Reading Rawls

It is obvious that no single book could ever do justice to the wide range of questions addressed by Rawls, to the detailed arguments and answers to criticisms developed in a body of work that spans over fifty years as well as to the huge secondary literature that accompanies it.[30] The aims of this introductory book are both to help the reader understand Rawls' main ideas and get a feel for the many challenges that he faces, and to offer a comprehensive and coherent interpretation of his core ideas and of how consistent his answers are. Ever since the publication of his essays from the 1980s and of his second book, *Political Liberalism*, in 1993, there has been a debate surrounding the existence and the nature of a major shift in his thinking, of a "second Rawls", more "contextualist" or "communitarian", no longer Kantian or universalistic but limited to contemporary Western democracies. Richard Rorty (1991) is a good example of such an interpretation.[31] My claim here is that such a shift did not really take place and that, from the start, the theory of justice had practical and political aims: a public conception of justice and its public justification within a democratic context. What happened, then, was a return to these aims that were in fact fairly clearly spelt out in *A Theory of Justice*, as Rorty himself recognizes. In *Political Liberalism*, Rawls realizes that his own attempt at some misleading doctrine of "rightness as fairness" (*TJ*: 15 and 95–6), that is, at a comprehensive doctrine of the good, would contradict citizens' autonomy. This would conflict with his main attempt at providing a conception of justice characterized by "doctrinal autonomy", or full independence from any particular view. One should understand that one of Rawls' unique achievements is this respect for democratic autonomy, not simply as a value but as a methodological and practical imperative of the doctrine itself.

How then should one read Rawls? This is certainly not an easy task in view of his often dense and off-putting prose and the numerous layers of discussion generated by his own seminars and by his extreme attentiveness to criticisms and improvements of his arguments, not to mention again the gigantic secondary literature that now exists. In view of all these difficulties, this guide proceeds simply through a series of themes that are chronologically organized and that cover most of Rawls' main books and articles. It requires reading Rawls as a whole, while being acquainted with the modifications he added over the years, modifications that do not represent, as I said, a radical shift, but more a return to the core ideas.

What are the major texts required for this introduction? In order to master Rawls' central ideas, one should dedicate most effort to reading the first part of *A Theory of Justice* (§§1–30), which is covered by the first three chapters of the book. One major addition to *A Theory of Justice* is his developed argument for the priority of basic liberties, which he offers in *Political Liberalism: Lecture VIII* and which is also essential reading. Then, Chapter 4 presents the "new" doctrine of political liberalism, in contrast to the comprehensive liberalism that Rawls seemed to be previously advocating. He explains the reasons for these modifications in the preface for the revised edition of *A Theory of Justice* (1999) and, even more clearly perhaps, in the introduction to the paperback edition of *Political Liberalism* (1996). These two texts are therefore useful, as is his 2001 *Justice as Fairness*, in which the main ideas of the revised theory are clearly spelt out in Part I (§§1–11). The 1996 edition of *Political Liberalism: Lecture IV* provides a useful answer to the question of political consensus, which forms the focus of Chapter 4. To these texts, one could add "The Idea of Public Reason Revisited" (1997, 1999), which gives a very good introduction to Rawls' own conception of deliberative democracy, a notion that has gained increasing popularity in political theory and that embodies the democratic impulse that I mentioned earlier.[32] This is presented in Chapter 4. Finally, one should turn to Rawls' conception of international justice in *The Law of Peoples*, the discussion of which is presented here in Chapter 5.

It would also be useful for the reader to become acquainted with Rawls' major interlocutors from the history of philosophy. As I mentioned earlier, Rawls was unusual among analytical philosophers in that he remained very interested in the history of philosophy. Martha Nussbaum quite rightly insists that

> Rawls always viewed his work not only as the articulation of a particular theoretical view, but also as an attempt to reclaim the space within which the great thinkers of the tradition worked ... His writing has revivified not only the social contract tradition and the tradition of Kantian ethics, but also the Aristotelian search for the well-lived life, Hume's and Rousseau's theories of moral development, and Henry Sidgwick's account of method in ethics.[33]

Hume's 1740 *Treatise* Part III, Rousseau's 1762 *Social Contract*, Kant's 1785 *Grounding for the Metaphysics of Morals* and his political writings of the 1790s, Hegel's 1821 *Philosophy of Right*, Mill's 1861 *Utilitarianism*, and Sidgwick's 1874 *Methods of Ethics* are constantly present in his arguments.

Finally, the reader should become acquainted with a selection from the major debates in contemporary philosophy surrounding Rawls' work, even if I can only mention here but a few among the most important. In Chapter 1, I discuss Ronald Dworkin's (1977), Jean Hampton's (1980), David Gauthier's (1986) and Martha Nussbaum's (2006) very different critiques of the use of the social contract as well as Brian Barry's (1989 and 1995a) critique of justice as reciprocity and mutual advantage and Michael Walzer's (1983) critique of a unified conception of justice. In Chapter 3, I examine G. A. Cohen's critique of Rawls' egalitarianism and Robert Nozick's libertarian critique of distributive justice as well as John Harsanyi's (1976) discussion of Rawls' *maximin* criterion and Joshua Cohen's important 1989 defence of Rawls' egalitarianism. In Chapter 4, I discuss Jürgen Habermas' (1995) critique of Rawls' political liberalism. In Chapter 5, I discuss the cosmopolitan critique of Rawls represented by various authors, such as Thomas Pogge (1989 and 2002), Charles Beitz (1975 and 2000) and Kok-Chor Tan (2004).

The book is roughly divided into two parts. In the first one, Chapters 1–3, I comment on Rawls' conception of political and social justice and its justification and I follow his own presentation in the first part of *A Theory of Justice*, including some references to changes made in more recent works, in particular *Political Liberalism* and to *Justice as Fairness*, and to the major debates. In the second part, Chapters 4–5, I focus the analysis on Rawls' more practical concerns for stability and political consensus, citizenship and international justice, showing the continuity with the first part of his work.

Chapter 1, after some elucidations of the concept of justice, is dedicated to understanding Rawls' moral philosophy and its core thesis, the *primacy of justice*, as the proper moral answer to the evils that contemporary democracies have had to confront: totalitarianism, fascism, the Jewish Holocaust, genocides, crimes against humanity, mistreatments of minorities and ethnic cleansing, famines and misgovernment, added to the evils of wars and terrorism. As Collingwood once wrote: "The chief business of twentieth-century philosophy is to reckon with twentieth-century history".[34] This is exactly what Rawls embarks upon. I examine Rawls' moral doctrine in its three dimensions. First, I explain that it is a *deontological* thesis on the nature of the right and the good, which means that, inspired by Kant, it argues for the independence of the right from the good as a way of fully protecting the priority of freedom and the moral conception of the person as autonomous. It rejects any derivation of a conception of justice from a shared moral or religious doctrine of the good as a limitation on freedom. Rawls' doctrine is both liberal and deontological; it is a "deontological liberalism" and it opposes teleological doctrines such as utilitarianism, which maximizes utility without first securing rights. Secondly, I show the sense in which it is a *contractarian* conception modelled on the idea of the social contract: justice is not derived from a prior and independent authority such as God, nature or reason, but is the result of a rational agreement or contract between the parties concerned. As a consequence, it may also be understood as a *constructivist* conception that is not derived from facts about nature as naturalistic conceptions would be or as moral realism claims, but that aims solely at constructing a reasonable account of the right recognizable as such by rational and reasonable citizens. Thirdly, I analyse the sense in which justice is, for Rawls, the first virtue of social and political institutions, that is, of *the basic structure of society*. I show how his "holistic" social ontology sets him apart from most liberal thinkers and what its controversial consequences are. I conclude with an analysis of the relation between the theory of justice and *practical reason*. I claim that, in spite of its title, the theory of justice should be understood not as "theoretical", but as essentially practical in the sense that it is an empowering conception of justice. This creates major difficulties that I analyse in the concluding remarks.

Chapter 2 presents a detailed analysis of the various alternative principles or conceptions that best express our sense of justice as citizens of a functioning democracy. It first explains how Rawls' constructivist method is applied and leads to comparing three main groups of principles: deontological, teleological and intuitionist. Then, I go through Rawls' own deontological conception of *justice as fairness* and its two principles, with their priority rules. In particular, I explain why, for him, rewarding *merit* cannot be a principle of justice. Following that, I examine the teleological principle of utility as well as the mixed conceptions that combine it with other principles. I continue with an analysis of perfectionism or the derivation of the right from the claims of human excellence. In the last section, I briefly address the question of intuitionism. Noting that all the principles examined are taken from major moral theories and that Rawls presents us with a Kantian interpretation of principles of justice as categorical imperatives, I conclude with a major concern: is Rawls not confusing moral and political principles? Is it not highly questionable that political morality should be simply an extension of personal morality – a prospect firmly rejected by Kant, for instance, and questionable for Rawls himself as his justification method clearly shows?

Chapter 3 partly answers that concern and presents in some detail the argument from the Original Position. It examines how disagreement among these different principles is to be settled by the justification process, which includes the device of the Original Position with the additional help of independent arguments. I start by defining the Original Position as an interpretation of the idea of a reciprocal social contract and a way of giving objectivity to moral judgements of justice: justice is the result of a rational agreement. I then discuss the particular set-up of the Original Position: the features of the contracting *parties*, and the two series of conditions that apply to them: the *veil of ignorance* and the *primary goods* as *distribuandum*. Thirdly, I explain the structure of the argument and the use of the *maximin* criterion in view of Harsanyi's criticism: justice and efficiency recommend maximizing the benefits for all social positions, especially the position of the worst off, as we ignore which position we will eventually end up in. This leads to a firm rejection of the utility principle under its various forms and to the defence of the principles of equal liberty and of democratic equality. I also examine two of the most important critiques of Rawls' method and principles: the libertarian critique of Robert Nozick and the Marxist critique of G. A. Cohen, as well as Rawls' answers and Joshua Cohen's defence of Rawls. I conclude that, far from being redundant, as many critics have maintained, the device of the Original Position plays a crucial role in the economy of the whole theory and expresses its core ethical content as part of an empowering conception of justice, and can be reinterpreted as an educational device for citizenship.

Chapter 4 turns to the question of feasibility: on what conditions can a public conception of justice be not solely attractive but also feasible and realistic, playing its role at strengthening just political institutions and empowering citizens resisting injustice? I give an overview of the reasons that led Rawls to modify his argument and to produce his later work, *Political Liberalism*, which has been interpreted by many as narrowing the scope of *A Theory of Justice*. I show instead that, contrary to this interpretation, what led Rawls to change his view was an increased concern over questions of justification. As a consequence of their exercise of democratic expressive and associative liberties, citizens can no longer share the same conception of the good, which could justify the principles of justice and their coercive dimension. This is "the fact of reasonable pluralism", which means that people may disagree not only irrationally, given conflicts of power and of ideologies, but also "reasonably", and that dissent, not as a failure but as a fact of reasonable disagreement, is at the heart of democratic and free societies. Justification must take this fact into account. People who do not share the same democratic background culture are still able to understand it and to support their "just" institutions. The demands of *doctrinal autonomy* are thus even more pressing in *Political Liberalism* than in *A Theory of Justice*, and lead to Rawls' notion of a political, not comprehensive, liberalism. From that angle, I address the communitarian critique of Rawls' abstract individualism and the ensuing debate, emphasizing the numerous misunderstandings that characterize it. In the next section, I present Rawls' argument for the possibility of an "overlapping political consensus" in the context of moral disagreement, with a focus on religious conflicts and multiculturalism. The role of *public reason* in providing a strong basis for such a political consensus is examined in the following section, as well as Habermas' critique of political liberalism and Rawls' own "Reply to Habermas" (1995). I conclude with some remarks on the main remaining objections to political liberalism.

In Chapter 5, I discuss Rawls' proposals for international justice, that is, for shared normative principles that would regulate international relations and international public law, or *jus gentium*. I examine first how Rawls came to extend his conception to justice beyond borders and the opposition he faced from both *cosmopolitanism* – or the generalization of justice to any individual on earth – and *realism* – or the belief that justice has no role to play in international relations. I then present his complex position and the many objections it raises. To test it, I turn to three central issues: the cooperation among peoples, including non-democratic ones, and the protection of *basic human rights*; the question of war and the idea of *democratic peace*; and the duty of assistance and of *global distributive justice*. I conclude that, in spite of its many weaknesses, Rawls' conception offers a truly critical theory of how ethics could be applied to international politics in a discriminating way, avoiding the shortcomings of both cosmopolitan idealism and political realism that still objects to international intervention in the name of states' sovereignty.

Chapter 1

The primacy of justice

Each person possesses an inviolability founded on justice that even the welfare of society as a whole cannot override.   (*TJ*: 3)

Introduction

What is characteristic about democratic societies? What is their ambition? Is it to increase welfare and prosperity or happiness or liberty or some other value? For Rawls, it is *justice* and equal respect for persons that is the main distinctive concern, a concern that overrides other legitimate values. "I have tried to set forth a theory that enables us to understand and to assess these feelings about the primacy of justice" (*TJ*: 513).

In this chapter, I explain the main philosophical thesis that is the backdrop for the primacy of justice.

I start with some remarks on the meaning of the *concept* of justice and on the distinctions made by Rawls at the beginning of *A Theory of Justice* and in his later work between conceptions, precepts and principles of justice. In particular, I explain the meaning for Rawls of a conception of justice as impartiality, as mutual advantage and as reciprocity and I discuss Brian Barry's interpretation of Rawls' two theories of justice (Barry, 1989: Ch. 4). I also explain why Rawls refers to Hume's analysis of "the circumstances of justice" (Hume, 1740: III).

In the following sections, I examine three different aspects of the priority of justice. In Section 2, I analyse in what sense Rawls' conception is deontological, that is, claims that justice is prior to the good and independent of it. He argues that this view is distinctive of the political culture of constitutional democracies whereas other societies would derive justice from religious or ideological beliefs.

> Justice cannot be specified by an authority distinct from the persons cooperating, say, by God's law... by reference to a moral order of values, say, by rational intuition, or by reference to what some have viewed as natural law. (*JAFR*: 14–15 and *PL*: 97)

As a consequence, Rawls rejects the *teleological* doctrines of utilitarianism and perfectionism.

In Section 3, I examine two main features of the theory: *constructivism* as a philosophical conception of moral truth, and *contractarianism* as a conception of justification modelled on the idea of a social contract. Principles of justice are constructed by human beings as guides to action in a way that can be rationally justified without appealing to natural rights. The whole scheme should appear to us as if we had chosen it and we should therefore willingly comply with it, even if no society can, of course, be a scheme of cooperation that men enter voluntarily in a literal sense (*TJ*: 12).

In Section 4, I focus on Rawls' claim that justice is "the first or most important virtue of social and political institutions" (*ibid.*: 3). Its subject matter is the system formed by these institutions or what Rawls calls the *basic structure of society*, distinct from the many different individual situations and associations within it that call for "the local justice of associations".[1] Deep injustices originate not solely from individual interactions, but mostly from the basic structure of society. The emphasis on institutions and the social structure is one of the most striking features of the theory that distinguishes it from most liberal views.

Concluding this presentation of Rawls' moral philosophy in Section 5, I reflect on the way Rawls provides a unified conception of justice as a way of empowering citizens and I stress the *practical* dimension of his view that has often been overlooked. Finally, I insist in Section 6 that major difficulties remain, especially in the appeal to instrumental rationality and to the idea of the social contract.

1. Some remarks on the concept of justice

In this introductory section, I present some general remarks on the meaning of justice. If Rawls starts in *A Theory of Justice* with a fairly standard definition of justice, he has enriched it greatly during the course of his thinking. The indeterminacy of the concept of justice calls for many different interpretations and illustrates how political concepts differ widely from philosophical concepts. In particular, Rawls' own concept of justice as fairness is open-textured and, in that sense, ideally suited to its political and practical roles. Its indeterminacy should not be understood as a defect, but given Rawls' *constructivist* and anti-realist view of moral judgement, as an appeal to democratic constructivist interpretations and discussions.[2] Rawls' claim that the process of arbitrating among these competing views should be democratic is consistent with his defence of autonomy; it should be left to the people themselves and should not impose preconceptions. This is the reason why an *a priori* definition of justice is impossible: it is an ongoing process and we need to add more interpretations as we go along, finally reaching a three-dimensional concept of justice as fairness understood as impartiality, mutual advantage and reciprocity, in Rawls' later work.

I analyse first the traditional understanding of justice as both a *personal* and a *social virtue* (1). I move then to the specific *"circumstances of justice"* that give meaning to the concept of justice (2). I explain Rawls' important distinctions between the *concept* and conceptions of justice as well as what he means by theory, doctrine, principles, precepts and criteria of justice (3). I conclude with a discussion of the motivational bases for justice, which helps clarify further the different meanings of justice: justice as impartiality, as mutual advantage and as reciprocity, and I discuss Brian Barry's interpretation of these three concepts (4).

The virtue of justice

Rawls starts his analysis with the traditional or Aristotelian definition of justice as a personal virtue, "a steady and effective desire to act justly", that is, to give each her or his due, whatever that is, but no less and no more. It is the opposite of *pleonexia*, "of gaining some advantage for oneself by seizing what belongs to another ... or by denying a person that which is due to him" (*TJ*: 9–10). Justice is also quite distinct from care, compassion or charity, of supererogatory acts, as it implies a measure of reciprocity and the application of consistent rules. However, justice cannot be simply a personal or private virtue as it presupposes a social conception of what persons are duly entitled to, of their legitimate expectations, as derived from social rules and institutions. Therefore, for Rawls, "justice is the first virtue of social institutions" (*ibid.*: 3). It is the norm that enables assessing how societies fare, exactly in the way truth is the criterion that assesses the validity of judgements, discourses, arguments, theories, etc.

Now, one main idea, to be found for instance in Plato's *Republic*, is that just societies are ordered or stable in the sense that peace is the result of just laws and institutions that people accept and comply with. Justice is instrumental to public order and generates respect for the laws. One sees that justice is tightly connected with ideas of compliance, acceptability and legitimacy. Imagining an idealized situation of strict compliance or an "ideal case" situation, Rawls aims at understanding what a perfectly just society would be like. Three cases are possible. In the first case, order is generated through the pressure of authority, authority of the church, of the state, etc., and justice is said to be derived from an antecedent principle, be it God's will and design, natural law or reason itself. This Rawls describes as the "morality of authority" (*TJ*: §70). In a second case, compliance is the result of the needs and pressures of social cooperation itself: the law is just because it is seen as a source of mutual advantage and social peace, allowing the reconciliation of conflicting passions through appeals to common interests. This is the "morality of association" described by Rawls (*ibid.*: §71). In the third case, or "the final stage of morality as morality of principles" (*ibid.*: §72), people obey the law freely because they reason and understand it as just, not as God's will or as the majority's interest. Justice is disconnected from social order or personal gains and it becomes an independent notion that reflects people's rational autonomy. In Kant's words, this is a stage where people submit to justice for justice's sake.

What is characteristic of the virtue of justice in a democratic society, for Rawls, is that it combines the last two meanings, but excludes the reliance on an independent authority. His main thesis is that justice is the result of an agreement between free and equal persons who wish to protect their main interests both as rational self-interested beings and as moral persons, moved to act through moral imperatives. We should then demystify justice and simply treat it as the result of an agreement under specific conditions on what defines each person's due, or as *pure procedural justice.* "Pure procedural justice obtains when there is no independent criterion for the right result: instead there is a fair or correct procedure such that the outcome is likewise correct or fair, whatever it is, provided that the procedure has been properly followed" (*TJ*: 75).

A good comparison would be with conceptions of truth. If the correspondence theory of truth assumes the existence of an independent basis for valid judgements, of an "authority" in nature or God's design, a consensus conception of truth rejects such an assumption and sees convergence or agreement as the main criterion. Universal suffrage is the guide to truth. Similarly, for Rawls, justice is the result of an agreement reached under specific conditions of fairness, equality, reciprocity, publicity and impartiality, and derived from a normative conception of persons as free and equal. Another such conception would be Jürgen Habermas' *post-metaphysical* communicative ethics (Habermas, 1999: 34–46), which answers similar concerns: how to ground public morality in interpersonal relations and interactions in the absence of any shared independent criterion?

The circumstances of justice

Reasoning about the virtue of justice necessitates a proper understanding of the circumstances of justice[3] or of "the normal conditions under which human cooperation is both possible and necessary" (*TJ*: 109).[4] "Unless these circumstances exist, there would be no occasion for the virtue of justice" (*ibid.*: 110). For Hume, "it is only from the selfishness and confined generosity of man, along with the scanty provision nature has made for his wants that justice derives its origin" (*Treatise*: 495). For Rawls, rough equality of powers and capacities and competition for rare resources, on the one hand, and the necessity of cooperation against conflicting interests and needs, on the other, lead human beings to agree on the binding rules of justice. Without these conditions, the concept of justice loses substance and meaning.[5] We would be reasoning either for a world of continuous struggles and zero-sum games, or for an angelic realm where justice does not make sense. We should instead think in terms of conflicts that need to be arbitrated.

> Although a society is a cooperative venture for mutual advantage, it is typically marked by a conflict as well as by an identity of interests. There is an identity of interests since cooperation makes

possible a better life for all than any would have if each were to live solely by his own efforts. There is a conflict of interests since persons are not indifferent as to how the greater benefits produced by their collaboration are distributed, for in order to pursue their ends, they each prefer a larger to a lesser share.

(*TJ*: 4, 109 and 456)

The *subjective* circumstances are human vulnerability, relative equality of physical and mental powers, and limited altruism as well as the value and necessity of social cooperation against conflicting first-order interests and life plans. The *objective* circumstances are moderate scarcity of resources. However, Rawls does not strictly follow Hume's analysis on one major point. To these circumstances he adds, in his later work, a very important fact, "the fact of reasonable pluralism" or of the existence in open and free societies of insoluble ideological conflicts among citizens. As a consequence of the exercise of basic rights and liberties, expressive and associative liberties in particular, there exists a plurality of comprehensive but opposed doctrines as well as of forms of social cooperation (*JAFR*: 197). The historical and social circumstances of justice in modern democracies include the fact of reasonable pluralism, its permanence and the knowledge that only the oppressive use of state power might end it. Pluralism, as we shall see at length in Chapter 4, is the hallmark of modern democracies for Rawls. In this situation, reason itself is limited and cannot aim at unanimity: this is the fact of the "burdens of judgment"[6] as the source of reasonable disagreements in open societies.

The role of an appeal to the circumstances of justice is to ground firmly in reality our use of the concept of justice and to avoid the numerous confusions that surround it, in particular with care, compassion and humanity, or with peace and order. One of the many misunderstandings surrounding Rawls' conception is that it ignores an *ethics of care*, which is central, in contrast, for feminist ethics. One can argue that more than justice is needed and that care, compassion and humanity should not be discounted in the name of justice. However, this does not mean that justice should be conflated with care and humanity. As Martha Nussbaum and others have shown, care and compassion can be part of our sense of justice where emotions play a central role (*TJ*: 42); however, the meaning of the concept of justice is distinct from that of care or compassion.[7] We need justice for a social world where arbitration is needed between conflicting interests, but where people understand the value of cooperation, a world that is neither a utopian

Golden Age nor a state of senseless wars of all against all, but that is *ours*.

Concept and conceptions of justice

Let us now move on to the meaning for Rawls of the concept of justice and to the distinctions that he makes at the beginning of *A Theory of Justice* between the concept of justice, on the one hand, and conceptions, principles, precepts and theories of justice, on the other (*TJ:* 5–6).

The *concept* of justice has a core meaning on which we can all agree, says Rawls. "Institutions are just when no arbitrary distinctions are made between persons in the assigning of rights and duties and when the rules determine a proper balance between competing claims to the advantages of social life" (*ibid.:* 5). Whereas any rational and reasonable person can agree upon such a general idea, it leaves room for interpreting the meaning of arbitrariness and for disagreement as to how to specify this balance and what criteria to use. "Men disagree upon which principles should define the basic terms of their association" (*ibid.*). "Thus, it seems natural to think of the concept of justice as distinct from the various conceptions of justice and as being specified by the role which these different sets of principles, these different conceptions, have in common" (*ibid.*). We thus need something else to give a specific content to the concept of justice.

We need a *conception* of justice that is constituted of two parts: principles and criteria. First, we need general guiding *principles*. Principles are distinct from *precepts* even if they play the same role. Simple common-sense precepts of justice such as "to each according to his effort", "to each according to his contribution" or "to each according to his merit", or even Marx's precept "from each according to his capacities to each according to his needs"[8] do not possess the required consistency to function as first principles (*TJ:* §47–8). They are too contradictory. For instance, persons are fully equal as free agents, but at the same time, their contribution to society is necessarily different and unequal. Political principles are thus distinct from distributive principles. Secondly, we need *criteria* for departing from simply judging similar cases in a similar way, for what Henry Sidgwick called a "reasonable motive for justifying making distinctions".[9] We need "to single out which similarities and differences between persons are relevant in determining rights and duties and which division of advantages is appropriate" (*ibid.:* 5). A conception of justice should clearly single out the main *criteria* for applying the general principles to specific situations.[10] Mill, in his 1843 *System of Logic*, equally appealed to intermediate principles or *axiomata media* as intermediaries between the general normative principles and specific applications. Rawls' *maximin* rule, or the requirement to improve the situation of the worst off, is such a criterion.

Conceptions of justice are the various interpretations of the concept of justice that are immanent in the political culture of different societies. Theories of justice, however, try to systematically spell out the different principles and criteria that correspond to people's actual and often confused sense of justice and to their considered opinions in a convincing and coherent way, so that citizens can recognize more clearly what they share and what they disagree upon. "One may think of a public conception of justice as constituting the fundamental charter of a well-ordered human association" (*TJ*: 5). Rawls' ambition, here, is both philosophical and practical: to bring about a clarification of what we mean by justice and to show how this clarification helps us assess our institutions.

There are several possible interpretations of the core meaning of a shared concept of justice because our own *considered judgements*, however confident we may be of their value, are not always convincing for other members of society. Considered judgements of justice stem, for instance, from our indignation at the injustice of and condemnation of slavery and serfdom, of religious persecution and the subjection of the working classes, of the oppression of women, of unlimited accumulation of vast fortunes, of the hideousness of torture and the evil of pleasure of exercising domination (*TJ*: 17–18 and for an inclusive list, see RH: 431). These are non-negotiable emotions and strong feelings that we cannot always account for in arguable terms. They can also clash with first principles that we ourselves still recognize as convincing. An *intuitionist* philosopher will claim that a conception of justice is simply made up of a bundle of intuitions that cannot be explicated and systematically organized. A *constructivist* philosopher such as Rawls claims that this is not enough and we need to construct a more unified and systematic account of our intuitions and of our principles, because they are open-textured and hence stand in need of interpretation. More importantly, they are in conflict and need to be reconciled for democracies to develop peacefully. Theories of justice have therefore both theoretical and practical objectives.

A theory of justice should then help to establish a convincing *reflective equilibrium* between intuitions and principles, and also among fellow citizens; this is an equilibrium reached through reflection, which adjusts intuitions and principles. Inspired by Nelson Goodman, Rawls sees reflective equilibrium as the result of a two-way process of evaluating principles against beliefs and beliefs against principles (*TJ*: 18–19). Reflective equilibrium, with the device of the Original Position and the use of public reason, are the three methods of justification that Rawls appeals to at various stages in his theory. This notion has become increasingly important for Rawls because it provides a template of what it means to be a reflective citizen. It also involves the role of public reason, discussion and deliberation in transforming citizens' judgements and in empowering them. I develop all these aspects of the importance of reflective equilibrium both here (Section 5) and in Chapters 3 and 4.

A theory of justice, then, is distinct from a conception of justice, in that it provides arguments, even if those are not final, for first principles that can serve as a "public conception of justice" and that are acceptable from different angles and viewpoints. Through its argument and justification process, a theory helps us to move from the level of intuitions and convictions to one of shared meanings and understandings between people with different sets of beliefs.

Rawls uses a vivid comparison to explain his point. "A useful comparison here is with the problem of describing the sense of grammaticalness that we have for the sentences of our native language" (*TJ*: 41 and n. 25). We, as native speakers of our language, possess an "ability to recognize well-formed sentences" or a "competence" – to use Chomsky's vocabulary – that is the starting point for any "theoretical constructions that far outrun the ad hoc precepts of our grammatical knowledge. A similar situation presumably holds in moral theory" (*ibid.*). As citizens of democratic societies, we possess a capacity for discriminating between just and unjust institutions or policies without distortion (*ibid.*: 42) that is the basis for philosophical theories of justice.

We end up with the following three-level structure.

(1) The "sense of justice" or the widespread moral sentiments[11] and considered convictions that exist in a democratic context at any point of time and place constitute a first level (*ibid.*: 17). These can even, says Rawls, "include views critical of the concept of justice itself (some think Marx's view is an example)" (*JAFR*: 31).[12] Let us call this the level of the *given*, as Rawls' constructivism is a weak form of constructivism that starts with given

facts from social and historical developments and human nature. These intuitions may be fairly organized within the political culture of various societies and expressed in "general" conceptions of justice in various and sometimes conflicting manners, illustrated in the history of democratic thought (*TJ*: 54–5). They provide various precepts and maxims.

(2) At the level of philosophical construction, we find various theories of justice that articulate the distinct structure of these conceptions, Rawls' being one of them. They include first principles as well as *criteria* of justice in order to apply the general principles (*PL*: 16; *JAFR*: 97). They vary greatly between *intuitionism*, where no ordering is possible; dominant-end conceptions, where one single principle applies to the whole social system (such as *utilitarianism*); and *pluralistic* conceptions such as Rawls' justice as fairness, where the various principles are lexically ranked and questions of priority, priority of liberties over equality, for instance, find an answer. Isolating this structure help citizens to decide which is the preferred alternative.

(3) Finally, once they see more clearly which is the best option, it is the responsibility of citizens to order their personal convictions and the public principles of justice in a rational and reflective way, to place them in *reflective equilibrium* through the use of public reason so that they acquire the required stability.

Note that levels 2 and 3 are absent from undemocratic and illiberal societies and regimes where the common conception of justice is neither publicly agreed nor discussed. In contrast, citizens of a well-ordered democratic society may affirm the same conception of justice, not however as the result of dominant shared values, which would contradict their political and moral autonomy, but as the "mutual adjustment of principles and considered judgments" (*TJ*: 18–19 and *JAFR*: 29–31). Rawls insists that the mediation of a public conception of justice is the main feature of a *well-ordered society*, whereas a society may be ordered by a dominant religious or philosophical ideology and still be unjust because it does not appeal to people's public reason. "A society is well-ordered when it is not only designed to advance the good of its members but when it is also effectively regulated by a public conception of justice" (*TJ*: 4).

This means that once the various guiding principles are institutionalized (*ibid.*: Part II) and become part of the public culture, the sense of justice develops and progressively shapes citizens' moral understanding of their political world (*ibid.*: Part III). Through that complex route of both public and personal ethics, Rawls believes that justice may lead to stability and social order, not in an instrumental but in a constitutive way, in keeping with people's autonomy.

The motivational basis of justice: mutual advantage, impartiality and reciprocity

One additional difficulty remains: what motivates us to be just, to comply with just laws, institutions? Justice is not only a vague open-textured and "contested" concept that constantly needs interpreting, even negotiating; it also features very different motivational bases. Whereas in authoritarian societies, fear of punishment, of exclusion and banishment would be the main motivational basis, democratic societies appeal to three very different ideas that need reconciling: justice as mutual advantage, impartiality and reciprocity. Such reconciliation has become increasingly important in Rawls' later work and has been contested by Brian Barry's critique of Rawls (*PL*: 16–17; *CP*: "Justice as Reciprocity").

Justice as mutual advantage

The first aspect of the concept of justice is *prudential*, and its motivational basis would be expected mutual advantage or the promotion of our wellbeing at an acceptable cost to ourself and to others. Rawls agrees with a long tradition of moral and political philosophers that, without justice as a mutually beneficial cooperative scheme, societies cannot flourish and, still less, survive, and the interests of the self are thus harmed. Justice represents a rational and prudential sacrifice of part of our good for the sake of a greater good: more security and stability. Its motivational basis is thus firmly grounded in the "goodness" or "usefulness" of justice. Without certain binding rules and "a system of cooperation designed to advance the good of those taking part in it" (*TJ*: 4), societies cannot survive because of the conflicts inherent in them. As Socrates famously replied to Thrasymachus in the *Republic*, "do you think that a band of robbers and thieves, or any other gang of evil-doers could act at all if they injured one another?"[13] Even they need justice in that etiolated sense! Glaucon reminds us that justice is a necessary price to pay and a rational constraint on our pursuits, in order to gain social peace and order. "It pays to make a pact neither to commit nor to suffer injustice. It was here that men began to make laws and covenants, and to call whatever the laws decreed 'legal' and 'just'. This is ... both the origin and the essence of justice" (*Republic*, II 359a–b). In that limited sense, justice equates with order. It means stability or security measured by the advancement of the good of individual persons and the avoidance of destructive conflicts between them. Even unjust persons, who cannot act for justice's sake, says Socrates to Thrasymachus, will recognize the virtue of justice as an indirect source of *mutual advantage*. It leads to a lesser good, as Glaucon says to Socrates, than if we were totally free to act, but to a greater good than if we were threatened all the time by other members' pursuits: "Justice is a compromise; it is not cherished as a good, but honoured out of inability to do wrong" (*ibid.*). As Brian Barry says, "Justice is the name we give to the constraints on themselves that rational self-interested people would agree to as the minimum price that has to be paid in order to obtain the cooperation of others".[14]

Justice as impartiality

A second aspect of the concept of justice for Rawls is *ethical* and refers not only to the fact that a society is ordered, but also to how *well* it is ordered. Impartiality or fairness as the requirement that we "treat like cases alike and different cases differently"[15] is a motivational basis for justice, as we know that the laws are not biased or arbitrary. In a well-ordered society, there is agreement on a "common point of view from which ... claims may be adjudicated" (*TJ*: 4). This impartial point of view is called by Rawls "an Archimedean point for assessing the social system ... a standard for appraising institutions and for guiding the overall direction of social change" (*ibid.*: 230–31). "In a well-ordered society, effectively regulated by the principles of justice, everyone has a similar sense of justice and in this respect a well-ordered society is homogeneous. Political argument appeals to this moral consensus" (*ibid.*: 232). In the end, "everyone accepts and knows that the others accept the same principles of justice and the basic social institutions generally satisfy and are known to satisfy these principles" (*ibid.*: 4).

What is distinctive of justice as a moral value is that the system of rules it establishes is not contingent on its outcomes and on the benefits that it yields for some. It is a publicly agreed system that is valued *in itself*, that can survive interpersonal conflicts, even if it might hurt personal interests. Justice is a moral imperative that characterizes well-ordered societies that are not satisfied simply with stability and order, but that call for a *justified* order. The primacy of justice is tightly connected with the self-representation of democratic regimes as being well ordered in that sense and with a conception of the person as having the capacity to understand and to abide by the law, having two moral powers, according to which principles of justice have, in Rawls' view, the force of moral categorical imperatives (*TJ*: 222–3).

We make clear distinctions between a rational scheme of cooperation and one that is fair or just. However, this does not mean that the one can go without the other and that this would support a conception of moral motivation where we could be moved only for justice's sake! As I show in the next section, Rawls does not accept Barry's criticism that the two aspects are incompatible.

Brian Barry's criticism

For Brian Barry, the existence of two conceptions of justice in Rawls' theory (1989: ch. 4), one based on justice as mutual advantage and one based on justice as impartiality, creates a major confusion.[16] In a well-known argument, based on the nature of moral motivation, he claims that "the motivation for being just is the desire to act in ways that can be defended to oneself and others without appealing to personal advantage" (*ibid.*: 359). In other words, he denies "that the motivation for being just has to be its prospective advantageousness" (*ibid.*: 362). "That something is just can be in itself a good reason for doing it" (*ibid.*: 363), "Self-interest cannot be expected to bring about just institutions in general" (*ibid.*: 366). As a consequence, the whole process of justification of the principles of justice is redundant because moral motivations are enough to justify them and to lead to a just society where selfish first-person motivations tend to weaken.

Against these claims, I would like first to say that, for Rawls, the prudential aspect of justice is not fully covered by the idea of self-interest and of mutual advantage, as Barry ultimately recognizes (Barry, 1995a: 60, n.b). Secondly, his understanding of the moral aspect of justice is distinctive and does not simply equate justice with impartiality, as Rawls rejects the thick altruistic assumptions of such a concept. Instead, Rawls' concept of justice includes both aspects but in an innovative way, in what he calls "justice as *reciprocity*", which combines more satisfactorily concerns for the self and for others, in the ideal of justice (*PL*: 16–18). It goes beyond the limits of this book to fully explore this controversy. My interpretation maintains that, for

Rawls as for Sidgwick (preface to the sixth edition of the *Methods of Ethics*), the two aspects of practical reason, the Prudential or Rational and the Ethical or Reasonable (*PL*: 48–54), are inseparable but cannot be translated into the two simple concepts of mutual advantage and impartiality. Justice as *reciprocity* is the conception that, for him, combines the prudential value of cooperation with the moral value of equal respect, of treating each other impartially. Rawls is clearly inspired by a long tradition of political philosophy acutely aware of the entanglement of these two dimensions and does not want to sacrifice one to the other.

Justice as reciprocity

The third aspect of the concept of justice, justice as reciprocity, is *societal*. It denotes as a motivational basis our higher-order interest for a just or fair cooperative scheme, not simply as an instrument of mutual benefit, or as an impartial treatment of persons, but as constitutive of a valued social world. Let us say, to clarify, that whereas justice as mutual advantage is concerned with individual interactions, and justice as impartiality with the moral treatment of persons as equal in dignity, justice as reciprocity focuses on the social aspect of human nature and on the reasonableness of social links.

The difference between mutual advantage and reciprocity is much clearer if we contrast mutual benefits as the results of inter-individual interactions with reciprocity as a feature of the social world itself. Reciprocity is built into the system of rules and practices that regulate social institutions and create social cohesion, and it is not left to individual decisions. It is, in other words, a structural feature of the well-ordered society. The reciprocal scheme has structural value as a system of rules, not simply in view of its *outcomes*. A society that accepts slavery could be mutually advantageous but it excludes reciprocity. The emphasis on reciprocity as distinct from mutual advantage has become even more important in Rawls' later work and in his reflections on the stability of democracies and on a just world order.

> The idea of reciprocity lies between the idea of impartiality, which is altruistic (being moved by the general good), and the idea of mutual advantage understood as everyone's being advantaged with respect to each person's present or expected future situation as things are. (*PL*: 16–17 and n. 18)

The originality of Rawls' approach, as I have already stressed, lies in the importance, for him, of social structures, of *institutionalism*, and this is the best way to understanding his appeal to reciprocity.

The emphasis shifts towards the *public* justification of the system of rules. Our self-interest is mediated and mitigated by a desire to cooperate on a fair basis. Rawls quotes Scanlon's criterion for moral motivation, that is, "the desire to be able to justify one's actions to others on grounds they could not reasonably reject".[17] This means that we now consider not only everyone's individual advantage but also what makes society as a whole function well. The social scheme of cooperation is recognized as just or fair, not simply as mutually advantageous, from a viewpoint that is no longer personal (or non-public), but societal and public.

How does Rawls combine these three requirements of justice? Does "justice as fairness hover uneasily between impartiality and mutual advantage?" (*PL*: 17, n. 18). I think that the answer to Brian Barry's criticism is straightforward: Rawls seeks to combine the three ideas and to advance a theory fit for our ordinary social world and for the types of motivation that are really effective in it. He is quite clear on that point.

> [For] as we have seen, the reasonable (with its idea of reciprocity) is not the altruistic (the impartial acting solely for the interests of the others) nor is it the concern for self (and moved by its ends and affections alone). In a reasonable society, most simply illustrated in a society of equals in basic matters, all have their own rational ends they hope to advance, and all stand ready to propose fair terms of cooperation that others may reasonably be expected to accept, so that all may benefit ... This reasonable society is neither a society of saints nor of the self-centred. It is very much part of our ordinary human world. (*Ibid.*: 54)

However, making room for all these aspects of justice is a daunting task that leads Rawls into major difficulties, the main one being how to accommodate the motivational bases for compliance with justice and the defence of autonomy and equal respect, that is, the deeper theory of justice that I mentioned in the previous section. If among these motivations we include mutual advantage, we seem to contradict a conception of motivation that sees acting for justice's sake, not for its outcomes, as the embodiment of our autonomy.

2. Autonomy and the priority of the right over the good

After these exploratory remarks, I now turn to explaining in fairly general terms the philosophical conception of autonomy that supports the priority of justice and its political consequences for the conception of constitutional democracy. However, it would be a serious misunderstanding of the whole Rawlsian project to see this "deeper doctrine" of autonomy as a starting point. Instead, the aim of the theory is to provide a satisfactory justification for it. One should thus keep in mind that here we are simply introducing the basic idea of the priority of justice, not looking into its justification.

I explain first in what sense Rawls' philosophical doctrine is *deontological*, not *teleological* (1). I then show its consequences for political and moral autonomy and how Rawls' view relates to the Kantian doctrine (2). I show how the priority of justice excludes doctrines such as utilitarianism that can no longer be seen as protecting basic rights and liberties as a matter of priority and as the favoured conception of justice for constitutional democracies (3). I conclude that for that reason Rawls' doctrine of deontological liberalism is firmly embedded in the ideal of constitutional, not majoritarian democracies (4).

Teleological and deontological doctrines

For most moral philosophers, the two main concepts in moral philosophy are the right, or what we ought to do, and the good, or what has value in itself.

> I have tried to distinguish clearly two kinds of question, which moral philosophers have always professed to answer, but which, as I have tried to show, they have almost always confused both with one another and with other questions. These two questions may be expressed, the first in the form: What kind of things ought exist for their own sakes? The second in the form: What kind of actions ought we to perform?
>
> (G. E. Moore, *Principia Ethica:* vii–viii)[18]

Now, the main distinction among various philosophical doctrines is in the balancing of these two concepts. Two possibilities exist. Deontological doctrines affirm the priority of the right over the good. Teleological doctrines derive the right from the good. Rawls' doctrine is a *deontological liberalism*: it separates the two main concepts and affirms the priority of the right over the good in the name of the priority of liberty. Such a philosophical doctrine supports the political conception of constitutional democracy where basic rights and liberties are enshrined in the constitution and fully protected against majority rule.

Teleological doctrines affirm the existence of a supreme good, an ultimate end or *telos*, with justice as what maximizes this all-important end. For ancient teleological doctrines such as Epicureanism, etc., this good is pleasure or happiness and is given by nature and knowable by reason or rational intuition. The moral person is the good and wise person, who knows what is good and pursues it. For modern teleological doctrines, in contrast, such as utilitarianism, this good is man-made in the sense that it is not given by nature unless "by natural we understand what is common to any species" (Hume, *Treatise*: 484). Note also that the good that is maximized is *subjective* and is thus more fitting for a democratic society.[19] The goods that are protected and distributed are those that satisfy people's preferences as expressed and measured by their choices. It is therefore not knowable *a priori* by reason, but only by experience, trial and error in the consequences of our actions, which eventually indicate what the good is. Modern teleological doctrines such as Mill's are *consequentialist* and action-centred, not intuitionist: they assess the good according to the consequences of actions, not according to an independent factor such as an ideal of virtue or of the good character of the agent or her intentions. Justice then is that which maximizes that dominant good. "In a teleological theory, the good is defined independently from the right ... the right is maximizing the good as already specified" (*TJ*: 21–2). In that sense, modern teleological doctrines reject the priority of justice and have difficulties accounting for individual choices and liberty. Questions of justice, according to Rawls, are accommodated by teleological doctrines in a simple way as the right is derived from the good and duties and rights are respected not as natural or *a priori* rights, but for their beneficial consequences. They do not require extra-empirical arguments to explain why they are right. Such a simple principle also has the benefit of avoiding any priority problem: all our considered convictions can be systematically organized and ranked around it and no unaccounted for appeal to intuition is needed (*ibid.*: 36). However, for Rawls, teleological doctrines relate the right and the good in the wrong way, as they can make no room for autonomy as the capacity to choose one's own ends and good.

Deontological doctrines such as Kant's, in contrast, affirm the priority of the right over the good as the priority of individual freedom over empirical and heteronomous ends such as happiness, and either do not specify the good independently from the right, or do not interpret the right as maximizing the good. A deontological doctrine is focused on duty and the value of moral obligation in itself. A good example is Kant's ethics. In contrast, a teleological doctrine such as utilitarianism is consequentialist and affirms that the value of the duty of justice depends on the goodness of the consequences it brings about (*TJ*: 26). Commenting on Kant's practical philosophy, Rawls writes: "Kant believes that once we start from the good as an independent given object, the moral conception must be heteronomous ... In these cases what determines our will is an object given to it and not principles originating in our pure reason as reasonable and rational beings" (*CP*: 509; *PL*: 99). Kant, for instance, writes in "Theory and Practice" (1792):

> No-one can compel me to be happy in accordance with his conception of the welfare of others, for each may seek his happiness in whatever way he sees fit, so long as he does not infringe upon the freedom of others to purse a similar end ... he must accord to others the same right as he enjoys himself. (Kant, 1991: 74)

This does not mean that deontological doctrines are not consequentialist. The rightness of institutions or acts cannot be characterized independently from their consequences. All ethical doctrines worth our attention, says Rawls, take consequences into account in judging rightness. The priority of the right over the good means above all that preferences cannot dictate what is just and that "the interests requiring the violation of justice have no value" (*TJ*: 28; *PL*: V).

Rawls and Kant

Deontological liberalism claims that justice cannot simply be instrumental for social order or personal gains or for the implementation of a particular conception of the good, but that it has value in itself as an independent imperative that can motivate us as such. The capacity to act for justice's sake expresses a conception of persons as autonomous and as deserving equal respect. Such a conception of autonomy is the regulative moral ideal of contemporary democracies and of the protection of equal basic liberties and rights, in contrast with hierarchical or traditional societies. It expresses a *moral* recognition of human dignity and personality[20] grounded in its nature as free and autonomous that overrides any other concerns such as welfare or happiness in qualifying the good society.

In the context of dominant utilitarianism, the claim that justice comes first and cannot be derived from any specific conception of the good is controversial. For utilitarianism, there exists a *summum bonum*, in the sense of happiness, welfare or preference satisfaction that is both descriptive and prescriptive. It describes what people desire and prescribe what just social arrangements should be: those that benefit most the greatest number. In contrast, for Rawls, justice simply cannot be derived: it is a requirement of duty for duty's sake to moral persons, imposed without prior justification be it based on general welfare, utility, interest, or on an ideal of human perfection. Justice cannot be instrumentalized. Rights are prior to welfare or happiness. They are unconditioned and prior to majority preferences. The intensity of preferences cannot determine what is just.

> Each person possesses an inviolability founded on justice that even the welfare of society as a whole cannot override. For this reason, justice denies that the loss of freedom for some is made right by a greater good shared by others ... the rights secured by justice are not subject to political bargaining or to the calculus of social interests. (*TJ*: 3–4)

This is a view of justice obviously inspired by Kant, as Rawls recognizes (*ibid.*: 28, n. 16). The priority of justice is formulated by Kant in *Perpetual Peace* in 1795 in the following way:

> the political maxims adopted must not be influenced by the prospect of any benefit or happiness which might accrue to the state if it followed them ... they should be influenced only by the pure concept of rightful duty, i.e. by an obligation whose principles are given *a priori* by pure reason. (Kant, 1991: 123–4)

The problem, in Kant, is that the priority of justice is based on a seemingly obscure transcendental argument that contrasts the empirical world of *phenomena*, or things as they appear in space and time, with the intelligible world of *noumena*, or the things as they are in themselves, while the priority of justice expresses the priority of the noumenal self over the empirical and causal world. Kant was well aware of the difficulties of his view. He nevertheless writes

> The proverbial saying *fiat justicia, pereat mundus* (i.e. let justice reign, even if all the rogues in the world must perish) may sound somewhat inflated, but it is nonetheless true. It is a sound principle of right ... and should be seen as an obligation of all those in power not to deny or detract from the rights of anyone.   (*Ibid.*: 123)

However, Rawls detaches himself from Kant as he consistently rejects any appeal to the transcendental argument in order to solve the antinomies of freedom (*LHMP*: 86–8). He has instead built up a very sophisticated argument to overcome Kant's difficulties and to disconnect the primacy of justice from the liberal defence of individual autonomy. The defence of autonomy is indirect. It is the outcome of a justificatory process that addresses people's own powers of judgement and capacities for choice, that is "doctrinally autonomous" in that sense. Rawls' innovative doctrine is both theoretically and practically a defence of autonomy that cannot be seen as the imposition of a dominant good or value.

Still, this ambition has not always been fully understood. The question remains whether Rawls is limited to that type of individualistic liberal doctrine or whether he offers a different take on liberalism, as I will suggest. This is a major issue that has nourished the debate between liberals and communitarians and has inspired Michael Sandel's perceptive criticism of Rawls that I examine in Chapter 4.[21]

The rejection of utilitarianism

The priority of justice, that is, the affirmation of the inviolability of persons, even in the name of welfare and utility maximizing, leads to the rejection of utilitarianism, which is one of the great achievements of Rawls' theory of justice as fairness, given the central role of utilitarianism as the main public philosophy that has shaped the self-understanding of most liberal democratic societies as welfare maximizing in the Anglophone world at the time. In this section, I simply sketch the main reasons for opposing utilitarianism in the name of the priority of justice, leaving a comprehensive account of the detailed argument for the next chapters. This argument spans most of Rawls' work.[22] It functions as a sort of "master argument", with the rest of the theory developing and deepening its major ideas. Let us simply say at this stage that, in spite of its many attractions, utilitarianism suffers, for Rawls, from two major defects: it does not respect the separateness of persons and their autonomy, and it does not recognize the pluralistic nature of the good, two constitutive elements of liberalism; whereas a conception of justice as fairness is *fair* to all citizens as it seeks to respect their distinct and opposing aims and life plans and does not impose certain specific values or ends as dominant.

First, utilitarianism has no concept of fairness to persons because it fails to treat them as *distinct* beings, characterized by determinate first-order conceptions of the good.[23] It has no respect for their autonomy and their distinctive choices. "The idea that political community should rest on this sort of mutual respect belongs at the heart of Rawls' philosophy" (Larmore, 2003: 374). Utilitarianism is not fair to persons. This is true of the average utility principle that aims at maximizing average utility and tends to treat persons as "bare-persons" (*TJ*: 152), as having no definite character or will. It is unable then to understand conflicting claims for scarce resources, that is, the main circumstance of justice. It cannot work as a principle of justice in the precise sense that we defined earlier. This is also true of the classical principle that aims at maximizing general utility, and sees persons as interchangeable. It does not take seriously into account the plurality and distinctness of individuals (*ibid.*: 26). Because it uses an aggregate measure of satisfaction, it fails adequately to consider citizens' first-order interests and conceptions of the good as distinct pursuits. It assumes that the satisfaction of one person can be added to another one, and that aims are exchangeable. "In calculating the greatest balance of satisfaction, it does not matter what the desires are for" (*ibid.*: 27). As Bentham famously said, "a game of pushpin is as valuable as poetry". This is unacceptable as we saw that, in virtue of the democratic ideal, in a just society, all should benefit personally and not simply as exchangeable parts of an aggregate. What Rawls discovers in a most illuminating way is the paradox of the general utility principle. On the one hand, it is individualistic in that, according to its conception of society, separate individuals are thought of as different lines along which rights and duties are to be assigned and scarce means of satisfaction allocated (*ibid.*: 24). On the other hand, it does not recognize the separateness of persons: that their satisfaction is not exchangeable, that they have distinct, perhaps not only competing but also incompatible first-order interests, even if they share higher-order interests.

As a consequence of this lack of distinction between persons, the utility principle would happily propose that benefits for some might compensate for hardship on others. Moral relations between persons as members of a joint undertaking are not taken into account (*CP*: 65–6 and 217). Social unity and justice are the results of a higher-order administrative efficiency, not of the agents themselves.[24] Individual preferences are a given and have value as such (*CP*: 66, 70; *TJ*: 27). Preferences and interests, desires and needs are given independently of the social structure and of any moral relation between the persons. More importantly, justice and equality do not enter into the formation of our preferences. Because the good is given, there is no room for transforming preferences in view of others' preferences or good. There is no room for reciprocity, no moral relations such as a concern for equality that shapes desires and interests. In other words, utilitarianism does not recognize the presence of embedded concerns for justice in our system of preferences (*TJ*: 27), or the existence of higher-order moral sentiments (*ibid.*: 167). We can see that the utility principle has no concern for preserving and developing the sense of justice of the persons represented, nor for strengthening it. What is missing in the end is the *social* dimension of a concern for justice. This is equally striking when one looks at justice among peoples, at the international level. Because it has no notion of the singularity of one people contrasted with the others, utilitarianism would reason as if, in the distribution of resources, one people could agree that "the benefits for another people outweigh the hardships imposed on itself" (*LOP*: 40).

Secondly, as a teleological doctrine, utilitarianism fails to understand the modern condition of freedom: the plurality of choices made possible by the pluralistic nature of the good. In the modern context, there cannot exist a dominant end that all endorse and there is no hope of reconciliation of the many valuable human ends. Utilitarianism is incompatible with the values of a constitutional democracy, mainly autonomy, because it does not understand the pluralistic nature of the good. This should be stressed as the most important critique. Therefore it does not provide an adequate protection of rights and liberties and can justify the sacrifice of the rights and liberties of some in the name of social utility. In contrast, the primacy of justice is tightly connected with the self-representation of democratic regimes where the protection of basic human rights is constitutive of well-ordered just societies.

Justice, tyranny of majorities and constitutional democracy

From all these remarks, we can see clearly that the priority of justice corresponds to a certain political regime that Kant could only have dreamt of, a regime that we have come to call *constitutional democracy*: the alliance of democracy and liberalism, of universal suffrage, popular sovereignty and representative government, on the one hand, the rule of law, limited government, constitutional checks and balances and a Bill of Rights, on the other. Let us conclude in examining briefly Rawls' political claim that "our intuitive conviction of the primacy of justice" (*TJ*: 4) – that justice should not be sacrificed in the name of welfare or any other aim – is distinctive of constitutional democracies, in contrast with other forms of democratic or undemocratic regimes.

Without the protections and checks of rights and justice, the unconstrained search for happiness or prosperity can lead to dangerous situations, which contradict our sense of justice and our considered moral convictions as expressed in a democratic constitution's main articles and amendments. We can think of situations where minorities, such as illegal migrant workers, single-parent families, gay couples, etc., are not protected against hostile majority interests or opinions, and their basic human rights are simply sacrificed to the majority's belief systems and preferences. Their basic constitutional rights are not protected, whatever the reasons, good or bad, for such treatment. Such situations are destructive of democratic societies even if they satisfy the preferences of the majority of citizens; they threaten the status of citizens as equal and free moral persons. To affirm the priority of justice is to affirm that majority feelings and opinions are not enough to protect citizens' rights and that we need valid regulating rules of a democratic society over simple majority rule such as a Constitution and a Bill of Rights. Understanding the meaning of justice and of the priority of rights is of paramount importance for the continuity and stability of such a regulating system. We should, therefore, keep in mind this intuitive understanding of the priority of justice and the deep personal worries that Rawls expressed many times about the future of a democracy, which is progressively turning into a "market democracy" as the contemporary form of the "tyranny of majorities" deplored by Mill. Democratic politics in the United States and elsewhere is increasingly trivialized through confusing the forum and the market, the citizen and the consumer. The worry is that the "tyranny of majority preferences" is taking us further away from the conceptions grounding the American Constitution: above all, the provision of equal liberty for all – even at the cost of the welfare or the interests of the majority. What is at stake here is the moral and social inspiration of constitutional democracies and how it is threatened by the reign of special interests and lobbyists.

3. A contractarian and constructivist view of justice

Rawls' *constructivist* and procedural[25] view of justice inspired by social contract theories revolutionized the debate when *A Theory of Justice* appeared in 1971. As he says, his aim is to generalize and carry to a higher order of abstraction the traditional doctrine of the *social contract*. Justice is defined as *fairness*[26] because it is the result of a fair procedure, respecting persons' equality and autonomy,[27] and unbiased by social circumstances and natural contingencies. "Acting from this precedence of the sense of justice expresses our freedom from contingency and happenstance" (*TJ*: 503).

I interpret the priority of justice as meaning that justice cannot be derived from some facts over human nature as independent features of the world. Rawls' theory is not naturalistic in that sense and rejects *moral realism* or "the affirmation of a moral order of values that is prior to and independent of our conception of the person and society and of the public social role of moral doctrines" (*CP*: 511). This does not mean either that it is a form of moral relativism. If Rawls agrees that justice, as Hume famously said, is an "artificial virtue"[28] and has its source in conventions or contractual arrangements, this does not mean that it cannot be justified in a rational way. Rawls constructs a reasoned account of the right and of justice, not a conventionalist one like Hume's, but a contractarian one.

The priority of justice is best expressed in a *contractarian* view of political legitimacy, that is, through the idea that a fair *contract* between free and equal agents, not an independent authority, should determine the just social and political arrangements. Given that the consequence of democratic freedom is that we have no access to an antecedent and independent criterion of justice based either on superior divine authority or on "natural law" and that, even if we had, no consensus on it would be possible in a pluralist society divided by so many different creeds and doctrines, we should simply treat justice as the result of a process or as *pure procedural justice*. This is the only way of giving a political expression to the idea of freedom as autonomy or of treating human beings not solely as means but as ends in themselves, as Kant says. And similarly, Rawls writes: "On the contract interpretation treating men as ends in themselves implies at the very least treating them in accordance with the principles to which they would consent in an original position of equality … The contract view as such defines a sense in which men are to be treated as ends and not as means only" (*TJ*: 156–7). The simple and elegant solution that Rawls proposes is to transform the problem of justice into a problem of choice where, if the terms and conditions are properly specified, a satisfactory solution should follow.

> My aim is to present a conception of justice which generalizes and carries to a high level of abstraction the familiar theory of the social contract as found in Locke, Rousseau and Kant ... the guiding idea is that the principles of justice for the basic structure of society are the object of the original agreement. They are the principles that free and rational persons concerned to further their own interests would accept in an initial position of equality as defining the fundamental terms of their association ... This way of regarding the principles of justice I shall call justice as fairness ... Imagine that those who engage in social cooperation choose together, in one joint act, the principles which are to assign basic rights and duties and to determine the division of social benefits ... The choice which rational men would make in this hypothetical situation of equal liberty, assuming to the present that this choice problem has a solution, determines the principles of justice.   (*TJ*: 10–11)

The main idea of the theory of justice is the idea of the social contract. Hence Rawls' conception of justice can be described as contractarian.

The appeal of social contract doctrines

The appeal of social contract doctrines is obvious for a deontological theory such as Rawls' because they place freedom as autonomy at the centre of the legitimating process. Among those, it is Rousseau's conception as expressed in *The Social Contract* of 1762 that has been most influential for Rawls.[29] As Rousseau said, it is the freedom of the parties in the contract that gives legitimacy to its result and to their decisions because "if you take away all freedom of the will, you strip a man's actions of all moral significance" (*Social Contract*, I, 5). In a formula that was to define Kant's own conception of moral autonomy, Rousseau famously claims: "the obedience to a law one prescribes to oneself is freedom" (*Social Contract*, I, 8). Another reason for the attraction of social contract doctrines for Rawls is that they have been heavily criticized by utilitarians, by Hume (1740: *Treatise*, III ii 9 and III iii 1), and most famously by Bentham (1776: ch. 1, §§36–48) and Mill

(1861: ch. V). For them, either a contract is a *real* contract – meaning that we should gain something from it, in which case being rational, we should consent and accept it as final – or it is not. In that case we cannot consent. The argument shows clearly that the value of a contract is in the beneficial consequences, not in a so-called consent that adds nothing to it. A hypothetical contract with no benefits or gains, no matter if it is "free", is for Bentham "a non-sense on stilts", as are natural rights. In his desire to mount a definitive attack on utilitarianism, it was natural for Rawls to go back to this vilified idea and to try to rework it in his own terms. In what follows I explain the main features of social contract doctrines and I cite three reasons that Rawls advances for his choice.

The fiction of a social contract is the device used by a long line of philosophers from Hobbes and Locke to Rousseau and Kant as a way of legitimizing political authority and of explaining political obligation on the basis of free and rational agreements, in the absence of religious or natural law justification. Rawls, in contrast, is not so much concerned with the best form of government as with the best public conception of justice and with its justification process (*JAFR*: 16, n. 16). Social contract arguments purport to have prescriptive force when they maintain that we ought to do that which appropriately rational and free human beings "could agree to". There are two kinds of prescriptive argument to which the contractarian metaphor has given rise, the first having its roots in Hobbes and the second in Rousseau and Kant.

Hobbesian contractarian theory almost exactly parallels the structure of social contract arguments with respect to the state. It is committed to the idea that the state is a human-made institution, which is justified only to the extent that it effectively furthers human interests. What we could agree to has prescriptive force for Hobbesians, not because make-believe promises have any force, but because this sort of fictional agreement reveals the way in which the agreed-upon outcome is *rational* for all of us. A deduction of practical reason determines which policies are mutually advantageous. However, in Hobbesian contractarianism freedom is subordinated to rational advantage.

Kantian contractarian theory is the result of Kant's admiration for Rousseau and for the idea of a hypothetical social contract between free and equal citizens as a source of legitimacy for political power as the power of the people. In a late work, "The Theory of Right" (1797), following Rousseau, he writes: "The legislative power can belong only to the united will of the people. For since all right is supposed to emanate from this power, the laws it gives must be absolutely incapable of doing anyone an injustice".[30] Like Rousseau, he believes that make-believe agreements have moral force because of the process itself that reveals citizens' autonomy, their "general will" distinct from their particular interests, not because of the actual benefits. The idea of a social contract, therefore, brings together the two dimensions of justice: prudential rationality as we cannot agree to harmful or unjust laws, and ethical rationality as the process of legitimation rests on its universalizability. It could be universalized to all human beings and it is respectful of each as an end in herself. The contract seeks to establish what fully rational people would agree to, each being concerned to get her due, and none being affected by prejudices or the distorting powers of passion. Kant believes that we can thus determine laws that are just in the only way they can ever be.

Rawls espouses the Kantian version of the contract and argues that when we reflect upon what (suitably defined) people could "agree to", we are reflecting from an "Archimedean point", surveying the terrain of morality from an acceptably impartial and morally revealing vantage point.

The main problem now is to understand how the social contract framework can provide such a vantage point, how it can guarantee impartiality and that citizens' considered judgements become immune to biased ideas or intuitions. Rawls' answer is the device of the Original Position. We are to choose the principles of justice in conditions that reflect the two main ideas of democratic societies: citizens are equal and free, and they agree to cooperate on fair terms so that all benefit from cooperation. Here again, Rawls is following Kant when he writes in the *Metaphysics of Morals*:

> The three rightful attributes which are inseparable from the nature of a citizen as such are as follows: firstly, lawful *freedom* to obey no law other than that to which he has given his consent. Secondly civil *equality* in recognizing no-one among the people as superior to himself ... and thirdly, the attribute of civil *independence*. (Kant, 1991: 139)

There are three main reasons for preferring the social contract approach to views such as utilitarianism, intuitionism or perfectionism: contractarianism embodies the three requirements of moral, political and doctrinal autonomy.

51

First, the social contract approach is compatible with the conception of the person as *morally* autonomous, which characterizes democratic societies. It treats them as moral persons,[31] as free and equal, rational and reasonable beings who are capable of justice, of acting not only *according to* the moral law, but also *from* the moral law. It expresses the need to protect them from the coercion of *heteronomous* doctrines and from illegitimate interference by others. The primacy of justice is thus the basis for social contract doctrines. Justice is not derived from some antecedent authority; it is that form of coercive law to which rational and reasonable citizens can consent, for justice necessarily implies coercion and certain constraints and limitations on the pursuit of interests and one's conception of the good. As I have shown, being able to recognize these constraints as a source of obligation and to act freely upon them is one of the main moral powers possessed by free and equal citizens.

Secondly, the contractarian process guarantees the *political* autonomy of citizens inasmuch as it respects their most important interests and values. The authority of the state is not something that can be derived from any sort of natural or innate authority that might be possessed by some set of supposedly superior persons over others, nor is it derived solely from the word of God. Instead, the authority of the state is the creation of the sovereign people who constitute it. It is conventionally generated and supported because its institutions are perceived to be mutually advantageous. The social contract situation means that control is possible at any time. It is a fair process whereby I submit only because I know that the others also submit knowing in their turn that I do. This reveals the crucial *publicity* requirement of a fair contractual situation and connects it with justice as reciprocity. It creates a public sphere of trust and reciprocal justification where citizens not only deliberate together and modify their views and political decisions accordingly, but they also know that all recognize the same binding rules and share in the same political power.

Thirdly, there is another even more important reason in favour of the social contract device, which is explained at length in *PL*: 98 and in *The Lectures on the History of Moral Philosophy*. This is "doctrinal autonomy" or autonomy as a feature of the practice of justification, not simply as a theoretical value. Thanks to his method, Rawls not only provides a conception of justice externally compatible with moral autonomy as a comprehensive value of the sort advocated by Kant. He is, more fundamentally, providing a conception that is itself *doctrinally* autonomous.

A view is autonomous then because in its represented order, the political values of justice and public reason (expressed by their principles) are not requirements *externally* imposed. Nor are they required of us by other citizens, whose comprehensive doctrines we do not accept. Rather, citizens can understand those values as based on their *practical reason* in union with the political conceptions of citizens as free and equal and of society as a system of fair cooperation. In affirming the political doctrine as a whole, we, as citizens, are ourselves autonomous, politically speaking. (*PL*: 98, emphasis added)

Autonomy is not a *value* advocated in contrast to, let us say, utility. Autonomy is a *practice*, a mode of being, of acting and thinking, which should reverberate in the theoretical conception itself. It is this feature of the social contract doctrine that makes it an empowering political conception in the sense that citizens anxious to understand the political system in which they live can assess the institutions of justice following the method developed in *A Theory of Justice*. The theory of justice empowers citizens because it sees them as taking control, both intellectually and politically, of their most important institutions, of the system to which they are normally subjected, thanks to the thought-experiment of the social contract. This view is most clearly presented by Rawls in his 1995 "Reply to Habermas", on which I briefly comment in Chapter 4.

A parallel universe

It is such a move that makes Rawls' theory of justice stand apart as a work of exceptional philosophical imagination. Like so many philosophical discoveries, it leads us to consider external and coercive realities as the results of voluntary decisions, not as the result of fate or nature. We are asked from the start to enter a *parallel universe*, to open up our minds to new possibilities and to look at our own world from new perspectives.[32] Rawls here joins a prestigious tradition of philosophers and utopian writers who have used rational imagination and counterfactual reasoning to great effect. Plato asked us to look at our social and political world as if it were a mere collection of shadows and to envisage a more rational world beyond the Cave. Thomas More took us on a journey to Utopia (or "Nowhereland") where men hate gold and private property, and are united by brotherly love, and asked us to contrast it with our actual world. Descartes asked us to look at the world as if we were deprived, by some magical trick, of our bodily apparatus and to see whether it still had any reality. Rousseau asked us to judge our social and political institutions as if they were the results of an original fair contract and to compare that fiction with our actual experience.

However, the main model here for Rawls is Kant and his doctrine of the categorical imperative. In order to discover what a truly moral action is, "Kant tells us to test our maxim by considering what would be the case were it a universal law of nature ... and we did not know our place in this *imagined* system of nature" (*TJ*: 118, n. 11, my emphasis). The exercise of rational imagination leads us to discover our "reality" from a new perspective. In spite of his sober vocabulary and his use of rational choice theory, Rawls likewise takes us on a voyage where what seems to be a "given" is discovered to be a result of human action.

> We may reflect that the world is not in itself inhospitable to political justice and its good. Our social world might have been different and there is hope for those at another time and place.
>
> (*JAFR*: 38)

The test for democratic legitimacy resides in the possibility of an imaginary process according to which any political institution and practice in a democratic regime results from general consensus, even if we only vote for a fraction of them. As Ronald Dworkin argues, the value of the contractual method is in the end not simply to justify Rawls' own principles of justice, but "to represent a specific mental process present in most or perhaps all human beings".[33]

Rawls and constructivism

Another main feature of Rawls' theory, as a consequence of the priority of justice and of its contractarian model, is *ethical constructivism*. This view is developed first in *TJ*: §9 and then presented more systematically in an important paper, "Kantian Constructivism in Moral Theory", (*CP*: 305–48, redeveloped in *PL*: Lecture III). It obviously goes beyond the scope of this book to examine all the aspects and difficulties of Rawls' meta-ethics and constructivist methodology, on which there exists a huge secondary literature.[34] Let us simply note some useful points that bear upon the overall nature of Rawls' project as basically *practical*, as a construction of justice, empowering citizens.

First, Rawls rejects any notion of *moral realism*. Ethical principles, and principles of justice in particular, are constructions of human agents. Their objectivity is not based on a reflection of nature, on "moral facts", but on public procedures of reasoned justification. Secondly, he equally rejects *moral relativism*. Rawls claims that if moral principles are the result of constructions, they are nevertheless not arbitrary.[35] They are supported by a wide range of philosophical and religious views. Constructivism is thus closely connected with Rawls' ideals of deliberative democracy and public reason (see Chapter 4). Thirdly, a doctrine that is practically autonomous must proceed from a *construction of justice*, that is, from our own considered views on justice. There is no further court of appeal. We cannot go beyond our shared practical reason and our own considered beliefs mutually adjusted with our principles in reflective equilibrium. As long as these views are not publicly constructed, they lack authority. Like Kant, Rawls thinks that the authority of reason must be constructed or instituted by human agents. This is the exact meaning of practical reason, in contrast with theoretical reason. Theoretical reason is defined as concerning the knowledge of given objects whereas practical reason concerns the *production of objects* in accordance with a particular conception of them (*PL*: 93; *LHMP*: 217–18, and Kant, *CPrR*: 89, emphasis added). Constructivism produces social and political norms on the basis of our own conceptions of justice as members of a functioning democracy, and whether they are correct or not is not a function of their truth theoretically assessed, but rather of their reasonableness practically assessed. It emphasizes the practical aims of a theory of justice and refuses any foundational derivation of norms from an independent moral order that would contradict persons' autonomy.

Rawls' constructivism is Kantian in its inspiration, but is distinct from Kant's in many ways. It would be impossible within the limits of this book to give full justice to such an important philosophical discussion that would uncover the deep metaphysical foundations of Rawls' work and its roots in both Kant's and Hegel's philosophy of history. Suffice to say that it is a *political* constructivism designed for citizens, not for moral persons, and for the social world, not the personal one. It is not a general method, but is limited to justice: we can construct an account of the right derived from practical reason, not of the good. The main difference from Kant is that reason for Rawls may be anchored in the norms of a specific existing community: for instance, in existing constitutional democracies. As Onora O'Neill (2003: 359) very perceptively notes, this is why Rawls hopes that an overlapping consensus of citizens of an ethically diverse polity may be constructed, whereas, for Kant, *universalizability*, not actual consensus, is the supreme principle of practical reason. Kant preserves the purely regulative nature of the principles of justice and the duality of nature and freedom in refusing their construction on the basis of given empirical and historical beliefs and intuitions. In that sense, Rawls' constructivism is probably more Hegelian than Kantian. "Kant's public is not the Rawlsian public consisting only of fellow citizens in a liberal democratic society: it is unrestricted" (*ibid*.: 362). This is exactly what Rawls' constructivism would reject in the name of a situated practical reason.

4. "Justice as the first virtue of social institutions"

Lastly, the priority of justice expresses the fact that "justice is the first virtue of social institutions" (*TJ*: 3). Rawls shares the Aristotelian view of justice as a social virtue, the most important indeed of all social virtues that helps society to function as efficiently as possible and to realize its potential. In imposing constraints on the pursuit of self-interest, it regulates human interactions and makes social life possible. "The effects of the basic structure on citizens' aims, aspirations, and character, as well as on their opportunities and their ability to take advantage of them, are pervasive and present from the beginning of life" (*JAFR*: 10 and 55). In that sense, justice plays a primary role in our life plans and prospects. It is instrumental for our happiness and flourishing, and should be our primary concern when we look at our life from that *social* point of view. One of the striking features of Rawls' theory is its focus on institutions, not on individual positions. His "holistic" social ontology is closer to Hegel and Marx than to the tradition of methodological individualism predominant in the history of liberal thought.[36] The aim of the public conception of justice is to correct structural injustices, not to meet individual demands for retribution, redress or recognition of merit. Note here that there may exist a tension between this holistic view of justice and Rawls' moral individualism expressed in his affirmation of the priority of the right over the good and of persons' autonomy.

A public conception of justice

One of the most powerful features of Rawls' theory is his emphasis on the role of a *public* conception of justice. This is what sets him apart from most contemporary writers, either libertarians – who do not fully acknowledge the societal dimension of justice – or communitarians – who derive the conception of justice from a pre-given shared doctrine of the good. Not only is there agreement in a well-ordered democratic society to accept justice rather than force to solve conflicts, but also this agreement is public in that everyone knows that everyone else accepts the same rules. Agreement is necessary because the binding rules of justice cannot be simply forced upon free and equal citizens, they have to be freely discussed among equally rational and reasonable members. The condition of publicity is equally crucial to prevent arbitrariness and mistrust. In a well-ordered society, then, there is agreement on the necessity of relying on a common conception of justice to solve antagonisms and conflicts.

Societies that reach such an agreement are not simply cooperative organizations, but they are structurally stable and lasting ones, as they do not rely exclusively on force or on fluctuating self-interests to reach a certain level of order and stability. They are ordered "from within", so to speak. These societies understand that conflicts characterize social life, but they can be solved through peaceful processes, based on recognized principles: they acknowledge and value "the rule of law". They are well ordered because their stability does not rely on violence, fear or brainwashing. This is their distinctive feature in contrast to what Rawls has later described in *The Law of Peoples* as "outlaw states" where the rule of law does not apply, and with "burdened societies" which are too poor to afford fair institutions.

> Among individuals with disparate aims and purposes, a shared conception of justice establishes the bonds of civic friendship ... One may think of a public conception of justice as constituting the fundamental charter of a well-ordered human association ... In the absence of a certain measure of agreement on what is just and unjust, it is clearly more difficult for individuals to coordinate their plans efficiently in order to insure that mutually beneficial arrangements are maintained. Distrust and resentment corrode the ties of civility and suspicion and hostility tempt men to act in ways they would otherwise avoid. (*TJ*: 5–6)

This agreement is both functional and moral. In that sense, Rawls starts with a concept of justice that unites rationality and morality, without reducing morality to rationality. This creates, as we shall see later, a web of difficulties and dilemmas that Rawls is possibly unable to address fully. Nevertheless, the strong point of his theory is that the prudential aspect of justice and its moral aspect cannot be disentangled. In his later work, he is more rigorous and establishes that the public agreement is both *rational*, in the sense that it fosters order and stability that are beneficial at the individual level, and *reasonable*, in the sense that it avoids a mere *modus vivendi* and is based on a shared moral concept of justice, beneficial at the social level (*PL*: 48–54). Another useful clarification is that this agreement differs from agreements on shared values or conceptions of the good – on what Rawls labels in his later work as "comprehensive doctrines" (*ibid.*: xviii). This is an agreement strictly on justice, not on conceptions of the good, that leaves open the question of the plurality of its interpretations in specific cases and in various cultures. In that sense, it is an agreement that takes place in a free public sphere, distinct from the associational world and of its conflicting interpretations of the good – the kind of space that is lacking in non-democratic societies.

Now, one could raise the following objection. Which historical societies correspond to Rawls' analysis of the well-ordered society in contrast to simply ordered societies? Is he talking in the void or has he specific historical and political contexts in mind? It is obvious that the only societies possessing these features, especially a public conception of justice, are democratic or quasi-democratic. These conditions are absent from societies where there is no free public debate or public space, no recognition of the status of citizens as free and equal persons. Unfortunately, in *A Theory of Justice,* this fact is not fully elucidated. Rawls himself recognizes in the introduction to *Political Liberalism* (1993: xvi) "the unrealistic idea of a well-ordered society", that is, of a society where all citizens endorse the same conception of justice. Conflicting ideas about justice as they develop in contemporary free societies are not fully taken into account. The analytical definition of justice sounds as if it applied to any functioning society, as if it were not context-relative. Rawls at this stage does not make explicit the distinction between democratic and non-democratic societies. Nor does he make a distinction between public conceptions of justice and non-public conceptions of the good or the "comprehensive" doctrines that citizens may hold. This distinction will appear only later. His definition seems to be *a priori*, and this will in turn lead to many criticisms and misunderstandings, especially from his communitarian critics as it is perfectly clear that, for many societies, justice is not prior to other virtues such as solidarity, community or cohesion.

What I would like to suggest here is that, in effect, Rawls' conception is, from the start, much more *context-dependent* and historical than is generally recognized because of the role of a public conception of justice in defining a well-ordered society. In fact, justice is the first virtue not of any given social organization, but of "well-functioning" social arrangements. Without such a clarification, the meaning of the primacy of justice may be too broad. In my view, Rawls is talking here of a universal ideal that is also firmly grounded in a *specific* case: the historical fact of two centuries of functioning constitutional democracies. Justice should be the first virtue of social institutions, but it is only in democratic societies that this is recognized and conceptualized as such. History fashions the way we think of justice as primary. It is interesting that, in his later work, he mentions historical facts such as the "fact of reasonable pluralism" as the context for the concept of justice. In contemporary democratic societies, not only conflicts of interests, but also "deep religious and moral conflicts that only the oppressive use of state power could overcome", divide society and lead to the adoption of principles of justice. The circumstances of justice are possibly not universal, but "the historical conditions under which modern democratic societies exist" (*JAFR*: 84).

Rawls assumes here that the concept of justice itself is transformed and enriched when it is at work in a democratic or, at least, "decent"[37] society, where an agreement on a public conception of justice is necessary for justice to fulfil its function. A superficial reading, here, would lead one to think that Rawls is giving a definition of justice and of its primacy *sub specie aeternitatis*, because these implications are not fully analysed. The communitarian critique of Rawls has spread such misconceptions. But the insistence on the central role of a public conception of justice shows beyond serious doubt that for Rawls the concept of justice is context-dependent, a view that should not be confused with any form of moral relativism, as we shall see later.

One could even say that the public culture of democracies is developed in order to make sense of the concept of justice, in order to create and develop different interpretations of it that can be understood and accepted by the citizens themselves who will have to abide by them as well as by the judges and politicians who produce them. Interestingly, such a production and discussion of law and justice is for Rawls the main point that separates democracies or quasi-democracies from the rest. Principles of justice and the consistent conceptions that make sense of them are not pure abstract constructs, but are the building blocks of public ethics in the public forum. This shows how misplaced the communitarian critique of Rawls is: far from being an abstract and non-political, non-historical "theory", we can already identify one of its main aims as clarifying the considered convictions or values of the public cultures of functioning democracies. The elaboration that transforms mere binding rules of conduct into legitimate laws is founded on a capacity to act on the basis of principles and to understand how principles cohere into a single overall conception. The important element in Rawls' analysis, which is not obvious at first reading, is that it is only in well-ordered democratic or, at least, "decent" societies, that public conceptions of justice play a role. "Theories" of justice only have a meaning in those specific contexts where theorizing is allowed and necessary. In contrast, "common good conceptions of justice"[38] have no need for theorizing and conceptualizing their considered judgements on justice as those are not distinct from the common conception of the good and are not characterized by deep conflicts and disagreements within society.

It is obvious, however, that if we do not place the emphasis on the distinction between the two aspects – prudential and moral – of the concept of justice, and on the role of a public conception of justice, we are bound to misunderstand Rawls and to treat his theory as being abstract and context-free. Rawls himself is not always clear and consistent in this respect, as he mentions the possibility of an agreement on a common conception of justice when he means an agreement on a common concept of justice (*TJ*: 4). By contrast, the interpretation that I propose here is that, for Rawls, even the basic concept of justice is shaped by a historical and political context, that of contemporary constitutional democracies, a claim that is assumed, but not fully elucidated in *A Theory of Justice*, but that will become more and more important in the subsequent developments of the theory. Rawls assumes that the primacy of justice is not only an important moral thesis; it also tends to be the main political feature of most well-ordered societies, in contrast to non-democratic, non-liberal ones.

With these clarifications in mind, we can better grasp the full implication of the primacy of justice as the first virtue of social institutions.

The basic structure of society as the main subject of justice

Now Rawls adds the very important idea that social institutions function as a system or scheme: "the basic structure of society". This is a highly significant aspect of Rawls' analysis of justice, which makes it unique in liberal political philosophy. This point has been well noted by Brian Barry when he writes:

> When we talk about the basic structure of a society, we are concerned with the way in which institutions work systematically so as to advantage some and disadvantage others ... Rawls's incorporation of this notion of a social structure into his theory represents the coming of age of liberal political philosophy. For the first time, a major figure in the broadly individualistic tradition has taken account of the legacy of Marx and Weber.[39]

Conflicts and inequalities arise among individuals that are the result not of individual actions, but of structural dysfunctions or injustices. We need to shift the focus toward structures and the distinction between the justice of *institutions* or practices as a system of rules, and the justice or injustice, of a particular *action* falling under them.[40] This is the basis of Rawls' "holistic" social ontology: the fact that social organizations are more than the sum of the behaviours of the individuals taking part in them and that the structural features of institutions exist independently as a whole and have lasting effects on their members. This also explains the possibility of a holistic conception of justice, covering all particular cases.

> It is a mistake to focus attention on the varying relative positions of individuals and to require that every change, considered as a single transaction viewed in isolation, be in itself just. It is the arrangement of the basic structure which is to be judged, and judged from a general point of view. (*TJ*: 76)

Rawls uses the expression "background justice" to describe the social factors that shape injustices and that could be acted upon in order to remedy them.[41] The main object of a conception of justice is the inequalities generated by the basic structure, not the particular social positions.

> The fundamental social and economic inequalities are the differences in citizens' life-prospects as these are affected by such things as their social class of origin, their native endowments, their

opportunities for education and their good or ill fortune over the course of life ... These inequalities are our main concern.

(*JAFR*: 40–41)

In order to illustrate this crucial distinction, let us take Rawls' example of the theory of punishment in his 1955 paper: "Two Concepts of Rules" (*CP*: 20–46). The justice of punishment is usually affirmed on the basis of two contrasting lines of argument. The *retributionist* view advocates punishment of the guilty as a way of compensating for past sufferings, according to a strict balance between crime and punishment, between the specific criminal action and the price that should be paid for it. This is the most widespread view, one that chimes with common-sense morality. "The state of affairs where a wrongdoer suffers punishment is morally better than the state of affairs where he does not" (*ibid.*: 22). The *utilitarian* view, most famously advocated by Bentham, holds that punishment is justifiable only by reference to its probable consequences on the social order, at large. "If punishment can be shown to promote effectively the interests of society, then it is justifiable, otherwise it is not" (*ibid.*). If the retributionist view seems to be limited to punishment of specific actions in specific cases, where the alleged offender has been shown to be guilty, the main difficulty with the utilitarian view is that it seems to justify too much, in particular the punishment of innocents if it is for the greater good of society. Utilitarianism then makes sense only if it makes a distinction between particular actions and the basic institutional structure as a practice or system of rules.

> One must distinguish between justifying a practice as a system of rules to be applied and enforced, and justifying a particular action that falls under these rules; utilitarian arguments are appropriate with regard to questions about practices, while retributive arguments fit the application of particular rules to particular cases. (*Ibid.*: 22)

In order to make sense of the concept of justice, we must make use of this distinction between particular actions and the system of rules under which they fall. The main subject of the concept of justice is the rules that regulate social institutions and the practices that can be deemed just or unjust. Conceptions of justice will then specify the way these rules and institutions function in a less than perfect world. An institution can be just at the social global level and have unjust consequences in particular cases. But knowing that the overall social scheme is just or quasi-just makes all the difference for citizens. They can still trust the system even when opposing particular effects in particular cases. For instance, they can recognize the general institution of punishment as just and useful in its principle and design while its applications in specific cases can be discussed with a view to their improvement.

Therefore the main subject of the concept of the justice is the basic structure of society, not the particular actions that occur within it. The basic structure of society comprises its main institutions "taken together as one scheme". "Thus the legal protection of freedom of thought and liberty of conscience, competitive markets, private property of the means of production and the monogamous family are examples of major social institutions" (*TJ*: 6). Now, focusing on the basic structure allows one to depart from the examination of the present state of affairs, of existing preferences and needs, and to take into account lasting and structural effects on people's chances in life, the "deep and pervasive inequalities" that a well-ordered society must fight. The basic structure is the locus of permanent or at least durable inequalities that individuals might not clearly grasp in the present moment. It is also the place where changes and improvements can occur. In that sense, Rawls' theory is a *historical* theory that takes into account duration, not simply the current situation. More precisely, it is "a social process view that focuses on the basic structure and on the regulations required to maintain background justice over time" (*JAFR*: 54).

By contrast, Robert Nozick's (1974) libertarian theory of justice is, for Rawls, "a historical process view that focuses on transactions of individuals and associations" (*JAFR*: 54). Nozick claims that his view is equally historical and takes into account how the basic configuration of initial entitlements is unjustly transformed through historical transactions. But his theory is individualistic and libertarian, whereas Rawls' theory is holistic and egalitarian. I will contrast Rawls and Nozick's conceptions in Chapter 3 on how they fare concerning the defence of basic liberties.

At this stage, we can distinguish two connected requirements of a public conception of justice: (1) that ultimately the content of the conception should faithfully express our most important beliefs as citizens; (2) that the process of justifying it should respect our moral and political autonomy and allow for the possibility of our coming to modify our initial beliefs.

To answer (1), the conception of justice should not add anything new to our own beliefs and convictions. It should solely put them in order, put them in a *reflective equilibrium*, as Rawls says, that allows for adaptation both of beliefs and principles, and makes them understandable and mutually acceptable. It is from within the main tenets of liberal democracy that we draw this conception and recognize it as fitting. In other words, the best conception is the one that is most capable of reconstructing in the best possible light our deepest moral convictions, and showing them to be compatible with our fellow citizens' equally deeply considered convictions. "A political conception of justice is formulated so far as possible solely in terms of fundamental ideas familiar from, or implicit in, the public political culture of a democratic society" (*JAFR*: 26–7). The two familiar ideas present in democratic societies from which we can construct the conception of justice are the conception of society as a fair scheme of cooperation (principle of reciprocity) and the conception of the person as free and equal and defined by her two moral powers.

In order to satisfy (2), the justification process should not be externally imposed or taught to citizens, as in the case of the "civil religion" that Rousseau advocates in his *Social Contract*, or as in many ideologies. The justification should be that we ourselves would choose the conception of justice when the relevant conditions are available or that we would agree to choose it in spite of not agreeing with all its requirements. In other words, the choice has to be autonomous, not based on beneficial outcomes, on mere preferences, appeal to authority or on an external conception of the good.

5. An empowering conception of justice

Having explained the three main interpretations of the priority of justice for Rawls, I now turn to its consequences for *power*. Citizens capable of constructions of justice find themselves in a situation where the power of the government is also their power, where the democratic ideas of a society of equals and of self-government find their embodiment. Justice as a constraint on our pursuits is the result of political power. The theory of justice reclaims this power for the citizens themselves as autonomous agents of the construction of justice and as having a social nature, as members of the basic social structure, not as isolated and divided individuals.

The aim of a public conception of justice is then to *empower* citizens with the capacity to assess their institutions and to initiate social change. It should provide them with a viewpoint from which to judge the polity's most important features and from where to resist its injustices, as in both cases of conscientious refusal and civil disobedience analysed by Rawls (*TJ*: §§55–9). This is why it is so important to define the subject matter of a conception of justice in terms of the social structure, not of individual positions. Also, a theory of justice, according to Rawls, should limit itself in matters of feasibility to the ideal case of strict compliance, going back to the more likely situations of non-compliance and injustices afterwards (*ibid.*: 8). The claim here is not so much that the ideal or theoretical level has precedence over empirical cases. This is a mistaken interpretation of Rawls' project that I mentioned earlier. Rawls' claim is rather that citizens in a constitutional democracy need a clear point of view, a clear standard, even if oversimplified, that empowers them and allows them to understand clearly the justice or injustice of their most important institutions. They can then decide whether to trust them, if the social structure functions according to the public rules and principles they know to be just and freely accept. Rawls is not so much concerned with the perfection of the design as with social cooperation, civic friendship and the political public culture that is their condition.

A unified conception of justice

One condition is that a public conception of justice should provide a justification of the standards that all could accept and that could unite society. In that sense, Rawls is trying to build what can superficially be described as a unitary conception of justice valid in all the different spheres of a democratic society. "Political philosophy may contribute to how a people think of their political and social institutions as *a whole* ... to a *unified framework* within which proposed answers to divisive questions can be made consistent" (*JAFR*: 3; emphasis added). I shall now examine the nature and the limits of such an ambition.

A common feature of philosophical theories of justice has been their ambition to provide a unitary conception that could effectively unite society and apply to both individual persons and the state, usually in a fairly dogmatic way. If we take Plato's *Republic*, his main claim was that the just man and the just society exhibit the same features and that these are in effect those of nature itself: harmony, order and measure in the midst of chaos, conflicts and violence. Aristotle in his *Politics* was possibly less dogmatic, but he too claimed that a good man and a good state have common features, even if he hesitated to argue that the good man and the good citizen were identical. Utilitarians, too, are remarkable in the way they think that a common principle could be applied to both individuals and society. This claim has been attacked by a long tradition of realist and illiberal thinkers from Machiavelli and Hobbes to Nietzsche and Carl Schmitt, who argue that moral philosophy has no understanding of the conflictual nature of social arrangements and political allegiances, that no theory of justice can replace passions and imaginary identifications in uniting societies.

Where does Rawls stand in this debate? Is he only another abstract thinker with little or no grip on reality? Or does he exhibit some sense of the "limits of moral philosophy", to use Bernard Williams' expression?[42]

We must now address Rawls' apparent claim that one single "public conception of justice" can answer all the different questions, dilemmas or conflicts that arise within the basic structure of society. This raises three different questions: (a) Could the range of questions be unified and how? (b) Is the conception of justice itself unified or do intractable conflicts remain? (c) Are the members of democratic societies themselves united thanks to their common conception of justice?

A conception of justice may be unified in the *first* sense if the range of questions addressed has unity. We must first examine *the range of questions* (*TJ*: 176) that the principles of justice should help to address. Rawls affirms that social institutions can be "taken together as one scheme" (*ibid.*: 6). At the same time, he is clear that "the social structure may be viewed as having two more or less distinct parts ... the assignment of rights and duties and the distribution of social and economic advantages" (*ibid.*: 53). Not only that, but the two parts are very different in the sense that the first one demands equality whereas the second one tolerates some level of inequalities in the name of fairness and efficiency. There is thus a tension within the range of questions addressed by the theory, and a unified conception cannot be understood as based on one single principle fit for all these questions. What Rawls means here is that the theory is unified in the sense that it should provide a unified understanding of how different principles, fit for different parts of the system, should relate to each other. He appeals to *rules of priority* to order them, rules that are missing in intuitionist theories and superfluous in dominant-end conceptions such as utilitarianism. A unified theory is certainly not a simple one.

Inspired as he says by inductive logic, Rawls moves from abstract and general analysis to more specific descriptions, from general theory to more specific principles, criteria and rules, and then to a workable political conception and to institutional design. We start with the most basic issues of justice, those of basic constitutional rights and of social inequalities, and with the principles that apply to them. "These principles, then, regulate the choice of a political institution and the main elements of the economic and social system" (*TJ*: 7). The range of questions covered is directed not so much by the search for truth, but rather by the needs of ordinary citizens when confronted with deep and lasting injustices at the political, social and economic levels such as discrimination, insecurity, poverty, loss of self-respect, violence, etc. As a tool available to citizens, a simplified but feasible theory is valuable, even at the cost of some vagueness and oversimplification.

> This indeterminacy in the theory of justice is not itself a defect. It is what we should expect. Justice as fairness will prove a worthwhile theory if it defines the range of justice more in accordance with our considered judgments than do existing theories, and if it singles with greater sharpness the grave wrongs that a society should avoid. (*Ibid.*: 176)

Because different types of questions, ranging from political processes to economic policies, can be addressed on the basis of similar principles, a common political culture could develop in spite of the various comprehensive doctrines that determine individual and collective choices. It is then in that sense that a unitary conception is necessary in view of the primacy of justice and of the indeterminacy of the concept of justice, a conception that could empower citizens beyond their own limited scope and information.

A conception of justice may be unified in the *second* sense if there is agreement on its principles in the background political culture and history. Now, the ideal theory has to acknowledge that, even under reasonably good conditions, political culture is generally not characterized by consensus.

> The course of democratic thought over the past two centuries or so makes plain that there is at present no agreement on the way the basic institutions of a constitutional democracy should be arranged if they are to satisfy the fair terms of cooperation between citizens regarded as free and equal. This is shown in the

deeply contested ideas about how the values of liberty and equality
are best expressed. (*PL*: 4; *JAFR*: 2 and 14)

In democratic thought, two main conceptions of justice exist that
assess differently the claims of equality and freedom. From a "continental" perspective, the traditional conflict has been between an
egalitarian or socialist conception of justice that gives priority to the
claims of equality and sometimes does not hesitate to sacrifice personal
or subjective liberties, and a liberal or libertarian conception, where
freedom has priority. But interestingly, Rawls only mentions the more
traditional conflict within the liberal tradition between the "liberties
of the Ancients" and "the liberties of the Moderns", an expression
coined by Benjamin Constant in his *Political Writings* (1819). The
liberties of the Ancients were basically the equal political rights of
citizens to participate in political power. For instance, for Rousseau,
political domination and inequality in the access to these rights were
the main obstacles in the conquest of liberty. In contrast, for Locke
and modern "libertarians", the liberties of the Moderns correspond
to individual freedom as an end in itself that should never be limited
except in the name of liberty itself. The protections of the person from
any interference take precedence over the search for political emancipation and equality. An explanation is probably that it was difficult
for Rawls in 1971 to see socialism as part of democratic thought and
that liberalism, not socialism, was the more progressive view for the
American "Left".[43] One has to understand the efforts of *A Theory
of Justice* against this historical and political background. As a consequence Rawls seeks above all to unify liberal democratic thought
and to advance principles of justice that unify the claims of liberty
and equality. This is not simply a question of intellectual clarity, but of
stability and survival for the ideal of constitutional democracy.

A conception of justice may be unified in the *third* sense if it can
unite a divided society. This is the most difficult question. In *A Theory
of Justice*, Rawls was fairly optimistic that there would be enough
agreement in the end to overcome the social and economic divisions
inherent in democratic societies. He was also fairly optimistic that the
main political divide in democratic societies and also in democratic
thought, between liberty and equality, would be properly addressed in
his conception. However, it is clear that already in *A Theory of Justice*,
his conception recognized the permanent existence of tensions and
conflicts of interests in free societies. He hoped that the justification

process would bring about an answer to these conflicts as important as the content of the conception of justice itself.

> Justification is argument addressed to those who disagree with us ... It presumes a clash between persons or within one person ... one of the aims of moral philosophy is to look for possible bases of agreement where none seem to exist ... Justifying grounds do not lie ready to hand.   (*TJ*: 508–9)

It is thus not satisfactory to understand *Political Liberalism* as adding the completely new dimension of pluralism to *A Theory of Justice*. The reference to incommensurable conceptions of the good is implicit in *A Theory of Justice* and the analysis of the circumstances of justice stresses that conflicts are here to stay. However, in *A Theory of Justice*, Rawls did not realize at the time how important *cultural* differences were and how crucial questions of identity and pluralism were becoming for members of free democratic societies. As he came to recognize it, "the idea of the well-ordered society as it appears in *Theory* was unrealistic" (*PL*: xviii). The critique of Rawls in the name of cultural pluralism, the so-called *communitarian* critique, developed along these lines and, for many commentators, gave rise to a "communitarian shift" in his way of thinking.[44] I shall address this problem in Chapter 4. Let us simply note here that democratic societies for Rawls are characterized by a dilemma. On the one hand, they need homogeneity and a strong consensus on justice, as we saw with the reference in Rawls to an "Archimedean point" as a shared basis for assessing our institutions impartially. In the absence of free agreement, the fear is that intervention of oppressive state power is the only alternative (*JAFR*: 34). On the other hand, "the fact of reasonable pluralism", which characterizes a society with free institutions, makes it impossible for it to be "a community, a body of persons united in affirming the same comprehensive doctrine" (*ibid.*: 3). In what sense, then, can the theory of justice provide a unitary conception properly applicable to the diversity of problems to be addressed, to the divisions within democratic thought and to the cultural fact of pluralism itself? In what sense is it different from any comprehensive conception of the good?

Michael Walzer's critique of the theory of justice

There are, obviously, formidable obstacles on the road to that ideal, some of which have been discussed by Michael Walzer, in his book

Spheres of Justice. Here Walzer claims that to treat human societies as a simple "distributive community" where one single point of access allows us to examine and assess the fairness and justice of all sorts of social arrangements is an illusion. It ignores the plurality of goods to distribute, the differences in times and places, in other words, the plurality of what he calls the different "spheres of justice".

> There has never been a single criterion or a set of interconnected criteria for all distributions ... I shall argue that the search for unity is to misunderstand the subject matter of distributive justice.
> (Walzer, 1983: 4)

His main arguments against Rawls' search for a unitary conception stem from an analysis of the plurality of social and symbolic goods to distribute among the different spheres of distribution: memberships and identities, security and welfare, economic rewards, offices, employment, free time, education, love and recognition, etc. His defence of pluralism has fuelled the major debates between liberals like Rawls and communitarians. Rawls has thus to explain that a unitary conception of justice does not necessarily need a homogeneous society. To these objections, Rawls opposes three main answers.

First, the unity of the conception does not mean that all questions of justice are similar as such. It simply means that it is possible to construct a *single point of view* from which we can clearly see the common features of our social institutions and of the basic structure of society, and assess their justice as well as their capacity to generate deep injustices. Rawls repeatedly talks in *A Theory of Justice* of a shared sense of justice among citizens of a well-ordered democratic society. In his later work, from 1980 onwards, he recognizes that unity can come from another corner than from common conceptions of the well-ordered society or of the good. Instead of being a static unity, based on given identities such as those formed through a common history and religious or even philosophical beliefs, it could be a dynamic unity, based on a transformative project, rather than on a given: the project of constructing and transforming institutions in agreement with our sense of justice. A unitary conception of justice is, then, an instrument that helps citizens to distance themselves from the advice of experts, and to become more and more confident in their own judgements and deliberations, even if the range of questions at stake goes beyond their own expertise and knowledge. The project will either fail or succeed at the level of the theory and the principles, not at the level of the resulting assessments. What is at stake here is the possibility of adopting the relevant point of view. The answer to this challenge is to be found in the method adopted by Rawls, in the device of what he calls the Original Position (see Chapter 3).

Secondly, the unity of the theory is not synthetic. It does not imply a levelling down of the historical, cultural and social diversity of the various contexts of justice. It is rather a *sequential unity* that Rawls presents in the second part of the theory, when the principles of justice are applied in a several-stage sequence: the constitutional convention, the stage of the legislature, and finally, the application of rules to particular cases (*TJ*: §31). The unity of the theory is not dogmatic, but a useful simplification to guide citizens in their appraisal through a several-stage sequence. "It is a conception for ranking social forms viewed as closed systems" (*ibid.*: 229). Rawls dedicates a great deal of effort to explaining how the theory works, because it is both unified and spread out in time.

Thirdly, the cohesion of democratic societies around a common conception of justice is not to be confused with the cultural homogeneity of a community. The public conception of justice is to be understood "as a *political* conception of justice rather than as part of a comprehensive moral doctrine" (*JAFR*: xvi, emphasis added). This means that it is limited in its scope to questions of basic political justice, that it does not rely on one single philosophical or moral doctrine, and that it can be accepted from different personal points of views as the whole demonstration in *Political Liberalism* shows.

Theoretical and practical reason

Let us conclude these remarks by saying that Rawls' main ambition is not purely theoretical, but *practical*[45] and political and that Rawls' "theory" of justice is not as theoretical as it seems. The "practical role" of political philosophy (*JAFR*: 1) is *empowerment*, even if the term itself is not used by Rawls, as he simply talks of the value of political participation, of "speaking with an equal voice in settling how basic institutions are to be arranged" (*TJ*: 205). He refers in the conclusion of *A Theory of Justice* to reaching "a standpoint that is objective and expresses our autonomy" (*ibid.*: 514). Its aim is not one of providing a dogmatic definition of justice valid anywhere, anytime, but of helping citizens assert their understanding of justice against political institutions and practices from which they may feel alienated. Rawls

71

is possibly more interested in empowerment than in truth. This has become much clearer in his later work, which lifts many of the ambiguities of *A Theory of Justice*. As a tool available to citizens, such a public conception could allow them to rely less on the advice of experts and more on their own considered judgements and deliberations. It would, in other words, redirect political power from governments to citizens and provide them with the means to resist unjust laws (theory of partial compliance), to initiate social changes and to intervene in external relations in the name of justice.

Experts and technocrats see efficiency as more relevant than justice in the assessment of institutions. Not only is this not a moral evaluation, but it is also a minority view, the view of the knowledgeable as opposed to that of the ordinary people. Important as knowledge is, the essence of democracy demands that, in matters of social structures and institutions, the last word belongs to those who must abide by the law. Conversely, if the assessment is simply that of the individual person, without the *mediation* of a public conception of justice, the citizenry is fragmented into an aggregate of particular preferences and the public good becomes the sum of particular goods. In that case, democracy degenerates into "market democracy" whose citizens are only as powerful as their coalitions or lobbies. In contrast, preferences informed by public reason and discussions are morally more responsible and political in the full sense of the term. The priority of justice means that preferences that are not compatible with justice carry no weight and that majorities, as such, have no legitimacy. The primacy of justice is inseparable from the empowerment of citizens.

6. A major difficulty with the priority of justice

Of the three interpretations of the primacy of justice, it is the contractarian one that has given rise to the most worrying objections. Most criticisms are addressed to the questions both of the nature and of the usefulness of the contract in the justification process. A full presentation of the usefulness of the contract appears in Chapter 3 on the Original Position as it explores the justification process in more detail. I simply conclude this introductory chapter with some details about the complex nature of the social contract approach for Rawls.

The nature of the social contract

For most critics, it is far from clear that the social contract model fully represents the priority of justice over economic interests in democratic societies. Martha Nussbaum, in her recent critique of Rawls (2006), convincingly argues that his use of the social contract and of a conception of the person as fully productive and cooperating over a whole life leaves so many unsolved problems and unaddressed injustices that it should be abandoned.

I have insisted that justice for Rawls has three aspects that need to be combined: mutual advantage, reciprocity and impartiality. The question is whether the social contract does not emphasize the demands of reciprocity and mutual advantage beyond the demands of impartiality. Jean Hampton (1980), in a very perceptive article, shows that Rawls seems unclear about the balance between two features of a contract. Is it primarily about *reciprocity* and the pressure that each party exerts upon the others? In that case, in place of a free agreement, "a give-and-take process will take place, a negotiation of conflicting interests" (Hampton, 1980: 116). There is not much ethical force in the device of the contract so interpreted. "The bargaining process would never end in a contract" (*ibid*.: 121). Or is it about the *commitment* involved in forging a contract not to change one's mind? In that case, reciprocity and the interests of the others drop into the background. "All we need now is an irrevocability condition; so why can't this constraint be stated directly?" (*ibid*.: 123). In the end, "an attempt to derive a fair justice conception from the circumstances of actual contractual agreements with actual people won't work" (*ibid*.: 122). Hampton concludes that Rawls is confused because he fails to include in his conception features that characterize real binding contracts: reciprocity and finality. She raises then the question of the usefulness of the contract in view of Rawls' perfectly valid non-contractarian selection procedure in the Original Position (*ibid*.: 129).

Ronald Dworkin's inspiring analysis of the difficulties of the social contract leads to similar conclusions (Dworkin, 1977: ch. 6). For him, "the contract cannot sensibly be taken as the fundamental premise or postulate of the theory of justice … it must be seen as a kind of halfway point in a larger argument as itself the product of a deeper political theory that argues for the two principles through rather than from the contract" (*ibid*.: 169). This "deeper theory", for Dworkin, is rights-based and "the contract does make sense in a rights-based deep theory … a theory that is based on the concepts of rights that are natural" (*ibid.*: 176). He concludes that "justice as fairness rests on the assumption of a natural right of all men and women to equality of concern and respect" (*ibid.*: 182). This is obviously the exact opposite of what Rawls is aiming at with the device of the social contract: a non-foundational procedural conception of justice in the absence of any reference to natural law.

Very differently, David Gauthier (1986) claims that Rawls is not sufficiently contractarian. His contractarian view of morality is half-hearted and indeed, in *Political Liberalism*, Rawls corrects his view in *A Theory of Justice* that the theory of justice was part of the theory of rational decision.[46] Instead a fully contractarian theory of morality would "generate morality as a set of rational principles for choice. We are committed to showing why an individual, reasoning from non-moral premises, would accept the constraints of morality on his choices" (Gauthier, 1986: 5). Obviously, Rawls is not contractarian in that sense. Let us conclude, for the moment, that possibly the social contract is more *a way of thinking* about potentially just arrangements as those that free and equal persons could agree to rather than a way of effectively binding people into an actual agreement on justice. The social contract for Rawls is not an actual contract, rather "a device of representation" for our considered judgements in reflective equilibrium. We still have to show the usefulness of such a method.

The prescriptive force of the contract

A second major difficulty concerns the authority of the social contract or the "compliance problem". If the principles of justice have the binding force, as Rawls claims, of "a categorical imperative" in the Kantian sense (*TJ*: §40), they must as such have power over people's motivations and effectively constrain their pursuit of the good and of their own satisfaction when and if it is contradictory to justice. The priority of justice means that justice comes first, not that it depends on agreeing to a contract from which one expects to benefit. There is a contradiction between the appeal to a contract based on self-interest and the affirmation of the priority of justice. The nature of *rationality* is not clearly spelt out in all its consequences. For instance, in *A Theory of Justice*, Rawls tends to use the term "rational" both for the rationality of self-interest and for the rationality of the moral law. Mentioning Kant's conception of morality, he says: "Kant begins with the idea that moral principles are the object of rational choice" (*TJ*: 221). This is extremely confusing and has been understood generally in the idiom of rational choice theory, which is contrary to Rawls' views on rationality. This major difficulty branches out into three distinct but related problems.

The first one is the *prescription* problem. How can people be moved to abide by the principles of justice, to recognize their authority? Rawls claims that the appeal to the social contract helps people to understand and to agree upon one single conception of justice. I have described the conception of justice as empowering and helping people to make choices and assessments and to understand why the laws are justified on the basis of a common conception of justice. But citizenship is not just about choices and exercising rights and freedoms. It is also about abiding by the law and fulfilling obligations and *duties*. It needs the backing of a conception of the person that would explain how real people move from being the source of the law to being subject to the law. We have still to explain why people would accept the principles as prescriptive, binding and authoritative. Providing an answer is the reason why Rawls dedicates so much space to the question of stability in the third part of *A Theory of Justice* and in *Political Liberalism*.

The second problem is the *motivation* problem. The only way to answer the prescription problem is to appeal to specific motivations. We need to understand how the principles of justice would motivate people to act without appealing solely to self-interest or, even more improbably, to justice itself as suggested by Brian Barry's interpretation of the moral motivation for justice (1989: 359). But Rawls also suggests that the social contract is based on justice as mutual advantage, on expected benefits. This would seem contradictory, unless we have a detailed conception of motivation. In other words, we need a conception of ethics as both personal and institutional.[47] Unless Rawls claims that reason in itself is a powerful agent for action and that understanding the justice of a decision, an institution, etc., is motivation enough to submit to it, we cannot see why two types of motivation, self-interest and a sense of justice, are called for. This is noted too by H. L. A. Hart's critique when he concludes that

> Rawls' argument for the priority of liberty purports to rest on interests, not on ideals, and to demonstrate that the general priority of liberty reflects a preference for liberty over other goods which every self-interested person who is rational would have … I do not think that it succeeds in demonstrating its priority.
>
> (Hart, 1975: 252)

Unfortunately, Rawls does not give such an explanation of why we should act, other than on the basis of self-interest. This is the line taken by Hobbes and his modern followers, such as David Gauthier,[48] who abandon the priority of justice. Morality can be based on a contract where expected benefits compensate for the limitations introduced by the principles of justice. Rational self-interest is the motivation that leads to agreement to the principles of justice. But, in that case, it is obvious that the claim of the priority of justice loses its force.

The third problem is the *realization* problem. How are the principles of justice to regulate our institutions? Do they have the authority of the moral law, as Rawls seems to suggest in §40 of *A Theory of Justice*, and nothing else to rely upon? In that case, we might be tempted to say to Rawls that the real world of politics is as far away from the idea of a moral law as can be imagined. Is there not a utopian trait here? Rawls seeks to adapt Kant's conception of the priority of justice to the political world without sharing Kant's political realism. He treats the social contract as a way of constructing both morality and the legitimacy of the state and of the law. Is this acceptable?

For Kant, the solution to all these related questions is to be found in the Transcendental Argument and in a metaphysical conception of the person that Rawls has never accepted.

The human subject, for Kant, belongs to two different worlds. On the one hand, as a natural creature, he is part of the empirical world of *phenomena*, or of things as they appear to us. In that realm he is submitted to the law of causality and to the two *a priori* forms of intuition: time and space. On the other hand, as a rational being, he is part of the intelligible world of *noumena*, or of things as they are in themselves, beyond time and space, but also beyond human rational knowledge. There, the causality of freedom reigns as time and space are not at work, and he understands himself as autonomous and as legislator in the kingdom of ends. The priority of justice means for Kant that we have the capacity to legislate in, and to act causally upon, the empirical world too: to obey the law that we have set for ourselves.[49] The moral law is the realization in the empirical world of our nature as free and rational agents. This is the solution to the prescription problem: the only law compatible with our freedom is the moral law. We obey the law as a categorical imperative on the basis of respect for humanity and reason in ourselves and in others, thus solving the motivation problem.

But the priority of justice for Kant applies exclusively to morality. The political situation asks for very different mechanisms, as men are not only rational beings, but also self-interested "devils", as he says in *Perpetual Peace* (1970: 112). "How, asks Kant, does nature guarantee that what man ought to do by the laws of his freedom (but does not) will in fact be done through nature's compulsion, without prejudice to the free agency of man?" (*ibid.*). The motivation and prescription problems cannot be solved, contrary to Rawls, through rational agreement, but with the aid of nature, i.e. self-seeking inclinations. This means that "the mechanism of nature can be applied to men in such a manner that the antagonisms of their hostile attitudes will make them compel one another to submit to coercive laws, thereby producing a condition of peace within which the laws can be enforced"(*ibid.*). Following Rousseau, Kant says that we can only alienate our freedom to a political authority that has its source in ourselves. But this is a *regulative* ideal of how republics should be regulated, not a description of the way actual political institutions function, even less a way of assessing their virtue. Kant is much more pessimistic than Rawls. The realm of morality is divorced from the political world. Only the law can mediate between the two.[50] This is Kant's solution to the realization problem. Compared to Kant, Rawls sounds over-optimistic and utopian.

However, Rawls rejects such an appeal to the Transcendental Argument because of the unacceptable dualism involved. He nevertheless thinks that the conception of the person that is at the basis of his argument should address all three difficulties. In *A Theory of Justice*, citizens are described as both rational self-interested agents and as moral persons, capable of obeying justice for justice's sake. The term "rational" is used in a very loose way. But later, in *Political Liberalism* and *Justice as Fairness*, Rawls makes a clear distinction between the Rational, or the capacity to rationally pursue one's self-interest, and the Reasonable, or the capacity for a sense of justice as impartiality. The priority of justice thus means the priority of the Reasonable over the Rational. We have to be alerted to this difficulty, which recurs in the conception of the person as deeply divided. Therefore, Rawls needs to appeal to the philosophy of education and the psychology of child development (Piaget, Kohlberg) in the third part of *A Theory of Justice* and in *Justice as Fairness*: §59, to answer satisfactorily the motivation and realization problems. The prescriptive power of the principles of justice, however, remains a major difficulty.

Philosophy of history

I suggest, to resolve this difficulty, another possible line of argument, which is that only a philosophy of history can answer the realization problem, but that this is only sketched in Rawls' later works: *Justice as Fairness* and *The Law of Peoples*. Here Rawls is nearer to Hegel than to Kant.[51]

Hegel was confronted with a similar difficulty when he rejected Kant's dualism and Transcendental Argument while affirming the centrality of freedom of both the moral agent and of the citizen in the description of the modern state. In *The Phenomenology of Spirit* and *The Philosophy of Right*, he thought that this duality could be overcome through historical processes of reconciliation between ideals and social realities, between Spirit (*Geist*) as individual freedom and Spirit as culture and institutions. Historical struggles and crisis progressively give reality to the noumenal world and to the Ideas of Reason. Rawls even quotes Hegel: "When we look at the world rationally, the world looks rationally back" (*JAFR*: 3; *LOP*: 124–7). It is amazing to see that the late Rawls quotes Hegel and the theme of reconciliation as an objective for political philosophy. Even more interesting is the term of "realistic utopia" applied to his attempt at a reasonable law of peoples and to the aims of political philosophy as a whole. Philosophy of history is possibly the missing link which would demonstrate the full potential of Rawls' realist utopia.

Conclusion

Let us conclude that the priority of justice is a revolutionary concept in that it leads to citizens' empowerment, but that it may be weakened or even contradicted by the appeal to instrumental rationality. This is the reason why, in his later work, Rawls hardly mentions justice as mutual advantage and develops instead the central value of reciprocity. He also rejects his previous interpretation of the theory of justice as a part of the theory of rational choice. In the end, the conception of rationality and of practical reason, which Rawls appeals to, has to be remodelled. The debate with utilitarianism as well as the central debate with H. L. A. Hart (Hart: 1975) are the occasions of such a clarification, as I now show in Chapter 2.

Chapter 2

Constructing the principles of justice

> The natural distribution is neither just or unjust; nor is it just or unjust that persons are born into society at some particular position. These are simply natural facts. What is just or unjust is the way institutions deal with these facts. (*TJ*: 87–8)

In this chapter, I examine how Rawls translates his *moral* doctrine of the priority of justice into *political* principles of justice. The method he uses to that end is *political* constructivism (*PL: Lecture III*). Constructivism, as I showed in Chapter 1, is Rawls' specific method, which avoids imposing personal moral criteria to collective guidelines and political principles, as dominant-end or teleological doctrines would do, thus disregarding citizens' autonomy. Constructivism generates instead from within, so to speak, a transformation of our considered moral intuitions into political principles during a two-stage process. In the first stage, we reconstruct moral *intuitions*: this is the focus of this chapter. In the second stage, we reconstruct the *reasoning*: this is the subject matter of Chapter 3, in which I examine the argument of the Original Position leading to the two principles of justice as fairness as the preferred alternatives. Note, however, that the moral intuitions and convictions in question are not apolitical from the start: they are the moral "fixed points" of citizens in a functioning constitutional democracy, a precision that was implicit, but probably not sufficiently stressed in *A Theory of Justice*, and that is crucial for the correct understanding of Rawls' project.

In what sense are principles of justice political? I have already noted how a theory of justice may seem far removed from the concerns of real politics and how difficult it is to establish the connection. Let us say, for the moment, that such principles are political in their *function*: they aim to regulate the design of democratic institutions, to influence political practices and to inform public political culture. They have a practical aim leading to collective choices and policies that contrast with the kind of abstract philosophical analysis that Rawls is providing in the first part of *A Theory of Justice*. This is obviously an area of great difficulty, where Rawls' challenges are at their greatest and where criticisms have been at their most ferocious.

In Section 1, I analyse the major difficulties of Rawls' constructivist method, and, then, in Section 2, I describe the requirements that principles of justice should meet to figure on a list of alternatives in the initial choice situation. In Section 3, I present Rawls' first principle of justice: the principle of equal liberty, and I show how distinctive it is, compared with traditional liberal views. I move on in Section 4 to the second principle, which is, in reality, made up of two principles: the principle of fair equality of opportunity and the difference principle. I explain the nature of Rawls' egalitarianism and the reasons for his rejection of merit as a basis for distributive justice. The reconstruction of the various utility principles – classical, average and restricted – figures next on the list in Section 5. Then, in Section 6, I briefly examine intuitionist and perfectionist principles as plausible candidates for a public conception of justice. I conclude in Section 7 by noting that two of the major difficulties still remain. It is far from clear that all the principles on that list are political principles of justice and that the conception of distributive justice presented in Rawls' second principle overcomes the tensions between liberty and equality. Indeed, his conception remains highly controversial, for both libertarians and egalitarians.

1. Three difficulties of constructivism

Before describing the list of principles that Rawls has selected, it may be useful to start by singling out three major difficulties of constructivism, while noting that, to be fair, we should wait until the presentation of Rawls' constructivist method is complete to make a final judgement. An overall assessment would be premature and will have to wait until the end of Chapter 3, where the second stage of the process is presented.

The first difficulty concerns the relation between ethics and politics and the nature of the principles of justice. In this first stage, Rawls *constructs* the various principles of justice as "an accurate account of our moral conceptions" (*TJ*: 45–6).[1] These are present both in the history of moral philosophy as observed by the moral theorist, and in our own moral experience, our moral sentiments and ideals, as citizens of modern constitutional democracies (*CP*: 288). The theory of justice, says Rawls, is "a theory of moral sentiments (to recall an eighteenth century title)" (*TJ*: 44). The aim is that, following Sidgwick's view, "the common moral thought of mankind may be at once systematized and corrected". These principles are obviously simplifications and approximations, and "we need to be tolerant of simplifications if they reveal and approximate the general outlines of our judgments" (*ibid.*: 45). However, these principles must also connect with the various background political conceptions and values that have conflicted within the history of democratic thought. They must be relevant in view of the general facts of, say, unequal access to political power and economic development, legal institutions, the organization of political parties and of social group interests, etc. As Joshua Cohen, in an important paper, notes: "politics and morality are different: moral thought is concerned in part with what *I* should do in a world in which other people do not see eye to eye with me, but democratic politics is concerned with what *we* should do when we do not see eye to eye with one another" (2003: 130). One main worry at this stage is that Rawls is examining moral instead of political principles. Principles that are to guide social and economic policies or to protect the rule of law are inspired in a complex and often unconscious way by personal moral principles that guide persons in their private lives. Policy-makers understood as moral agents are balancing various objectives using their own moral doctrines as criteria of efficiency, fairness and justice. Now, this is exactly what should be avoided in a *public* conception of justice and what Rawls finds unacceptable in utilitarianism: the *collective* aspect of political morality is ignored and that the same principle is used for individual and collective decisions. Obviously, a public conception of justice needs principles that are really political, not "applied moral philosophy". One main question that we have to keep in mind during the presentation of the principles in this chapter is: How can the constructivist method enable the move from traditional moral theories to real politics?[2]

A second major difficulty that I would like to underline from the outset is that Rawls does not draw a strict distinction between the *description* of the various principles of justice in the initial situation, and the *justification* of his own favoured interpretation.[3] He deliberately constructs the principles of justice in a way that favours his own view. In other words, in the same way that he does not distinguish between the examination of the history of moral doctrines by the moral theorist and his own self-examination, he does not distinguish between the expository process that informs the reader, and the justification process.[4] For instance, in an important section on moral theory, Rawls says that the comparison with utilitarianism is an expository device while, at the same time, it is an argument in favour of his alternative view (*TJ*: 46). Rawls creates some confusion by failing to establish a clear line between those two aims. He struggles to present the different alternatives in a fair light while, at the same time, claiming that his own interpretation of the initial situation, "justice as fairness", is to be preferred. This is possibly responsible for some of the many obscurities in the book. To lift this ambiguity, I suggest we approach the list of alternatives *as if* we were in the initial position, ignorant of Rawls' own preferences, the principle of utility being on a par with Rawls' own principles: simply as alternatives from which we choose. We may then take his claim seriously. We, the readers, are now embarking on that same voyage as the parties in the initial contractual situation and we have to make up our minds without being influenced by Rawls' initial claim.

A third and even more serious difficulty is that the principles of justice should be constructed in a way that addresses the claims of both liberty and equality. Now, there is an obvious tension between the two, a tension that the political debates between socialism and libertarianism perfectly illustrate. Once equal rights and liberties are guaranteed as the fundamental charter of a liberal constitutional democracy, some individuals will take advantage of them and fully exploit their threat advantage and bargaining power to gain greater benefits and positions of superiority. The priority of liberty generates inequalities due to the greater *natural* talents and endowments of some, inequalities that the liberal principle of equality of opportunity encourages and justifies, when it claims that once *social* circumstances are neutralized, individuals are fully responsible for their own choices, for instance to work more or less, even if that means increasing inequalities in their life chances and standards of living. The egalitarian response claims that the distinction between natural and social circumstances is not valid, that people's natural abilities are socially determined and that freedom, as a source of unjustified inequalities, should be reined in, even by state power, and its excesses corrected by redistribution. The conflict between liberty and equality has obviously been even more violent in the history of the non-liberal world than in Rawls' own context. This has created a great deal of interest, but also scepticism, towards his views. One important issue that unfortunately cannot be properly addressed within the limits of this book is whether Rawls' thinking about the conflict between freedom and equality has something to contribute to socialism, especially to liberal socialisms and social-democratic ideologies.[5] Let us conclude for the moment that we should look at Rawls' constructivism as a form of *liberal* political constructivism, reflecting the values of liberal constitutional democracies, which makes it both important and problematic for the non-liberal world.

2. The initial contractual situation and the list of alternatives

I shall now present the various alternatives available to us in the initial choice situation. We should thus imagine the principles that are to regulate a well-ordered or just democratic society as if they were the result of a hypothetical contract between all members concerned: all our basic political and social institutions and the distribution of power, as well as the rules regulating the market, the family, etc., the whole of the basic structure of society, should be designed in such a way that they could publicly win our agreement if we were asked for it. "We have to ascertain which principles it would be rational to adopt given the contractual situation" (*TJ*: 16). The whole scheme should appear to us as if we had chosen it and we should therefore willingly comply with it, even if "no society can, of course, be a scheme of cooperation which men enter voluntarily in a literal sense" (*ibid.*: 12). The idea of a contractual scheme expresses the constitutive element of the democratic ideal: that we should be treated as equal and free citizens, as autonomous and responsible agents, submitting only to principles and laws that we have ourselves agreed to. I said in Chapter 1 (Section 3) that Rawls uses the social contract paradigm in order to represent the principles of justice as grounded in freedom: this is the meaning of the priority of justice. The idea of the social contract models our understanding of what a free society is, that is, a fair scheme of cooperation between free and equal members who hope to benefit equally and fairly from it. This is the *general conception* of justice that is characteristic of a democratic society:

> All social values – liberty and opportunity, income and wealth,
> and the social bases of self-respect – are to be distributed equally
> unless an unequal distribution of any, or all, of these values is to
> everyone's advantage.[6]   (*Ibid.*: 54)

Cooperation and reciprocity are the characteristics of justice in a
society of equals with both conflicting and converging interests, capable of both limited altruism and moderate self-interest, as we saw in
the analysis of the circumstances of justice. One should not confuse
justice with charity, mere humanity or supererogatory acts. Contractarianism is thus the main feature of a conception of justice fit for a
well-ordered democratic society because it incorporates the ideas of
both reciprocity and freedom, at the possible price of overlooking the
tension between the two aspects, as I noted in Chapter 1.

The initial situation (TJ: §3)

The initial situation is a way of thinking about justice that clarifies
our considered judgements, the structure of moral doctrines and the
controversies surrounding distributive justice. It is the first methodological step leading to the idea of the Original Position. The assumption is that such an abstraction helps to detach us from the immedi-
acy and subjectivity of moral beliefs and to model political morality
in a clearer way. It is made up of three elements: the parties in the
contractual arrangement; the aim of the process; and the choice
conditions.

First, the parties in this initial situation are constructed by Rawls as
"representatives" of all concerned (*TJ*: 12; *JAFR*: §6). They are artificial persons, clearly distinct from existing citizens and from "you and
me", as actual readers of Rawls (*PL*: 28; *JAFR*: 45, n. 8). One common
mistake made by critics is to treat them as real persons, not as constructs in a device of representation, say, as characters in a play (*PL*:
27). The parties are representatives who act as trustees or guardians
entrusted with citizens' most important interests. Therefore they are
rational choosers in a very weak sense, borrowed from economic theory and involving no controversial ethical element. They want above
all to further citizens' conflicting rational first-order interests and conceptions of the good. They are mutually disinterested in the sense that
they are not interested in other people's interests, but they are neither
egoistic nor selfish, having interests *of* the self, not *in* the self (*TJ*:

111). Finally, they ignore envy and are not characterized by special psychologies (*ibid.*: 12).

Secondly, they are to choose the best principles of justice, not, as in the case of social contract doctrines, the best form of government (*JAFR*: 16). Note, however, that the two objectives are connected, as the constitutional stage where citizens choose the best constitution in view of the principles of justice is the immediate successor to the initial situation (*TJ*: §31).

Thirdly, it is the description of the situation that incorporates the idea of justice as impartiality and reciprocity, not the special psychology or rationality of the parties. Justice appears in an autonomous way, not as an antecedent criterion derived from the parties' moral doctrines. In this way, the parties can represent anyone and are a good way of representing anyone's thoughts on justice. The parties are to choose from a situation of equality where they are placed symmetrically. Reciprocity is the main condition: they cannot choose principles that they would not themselves abide by (*TJ*: 13). Their choice is final: they cannot change their mind according to unforeseen circumstances (*ibid.*: 11). However, the contract is hypothetical and non-historical, which contradicts its having a binding force (*CP*: 400, n. 19).[7] Finally, the choice is public, meaning that everyone concerned knows that the others know that they have agreed on the principles.

In this initial situation, we are presented with a list of alternative principles of justice. Remember that principles are not simply precepts, but belong to an organized conception of justice that systematically defines the contested concepts relevant for justice: liberty, equality, reciprocity and fairness. In the following stage, when we move from the initial situation to the Original Position, we must choose the best conception of justice, and the reasons and criteria for choosing it have to be made clear and public. Further down the line, constitutional arrangements are to be derived from these first principles and so on, in a four-stage sequence (*TJ*: 12 and §31).

The list of alternatives (TJ: §21)

I now explore the alternatives available in the initial situation. The alternatives offered suggest some initial questions. What is the origin of these doctrines? Why this specific list? Is it not arbitrary? Rawls' answer follows Sidgwick's *Methods of Ethics*, which identifies three main traditions: utilitarianism, intuitionism and egoism. "A list that includes the leading traditional theories is less arbitrary than one which leaves out the more obvious candidates ... the list used is not simply *ad hoc*: it includes representative theories from the tradition of moral philosophy" (*TJ*: 509). If this is correct concerning utilitarianism, perfectionism and intuitionism, it is less obviously so with regard to Rawls' own two principles, which may strike us as going beyond the limits of moral philosophy in having some implicit political content. The difference principle, for instance, is typically social-democrat whereas the first principle mirrors Mill's principle of liberty, which puts constitutional limits on democratic government. We can only suggest that they represent left-of-centre liberal or social-democratic views (*JAFR*: §41 and §49, 138–9). Rawls repeatedly says that he favours a property-owning democracy or "liberal socialism" in contrast to either right-of-centre libertarian views or the capitalist welfare state (*TJ*: xiv–xv; *JAFR*: 135–6 and 139–40). He also often suggests that his principles are compatible with state ownership of the means of production (socialism) or with private-property economy, as for him the right to private property is not a basic liberty (*TJ*: 239–42; *JAFR*: §52). The difficulty lies in the fact that the alternatives are presented in terms of moral philosophy whereas it would have been less problematic if they had been expressed in the traditional terms of political philosophy: socialism, conservatism and social democracy.

A second meta-ethical question concerns the *structure* of the conceptions and principles from which we have to choose. There are various kinds of normative conceptions. "The traditional moral theories are for the most part single-principled or intuitionistic" (*TJ*: 40). Single-principled or "dominant-end" conceptions are illustrated by the utility principle, which applies to both individuals and institutions. Intuitionist doctrines may propose a plurality of principles, but as a bundle, without any rules of priority to organize them. Finally, a plurality of principles can be proposed, but coordinated by priority rules. The two principles proposed by Rawls under the title "justice as fairness" are just that: a plurality of principles organized by various priority rules. The first principle is *lexically* prior to the second. This means that, as in the order followed by a dictionary, it must be fully applied before the second can be operative and so on. Such an ordering might represent the solution to the conflict between liberty and equality: liberty is lexically prior and equality can be implemented only within the limits of the priority of liberty, a solution that differs profoundly from the classical liberal conception and, of course, from socialism.

Requirements

Let us now summarize the main requirements principles of justice must fulfil to appear on the list.

First, the principles of justice are to be fit for a modern *democratic* society with a regulated free market economy, where the political convention is that everyone as a citizen should gain from its policies as formulated in the general conception of democratic justice.

> It is a political convention of a democratic society to appeal to the common interest. No political party publicly admits to pressing for legislation to the disadvantage of any recognised social group ... Since it is impossible to maximize with respect to more than one point of view, it is natural, given the ethos of a democratic society, to single out the point of view of the least disadvantaged and to further their long-term prospects.   (*TJ*: 280–81; *JAFR*: 133)

This excludes both socialism and libertarianism, which are too costly either for the better off or for the worse off.

Then, they should be principles of *institutional* justice that are to apply to the basic structure of society, not to individual positions. This excludes justice as reward for individual merit. They do not apply to private associations: different principles of *local* justice would apply to the family, churches, schools and universities, etc. This excludes also the case of *global* justice (*TJ*: 7).

A very important requirement is that they should apply to *both aspects* of the basic structure of society, even if the argument will take the two parts as constituting a whole (*ibid.*: 7). Remember that for Rawls these two parts are, first, the realm of *political justice*: matters of rights and liberties, duties and opportunities, the acquisition and the exercise of political power. The second part is concerned with *economic and social inequalities*. It deals with access to and distribution of economic resources and opportunities (*TJ*: 53; *JAFR*: 48). Rawls suggests that a first principle should cover the first part, that is, the protection of the rule of law and of basic political and civil liberties, and a second one the concerns of distributive justice. It goes without saying that this is an approximation that will gradually be refined, especially in order to better emphasize how very tightly connected the two domains are. This requirement excludes socialism, which does not fully protect the first part, and neo-liberalism or libertarian doctrines, which leave the second part to market forces and deal only with allocative justice.

They should cover *general* or normal cases of justice where the circumstances of justice apply and persons are fully cooperating members of society throughout their lives. This excludes situations where mental health problems, physical disabilities or other reasons, such as child-rearing needs, affect the cooperative capacities of persons. This question is the focus of Martha Nussbaum's critique of Rawls (2006) and of his incapacity to reach out to so-called unproductive people and their need for justice. *Special* principles of compassion or care are then needed. This distinction seeks to eliminate misunderstandings of the limits of Rawls' programme[8] (*PL*: 183).

They must be sufficiently *simple* and *rational* to be publicly understood by all and then agreed upon; they should not simply be *ad hoc* precepts that are at the wrong end of generality and cannot lead to reconciliation (*TJ*: 270).

They are to apply to the *ideal* (strict compliance) case of a well-ordered society (*ibid.*: 8). Non-ideal cases, such as conscientious objection or civil disobedience, are dealt with separately (*ibid.*: §§55–59).

The complete list of alternatives is given in *A Theory of Justice*: 107.

A. The two principles of justice as fairness (in lexical order)
   1. The principle of greatest equal liberty
   2. (a) The principle of (fair) equality of opportunity
      (b) The difference principle
B. Mixed conceptions. Substitute for A2 above
   1. The principle of average utility; or
   2. The principle of average utility, subject to a constraint, either:
      (a) That a certain social minimum be maintained, or
      (b) That the overall distribution not be too wide; or
   3. The principle of average utility subject to either constraints in B2 plus that of equality of fair opportunity
C. Classical teleological conceptions
   1. The classical principle of utility
   2. The average principle of utility
   3. The principle of perfection

    D. Intuitionistic conceptions
        1. To balance total utility against the principle of equal distribution
        2. To balance average utility against the principle of redress
        3. To balance a list of prima facie principles
    E. Egoistic conceptions (though strictly speaking the egoistic conceptions are not alternatives)
        1. First-person dictatorship.
        2. Free-rider: everyone to act justly except for myself, if I choose not to.
        3. General: everyone is permitted to advance their interests as they please.

In the following sections, I concentrate mainly on (A), (C) and (D).

3. The first principle of justice as fairness

The two principles presented by Rawls have been the subject of a secondary literature of gigantic proportions. They have been scrutinized by philosophers, lawyers, political scientists, sociologists and economists over a long period of time. It would go beyond the limits of this introduction to explore the various debates that they have generated and still continue to generate. Even providing a reading guide would be a huge task. Instead, I shall concentrate on Rawls' text and on his reactions to criticisms, on the reasons why he changed his formulation many times and on some difficulties of interpretation, especially concerning the balance between social circumstances and personal choices as sources of inequalities.

Equal liberty

The first principle of justice is the principle of equal liberty, which is first presented by Rawls in *A Theory of Justice* in quantitative terms.[9]

> Each person is to have an equal right to the most *extensive* scheme of equal basic liberties compatible with a similar scheme of liberties for others.   (*TJ*: 53 and 266, emphasis added)

Rawls has modified the statement of the first principle, following Hart's criticisms, which I explore in more detail in Chapter 3, and he gives the following final statement in *Justice as Fairness*: 42. The first principle now reads as follows:[10]

> Each person has the same indefeasible claim to a fully adequate scheme of equal basic liberties, which scheme is compatible with the same scheme of liberties for all.   (*JAFR*: 42)

This final statement conveys important clarifications. First, we should consider the priority of the overall *scheme* of basic liberties, not of liberty as such. It is not liberty as such that has priority, as many have failed to understand, but the scheme that has "an absolute weight with respect to reasons of public good and perfectionist values" (*PL*: 294). This again distances Rawls from classical liberalism and a maximization of liberty is certainly not what he has in mind in this first principle. Secondly, this scheme comprises many basic liberties that may clash with each other, such as freedom of thought and free speech (*ibid.*: 340–48). They need to be balanced against each other or to be regulated on the basis of a satisfactory criterion. Such necessary regulations are not restrictions. As a consequence, the quantitative presentation of the first principle has to be corrected. To talk of the most extensive liberty is not satisfactory. "It is only in the simplest and least significant cases that the criterion of the greatest extent is both applicable and satisfactory" (*ibid.*: 331). Regulations – not restrictions – of basic liberties have to be introduced. Finally, not all liberties are basic liberties. For instance, the right to private property is not a basic liberty (*TJ*: 242; *PL*: 338). The detailed argument for the priority of basic liberties is presented later in Chapter 3.

The following three important provisos or preconditions complement the statement of the first principle.

(1) *Reasonably favourable economic conditions* must obtain before any principle of justice can be applied (*PL*: 297; *JAFR*: 47). This means that poor or "burdened societies" (*LOP*: 105–6) cannot be required to apply the first principle until they reach a certain level of economic development.

(2) "This principle may be preceded by a lexically prior principle requiring that *basic needs*[11] must be met, insofar as their being met is a necessary condition for citizens to understand and to be able fruitfully to exercise their basic rights and liberties" (*JAFR*: 44, n. 7). Provision of a social minimum is a constitutional essential derived from the idea of justice as reciprocity

and of society as a cooperative scheme where all should benefit (*ibid.*: 48 and 130).

(3) Equal political liberties have a special status and are to be guaranteed their *fair* value (*TJ*: §36; *JAFR*: 149). Citizens then have an equal chance of influencing policies, irrespective of their economic and social class.

In his 1975 paper: "Equal Liberty and Unequal Worth of Liberty", Norman Daniels expressed the classic Marxist concern that *formal* liberties are no liberties at all. Rawls agrees "that the basic liberties may prove to be formal" (*PL*: 325) and "that the equal liberties in a modern democratic state are in practice merely formal" (*JAFR*: 148 and 177). The question is what their worth or usefulness to persons is if "social and economic inequalities in the background are ordinarily so large that those with greater wealth and position usually control political life and enact legislation and social policies that advance their interests" (*ibid.*: 148). Most people do not have the means to properly understand and exercise their rights, and these remain mostly formal possibilities. Rawls is so impressed by this criticism that he now claims that "Hegel, Marxist and socialist writers have been quite correct in making this objection" (*PL*: lviii) and that he should clarify his position. The first principle should incorporate a *proviso* that "is the guarantee that the political liberties and only these liberties are secured by their fair value" (*ibid.*: 327). The point is that political liberties are crucial to guarantee equal access to legislative power and to protect the fairness of the political process. "The fair value of the political liberties ensures that citizens similarly gifted and motivated have roughly an equal chance of influencing government's policy and of attaining positions of authority irrespective of their economic and social class" (*JAFR*: 46; *PL*: 358). "The guarantee of fair value for the political liberties is one way in which justice as fairness tries to meet the objection that the basic liberties are merely formal" (*PL*: 328). This necessitates that some institutions are in place, such as the public financing of elections, a certain fair equality of opportunity, especially in education and training, a decent distribution of income and wealth, long-term security guaranteed by society and basic health care (*ibid.*: lviii–lix).

I would like to mention here that the principle of the fair value of political liberties has recently entered British and American politics. The "stakeholder society" was one of the main ideas of Prime Minister Tony Blair during his 1997 campaign. Citizens should not be treated as passive recipients of benefits and welfare. They should be seen as having a stake in society, as being an active part of its cooperative arrangements and having correlative political responsibilities and duties: to vote, to participate in public-good issues and concerns and in public deliberations. In America, the political philosopher Bruce Ackerman has come up with two important initiatives inspired by Rawlsian concerns to give political liberties their fair worth. The first one is described in his controversial book, *The Stakeholder Society* (co-authored by Anne Alstott), where he suggests that in order for citizens to equally enjoy their political rights, they should all be allocated on civil majority a capital sum of $80,000 which would represent their guaranteed stake in society – society's help to correct the natural and social inequalities that distort the equal access to political power. In a second book, *Deliberation Day* (co-authored with James S. Fishkin), he proposes an even more controversial measure, that all citizens be given a holiday on the eve of major elections to participate in public deliberations in order to exercise in a responsible manner the full range of their political liberties.[12]

The pedigree of the first principle is obvious: it derives from the various historical bills of rights and declarations of the rights of man.[13] Rawls carefully avoids any mention of these historical declarations, as the specific conceptions of justice and of the good that inspired them are too confused and controversial to be used as building blocks in his demonstration. Moreover, they belong to historical ideologies such as the European Enlightenment, which might prove culturally divisive. If human rights are universal, they do not need a philosophical foundation, and the theory of justice is certainly not going to play that role.[14] Rather, for Rawls, these declarations, as part of the background culture of constitutional democracies, provide one formulation among others of the widespread convictions and beliefs that are the starting point for his theorizing on justice.[15] Remember that the role of the social contract method is to allow an independent reconstruction of such convictions that publicly clarifies the reasons for our agreement, allowing us to be fully active, not passive, citizens as we do not simply rely on historical traditions.

The first principle is designed to answer the question of the constraints on personal liberty imposed in the name of justice: how far should my own freedom be allowed to expand while still being legitimate, without becoming the expression of my own threat advantage, of my own will to dominate others? The traditional liberal answer has been that my personal freedom should extend as far as possible and be limited only in the name of liberty itself. Considerations of justice and inequality are not central for liberals, as liberty is seen, first of all, as a personal power, not a social one, and social cooperation is instrumental rather than constitutive of it. Freedom is understood as non-interference, not as non-domination (Pettit, 1997). In contrast, Rawls' concern for justice and equality leads him, as a disciple of Rousseau rather than Locke, thoroughly to transform classical liberalism by adding the equality requirement not simply as instrumental for, but as constitutive of, liberty: he moves from liberal freedom to *democratic freedom*.[16] The main reason for this is that, following Rousseau, he considers that "the fundamental status in political society is equal citizenship, a status that all have as free and equal persons" (*JAFR*: 132). The turning point in the theory of justice is the move to replace considerations concerning individual persons and their good with considerations concerning citizens and their relative positions in the basic structure of society. Choosing the basic structure as the subject of justice entails reasoning about social positions and injustices rather than about individual preferences. This is, of course, the transformation operated by Rawls' constructivist method: constructing moral intuitions valid for the social structure, not for individual situations, that are political in that specific sense. The consequence of this concern for social cohesion and stability explains why the first principle is strongly egalitarian and distances itself from classical liberalism. Equal rights and liberties are constitutive of personal freedom, not instrumental to it. This is a serious departure from classical liberalism and we can expect major objections to it for being too egalitarian.

The priority of basic liberties

The second important feature of the first principle is that it is *lexically* prior to principles that apply to the distribution of social and economic advantages. "The lexical order requires us to satisfy the first principle in the ordering before we move on to the second, the second before we consider the third, and so on ... A serial order avoids having to balance principles at all" (*TJ*: 37–8). The priority rule does not mean that liberty can only be restricted for the sake of liberty, as Rawls first misleadingly said (*TJ*: 220 and 266). It means that the whole scheme of liberties has absolute priority and reads as follows:

> The priority of liberty means that the first principle assigns the basic liberties, as given by a list, a special status. They have an

> absolute weight with respect to reasons of public good and of perfectionist values. (*PL*: 294)

What Rawls means here is (1) that these basic rights and liberties are *inalienable* (*ibid.*: 365–6) and (2) that no consideration of economic efficiency and growth should constitute a basis for *denying* these liberties to any social group (*ibid.*: 295). In other words, the priority of justice means the priority of liberty over other political and social values, of politics over economics. This is, in my view, the most striking feature of Rawls' conception of justice, a feature deeply misunderstood in mainstream interpretations.[17]

> This priority rules out exchanges ("trade-offs", as economists say) between the basic rights and liberties covered by the first principle and the social and economic advantages regulated by the difference principle. (*JAFR*: 47)

Two comments here. First, the priority of basic liberties is an effective way of transcending the debate within democratic thought between liberty and equality by claiming that *equal* liberty, not liberty as such, has priority and that it has priority over the claims of distributive justice. Indeed, this clarification constitutes one of the great successes of *A Theory of Justice*. Liberty and equality are not to be seen as opposed and there should be no trade-offs between them as claimed both by libertarians and socialists. The tension does exist, but can be overcome through a rule of priority. The rule of priority is parallel to the affirmation of the priority of justice over the good and is the central moral claim in *A Theory of Justice*: economic advantages or redistribution cannot justify infringements of the absolute claims of liberty (*TJ*: 55).

Secondly, the position adopted by Rawls may be interpreted as an attempt at controlling the negative effects of majoritarian democracy and of "market democracy". No consideration whatsoever can justify the sacrifice or the infringements of citizens' powers, of their constitutional rights and liberties. Their priority is embedded in the constitution itself. "It expresses the priority of the constitution and of constituent power" (*JAFR*: 46). In view of the tyranny of majorities and of the violations of human rights that so-called democratically elected regimes have perpetrated, this is a very important point. It opens up the debate between advocates of constitutional regimes and of majoritarian democracies.

Obviously, an important question remains whether all social resources will not be exhausted by the implementation of the first principle, especially by investing in education, health, housing, etc. to guarantee the fair value of basic liberties, leaving nothing for the application of the second principle.[18]

The list of basic liberties

However, I said earlier that, for Rawls, not all liberties are basic. The list of basic liberties includes:

(1) Freedom of thought and liberty of conscience.
(2) The political liberties and freedom of association and the freedoms specified by the liberty and integrity of the person.
(3) The rights and liberties covered by the rule of law.

"Liberties not on the list, for example the right to own certain kinds of property, (e.g. means of production) and freedom of contract as understood by the doctrine of laissez-faire are not basic; and so they are not protected by the priority of the first principle" (*TJ*: 54). They are to be dealt with at the legislative, not the constitutional, stage. In consequence, the debate between advocates of private or collective ownership of the means of production cannot be settled by reference to principles of justice, but only through political process, on the basis of "the traditions and social institutions of a country and its particular problems and historical circumstances" (*PL*: 338).

More precisely, for Rawls, the basic liberties are those that are essential for the ideal of citizens as free and equal persons. They are not arbitrarily selected, but they rely on a conception of the person and of society that is shared by citizens in democratic societies. Again, thinking about justice in a constructivist way means changing the moral outlook and moving from personal conceptions of the good to shared conceptions of the person and of society, conceptions that are political in that specific sense. Unfortunately, in *A Theory of Justice*, Rawls remains too vague on this point and on the political content of his constructivist method. He seems too often to be reasoning in terms of the rational agent, omnipresent in economic theory, who is both rational and apolitical. It is only in his later work, in *Political Liberalism* and *Justice as Fairness* that this is made clear, as I show in Section 5 of

Chapter 3. In *A Theory of Justice*, for instance, Rawls says that the first principle applies to the first part of the basic structure of society and to the assignments of rights and duties (*TJ*: 53). But this is too vague and apolitical. In *Justice as Fairness*, he is more specific. The first principle has priority because it applies to the "constituent power" of the people as superior to that of government, or to "ordinary power as exercised routinely by the officers of a regime"[19] (*JAFR*: 46). It has priority since it applies to more crucial matters: to constitutional essentials and to basic questions of justice. Constitutional essentials are those rules that are decided at the constitutional convention and that cover

> (a) The fundamental principles that specify the general structure of government and the political process; the powers of the legislature, executive and the judiciary; the limits of majority rule;
> (b) The equal basic rights and liberties of citizenship that legislative majorities must respect ... as well as the protections of the rule of law. (*JAFR*: 28)

We may conclude, then, that the first principle aims at reconciling liberalism and democracy, or the liberty of the Moderns with the liberty of the Ancients – which is exactly Rawls' programme.[20] In particular, the emphasis is on protecting constitutional rights from any threat from political majorities. Majoritarian or electoral democracies have always been seen as potentially dangerous for the rights of minorities, as they tend to give a different weight to the liberties of those in majorities. Even if the question of whether a constitutional regime is to be preferred to majoritarian democracy is not in the foreground, it represents the wider political context of the first principle. For Rawls, a just society is based on the liberal principle of legitimacy: its citizens are to be treated as moral persons, as having an equal moral status that forbids any unjustified restrictions on or interferences with them, a moral status that their political status should express. However, this political status, as we have seen, is not instrumental, but constitutive of personal freedom. This means that the freedoms enjoyed by others are equally important and that Rawls' first principle is more egalitarian than most liberal views. Still, strict egalitarianism too is a danger to be avoided, for not all inequalities are unjust for Rawls. Such is the narrow strait that he has to navigate.

Criticisms of the first principle

A number of objections and criticisms have been raised against Rawls' conception of the basic liberties and of their priority, which Rawls has addressed in his later work, along with the main Original Position argument. As usual, the result is a complex multi-layered reasoning. The main questions that we have to keep in mind are the following. Is not the priority of basic liberties a costly requirement, especially for poor countries? The answer lies in the *first proviso*: the first principle can be applied only if reasonable economic and social conditions obtain, not in desperate situations where survival is at stake (*JAFR*: 47). Another objection is that, once these reasonable conditions obtain, the protection of constitutional rights is expensive and requires a continually high level of economic and social development. If we were to take the lexical priority seriously, would this not mean that all resources had to be allocated to it, leaving very little for the second principle? This is the "liberal Paretian paradox" discovered by Amartya Sen: that rights-based considerations can be inconsistent with Pareto optimality.[21] Another objection is that, as we have seen, the basic liberties are treated by Rawls both as items on an index of primary goods and as non-negotiable constraints on the pursuit of economic welfare. Habermas in particular remarks that treating liberties as goods involves a serious contradiction. Liberties are not commodities and Rawls instrumentalizes them (Habermas, 1999: 54). To that, the following answer is suggested by Van Parijs (2003): Rawls considers opportunities, not outcomes, and basic liberties are required for their transformative powers. They are thus not inert goods, but productive conditions for opportunities. Again, Sen's criticism of Rawls' primary goods is helpful and forces him to reason in terms of possibilities or opportunities, not of actual goods. Other criticisms are more obvious. The priority of basic liberties is a liberal Western concept and has no meaning for different cultures. Rawls claims in *The Law of Peoples* that even non-democratic countries could accept them at the international, not the domestic, level. We will examine the solidity of this claim in Chapter 5. However, a more worrying objection is that Rawls strongly contrasts the basic liberties that are "constitutional essentials", and social and economic rights that are not enshrined in the constitution because they are too controversial and do not have the same moral and political priority. This contradicts the Universal Declaration of 1948 and we have to ask whether it is possible to complement Rawls' argument with an analysis of the link between basic liberties and the fight against poverty, as argued by Pogge (2002) – a link still denied by most.

4. The second principle of justice as fairness

We now move on from the protection of equal basic rights and liberties to the distribution of social and economic resources, that is, from *protective* to *distributive* justice. This is a much more controversial domain and few aspects of Rawls' thought have given rise to so many discussions and comments. In particular, the famous difference principle can be considered as epoch-making.[22] This is the principle that specifies the second half of the statement of the "general conception of justice": a distribution is justified if it is to everyone's advantage, especially the least fortunate, even if it is an unequal distribution (*TJ*: 54). It reformulates the economic principle of Pareto-efficiency that says that a distribution is efficient if all benefit from it and no one is made worse off. The need for redistribution of economic resources has many justifications beyond justice, such as economic efficiency, social stability and cohesion, and so on. However, for Rawls, redistribution is a *moral* imperative too in a sense that is mostly absent from classical liberalism: as constitutive of the status of equal citizenship. Rawls' second principle is more egalitarian than the liberal principle of equality of opportunity, which concentrates only on the social sources of inequalities and does not exclude as unjustified inequalities that arise from the free competition of natural individual talents. However, it is less egalitarian than a socialist principle of redistribution.[23] Rawls, instead, defends a *democratic* conception of equality where both natural and social circumstances are to be counteracted. This is the full meaning of justice as *fairness*. It is justified as a way of giving content to the general conception of justice (*TJ*: 54) and of "preventing the use of the accidents of natural endowment and the contingencies of social circumstances as counters in a quest for political and economic advantage" (*ibid.*: 14). It wants to address the distressing problem of eradicating unjustified inequalities, poverty and the existence of an underclass, unable to access full citizenship and the full benefits of membership in a democratic society.

The problem of distributive justice

As with the first principle, two aims collide: the creation of wealth and economic efficiency with the avoidance of divisive and unjustified inequalities. However, the main difficulty is that equality cannot have the same meaning when one deals with rights, on the one hand, and with distributive justice, on the other. Equal rights are bestowed on us in virtue of our common humanity and dignity. There is no room for hesitation about this, as Rawls shows, using the metaphor of points inside a circle.

> The property of being in the interior of the unit circle is a range property of points in the plane. All points inside this circle have this property although their coordinates vary within a certain range. And they equally have this property since no point interior to a circle is more or less interior to it than any other interior point.
>
> (*TJ*: 444)

We are equal in virtue of *who we are*, that is, as members of the same human race, possessing the same moral personality and deserving equal respect; and we cannot be more or less members of it. The ideal of equal democratic citizenship provides the political point of view from which to reflect on this and to appraise the distribution of income and wealth in order that the least advantaged find themselves treated as nearly as possible in accordance with this standard (*TJ*: 82). However, inequalities already start appearing with *what we do* with what we are, that is, with individual freedom as we are all differently endowed by nature. The major debate thus concentrates on the distinction between inequalities resulting from *choices* or from *circumstances*, on how far the second principle corrects the prevailing view that only social, not natural, inequalities are undeserved. The question is whether, as Kymlicka (1990: 70) claims, "Rawls himself leaves too much room for the influence of natural inequalities; and at the same time leaves too little room for the influence of our choices".[24] The traditional liberal claim is that some inequalities are justifiable in view of what people do with their natural assets and of the consequences of their actions for them and for the common good. Justice should ensure that, as long as what they do is their own choice, and that they have all the opportunities they need to make sound decisions, the inequalities that will inevitably result from these choices, for instance, to work less or more, to develop some valuable talents over some others or not, and so on, are justified. Such differentiations are, as we have seen, crucial to the idea of justice as *fairness* for Rawls. However, when should they stop playing a role? When are choices real choices and free from natural contingencies? We have seen that justice for Rawls is about social control and regulation of necessary unequal outcomes of apparently free choices, not about eradicating them (*TJ*: 88). In this way, for him, "the difference principle offers a way of seeing nature and the social world as no longer hostile to democratic equality" (*JAFR*: 76). This is a tall enough order and, as critics have noted, a sharp distinction between choices and circumstances remains extremely difficult to maintain.

The second principle is based on widespread social-democrat intuitions, familiar to most contemporary left-of-centre political parties and electorates, but still highly controversial, having been severely criticized from both the right and the extreme left. Such a radical principle leads to questioning the nature of inequality and its link with justice. It also leads to the rejection of familiar views of what a democratic process is, the role of merit, ownership of talents, etc. In one of his most significant analyses, Rawls shows how both socialist and libertarian ideologies have misunderstood the nature of inequality and how the clash between the demands of liberty and equality can be overcome. He draws his inspiration from the postwar historical experience of the welfare state in Europe and to a lesser extent in America, and from both their successes and their failures. Concerning its pedigree, Rawls does not give us much information. He simply says that "we should recognize that the difference principle is not often expressly endorsed; indeed, it may prove to have little support in our public political culture at the present time" (*JAFR*: 132–3). In spite of being costly and sometimes counterproductive, policies of redistribution are necessary because on its own the market is unable to regulate exchanges in a way that meets the two requirements of equality and liberty (*ibid.*: 44). Distributive or social justice is a demand that places social stability and cohesion, "fraternity" says Rawls (*TJ*: 90) and "reciprocity" (*JAFR*: 77), at the centre of its concerns so "that economic and social inequalities contribute to the general good or, more precisely, to the benefit of the least advantaged" (*ibid.*: 52). But at the same time, it "recognises the need for inequalities in social and economic organisations of which their role as incentives is but one" (*ibid.*: 68). Distributive justice then authorizes "social and economic inequalities necessary or else highly effective in running an industrial economy in a modern state" (*JAFR*: 77).

Two conceptions are thus excluded from the start. A strictly *socialist* egalitarian view is concerned not so much with improving the position of the least advantaged as with eliminating altogether inequalities or differences, even inequalities that are an engine for economic efficiency and that provide incentives for innovation and the creation of wealth. This conception of social equality is mostly irrational and based on envy.[25] It is not a matter of justice for Rawls, who is concerned with *democratic* equality (*TJ*: §81).

The second view, the *libertarian* doctrine that rejects distribution as an unjust interference with basic rights and the natural process of legal acquisitions, is dismissed from the start. Let us imagine a situation where property and resources are initially fairly equally distributed. We could then take it that any subsequent distribution resulting from fair and legitimate agreements or contracts between individuals was itself fair, and that any additional redistribution of resources would be an interference with our basic liberties. Such an ultra-liberal view was already present in Locke and has been famously re-actualized by Robert Nozick in *Anarchy, State and Utopia* (1974). It is discussed by Rawls at length, but cannot count as an alternative conception of distributive justice.[26] What is missing in such an extreme view, as a consequence of its individualism, is the concept of the social structure that, for Rawls, is fundamental to our present understanding of democracy. A just social structure can be undermined by

> the accumulated results of many separate and seemingly fair agreements ... Very considerable wealth and property may accumulate in a few hands and these concentrations are likely to undermine fair equality of opportunity, the fair value of the political liberties, and so on. (*JAFR*: 53)

Distributive justice as an "ideal social process" corrects this by concentrating on the basic structure and its institutions, "and on the regulations required to maintain background justice over time" (*ibid.*: 54). The difficult problem is, then, how to respect legitimate expectations and to avoid unacceptable interference and regulations. As in the case of the first principle, the situation is one of tensions between competing demands, and the aim is to find a compromise.

One last difficulty. Distributive justice is often confused with *allocative* justice. Allocative justice starts with a bundle of goods and commodities, and asks how it should be fairly distributed or allocated among given individuals who have not cooperated in any way to produce these commodities. "Justice becomes a kind of efficiency" (*TJ*: 77). But this is not satisfactory because it ignores the damaging and widespread inequalities that may stem not from individual positions in respect of that distribution, but from the basic structure of society itself. It ignores the role of background social institutions in creating or correcting inequalities. Allocative justice is not justice for Rawls

(*JAFR*: 50; *TJ*: 56). In other words, the transformation initiated by
Rawls results in taking seriously the idea of distribution and replacing
aggregation with equality.

Statements of the second principle

The second principle of justice reads as follows in its initial presentation in *A Theory of Justice*: §11:

> Social and economic inequalities are to be arranged so that they
> are both
> (a) Reasonably expected to be to everyone's advantage, and
> (b) Attached to positions and offices open to all.   (*TJ*: 53)

Here Rawls seems to advance two very traditional liberal principles:
the principle of Pareto efficiency and the principle of equality of opportunity. A distribution is Pareto efficient if it cannot be modified without
at least one person losing out: it is to everyone's advantage, worse- and
better-off members. Equality of opportunity means that the inequalities resulting from arbitrary social circumstances are unjust and should
be counteracted whereas those resulting from natural talents are
justified. Now, in *A Theory of Justice*: §12–13, Rawls presents what
he calls the *democratic interpretation* of these two principles. This
means that the formulation of (a) undergoes a major change, in that
"to everyone's advantage" now reads: "to the greatest benefit of the
least advantaged" and has become the controversial *difference principle* (*ibid.*: 72). The formulation of (b), the liberal principle of equal
opportunity, is equally modified. "Positions and offices open to all"
is transformed by the mention "under conditions of fair equality of
opportunity" and becomes the principle of *fair* equality of opportunity
(*ibid.*). This parallels the transformation of the first principle of equal
basic liberties, when the *fair* value of political liberties was added as a
crucial proviso, answering the Marxist criticism of formal justice and
requiring that "all should have a fair chance of attaining equality"
(*JAFR*: 43). One sees now more clearly what Rawls means by justice as
fairness.

> The democratic interpretation is arrived at by combining the prin-
> ciple of fair equality of opportunity with the difference principle.
> The principle removes the indeterminateness of the principle of

efficiency by singling out a particular position from which the social and economic equalities of the basic structure are to be judged.   (*TJ*: 65)

The *first* priority rule of the second principle thus requires that the difference principle, or (a), is subordinated to (b), the principle of fair equality of opportunity, and the final formulation to be found in *A Theory of Justice*: 266, has not varied since.

> Social and economic inequalities are to be arranged so that they are both
>
>> (a) to the greatest benefit of the least advantaged, consistent with the just savings principles, and
>> (b) attached to offices and positions open to all under conditions of fair equality of opportunity.

Now, we must not forget that the second principle is to be applied in tandem with the first principle at a further stage, the legislative stage. Like the first principle, it expresses political values and it would be a mistake to limit it to economic justice: it affects not only the market, but also the whole basic structure and its background institutions (*JAFR*: 48). This makes the whole argument in favour of distributive justice much more convincing, as it connects it with constitutional rights and liberties.[27] Following Joshua Cohen's analysis, I examine in Chapter 3 the argument in its favour as a political argument for democratic equality, not simply as a principle of redistribution (J. Cohen, 1989).

Legitimate expectations, desert and recognition

The next important clarification concerns the fact that the second principle may appear unfairly biased towards the least favoured and to ask too much of the more talented and diligent citizens (*TJ*: 88). It seems to ignore a central demand of justice, that merit or desert should be rewarded. The discussion of the place of merit among principles of justice is a good occasion to clarify how Rawls sees the articulation between what I have called his *social holism*, that is, the fact that he primarily considers the deep inequalities created by the social structure, not individual positions within it, and his defence of *personal autonomy*. Is not social determinism a way of nullifying the importance of personal efforts and responsibilities as sources of justified inequalities? What is the balance for him, in the origins of inequalities, between the weight of natural and social circumstances and the role of free choices and decisions? How much responsibility is left to individual persons if the social structure is determining?

There are two parts to the problem: natural endowments and social circumstances. First, it is obvious that we do not deserve our lot in the lottery of natural endowments (*TJ*: 89). Moreover, these natural gifts only acquire their superior value if (1) they are cultivated and (2) they are in demand in society. Natural talents are thus socially mediated for Rawls and never a "given". This is a first difference with both utilitarians and libertarians, who are not concerned with preferences' social formation.

Secondly, do we deserve rewards for the efforts we put into training and developing our talents to the best of our ability? Is diligence to be rewarded? A central tenet of our most basic intuitions about justice is that it is only what *we do*, and not what *we are*, as a consequence of the natural and social lottery, that counts for distributive justice. Merit and individual efforts should thus be rewarded and bad luck that prevents us from success should be compensated. Rawls' answer is complex and has two parts.

Below a certain level of social justice, when the principles of justice do not apply, it is obvious that these efforts are often a mere reflection of social circumstances: individuals are not equally autonomous and responsible for their fate. As a consequence, the efforts that the more talented put into training and developing their skills into socially valuable assets are morally unjustified and cannot claim reward as they rely on natural and social contingencies such as family and class background, health and education, etc. and are socially determined. Rawls' principle of difference singles out superior talents as morally justified on condition only that they are used in ways that contribute to the good of all, especially to the least fortunate. Individual talents have social consequences that a just basic structure should regulate for the benefit of all, especially the least fortunate. Does that mean, as some critics have suggested (Nozick, 1974: 228; Sandel, 1982: 78–80), that the distribution of native endowments should be regarded as a common asset (*TJ*: 87) and that society "owns" people's superior useful talents and skills? This is a misinterpretation and would breach the first principle of equal liberty as the better off would sacrifice what is their own for the benefits of the least advantaged. No such trade-offs are allowed. The main idea is that benefits and rewards are determined by a social scheme that is just and efficient if it is to everyone's advantage, and where people's talents work for the benefit of all, with priority given to those who are worst off. The better endowed do not abandon ownership of their talents for the benefit of the least advantaged. "To the contrary, the question of ownership of our endowments does not arise" (*JAFR*: 75). Such a misconception stems from a misunderstanding of justice defined as *reciprocity*. In the same way that talents and skills are only valuable insofar as there is a demand for them and in that they are beneficial to some segments of society, so benefits and advantages earned from these talents become a common asset if they benefit all, especially the least advantaged. People are rewarded "not for their place in that distribution, but for training and educating their endowments, and for putting them to work so as to contribute to others' good as well as their own. When people act in this way, they are deserving" (*ibid.*). "To be sure", as Norman Daniels writes,

> we may deserve some credit for the way in which we develop and exercise our marketable talents and skills, and we may acquire legitimate expectations about what we deserve from our talents and skills when we follow the rules set by a social scheme, but we do not deserve (and are not responsible for) the results of the combined social and natural lottery that contribute so much to our capabilities.[28]

Thus justice is not meritocracy and the second principle is not a principle of redress, aiming at compensating people for all social and natural contingencies; its ambition is certainly not to be an insurance policy and to completely level the playing field.[29]

In contrast, beyond that threshold, once just institutions are in place, it is up to individuals to develop and take advantage of these opportunities. When they do, the role of the basic structure is not to restrict their autonomy, but, on the contrary, to back it. This is why just institutions do not need indefinitely increasing economic prosperity. As a consequence of his rejection of "luck-egalitarianism", Rawls affirms: "such a principle does not require continual economic growth over generations" (*JAFR*: 63), as it is neither a maximizing principle nor a principle of *redress* (*TJ*: 86–7). It leaves the choice and the responsibility to determine the desirable level of resources to the people themselves. If they do not choose to develop further, like the surfer at Malibu Beach who prefers leisure to work, it is their responsibility as autonomous persons, and they have to accept that justice is not meant to compensate them for the consequences of their choices.

People who prefer leisure to work, such as "the Malibu beach surfers, must somehow support themselves" (*CP*: 455, n. 7; *JAFR*: 179). If the incapacity to work and support oneself is not the result of a choice, but of bad luck, then it is no longer a matter of justice but of care and assistance. As I show in Chapter 5, Rawls' analysis of the duty of assistance to poorer countries and the equally important duty to respect their autonomy supports my interpretation and shows clearly the limits of justice. Even when just institutions are in place, not all inequalities can be mitigated, only destructive and unjust ones. The principle indicates a tendency to equality, not full equality, because redress is only one among the different aims of a just social order. Rawls' second principle is a good example of "complex egalitarianism".[30]

Let us conclude that Rawls' position is consistently anti-individualist in its analysis of merit while respecting the value of free and autonomous choices and the limits of corrective justice. Either our merit is personal and reward is not a question of social justice, or it is measured against a social criterion of the value of our contribution, and then the criterion is not provided by merit itself, but by the institutional context. It is thus incoherent to claim merit for choices for which we are not fully responsible and that are socially, not personally, determined. If they exist, "real" entitlements are socially determined by recognized public rules and should be distinguished from vague and confused individual aspirations to rewards.

> There is no criterion of a legitimate expectation or of an entitlement, apart from the public rules that specify the scheme of cooperation ... Apart from existing institutions, there is no prior and independent idea of what we may legitimately expect, or of what we are entitled to, that the basic structure is designed to fulfil. (*JAFR*: 72)

However, it is highly likely that such a distinction between social circumstances and "free choices" is not as clear as Rawls would like it to be and that we should expect many controversies in this area.[31] For instance, for David Miller, meritocracy could be defended even by egalitarians like Rawls if they renounced determinism in their understanding of the talents that are the basis for reward. "Equality is arrived at not by dividing all advantages up equally, but by enabling different people to excel in different social spheres" (Miller, 1996: 300).

Three ideas of desert need to be distinguished (*TJ*: §48; *JAFR*: §20).

(1) *Moral* desert, in the strict sense, is measured against a comprehensive moral or religious doctrine. It has no place in a public conception of justice, as moral and religious views of what constitutes a worthy or righteous person conflict. "It does not provide a first principle of distributive justice" (*TJ*: 275). Appeals to justice in the name of merit are confusing, except in the general sense that as moral persons, we deserve equal respect for what we are, not for what we do with what we are. "The equal moral worth of persons does not entail that distributive shares are equal" (*TJ*: 275). It should, then, be clear that moral and social conditions should not be confused.

(2) When we move to the *social* concept of desert, we commonly presuppose that people's efforts to develop their useful talents should be rewarded. But, again, "it seems clear that the efforts a person is willing to make are influenced by his natural abilities and skills and the alternatives open to him. The better endowed are more likely to strive conscientiously" (*ibid.*: 274). Thus, the precept that recommends reward for efforts is not acceptable as a first principle of distributive justice since it ignores this fact, even if it can be used as a useful motivational incentive for economic efficiency and social stability. It should be replaced with a clear notion of legitimate expectations and entitlements, defined by reference to a scheme of social cooperation in order to measure corresponding rewards and acquisitions.

(3) Finally, deservingness is even more specific when it is measured against a system of public rules designed with a view to certain purposes, such as those of games, when we say that the losing team deserved to win. In this specific case, non-moral desert is meaningful. Only merit as defined in (2) and (3) is relevant for a conception of social justice.

It is remarkable though that, when discussing merit, Rawls does not connect this analysis with his later discussion of *self-respect* and with the twin notions of self-esteem[32] and social recognition in Part III of *A Theory of Justice*. One of the strong points of Rawls' analysis of self-respect is that he refers to it not simply as the Kantian notion of impersonal respect for persons and humanity in oneself, but also connects it with self-esteem in a new and interesting way that recent movements such as the politics of *recognition* and the work of Axel Honneth have also developed.[33] In particular, Rawls' analysis of moral psychology gives an important role to what he calls the Aristotelian principle of social interaction in the formation of preferences and choices.

> Human beings enjoy the exercise of their realized capacities (their innate or trained abilities) and this enjoyment increases the more the capacity is realized or the greater the complexity ... The companion effect to the Aristotelian principle is that the esteem and admiration of others is desired, the activities favoured by the Aristotelian principle are good for other persons as well. (*TJ*: 375–6)

Because self-respect, for Rawls, is not solely a subjective assessment of one's own worth, but requires intersubjective interaction and evaluation, it is a very important sign of the justice of social institutions. Self-respect is strongly connected with self-esteem and social recognition in the sense that we need the validation of others to continue having faith in our own abilities and endeavours. "Without it nothing may seem worth doing, or if some things have value for us, we lack the will to strive for them ... we need to find our persons and deeds appreciated and confirmed by others" (*TJ*: 386). Self-respect is thus one of the most important social values of a democratic society.

Now, if we try to understand the meaning of demands for merit to be rewarded, it is obvious that what people do demand is not simply for their merit (1) to be recognized in a vague and general way as moral persons, but that this recognition should also include their specific aims and achievements. The demand for justice is indeed a demand for recognition. Rawls' notion of self-respect as intimately connected with self-esteem and recognition should have provided him with a way of fully understanding the hidden side of meritocracy and of the demand for justice as a demand for recognition, not simply for respect. The notion of merit is certainly confused. It is a claim to certain rewards not simply and "rationally" because the rules allow them, but also in order to compensate for what a strict regime of rewards and duties misses: the social benefits of recognition for our self-respect. The recent development of the politics of recognition in both social movements and political philosophy is indeed connected with Rawls' major intuitions, putting in a new light the importance of moral psychology for social justice. Equally, Avishai Margalit's remarkable analysis of the "decent society" as a society that does not humiliate its members[34] shows how the claims of justice and the experiences of humiliation and shame are connected. We would not ask for merit to be recognized and rewarded if there was not a tendency for individual efforts to be discounted by the social structure.

It is fair to say that Rawls' holistic view of justice in the first part of *A Theory of Justice* tends to take him too far in one direction and to ignore the way in which individual demands for social recognition stem from the vulnerability of self-respect in a competitive society and from its foundation on self-esteem, a foundation that he himself describes quite clearly in Part III of *A Theory of Justice*.[35]

5. The principle of utility

The next principle on our list is the principle of utility in its three versions: classical, that general utility should be maximized; average, that average utility should be maximized; and restricted, that utility maximization requires a context of protected basic liberties and rights, the fair value of political liberties and fair equality of opportunity, that is Rawls' principles of justice less the difference principle. We know that utilitarianism is a conception that Rawls strongly opposes. Remember that, for Rawls, the history of democratic thought is characterized by two great debates. The first opposes "the liberties of the Ancients" to "the liberties of the Moderns", that is, equal political liberties and the values of public life, to personal liberty (*PL*: 4–5). The principles of justice as fairness try to address this divide. The second main debate opposes the social contract tradition to utilitarianism:

> In the history of democratic thought two contrasting ideas of society have a prominent place: one is the idea of society as a fair system of social cooperation between citizens regarded as free and equal; the other is the idea of society as a social system organised so as to produce the most good summed up over all its members ... The tradition of the social contract elaborates the first idea, the utilitarian tradition is a special case of the second. (*JAFR*: 95–6)

Rawls' reconstruction of the utility principle

The aim is to present a reconstruction based on our considered judgements of justice that is fair to utilitarianism. Is that feasible, given Rawls' ambition to replace utilitarianism with his own conception? In reality, one should note that Rawls himself started out as a quasi-utilitarian philosopher and that his early articles were still very much influenced by it as the dominant moral doctrine of the time. In 1955, for instance, he argues in favour of a modified form of utilitarianism, which applies to "rules of practices", though not to rules for actions taking place within a practice – a notion that anticipates that of the basic social structure. He claims, on the basis of this distinction, to "state utilitarianism in a way which makes it a much better explication of our considered moral judgments" (*CP*: 21). However, as early as 1958, he recognizes that utilitarianism is unable to account for justice as *fairness*.[36] *A Theory of Justice* is entirely based on an attack on the utility principle and on a vindication of the two principles of justice as fairness. It is thus difficult to find a fair statement of the utility principle in the initial choice situation, as it is always accompanied by Rawls' criticisms (*TJ*: §5–6 and §30). However, the utility principle was so well known, it occupied such a prominent position at the time as the only reliable and "scientific" normative principle, that such difficulties did not seem central. The situation since *A Theory of Justice* was published has changed dramatically and the fact that utilitarianism no longer figures prominently in the 2001 *Restatement* is revealing of the impact of Rawls' criticism. This does not mean that Rawls' critique of utilitarianism belongs to the past. Far from it! I would, for instance, suggest that it is particularly relevant for the debate with socialism and the argument supporting the priority of politics over economics that is characteristic of Rawls' thinking.

Still, I would like to add a word of caution. Even if Rawls' presentation of the utility principle is not a caricature, it weakens some of its most attractive features. I will mention two of these. First, utilitarianism is a form of *naturalism*. This means, as Rawls recognizes, that in the division of labour between general facts and moral considerations, "it is characteristic of utilitarianism that it leaves so much to arguments from general facts. Justice as fairness by contrast embeds the ideals of justice more directly into its first principles" (*TJ*: 138). It is based on observation of human nature, human behaviour and psychology and has no speculative element in it. It is a monism in that facts and values are simply correlated, following Mill's well-known statement that the "proof" of utilitarianism is to be found in the observation of normal or most frequent human attitudes toward pleasure and pain. "No reason can be given why the general happiness is desirable, except that each person desires his own happiness" (Mill, 1969, ch. 4: 36). This would be a fallacy, as G. E. Moore claimed, if the principle had *prescriptive* force, if it indicated a duty. However, this is not the case. The utility principle is a tool of assessment, designed to help in deciding in very general terms what the best course of action is. It does not indicate what everybody ought to do in specific cases or what a just and well-ordered society should look like. Its ambitions are very different from those of a theory of justice. For that latter purpose, very different guidelines are needed. Mill mentioned the role of *axiomata media* or intermediate axioms for the indirect application of the principle to specific situations. The principle of utility recommends, but does not prescribe. This is fully recognized by Rawls when he writes: "Rules of practices are not guides to help someone decide particular cases correctly as judged by some higher ethical principle"(*CP*: 38). In contrast, the claim of the priority of justice and of its independence from the good needs a complex metaphysical set-up to justify its prescriptive force. It needs something like Kant's constructivism and dualist transcendental argument and the divide between *phenomena* and *noumena* – between nature and liberty – that Rawls consistently rejects. Can his political constructivism then succeed in matching utilitarianism's balance between general facts and moral considerations?

The second feature of the utility principle that is somehow discounted by Rawls is its powerful reformist drive. Utilitarians, with the exception of William Paley and Henry Sidgwick, were not conservative. They fought against common-sense precepts of their times, against religious and traditional moralities, political and legal injustices, on account of their often dire consequences. They had a very robust conception of justice as a condition of universal happiness that helped them to fight the status quo, in favour of the abolition of capital punishment (Bentham) or the vindication of the rights of women (Mill). They also fought the indeterminacy of the idea of natural rights, replacing them with rights embedded in the general facts of human nature (*TJ*: 29).[37] Rawls recognizes that theirs was a reformatory project.[38] Still, this is not sufficiently stressed in his presentation. In contrast, Rawls' reliance on considered convictions and widespread moral beliefs might look ill founded and leading, as Richard Hare once said, to "appeals to the reflections of the *bien pensants* ... to a cosy unanimity with people generally, congratulating themselves on having attained the truth".[39] Many critics of Rawls have noted that his relationship with the status quo might sometimes look too cosy. Utilitarians in contrast do not shy away from controversy. Peter Singer's utilitarian argument in favour of animal rights is a more recent and powerful example of this reformist drive.[40]

Utility as a principle of justice *(TJ: §§5–6 and 30)*

The statement in *A Theory of Justice* of the principle of utility and of its variations is a reconstruction. It draws on the historical doctrine but, at the same time, deliberately ignores some of its most important recent developments. It retains only certain relevant features of the classical works of Bentham, Mill and, most importantly, Sidgwick, adding references to the contemporary work of John Harsanyi on rule-utilitarianism and average utility. In that sense it is not fully comprehensive.

The general principle reads as follows:

> The main idea is that society is rightly ordered, and therefore just, when its major institutions are arranged so as to achieve the greatest net balance of satisfaction summed over all the individuals belonging to it.
> *(TJ: 20)*

This statement defines utility as satisfaction, that is, as a subjective experience.[41] It assumes that interpersonal comparisons can at least be summed up at the margin. Applied to the basic structure, it maximizes the absolute weighted sum of the expectations of the relevant representative men. When the size of the population increases, so does general utility, no matter how low the level for the least advantaged has fallen (*ibid.*: 139). Note that the general principle is only concerned with aggregation, not with distribution and inequalities. It is concerned with *allocative*, not distributive justice. Traditionally, the utility principle has been seen as a prudential principle of administration of resources. As Rawls notes, "the only principle that can guide legislation on a large scale is the principle of utility" (*ibid.*: 285). How does the principle of utility transform itself into a normative principle of justice? How can universal moral duties be generated by a prudential principle of maximization of the aggregate good? This is the central difficulty that utilitarian authors have addressed in various ways and that Rawls describes as follows.

For Bentham, as Rawls notes, the utility principle is not a principle of justice, but "simply a working rule of legislation" (*ibid.*). However Mill is less clear and tends to derive justice from utility as general benevolence, and refers to justice as a "useful social illusion" in *Utilitarianism*, Chapter 5. Sidgwick, having read Kant, was more aware of the central difficulty and of the fact that benevolence could not be equated with justice. His solution is more sophisticated: justice for utilitarianism is impartiality. What best encapsulates the utility principle as a principle of justice is the metaphor of the "impartial spectator" familiar to readers of David Hume and Adam Smith.

> It is by the conception of the impartial spectator and the use of sympathetic identification in guiding our imagination that the principle of one man is applied to society ... Endowed with ideal powers of sympathy and imagination, the impartial spectator is the perfectly rational individual who identifies with and experiences the desires of others as if these desires were his own. In this way, he ascertains the intensity of these desires and assigns them their appropriate weight in the one system of desire the satisfaction of which this ideal legislator then tries to maximize by adjusting the rules of the social system.   (*Ibid.*: 24)

Such a conception makes no distinction between the two aspects of the basic social structure, the claims of liberty and right, on the one hand, and the desirability of increasing aggregate social welfare for all, on the other, but claims that a single principle can deal with both: utility maximization, be it the personal utility function or the social welfare function of individuals taken together.[42] The protection of liberty and rights is indirect: it is derived from the utility principle in virtue of its social utility. There are four main features that, for Rawls, make utilitarianism a strong contender: rationality, reliance on a single principle, maximization, and the role of sympathy. I will develop only the first point: rationality.

Utilitarianism is attractive because it "regards what is rational for one man as right for an association of men ... The principle of choice for an association is interpreted as an extension of the principle of choice for one man" (*TJ*: 21). For any rational person, this principle is "to achieve his own greatest good, to advance his rational ends as far as possible ... from the series of satisfactions that are experienced at different moments in the course of his life" (*ibid.*). Similarly, "the well-being of society is to be constructed from the fulfilment of the system of desires of the many individuals who belong to it" (*ibid.*). It was Henry Sidgwick who best formulated the reasoning at the basis of the utility principle, making clear the connection between rationality and morality.

> Just as the notion of the good of an individual is constructed by comparison and integration of the different goods that succeed one

another in the series of our conscious states, so we have formed the notion of the Universal Good by comparison and integration of the goods of all individual human – or sentient – beings ... By considering the relation of the integrant parts to the whole and to each other, I obtain the self-evident principle that the good of anyone individual is of no more importance, from the point of view (if I may say so) of the Universe, than the good of any other; unless, that is, there are special grounds for believing that more good is likely to be realised in the one case than in the other. And it is evident for me that as a rational being, I am bound to aim at good generally, not merely at a particular part of it.[43]

Rawls retains Sidgwick's explanation:

As Sidgwick maintains, rationality implies an impartial concern for all parts of our life. The mere difference in location in time is not in itself a rational ground for having more or less regard for it ... Just as the good of a person is constructed in comparison and integration of the different goods of each moment as they follow one another in time, so the universal good is constructed by the comparison and integration of the good of many individuals.

(*TJ*: 21 and 259)

Utilitarianism appears thus as "the most rational conception of justice" (*ibid.*: 20). Let us illustrate the basic utilitarian reasoning in two simple examples of allocation of scarce social resources.[44]

(1) The first example concerns preferential access to education for either
   (1a) Highly talented student or
   (1b) Mentally retarded student
(2) The second concerns preferential access to health care for either
   (2a) A fairly healthy person or
   (2b) A terminally ill patient

If we follow our common-sense intuitions of justice, we should agree that access should be given preferably to those for which it makes the greatest difference: (1b) and (2b). In contrast, it is the benefits for the aggregate good of society and the impact on the general welfare that count for utilitarianism, not justice. In spite of its going against our better moral judgement, the correct utilitarian decision should be to allocate the resources to (1a) and (2a) as the advantages for society will be greater: the talented student will be more creative and possibly contribute more to the well-being of others; the healthy person will live longer and bring more benefits to society. Notwithstanding the equal rights of each citizen, some members of society are more important than others in terms of social utility and the welfare of the latter may be sacrificed in the name of the overall good of society.[45] Rationality and justice lead to opposite results. Is this the price to pay to bring rationality into the moral sphere? This is obviously controversial. To lower the cost and to make rationality and morality more compatible, the utilitarian's answer consists in saying that the usefulness of equal respect and of the protection of equal rights more than counterbalances the violations that may be allowed in exceptional circumstances. Questions of justice can still be addressed indirectly and equality can be sanctioned by utility, not as a matter of principle, but as one of efficient application of the utility-maximizing principle.

The principle of *average* utility that maximizes not total, but average, utility (per capita) (*TJ*: 140) represents a more acceptable variant of the classical principle since it prohibits the very low level of well-being that is compatible with the general principle (*ibid.*: 140–41). It is more plausible as it guarantees some sort of floor. Not only are its consequences more satisfactory, but also its structure is markedly different from the classical principle in not being based on a teleological doctrine of the good (*ibid.*: 143). This more modern view was held by Mill and, more recently, by John Harsanyi (1982). Utility is not a measure of satisfaction, but is now understood as a way of representing the revealed preferences and choices of economic agents (*TJ*: 143). In that sense, it is more representative of a democratic society where people's individual choices should be respected. Finally, it resembles the difference principle in the sense that it leads "to weight more heavily the advantages of those whose situation is less fortunate" (*ibid.*: 144).

Thus, combined with the first principle of justice and a social minimum to specify the level of the floor, average utility leads to a mixed conception and a *principle of restricted utility* that could prove a strong competitor for the difference principle (*ibid.*: 120). The differences in their results are likely to be minimal (*CP*: 239). However, on the question of the defence of basic liberties and of the situation of the less fortunate, this latest version is still deficient, as I show in Chapter 3.

Similarities between utility and the two principles of justice as fairness

We should ask now whether there are any similarities between utility and the two principles of justice so that a comparison might make sense. Rawls does not spend much time on this question, as he is busy advocating his own views. I indicate the following points of comparison.

First, the principles share with utilitarianism a common concern for the *well-being* of all those concerned, but, for Rawls, the well-being of the least advantaged has precedence whereas the least advantaged have no particular role to play in utilitarianism. There is simply a recognition of equal distribution as more socially efficient and beneficial. So the relevant position of the least advantaged may be important, except when "the disadvantages of some may be outweighed by the greater advantages of others" (*TJ*: 29; *CP*: 50). The idea of weighing disadvantages for some (the better off, for Rawls) against benefits for others (the least advantaged) is common to both. They share the reference to Pareto efficiency. Note, however, that *reciprocity* is absent from utilitarianism: "even if it uses the idea of maximising the expectations of the least advantaged, the difference principle is essentially a principle of reciprocity" (*JAFR*: 64). The more fortunate not only work for themselves, but also to contribute to the good of all, in particular, of the least fortunate. "Reciprocity is a moral idea situated between impartiality, which is altruistic, on the one side, and mutual advantage, on the other" (*ibid.*: 77).[46] The general utility principle, in contrast, treats the good of all equally from an impartial point of view, as we saw with Sidgwick's conception of justice as impartiality, and supposes widespread altruistic motivations. In contrast, the difference principle does not ask for sacrifices from the better off to mitigate the condition of the worse off, as this would violate the first principle of equal liberty. It asks only that their greater benefits should also improve the lot of all, especially that of the least advantaged (Scheffler, 2003: 440).

Secondly, utilitarians as well as Rawls are interested in the justice of institutions or, as Rawls says (*CP*: 57), of "practices", not in the relative individual situations. They both advocate what Samuel Scheffler calls a *holistic* view of distributive justice (Scheffler, 2003: 445).

Thirdly, because of this holistic view, *merit* or desert plays no part in distributive shares for both. Neither Rawls nor utilitarians regard desert as a fundamental moral notion. Still, we should remember that Rawls claims that this does not lead him to treat individual talents as a collective asset whereas utilitarians who do not recognize the separateness of persons treat talents as collective goods.

6. Perfectionism and intuitionism (*TJ*: §§7 and 50)

The next two alternatives are perfectionism and intuitionism.

Perfectionism is a teleological doctrine directing society to arrange institutions in such a way as to maximize the achievements of human excellence in art, science and culture. In its strict variant, it is incompatible with democracy as the requirement of perfection can override the claims of liberty and equality (*TJ*: 286). However, there is a more moderate version of perfectionism that is not teleological, but merely intuitionistic. It says that perfection is one standard among several others that should be considered. It can be used to limit the redistribution of wealth and income and as a counterweight to egalitarian ideas. It is true that in an egalitarian and democratic society the values of high culture and excellence are often threatened and that they should not be totally sacrificed. Joseph Raz (1986) convincingly advocates such a moderate form of perfectionism and of state intervention in his conception which is based on a criticism of Rawls' anti-perfectionism. Curtailing the expenditures required to protect cultural values, for instance, is not compatible with the idea of a well-ordered society as judgements of value have an important place in human affairs. Can perfectionism serve as a principle of justice?

It is worth noting that this more moderate version shares some features with Rawls' first two principles. First, it conveys an ideal of the person that constrains the pursuit of existing desires. It establishes independently an ideal conception of the person and takes into account what a person seeks to be, not only what he or she actually is (*TJ*: 230–31). Secondly, it takes into account factors other than the net balance of satisfaction and how it is shared (*ibid.*: 287). It is thus opposed to utilitarianism. Moreover, it helps make an important distinction that transforms our conception of equality. The democratic ideal states that human beings have equal dignity, but "none of this implies that their activities and accomplishments are of equal excellence" (*ibid.*: 289). This should leave room for the appreciation of human excellence. "We would have to check whether the consequences of doing without a standard of perfection are acceptable" (*ibid.*: 291). The problem is how to recognize the need for such a standard without damaging the self-respect of those whose endeavours are less success-ful. We may recall the criticism of desert as a basis for redistribution. In the same way, excellence cannot serve directly as a basis for dis-tribution, as it singles out individual positions. Excellence should be appreciated from the point of view of the basic structure and the bene-fits that it may bring to it. A perfectionist principle should then be able to combine a recognition of people's equal value with the demands of ideal-regarding considerations. At this stage, all we can say is that "the criterion of excellence does not serve here as political principle ... the principles of justice do not permit subsidizing universities and insti-tutes, or opera and the theatre, on the grounds that these institutions are intrinsically valuable" (*ibid.*: 291–2). Perfection and the pursuit of excellence are subordinated to the establishment and protection of just institutions; they cannot be part of first principles of justice for Rawls.

The last series of principles on the list belongs to intuitionistic con-ceptions, which propose, among other possibilities, to balance total utility against the principle of equal distribution, or average utility against the principle of redress or, finally, to balance a list of *prima facie* principles (*TJ*: 107). They are remarkable not so much for their content as for their structure. For intuitionism, Rawls writes, "there is an irreducible family of first principles which have to be weighed against one another by asking ourselves which balance, in our con-sidered judgment, is the most just ... There exist no higher-order constructive criteria for determining the proper emphasis for the com-peting principles of justice" (*ibid.*: 30). Intuitionistic conceptions have two main features. They include (1) a plurality of competing principles and (2) no explicit method for weighing these principles against one another: we are simply to strike a balance by intuition in each case. We should note here that intuitionism, in contrast with all the other conceptions presented in the list, stands nearer to the kind of atti-tudes that are more congenial to practical politics than to political philosophy.

There are many kinds of intuitionism, which vary according to the level of generality of their principles. Firstly, common-sense precepts of justice used in the political realm differ according to the different issues that they have to deal with, such as fair wages, taxation, pun-ishment and so on. In such cases, the weighting of reasons is based on intuitions generally influenced by the demands of different social interests, while in order to reach general agreement, we need to move to a more general scheme (*TJ*: 31). We may, then, face the problem of justice by balancing various economic and social objectives such as greater allocative efficiency, full employment, a larger national income, more equal distribution and so on. The several distinct problems of taxation, fair wages, etc., may in that way receive their due emphasis, according to the various ends of social policy. Finally, intuitionist philosophical conceptions are the most general. According to them, however, no priority rule for weighting lower-order ends and principles can be provided. We can only use our intuition to balance them in the most rational way, as no constructive criteria exist.

Rawls examines, then, what he calls "mixed conceptions" (*TJ*: §49). These are conceptions that accept the priority of the first principle, but that operate various modifications that substitute, for instance, for the second principle, (1) the principle of average utility; or (2) the principle of average utility, subject to the constraints either (a) that a certain social minimum be maintained, or (b) that the overall distribution not be too wide; or (3) the principle of average utility, subject to either constraint, plus that of equality of fair opportunity (*ibid.*: 107). These conceptions should be more appealing than a principle of general utility. Unfortunately, according to Rawls, all these various combinations suffer the same difficulty as intuitionistic doctrines in general. They do not provide clear priority rules and rely on computations and comparisons that are very difficult to justify and that, only too often, are influenced by contingencies that are arbitrary from a moral point of view (*ibid.*: 278 and 284). We need to find a method for choosing between these various alternatives that avoids the difficulties connected with intuitionism, while still respecting the complex nature of political ends and interests.

Rawls' own constructivist philosophy opposes intuitionism, while recognizing that "there is nothing intrinsically irrational about the intuitionistic doctrine" (*TJ*: 34).[47] "We must recognize the possibility that there is no way to get beyond a plurality of principles" (*ibid.*: 36). However, we should do what we can to reduce the direct appeal to intuitions and judgements. Constructivism is one way of reducing the appeal to intuition and of finding an answer to the priority problem. The advantage of a plurality of principles following priority rules, such as the two principles of justice as fairness in lexical order, is that they combine a concern for the complexity of political issues and social choices with the possibility of reaching agreement as to how the principle should be balanced (*ibid.*: 37). "The task is that of reducing and not of eliminating entirely the reliance on intuitive judgments" (*ibid.*: 39).

7. A problem of interpretation

Having been through the whole list of alternatives, the reader might by now be rightly puzzled and ask whether the difficulties that I indicated at the beginning have been addressed and resolved.

The first question I asked was whether the options on offer were all authentic political principles of justice. The constructivist method has indeed succeeded in moving toward *political* morality, even if we are not yet dealing with political principles. Concentrating on the basic structure, it excludes principles that would be limited to guidelines for personal life, simply applied to politics, and it focuses on citizens, not individual persons. It eliminates considering outcomes of non-cooperative schemes, such as merit, bad luck, etc. Most importantly, it insists that personal preferences can be transformed and does not treat them as a given, independent of social and political institutions, as utilitarians do. It creates a distance and is a useful abstraction from historical traditions and common-sense morality, which leads to putting them in perspective, and it has a critical effect on our considered convictions, such as merit. Let us then conclude that political constructivism is the method that may transform moral intuitions and doctrines into political principles.

We may also begin to understand how Rawls expects to overcome the conflict between liberty and equality. First, the rules of priority clarify the priority of equal basic liberties over economic advantages and tightly connect the two values. Then, the proviso of reasonable economic conditions restricts the application of the two principles and denies that economic development could justify the sacrifice of basic liberties. Finally, freedom and fully responsible choices are only possible if the basic structure is just or quasi-just. The natural differences among human beings will always create inequalities. However, the hallmark of a democratic and just society is that agreed-upon principles regulate and restrict these inequalities to morally justified ones, even if they cannot address all sources of inequalities. Having a limited ambition and connecting tightly the two ideals, Rawls' conception of justice may offer an answer.

However, a difficulty remains. Are principles simply guidelines or do they have a prescriptive force? Principles of justice, as we saw earlier, should not merely recommend a certain course of action as preferable to others, but should actually prescribe it as just, not simply beneficial or efficient. They contain an imperative and moral force that defines the priority of justice in Rawls' own terms: "laws and institutions no matter how efficient and well-arranged must be reformed or abolished if they are unjust" (*TJ*: 3). Justice is an imperative, it commands duties; it is not a matter of choice or of preferences. The worry, now, is that Rawls has presented the different options as objects of choice or preference, whereas our considered convictions about justice convey a sense that some options are too unjust to be considered while other elements are not negotiable. Religious intolerance and racial discrimination, for example, are clearly unacceptable; but though the proper distribution of wealth and authority is less obvious, this too needs to be decided as a matter of prescriptive justice (*ibid.*: 17–18). The question we are left with is whether all the principles listed here have the relevant moral authority. Later, presenting a Kantian interpretation of the two principles in *A Theory of Justice*: §40, Rawls says that: "the principles of justice are analogous to categorical imperatives" (*TJ*: 222). He means that they have a binding power that constrains our freedom of choice. "To act from the principles of justice is to act from categorical imperatives in the sense that they apply to us whatever in particular our aims are" (*ibid.*: 223). If the Kantian interpretation is right, then, the binding power originates in the moral force of the principles. But this is impossible, as laws and political decisions have little in common with moral imperatives. To suggest otherwise would lead Rawls to mere utopia. We certainly need some clarification as to the relation between rational agreement and politically or legally binding arrangements. Rawls briefly attends to this problem at the end of *A Theory of Justice*: §4. He says that the initial situation of choice is purely hypothetical. In the end, all the list and the initial situation can provide is *de facto* agreement, but not full compliance. There is a worrying confusion here, between a rational agreement and a binding contract, one being intellectual and the other practical. Even more worrying is the fact that some of the principles listed are not, properly speaking, principles of justice, but simply guidelines for efficient or good social arrangements; perfectionism or intuitionism certainly constitute such guidelines; utilitarianism, as we have seen, cannot be treated as a conception of justice unless we add complementary intermediate principles, etc.

The device of the Original Position, which I examine in Chapter 3, should then clarify both of the following points. First, what are the democratic credentials of all the candidates on the list: will they pass the test of being fitting for a democratic set-up? Secondly, what is the connection between moral principles of justice and political and legal institutions? As Habermas rightly remarks in his 1996 book, *Between Facts and Norms*, a crucial piece of the jigsaw is missing in

Rawls' analysis: the relationship between morality and the political/legal coercive order.[48] One should note that utilitarians, most famously Bentham, John Austin and then H. L. A. Hart, addressed the problem and that the principle of utility was never claimed to have more than advisory value. "Utility is not law"[49] (Bentham in Parekh, 1973: 151). For Bentham, the role of sanctions was crucial for the implementation of what Élie Halévy (1955) called the "artificial identification of interests". Moreover, sanctions of conscience – and we can treat the Rawlsian principles in their Kantian interpretation as such sanctions – had to be complemented by the duty-and-interest principle. Rawls, in that respect, seems to be too idealistic and to still believe in some sort of "natural fusion of interests", once people are all convinced of the value of the principles of justice and agree to them. To agree is not necessarily to accept sanctions, especially where major interests conflict. Rawls does not account for the imperative force of the law and not enough provision is made for the evil sides of human nature. Is Rawls not too optimistic? The reader will have to wait until the second part of the theory of justice to be persuaded that principles agreed upon on the basis of their rational credentials can be transformed into imperative constraints on our desires and preferences, into laws and institutions. If not, we will have to agree with those critics who claim that Rawls only furnishes us with moral, not political, principles of justice.

Chapter 3

Defending democratic equality: The argument from the Original Position

> The difference principle as agreed in the original position, offers a way of seeing nature and the social world as no longer hostile to democratic equality. (*JAFR*: 76)

In this chapter, I present the second part of Rawls' argument: the *reasoning* that leads to adopting the two principles of justice as fairness and to rejecting the other alternatives, mainly the utility principle in its various forms. As important as the reasoning itself is its setting in an Original Position (OP hereafter) where the parties, placed behind a "veil of ignorance", reflect on how best to distribute "primary goods" among the persons they represent, goods that are not simply welfare, but include wealth and income as well as the basic liberties and the social bases of self-respect (*TJ*: 54–5). How can such a constraint on information lead to rational and effective arguments? Many critics have argued that the theory of justice would be more convincing without the cumbersome device of the OP that hides and even undermines Rawls' deep commitment, beyond the metaphor of the social contract, to public justification and the ideal of equal respect.[1] Conversely, some, such as David Gauthier, have claimed that the OP fails to exploit fully the resources of rational choice theory for deriving principles of justice from principles of rationality.[2] The aim of this chapter is to explain why, in spite of widespread criticisms, OP arguments still constitute the heart of the doctrine, even if they are complemented by independent arguments and have been often misunderstood.

In Section 1, I suggest that, to fully understand them, one must remember that Rawls is seeking to defend the principles of justice through a *constructivist* method that expresses people's autonomy not solely as a moral and political value, but as a doctrinal requirement: the way people reason and adopt the conception of justice must reflect their nature as autonomous persons, a nature that is at the centre of the democratic ideal of a society of equal and free citizens. The device of the OP is meant to represent this ideal of doctrinal autonomy, as citizens endeavour then to reason independently of their own conception of the good and of their personal interests. In contrast, teleological doctrines would present the two principles as an independent and prior criterion of justice, based on a common conception of the good, a presentation that would not respect them as autonomous persons. My interpretation is that, if one takes seriously Rawls' commitment to doctrinal autonomy, the device of the OP makes perfect sense and cannot be interpreted as redundant or contradictory.[3] However, a number of questions must be asked, following the analysis of the priority of justice that was developed in the first chapters.

How *contractarian* is Rawls' view? How does his use of the social contract model compare with classical or modern contractarianisms such as Hobbes' or Gauthier's, that claim that the basis for justice can only be "constrained maximization" of self-interest? How does it fit in with the Kantian interpretation I advance here? Is the idea of a social contract not mostly to represent rational maximization and justice as mutual advantage, not the requirements of justice as reciprocity and impartiality? I explain in Section 2 how Rawls departs from his initial view of the theory of justice as being a part of rational choice theory and how he embeds moral considerations for justice in the very conditions of choice in the OP: the veil of ignorance and the distribution of primary goods.

How *egalitarian* is the theory of justice and how far does it distance itself from the liberal view of equality? In Section 3, I present the Marxist critique of Rawls and I explain why Rawls uses the *maximin* criterion of maximizing the worse-off situation and why this is not contradictory with his democratic ideal of equality, while taking him further away from classical liberalism.

How *political* is the OP? By this I mean that the reasoning leading to the principles of justice might be seen as too distant from real political argument. It might be interpreted as an exercise of "monological reason" (Habermas). It might be that "justice as fairness assigns too large a role to an exercise of philosophical reason and too small a role to public-political argument" (J. Cohen, 2003: 112). I seek to answer this final difficulty in Section 6 in showing the role of the OP in "creating citizens" and transforming their preferences.

To conclude, I ask how satisfactory the overall OP argument is. Remember that the chapter on the OP is where revisions have been most numerous (*TJ*: xiii–xiv). How is Rawls to overcome the *conflict between liberty and equality* in the argument itself? I explain, in the course of the chapter, how he has had to reshape the defence of the principles in his later work and how this should now be understood as "a unified rationale" (J. Cohen, 1989: 729). Equal liberties, fair equality of opportunities and the difference principle are all part of the democratic ideal of citizenship and have a unique source in it.

1. From the initial situation to the Original Position

I first present the differences between the OP and the initial situation that was the starting point for the construction of the principles of justice (see above, Chapter 2, Section 2). I then examine how Rawls' ideas have evolved and how he eventually sees the relation between rationality and morality in OP's dual structure. I conclude with a short comparison between the "impartial spectator" and the "Original Position" as two devices for expressing moral objectivity without reference to independent criteria of justice.

Interpreting the initial situation

What is the difference between the OP and the initial contractual situation? Obviously, a contractual situation can only model the idea of justice as *mutual advantage*, that is, "as everyone's being advantaged with respect to one's present or expected situation as things are" (*PL*: 50). It considers strictly individual interactions, not the societal aspect of justice: *reciprocity*, that needs the whole social structure to function as a cooperative scheme, fair and acceptable to all, or the moral aspect of justice: *impartiality*, that social and natural circumstance should be nullified as distributive criteria.[4] The challenge, for Rawls, is to transform the social contract situation into a proper argument for principles of justice and to clarify the difference between the OP and a mere prudential choice.[5] Now, social contract doctrines, as we saw in Chapter 1, had a more limited ambition: an agreement on the best form of government. They did not mention a moral or societal content. This moral content, for Rawls, is now defined by a concern for both citizens' autonomy and reciprocity, not solely for their gains and benefits, and should transform the idea itself of a contract.

Remember how in Chapter 1, Section 3, we described Rawls' *contractarianism* as an expression of the priority of justice: only criteria of justice that are derived from citizens' own agreement, and that are not given prior to and independently of this agreement, are compatible with a democratic context. As a consequence, in Chapter 2, Section 2, we described the initial situation as expressing the parties' rationality. It is a contractual situation leading to a rational agreement between symmetrically situated parties, hoping to benefit equally from a distribution of the benefits and burdens of collective life. This imaginary situation represents "the political convention of any reasonably just democratic society, a convention no political party normally dares openly to violate, namely, that everyone as a citizen should gain from its policies" (*JAFR*: 133). No one should be unfairly left out or discriminated against and all should benefit from the political scheme. However, such a requirement is not specific enough to lead to principles of justice. The initial situation may be defined in various ways, leading to various results. Depending on the description of the parties involved, on the nature of their interests, on the conception of cooperation and benefits, etc., we would have various possibilities, not all of them just, in spite of our intuitions. We need to refine our instrument so that the various alternatives appear in a much better light and that we are more aware of their consequences. Moreover, we need a better understanding of what it means to benefit *rightly* from the political scheme. It is now clear that a simple contract will not deliver such a result, because it is concerned only with a fair agreement between the parties concerned and not with an agreement on principles of political justice for the basic structure. It defines justice as mutual advantage and ignores the weight of natural and social contingencies. We need, says Rawls, to adjust the circumstances of the initial situation and to redefine the proper Original Position where this selection and agreement take place.

Rawls' interpretation of the initial situation is *dualist*: it has two parts corresponding to the distinct demands of the Rational and the Reasonable – of the prudential meaning of justice, and of its societal and ethical meanings.

The demands of *rationality*, that all should benefit from the social arrangements and policies, are expressed in the description of the parties to the contract. Rawls describes them as "rationally", not fully, autonomous (*PL*: 72–5). This means two things. First, they are rational in the sense that they are not characterized by specific moral motivations, altruistic or egoistic, only by the defence of the interests of those they represent. Remember, as we saw in Chapter 2, Section 2, that Rawls describes them as "mutually disinterested". Secondly, we cannot attribute to them specific motivations, as this would contradict their autonomy and their freedom to choose the best principles. Another reason that Rawls advances in his later work for the absence of moral motivation in the parties is that, given the diversity and likely incompatibility of people's conceptions of the good – what he calls "the fact of pluralism" (*PL*: 36–8) – such motivations would prevent reconciliation. Remember also that the contract is a case of *pure procedural justice*, where the parties have no independent criterion for the right result, be it God, moral truths or natural law (*JAFR*: 14–15), and the fair procedure is solely responsible for the correct result (*TJ*: §14, and above Chapter 1, Section 1). The description of the parties avoids value judgements and insists that they are only very thin "artificial" entities with very few properties, basically rational choosers. One is thus tempted to understand the theory of justice, at that level, as part of the theory of rational choice (*TJ*: 15). One should also note that Rawls himself describes rational agents as lacking the "moral sensibility that underlies the desire to engage in fair cooperation" (*PL*: 51).

Rawls addresses the demands of the Reasonable, that is, of the ideals of fair social cooperation, reciprocity and impartiality, but at a different level. They are now embedded in the very *conditions* within which the parties are making up their minds. It is, first, the information condition that guarantees that the parties will choose the best available principles, because they will not be biased by specific information: they will choose impartially. "The fact that we occupy a particular social position is not a good reason for us to propose or to expect others to accept, a conception of justice that favours those in this position" (*PL*: 24). The veil of ignorance is responsible for fairness and impartiality. Secondly, the *goods* that are distributed are not simply income and wealth, resources and commodities, but also include in a list of primary goods the necessary conditions for the full autonomy of citizens: equal basic liberties and rights and the social bases of self-respect. Justice as reciprocity and justice as impartiality complement the prudential concept of justice as mutual advantage, and this distinction is paralleled in the two-part method used by Rawls. To that we should add another important clarification concerning the nature of the *interests* that the parties are entrusted with. These are fundamental legitimate and non-negotiable interests, derived from a conception of the person, not simply first-order interests.

The OP is thus a combination of two very different elements: the *prudential* dimension of any contractual arrangements where the parties are expected to benefit and to satisfy their self-interest, and the *societal* and *ethical* dimensions where the parties cooperate on a fair basis and reason impartially as if they were, as Kant would say, both legislators and subjects in the kingdom of ends. It is this very unusual combination and the tensions within it that characterizes Rawls' argument in favour of his two principles of justice and his rejection of utilitarianism. It is a problematic method and one obviously cannot be sure that it can work.

The meaning of the OP in A Theory of Justice and in Political Liberalism: *between theoretical and practical reason*

I would like now to present how Rawls' thought has evolved on the question of the OP. There have been many misunderstandings of its exact meaning and Rawls has spent much time clarifying it that it is worth taking some time to understand what it is designed to achieve. The question is whether the aim of the OP is *theoretical* and cognitive, that is to simply represent our considered judgements in order to select the best corresponding principles, or primarily *practical* and political, that is to reach unanimous agreement on them and to justify them politically. Theoretical reason is defined as concerning the knowledge of given objects whereas practical reason concerns the production of objects in accordance with a conception of these objects[6] (*LHMP*: 217–18 and Kant, *CPrR*: 89). I claimed in the Introduction that one of the main difficulties in Rawls' thinking has been his hesitation between an appeal to theoretical reason, hence the title "*A Theory of Justice*", and a recognition that practical, rather than theoretical, reason is at work in political justice. The hesitations and ambiguities in the descriptions of the OP reflect this crucial dilemma, especially Rawls' definition of the OP as a "device of representation", which is an ambiguous formula as it can be both cognitive and practical.

First, we must note that the selection of the best principles is tied up with the description of the OP. As Rawls says, the OP is tailored to give the expected results: the superiority of the two principles of justice as fairness, and the rejection both of the utility principle and of the other alternatives, perfectionism and intuitionism. "We want to define OP so that we have the desired solution" (*TJ*: 122). Another description would give different results. It is a circular set-up where the outcomes that we want to generate are built into the initial assumptions. Therefore, it would be misleading to expect the OP to produce a *deductive* argument in favour of the principles, given that it is obviously biased in their favour from the start.[7] Thus the main point is that the OP is normatively oriented to accurately represent our best judgements as to what a democratic society/regime should look like; it is not designed to apply to simply any political regime. It includes normative ideas, and does not present itself as a mere rational argument, similar to those found in social or economic theory, even if there are some similarities.[8] The mistake made in *A Theory of Justice* was to assume that deductive reasoning was at work, or, rather, not to balance the weight of deductive argument against normative reasons, where moral constraints are built into the choice conditions. This is fully clarified in *Justice as Fairness*: §23.

> Our aim is to uncover a public basis for a political conception of justice, and doing this belongs to political philosophy and not social theory. In describing the parties we are not describing persons as we find them. Rather the parties are described according to how we want to model rational representatives of free and equal citizens. In addition we impose on the parties certain reasonable conditions.
> (*JAFR*: 133–4)

Secondly, as a consequence, Rawls modifies the presentations of the OP in *Political Liberalism* and *Justice as Fairness* to answer this point in adding to the information available behind the veil of ignorance the *two normative ideas* of citizens as having a moral personality, and of society as a fair system of cooperation, ideas that were either left too vague or were simply missing in *A Theory of Justice*, and with the precision that *two* agreements must be reached: one on the principles of justice and a "companion agreement on the guidelines for public inquiry, on the principles of reasoning and the rules of evidence" (*JAFR*: 89).

Now, this does not mean that we cannot reach a unanimous agreement, even if we do not use theoretical reason. As Kant has shown, practical reason can lead to unanimous agreement as in the case of the categorical imperative argument.[9] If the OP is properly designed, people in similar conditions should reason in the same way and be convinced by the same argument (*TJ*: 120). A unanimous agreement would still be a sure sign that the principles selected are the best, given the conditions. However, we should avoid the following confusion, noted by Rawls, between rational choice and rational agreement.[10] The principles might be unanimously selected, but "the class of things that can be agreed to is smaller than the class of things that can be rationally chosen" (*CP*: 249). Beyond rationally choosing a set of principles, the parties in the OP should commit themselves to an agreement in good faith, one they have reasons to believe they can honour and which is publicly binding and final; and this is a very different picture from one of mere rational selection. How do we achieve such a result? Is the force of reasons in favour of the selected principles sufficient to constrain us into compliance? Certainly not, and Rawls is clear that the rational selection process in the OP and the resulting agreement are only part of the whole justification process, which is more inclusive. We need to add a second part to the theory of justice, one that is even more practically oriented towards stability and political consensus and which is developed by Rawls in *Political Liberalism*.

Another crucial element is that the OP, on its own, is not sufficient, but needs to fit in with our considered judgements in *reflective equilibrium* (*TJ*: 18–19; *PL*: 28).[11] Reflective equilibrium is a process of mutual adjustment of principles and considered judgements that is crucial for practical theory, in contrast with deductive knowledge. It is obvious that principles have to be interpreted and tested against our considered convictions, duly adjusted and pruned. Reflective equilibrium is the other idea of justification that Rawls uses and the OP should then be clearly understood as only one part of the whole complex process, which is not simply intellectual, but also political and empowering, as I have claimed from the start.[12] This is a crucial part of the deliberative democratic process where preferences and opinions are transformed by deliberation and by the appeal to first principles of justice.[13] In the end, "OP is only a selection device" (*JAFR*: 83). If the principles agreed upon are found wanting, a new procedure has to be started whereby principles and intuitions are weighed against each other and readjusted or reformulated. Rawls follows a *coherentist* conception of justification,[14] not a deductive one. Even if he has hopes of reaching a kind of "moral geometry"[15] in his demonstration, political life and issues of justice are too messy for that. As he says, "I do not see how to avoid rough and ready methods" (*TJ*: 106). In the end, the balance of reasons in the OP rests on "judgment" (*JAFR*: 134). This is an acknowledgement that justice, as most political concepts, is an "essentially contested concept" and that political philosophy should remain modest in its claims to be able to clarify such a minefield. We may only manage to eliminate certain alternatives without succeeding in selecting the best ones. Still, the method will have helped to clarify our intuitions and to sharpen our judgements in matters of justice, even if we do not agree with the results of the OP. It has educational value. "The contractarian method is a useful way of studying ethical theories and of setting forth their underlying assumptions" (*TJ*: 14). The process is comparable to scientific experiments that aim at demonstrations through falsification tests and trials and errors. Truth is neither a given nor a construct, but the result of a competition between candidate explanations selected through an agreed process with an agreed criterion. Justice is the result of a similar process, but without an agreed criterion: the OP is a case of pure procedural justice.

The adjustments to his account of the initial situation have been the result of a long process in Rawls' thinking and constitute probably the most important contributions to his theory of justice. There are at least four layers in his presentation of the OP.

In the first phase, to be found in *A Theory of Justice* and in his previous publications, Rawls is still very much influenced by economic theory and sees "the theory of justice as a part, perhaps the most significant part of the theory of rational choice" (*TJ*: 15). He presents the OP as a selection method very similar to methods familiar in economic and social theory. He avoids introducing any controversial ethical elements in the OP. He is appealing to pure theoretical reason and even mentions "moral geometry" as his model. The division of labour between general facts and moral considerations is still close to that present in utilitarianism, and Rawls is not clear whether practical or theoretical reason is mostly at work.

But in 1980, in his "Kantian turn", he introduces a very important clarification. The OP appeals to both theoretical and practical reason. Theoretical reason helps to analyse the different options open to rational choosers. However, it is practical reason that dictates the kind of normative restrictions that apply to their choice so that the results are just and not simply rational.[16] The Kantian interpretation of the OP is strengthened by the distinction between the Rational and the Reasonable operating in *Political Liberalism*. The division of labour between the Rational and the Reasonable reflects the dual structure of the OP: the parties are described as rational in the usual sense whereas the conditions of choice are reasonable, meaning that they

131

impose moral constraints on rational choosers without imposing a conception of morality. The normative conditions imposed on the choice in the OP represent the Reasonable: the idea of free and equal citizens having a moral personality defined by two moral powers: a sense of justice and a capacity for a conception of the good, and the idea of society as a fair scheme of cooperation.[17]

In 1985, in his "political turn", the OP is further redefined to accommodate the "fact of reasonable pluralism" and is severed from any pre-existing comprehensive doctrine that aims to regulate both the personal and the public spheres.[18] It also emphasizes even more strongly the autonomous nature of the selection process and choice. The OP can convince citizens from various conflicting backgrounds and contribute to the construction of an "overlapping consensus". It simply represents a method for describing or representing our deep-seated convictions as members of a functioning democratic society, independently of any personal comprehensive doctrine. The OP does not offer a "proof" for the principles or a deduction or even a full justification on the basis of a particular comprehensive doctrine. It is simply a thought-experiment that could be entered into by anyone at any time, even members of non-democratic but "decent" societies (*LOP*: 10).

Finally, in *Political Liberalism* and in *Justice as Fairness*, he gives a thorough presentation of the first part of the OP argument in favour of the priority of the basic liberties and encourages the reader to repeat the exercise for the defence of the difference principle, cautioning us that we may find it more difficult to defend, especially because some improved form of the utility principle, the "restricted principle of utility", might be a serious contender.

It should then be clear that the OP is "no general argument" (*JAFR*: 95 and 134) and that "OP serves other purposes as well" (*ibid.*: 81).

The "impartial spectator" and the Original Position

A comparison will help our understanding of what the OP aims to achieve. Its objective is to select moral principles of justice on the basis of both impartiality and appeal to judgement without appealing to an independent moral criterion. This is what both David Hume and Adam Smith tried to achieve with the device of the "impartial spectator".[19] If moral judgements are not propositional or do not state facts as assertoric propositions do, we must find some other way to give them objectivity and to eliminate arbitrariness. Appealing to theoretical reason alone will not give the requisite result, as moral judgements are prescriptive and initiate action. The turning point, for Hume, is to address instead the motivational problem and to base the moral point of view not on reason, which cannot initiate actions, but on sentiment. The universal capacity for sympathy and benevolence as well as for self-interest or self-love is the basis of morality and virtuous behaviour. Natural sentiments are moralized by education and progressively acquire the kind of impartiality and objectivity that we normally associate with theoretical reason. This appeal to sentiments and sympathy is encapsulated in the device of the "impartial spectator" as presented by Rawls.

> It is this spectator who is conceived as carrying out the required organisation of the desires of all persons into one coherent system of desires. Endowed with ideal powers of sympathy and imagination, the impartial spectator is the perfect rational individual who identifies with and experiences the desires of others as if these desires were his own. (*TJ*: 24)

In the OP we should aim at reaching the same impartial moral viewpoint, at discounting biases and bargaining advantages, but the important point to note is that "instead of defining impartiality from the standpoint of a sympathetic observer, we should define impartiality from the standpoint of the litigants themselves" (*TJ*: 165). If justice as fairness is an alternative to utilitarianism, then the OP must be an alternative to the "impartial spectator".

2. The choice conditions in OP

I now examine how contractarian Rawls' method is and how he has changed his view that "the theory of justice is perhaps the most significant part of the theory of rational choice" (*TJ*: 16). I show that this was a mistake and that, already in *A Theory of Justice* and more clearly in the later work, Rawls makes a distinction between rational and reasonable constraints on choices such as the constraints of a veil of ignorance and of a list of primary goods. Combined with the formal constraints of the concept of right, they distance the OP from the contractarian model, defined by Gauthier as follows: "To choose rationally, one must choose morally ... Morality can be generated as a rational constraint from the non-moral premises of rational choice" (1986: 4).

Rawls' contractarianism is obviously fairly weak and I would insist instead on a Kantian interpretation of OP arguments.

I first examine the formal conditions of choice. I then present the content and extent of the veil of ignorance that affects the choice. I conclude with a presentation of the *distribuandum*: the list of primary goods that the principles of justice have to distribute.

The formal constraints of the concept of right

The parties are required to evaluate the alternative principles of justice from a suitably general and properly ethical point of view. Remember that the set-up of the OP, not the motivations of the parties, should represent the moral constraints on our pursuit of the good. The formal constraints of the concept of right (*TJ*: §23; *JAFR*: §24) prevent the parties from promoting principles that would serve particular interests. They are commonplace in moral philosophy and apply to the OP as the necessary, but not sufficient, constraints that guarantee an ethical outcome to the selection process. They are not specific to justice, but hold for the choice of any ethical principle. However, these are only formal and weak constraints that must be completed with stronger conditions.

There are five constraints: *generality, universality, publicity, ordering and finality*. "By themselves these five conditions exclude none of the traditional conceptions of justice" (*TJ*: 117). However, "they exclude egoism as the generality condition eliminates proper names, and thus first-person dictatorship or free-rider forms of egoism" (*ibid.*: 117). (Egoism is already excluded from the list of alternatives by the description of the parties as mutually disinterested.) As a consequence, these formal conditions exclude the application of games theory to ethics because the universality and generality conditions rule out the introduction of players' threat advantages. For instance, using Braithwaite's famous example,[20] Matthew the trumpeter has a threat advantage over Luke the pianist because he does not mind Luke playing at the same time whereas the same is not true for Luke. Thus he thinks it fair if he can play whenever he likes, while he obviously does not care whether Luke plays or not. The outcome of the game in those conditions cannot be fair and ethical (*TJ*: 116, n. 10). Formal conditions rule out this kind of non-ethical consequence from the start.

Publicity, of course, is more than a formal constraint. It is a central requirement for the legitimacy of a conception of justice and involves the role of *public reason*. Public reason is a major concept in Rawls' later work and is defined as the equal reason that citizens share in their public debates about constitutional essentials and basic justice.[21] This means that agreements on principles of justice should be publicly recognized. This eliminates doctrines that would be accepted only on condition that they would not be publicly endorsed. This is the case with utilitarianism, for instance, as a doctrine acceptable for the governing elite, but not for the people.[22] Note that Rawls' use of the term public reason is not very rigorous, as he constantly moves from reason as a type of argument (giving one's reasons in public) to reason as a faculty (public modes of reasoning). The publicity requirement should then be completed by a companion agreement on public modes of reasoning and the rules of evidence that can be used. We need to be much more rigorous in our description of the parties' modes of reasoning, making a strict distinction between appeals to comprehensive doctrines or sets of values, and to public or political sets of reasons. The forms of reasoning allowed to the parties are thus restricted in the following way to "the general beliefs and forms of reasoning found in common sense, and the methods and conclusions of science, when not controversial ... This excludes comprehensive religious and philosophical doctrines (the whole truth, as it were) from being specified as public reasons. This holds for elaborate economic theories of general equilibrium and the like, if these are in dispute" (*JAFR*: 89–90). This restriction on their mode of reasoning reflects the fact that citizens should mostly use public reasons, not comprehensive doctrines, when they make their case for the legislative and public policies that they want support. They thus respect their *duty of civility* to one another. Note that the wide view of public reason accepts arguments from comprehensive doctrines for dealing with non-ideal circumstances (*ibid.*: 90, n. 12). What Rawls means in the end is that appeals to comprehensive sets of values or doctrines have little or no room among the acceptable ways of public reasoning, even if they are reasonable values or doctrines.

Finality is the other important formal constraint on the parties' reasoning. They must reason as if the principles they adopt are final and the contract they enter into binding: no change or modification should be allowed at a later stage, once they have access to full information and would obviously wish they had chosen different and possibly more advantageous principles. This is impossible. We accept that a contractual agreement necessitates a commitment to abide by the public rules as binding and final. Alternatives can then be ranked according to the level of final commitment that they ask. Citizens will obviously avoid those that they can adhere to in good faith only with great difficulty. Rawls introduces the useful concept of the *strains of commitment* (*TJ*: 153–4; *JAFR*: 128–9) to describe the price that the requirement of finality exacts from conceptions of justice. The parties select the consequences of the various options and examine whether they are reasonable in terms of commitments, that is, of acceptable social minimums and decent standards of living, but also of alienation and potential crisis and revolts. In the name of realism and social unity, they should select the least damaging principles. The problem of commitment is also dealt with through the institutional process, which is presented at length in Part II of *A Theory of Justice*.

Note here an apparent contradiction in Rawls. He indicates that, when the parties accept the condition of finality, they show a capacity for justice (*TJ*: 153), illustrated by their capacity to take into account the strains of commitment. This seems to contradict the description of the parties as rational and as having only a conception of the good, not a sense of justice. The only way to avoid this difficulty is to understand this capacity for justice in weak terms as a department of rationality: it would be irrational and absurd to agree to principles that (1) you find impossible and too costly to implement and (2) you can change as a consequence of their disutility. Thus it is not in the name of justice, but of rationality and consistency that the parties accept the importance of taking account of the strains of commitment. Note, however, that the appeal to the strains of commitment to condemn some conceptions of justice such as utilitarianism as too costly in terms of inequalities in well-being might make the OP redundant, as Barry claims (Barry, 1995: 61–7). The formal constraint of finality is such a strong limitation on the choice of principles that it may be sufficient to describe the demands of justice: a level of inequality as low as possible to be acceptable to those who are at the losing end of them.

Still, Rawls claims that the formal constraints are not sufficient to yield the required outcome and to reach a unanimous agreement (*TJ*: 121). We need to add two more powerful constraints: the veil of ignorance and the list of primary goods.

The veil of ignorance

The main feature of the OP is the imposition of restrictions on the information available to the parties during the selection process.[23] The parties are to choose behind a "veil of ignorance" that guarantees the impartiality of their decision and nullifies the effects of natural and social contingencies (*TJ*: §24; *JAFR*: §25). The veil of ignorance is the answer to the "impartial spectator" model for moral judgement, an impartial and sympathetic observer who, like God, knows everything and everyone, loves them all equally and is not biased by passion or ignorance. Like the sympathetic spectator, the parties know nothing specific and neither love nor detest their fellow citizens. They thus occupy the relevant impartial moral ground for arbitrating conflicting claims. As an echo of Sidgwick's definition of fairness, Rawls writes: "The fact that we occupy a particular position is not a good reason to propose a conception of justice that favours those in that position" (*PL*: 24).

The idea of a veil of ignorance is not a novelty. It appears already in Kant (*TJ*: 118, n. 11 and 121) and, I would add, in Rousseau, when citizens have to decide on the best laws without communication among themselves and specific information (*SC*: II, 3). John Harsanyi was the first to use it to advance an equiprobability model of moral choice.[24] It is a powerful symbol of justice in the common iconography, where justice is represented as a blind woman. In British criminal courts, juries are banned from having access to certain facts concerning the past of both the accused and of the victim for fear that this might distort their judgement. These facts are revealed only after a verdict has been reached. However relatively commonplace the idea of a veil of ignorance may be, it is its relative "thickness" or scope that is at stake in the debate. It is also the kind of probability that we could infer from the lack of information that is in question. For Harsanyi, a "thin" veil of ignorance leads to assume equal probability for occupying any social position. Behind Rawls' thick veil of ignorance, we should reason as if our worst enemy were assigning us a place in the distribution of natural and social assets. The veil of ignorance seems to favour an aversion to risk that might be irrational and contradict the rationality of the parties (Harsanyi, 1976). It is then very difficult to figure out just how to make a rational choice if we are deprived of the relevant information.

Rawls' answer to these questions is that the parties are prevented from accessing information on *particular*, not general, facts.

(1) They do not know their specific place in society, their social class or status. This protects the impartiality of their choice against the weight of *social* contingencies.

y are unaware of their fortune in the distribution of *nat-*
l assets and abilities, of their race or ethnic group, gender,
elligence and physical strength, and so on. This again pro-
ts against such bargaining advantages as superior power or
intelligence.

(3) They are ignorant of their personal conception of the good, their comprehensive moral, religious or philosophical doctrines (*JAFR*: 88), as well as of the particulars of their rational plans of life and of their final ends.

(4) They are ignorant of the special features of their psychology, in particular the degree of their aversion to risk or their liability to optimism or pessimism, or will to dominate.

(5) They are ignorant of the particular political and economic circumstances of their society or of the level of civilization or culture it has been able to achieve (*TJ*: 118). The parties have no knowledge of the list of rights and liberties protected in historically more successful regimes (*JAFR*: 45). They know only that they have to choose principles fit for a democratic regime.

(6) The only particular fact that they know about their society is that it is subject to *the circumstances of justice* whatever this implies.

(7) However, they do have access to all relevant *general* facts about human society and nature: political affairs and principles of economic theory, the basis of social organization and the laws of human psychology. "There are no limitations on general information" (*TJ*: 119). They have full access to humanity's political culture defined as the "repository of the working out of men's sense of right and wrong" (*CP*: 5–6 and 12). They know that they have to select democratic, not any, political principles. From the history of social and economic facts, the parties may learn a conception of what a well-ordered democratic society should look like.

(8) Most importantly, they have access to a list of *primary social goods* that shape their demands on society (*TJ*: 123; *JAFR*: 88). They do not know which particular social primary goods they prefer but they have enough knowledge to rank the alternatives.

They know that in general they must try to protect their liberties, widen their opportunities and enlarge their means for promoting their aims whatever these are. (*TJ*: 123)

The aims of the OP can now be reformulated in terms of the parties being able to decide which principles are the most effective in:

(1) Protecting citizens' fundamental interests and determinate conceptions of the good (*PL*: 311).
(2) Guaranteeing stability for the first moral power (*ibid.*: 316).
(3) Protecting self-respect and limiting the strains of commitment (*ibid.*: 318).

There are several possible objections to the imposition of a veil of ignorance.

First, it may be objected that in the OP, the parties do not know enough to make an informed rational decision (*TJ*: 120). They are assumed to be rational but in the absence of specific information, a rational choice may prove impossible. "While they know that they have some rational plan of life, they do not know the details of this plan" (*ibid.*: 123). In reality, they have all the information that they need, but they cannot use knowledge of certain specific facts to their advantage. In particular, they cannot select a principle of justice that would advance their specific conception of the good or their particular abilities.

Secondly, the OP is apparently a *monologue*. This is, for instance, Habermas' criticism.[25] Rawls seems to say that any person behind the veil of ignorance would reach the same conclusions. "We can view the agreement in OP from the standpoint of one person selected at random ... assuming the deliberations of the parties must be similar" (*TJ*: 121). In the end, we only need to imagine one person behind the veil of ignorance, similar to the "impartial spectator". The veil of ignorance guarantees that, since the parties are equally rational and similarly situated, and they have access to the same restricted information, each is convinced by the same argument and a unanimous verdict can be reached. To that objection, Rawls answers that, given the complexity of the general information, of the rules of reasoning and the existence of the "burdens of judgment", it is highly probable that the parties will have to discuss and to progressively eliminate some alternatives with the aid of a referee (*ibid.*: 120). In fact, as he says, the OP is not a monologue, but an *omnilogue*, that is, a discussion where each of us can occupy the position of the parties.[26] As Samuel Freeman notes, it is important to understand that "OP is a collective, not an individual perspective" (2003: 284).

Thirdly, since the parties know that they are contemporaries, they can decide to favour their generation and not to save for future generations, which is extremely unfair (*TJ*: 121). They may use their information as a threat advantage to future generations and nothing constrains them to make any savings at all. To meet this difficulty, Rawls answers not very convincingly that as they do not know to which precise generation they belong, they will choose principles that do not advantage one generation over another, but are equally fair to all. This needs the additional constraint that "they wish all preceding generations to have followed the very same principles" (*ibid.*: 111). Is such a constraint compatible with the veil of ignorance and the OP? Rawls in fact changed his view in the revised edition of *A Theory of Justice* and advances a less egalitarian just savings principle that is distinct from the difference principle discussed in the OP.[27]

The distribuandum: *primary goods*

At this stage, an important clarification concerns the basis for redistribution: what are the goods to be distributed?

The first and most intuitive answer is a conception of *basic needs* as developed in both Marxist and socialist economic theory.[28] Human beings cannot be compared except in respect of their common basic needs: food, shelter, heating, health care, education, etc. Basic needs represent our common humanity. The notion possesses objectivity: needs can be measured and satisfied efficiently. It possesses neutrality in the face of existing social and economic inequalities and conflicts: rich or poor, all human beings have the same basic needs. It possesses impartiality: basic needs are not biased by cultural, religious or subjective views. It leads to a simple and effective conception of justice: to each according to their needs. The obvious difficulty is that basic needs do not exist, they are a myth, as is the Marxist notion of the "generic man": a man freed from any individual or cultural characteristics who would be the "pure" representative of the human genus. What is properly human about us is *both* our individuality and our belonging to a cultural world. These two features are missed by the notion of "basic needs". Even more important is the fact that no interpersonal comparisons of well-being can be made on the basis of basic needs because these are mediated and reinterpreted by both personal and cultural parameters.

In contrast, libertarians such as Nozick (1974) insist that only the agents themselves may define welfare, and that welfare economics cannot have access to a substantive, only to a formal, notion of the *distribuandum*. Human beings do not have needs; they have desires and preferences that they seek to fulfil as they see fit because they are essentially free and autonomous agents. A list of basic needs is meaningless, as it would immediately be contested in the pluralist setting that characterizes free and open societies. Welfare is the result of free and legitimate transactions among free agents. As soon as the transactions are interfered with, they cease to provide welfare in an autonomous way. Need-satisfaction without the freedom to define what we really need and how best to meet these needs is worthless. Thus welfare cannot as such be objectively defined. However, the conditions of welfare and individual satisfaction are well known: they are for Nozick free markets of resources and labour, freedom of transactions, minimal state, etc. The only provisos accepted by libertarians concern public goods such as water, air, etc., the private acquisition of which can be damaging and interfere with free transactions and acquisitions (Lockean proviso). The idea of free transactions seems to combine in a satisfactory way both the liberal or moral element of welfare: respect for individual and free decisions, which was missing from basic needs conceptions, and objective measurement, as it is fairly easy to check whether transactions are actually free and fair whereas it is impossible to define what basic needs are. A procedural conception of welfare is all we should aim at.

Traditionally economic theories and, most importantly, welfare economics define the *distribuandum* as general or average utility, but have had major difficulty with a central question: how to define and measure welfare, both collective and individual, in objective and unequivocal terms, something crucial to policy success. Welfare for modern utilitarians is thus defined by ordinal preference-satisfaction, by revealed preferences. We cannot access individual consciousnesses of pleasure and pain. However, individual behaviour as instantiated in choices and preferences can be measured. Preference utilitarianism, as Harsanyi (1982) suggests, combines successfully freedom of choice with objectivity.

This is where Rawls' conception of primary goods represents a turning point. Against preference utilitarianism, primary goods serve as the basis for objective comparisons between individual positions – what economists call interpersonal comparisons of well-being. "For questions of social justice we should try to find some objective grounds for these comparisons, ones that men can recognize and agree to" (*TJ*: 78). We now start with a list of objective goods that can be compared whereas people's expectations and satisfaction cannot. However, is a list of primary goods similar to a list of goods that satisfy basic needs? No, because the list includes the basic rights and liberties that may be violated in the name of basic needs. It is not a list of what is needed for mere survival, but for leading a decent and worthwhile life, in particular for cooperating fully in democratic politics and decisions as citizens. Thus the notion of "primary goods" represents a major improvement as it combines *freedom of choice* – primary goods are those goods that any free and equal person would prefer to have more of – and *objectivity* – these are the goods that are necessary not simply to human life and survival, but to a satisfactory life, for the welfare and satisfaction of each person's potential. Amartya Sen's and Martha Nussbaum's notion of *capabilities* goes even further in defining welfare in terms of "a person's ability to do valuable acts or reach valuable states of being, the various 'functionings' he or she can achieve" (Sen, 1987: 159–61; Nussbaum, 2000 and 2006).

In *Political Liberalism*, Rawls is even more explicit: primary goods are the goods that are necessary for each person to function as a *citizen*, not simply as a human being, and to exercise her basic rights and freedoms. The power of the notion of "primary goods" is that it belongs to both the liberal tradition, missed by basic needs conceptions, and to the social-democrat tradition, missed by utilitarianism and libertarians. It also gives an account of collective and individual welfare. Finally, as an ideal-based or deontological conception of welfare, it combines rationality and the ethics of justice in rejecting the illusions of the invisible-hand model applied to distributive justice.

Rawls has modified his definition of primary goods in an important way. In *A Theory of Justice*, he talks of "the things which it is supposed a rational man wants whatever else he wants" (*TJ*: 79). To summarize, these are the goods defined by a "thin" theory of the good that is not controversial and that can be adopted indifferently by utilitarians or by contractarians. "The main idea is that a person's good is determined by what is for him the most rational long-term plan of life given reasonable circumstances" (*ibid.*: 79–80). However, in his later work, Rawls does modify not so much the list as its basis, replacing the reference to the "rational man" with the "citizen".[29] He now says: "these goods are things citizens need as free and equal persons living a complete life; they are not things it is simply rational to want and desire, or to prefer or even to crave" (*JAFR*: 58). Primary goods clearly are the things that are needed *socially* to lead a fulfilling and meaningful social life, not simply to live as an individual entity. Primary goods are not simply distributed; they are also produced through social cooperation. "Social

cooperation, we assume, is always productive and without cooperation there would be nothing produced and so nothing to distribute.
This assumption is not emphasised sufficiently in *A Theory of Justice*,
§§12–13" (*JAFR*: 60). Finally the notion of primary goods is compatible with "the fact of pluralism". Given the plurality and, possibly, the
incommensurability of people's conceptions of the good, primary goods
are not dependent on a specific doctrine, as basic needs or teleological
doctrines would be, but are compatible with most and "belong to a
partial conception of the good" (*ibid.*).

I leave aside the many controversies surrounding the meaning of
primary goods,[30] in particular the criticism that primary goods are
still goods and that Rawls is a resource-egalitarian, and I list these as
follows:

(a) The basic rights and liberties described in the first principle
    of justice.
(b) Freedom of movement and free choice of occupation against a
    background of diverse opportunities: this gives an actual, not a
    formal value to these basic rights and liberties and to equality
    of opportunities.
(c) Powers and prerogatives of offices and positions of authority
    and responsibility.
(d) Income and wealth, understood as all-purpose means (having
    an exchange value).
(e) The social bases of self-respect,[31] understood as those aspects
    of basic institutions normally essential if citizens are to have a
    lively sense of their worth as persons and to be able to advance
    their ends with self-confidence.   (*JAFR*: 58–9)

Access to primary goods defines the relevant social positions from
where to appraise the justice of the distribution. "The least advantaged
are those who are least favoured by each of the three kinds of contingencies" (*TJ*: 83): social circumstances, natural endowments and
fortune or luck in the course of life. It is assumed, for reasons of sim-
plicity, that "physical needs and psychological capacities are within the
normal range, so that questions of health care and mental capacity do
not arise" (*ibid.*). As a result, the least advantaged have less of these
social primary goods, measured on an index. More precisely, given the
priority of the first principle, "the only permissible difference between
citizens is their share of primary goods (c), (d) and (e)" (*CP*: 363).
These are the inequalities subjected to the difference principle that

indicate the least advantaged as "those belonging to the income class with the lowest expectations and represented by reference to their share in the output and not as individuals identifiable independently of this scheme of production" (*JAFR*: 63). This is an important point that makes it difficult for Rawls to consider race and gender as relevant social positions for appraising the distribution, as, within these categories, wide discrepancies make it impossible to talk objectively of the least advantaged.[32]

I would like to conclude with the following objection. Rawls indicates that a cooperative scheme that "gives a greater return to the less advantaged for any given return to the more advantaged" is more effective (*JAFR*: 63). The difference principle "directs society to aim at the highest point of the most effectively designed scheme of cooperation" (*ibid.*). What he means here is obviously that the scheme is both more effective and just. However the conflation of efficiency and justice is worrying in view of the contrast he established earlier between the two. Justice is a social concern because people's decisions affect the whole basic structure and not simply their own lives. Primary goods are thus socially crucial. However, efficiency in the context of competitive markets is an individual matter whereby people try to maximize their returns on their investments in money, efforts, time, contributions, etc. Rawls thus declares: "the priority of liberty means that ... what kind of work people do and how hard they do it, is up to them to decide in light of the various incentives society offers" (*ibid.*: 64). Unfortunately, using the liberal idea here is both wrong and contradicts Rawls' notion of primary goods. It is not true that people are free in that abstract sense as a consequence of the first principle, even if fair equality of opportunity applies. Such a concept of liberal freedom contradicts the role Rawls attributes to the basic structure and to social determinants. It also contradicts the emphasis he put on fraternity (*TJ*: 90–91). There is seemingly here a tension between the individualistic understanding of economic efficiency and the social understanding of primary goods and justice. Rawls uses the traditional individualistic and quantitative conception of efficiency as depending on "people's decisions as to how to lead their lives" (*JAFR*: 64). This is even clearer when he says: "the difference principle requires that however great the inequalities ... may be ... they must contribute effectively to the well-being of the least advantaged ... even if it uses the idea of maximising the expectations of the least advantaged, the difference principle is essentially a principle of reciprocity" (*ibid.*). The question we should certainly ask at this stage is whether the reference to citizenship and social cooperation is not contrary to the traditional use of the concept of economic efficiency. An efficient scheme should be one that ensures social cooperation and stability in the long run, not only because the least advantaged are better off in terms of their own expectations, but because they are part of a fairer scheme of cooperation. As Rawls says, "the share of primary goods that citizens receive is not intended as a measure of their psychological well-being" (*CP*: 370). Efficiency is a necessary, but not a sufficient, condition of equity, unless it is described in terms of social, not simply individual, returns. This is exactly what the introduction of primary goods was meant to achieve, and I am wondering whether Rawls has gone far enough in that direction and why any reference to citizenship and to social and political institutions has disappeared in the description of an effective social scheme.

3. The structure of the OP argument and the *maximin* criterion

I now turn to the structure of the argument and to its most important feature: the *maximin* criterion or maximization of the situation of the worse off. I first present the intuitive reason why the parties would prefer equal distribution to liberal equality of opportunity. I then explain their reasons for appealing to the Pareto argument for efficiency corrected by the maximin: that all should benefit, but that the situation of the worse off should be improved. I conclude with a presentation of the many criticisms and misunderstandings that the use of the maximin has raised, and with Rawls' answers.

We now reach the most remarkable part of Rawls' demonstration: his defence of the two principles of justice in terms that the parties behind the veil of ignorance can agree to. The reasoning is remarkable because it aims at demonstrating that social and economic inequalities, against a background of equal basic liberties and fair equality of opportunity, should be evaluated in terms of how well off they leave the worst off (the maximin criterion), and not in terms of how much they increase the general or average welfare or equalize the situation of all at any price. The concern for the *least fortunate*[33] is built into the conditions of reasoning in the OP, instead of being the result of a specific Christian or Kantian morality, heteronomously imposed on the choice of principles. We should note that the maximin rule used here by Rawls has usually been interpreted in normative economics in total abstraction from its application to the institutions of the basic social structure.[34]

This ignorance of Rawls' holistic conception of justice leads to deep misunderstandings of the OP argument, which considers the position of the least fortunate, not solely from the economic point of view of access to resources, but primarily from that of access to rights and opportunities, to self-respect and to the possibility of full participation as a citizen, that is, to social primary goods in the widest sense. What has been misunderstood is that the maximin is not simply a criterion of economic, but also of political, justice, of *democratic equality*, as Joshua Cohen shows.

> We should seek to address distributive controversy by extending to that controversy the democratic ideal of a political association based on the mutual respect of free and equal citizens ... Ideals that are ingredient in the democratic tradition ... provide a *unified rationale* for principles requiring equal liberties, fair equality of opportunity and maximin. The argument from the original position presents that rationale. (J. Cohen, 1989: 728–9)

The structure of the argument is threefold: (1) the parties use an intuitive argument for equality and, then, (2) appeal to the Pareto principle of efficiency and (3) correct it with a maximin rule for choice under uncertainty that favours the situation of the least fortunate.

Preference for equality: the intuitive argument *(TJ: §26)*

We start with a fairly intuitive idea: the overall preference of the parties for an equal distribution of social primary goods, basic liberties and opportunities, etc., as a benchmark for assessing the various options. Knowing that they belong to a democratic society in which citizens see themselves as free and equal persons, but that, because of the veil of ignorance, they have no way of knowing how they could gain special advantages over others or burden some with special disadvantages, the parties will intuitively use *equality* as the benchmark for a just distribution. Ignorance leads to preferring equality. "The sensible thing is to acknowledge as the first step a principle of justice requiring equal distribution ... equal basic liberties for all, as well as fair equality of opportunity and equal division of income and wealth (*TJ*: 130). Equality does not need any more justification: it is the starting position for the parties as rational beings in the OP. It is obviously not a *moral*, but a rational, requirement at this stage, securing a minimum level of primary goods for all, what Rawls calls a "guaranteeable level" (*JAFR*: 98). All social values and benefits should be distributed equally among cooperating members as long as there is no justifiable reason for making differences. The main primary goods, basic liberties and fair equality of opportunity, freedom of occupation, income and wealth, responsibilities and prerogatives, the social conditions of self-respect, should be equally distributed, as the main concern is to serve every citizen's interests as well as possible. The parties decide to assess the different alternatives against this benchmark of equal distribution. Equality understood in such a way is constitutive of the democratic ideal of a society of equals. Rawls' egalitarianism is a strong claim that distances him from classical liberalism and from equality of opportunity understood as a corrective to unjustified unequal social circumstances, but not to unequal natural endowments. Remember how Rawls opposes both meritocracy and justice as redress for bad luck and misfortune (see above, Chapter 2, Section 4 and *TJ*: §17).

However, it is immediately obvious that not all primary goods can be measured in a simple way. For instance, it is simpler to assess equal basic liberties, wealth and income. This is why the easiest method would be to compare the different alternatives on our list of principles in terms of the minimum social conditions that they can guarantee. Access to positions of power and responsibility, not always connected with income, and to other social goods, is more difficult to measure. Again, various primary goods can be weighed against each other. This will call for different ways of comparing and measuring them.[35] Note, however, that Rawls defines the relevant positions for measuring equality in terms not only of wealth and income, but also of positions of responsibility and power even if he does not go as far as Sen in terms of "capabilities" or "functionings". Note also that he takes lifetime expectations, not simply immediate outcomes, as the benchmark for a just distribution. The benchmark is thus equality of primary goods, not of outcomes. The social minimum for the parties is thus much wider than the usual index used by capitalistic welfare states. It includes a "social equilibrium" in which self-respect and stability of cooperation are as important as welfare (J. Cohen, 1989: 274). The important point to emphasize is that the focus is on equality and that the more egalitarian a scheme of cooperation and redistribution will be, the more just, as assessed in the OP behind the veil of ignorance. This has been misunderstood because the presentation used by Rawls tends to cut short that important preliminary stage of the argument and to rush on to the next stage, the justification of socially beneficial inequalities. The OP is the central argument for democratic egalitarianism.

The Pareto argument for inequality

We said earlier that the more egalitarian principles would be chosen by the parties, unless there are good reasons for justifying inequality, that is, unless they can advance robust *moral* reasons that are acceptable from an impartial point of view, as Sidgwick said. For many critics of Rawls this represents a contradiction. Inequalities can never be morally justified, as we saw with merit, as possession of talents is mere good luck; they can only be justified in the name of efficiency. And this is exactly how the parties seem to proceed at first. Being rational and being trustees of citizens' interests, the parties will ask whether any departure from equality may be justified. One obvious rational justification would be that some departure from equality would indeed benefit all, for instance inequalities of income and benefits as *incentives* for the more talented to work more and improve the lot of the worse off. In other words, some inequalities might be justified in terms of general welfare. The parties have, of course, to consider such a powerful argument. For instance, they will ask whether an unequal distribution may be to everyone's advantage, improving the lot of *both* the worse off and the more fortunate, talented, hard-working, etc., whether it can improve the situation of all both socially and personally, or, in more utilitarian terms, whether it can increase the general well-being of all the people concerned, without anyone having to be sacrificed. This is the democratic character of the criterion used by the parties as an echo to the political convention that all should benefit. They will favour an efficient distribution against a less efficient one. Such reasoning leads to taking into account Pareto efficiency or Pareto optimality. Rawls adapts the Pareto principle of efficiency and says: "The principle holds that a configuration is efficient whenever it is impossible to change it so as to make some persons (at least) one better off without at the same time making other persons (at least one) worse off" (*TJ*: 58).[36] The move has seemed so convincing that "the persuasive power of Rawls' defence of inequality has helped drive authentic egalitarians, of an old-fashioned, uncompromising kind, out of contemporary political theory" (G. A. Cohen, 1995: 160).

Now, efficiency is certainly not a good moral reason for departing from equality. Rawls describes the parties as robust egalitarians and the only way to move them towards "justified inequalities" is to add another criterion: the maximin, to complement the Pareto argument for inequality. Not all Pareto-efficient distributions are just. The new move introduces the situation of the worst off as a relevant criterion of selection between different levels of inequalities. It therefore introduces an altruistic element of solidarity in the OP, which is the equivalent of the full moral motivation denied to the parties. This concern for the worse off, which should at the same time be not too costly for the more talented, is what makes the argument for unequal distribution *morally justified*. It is also a move in the direction of *fairness*, of the recognition of the diversity of natural talents and abilities but also of handicaps and difficulties that should be treated fairly.[37]

Favouring the least fortunate: the maximin criterion (TJ: §26 and JAFR: §28)

In the third and "more systematic" part of the argument (*TJ*: 132), the parties use the maximin criterion to help them pin down the still vague notion of "justified inequalities". The maximin ranks alternatives by their worst outcomes: a *maximum minimorum* (*ibid.*: 133). The maximin rule is well known to economists as a rule for decision under conditions of risk and uncertainty. Can it apply to the situation behind the veil of ignorance? John Harsanyi, immediately after the publication of *A Theory of Justice,* reacted strongly in saying that the use of the maximin criterion in the OP would contradict the assumed rationality of the parties. Rawls would seem to endow the parties in the OP with a special psychology: a high level of risk-aversion not compatible with their rationality. Appealing to the maximin as a rule for choice under conditions of risk and uncertainty would prove them to be risk-averse and hence irrational, in that they would prefer a lower overall gain to taking more risks.[38] Being rational, the parties instead should try to score the highest gains for the persons they represent. As a consequence, they should prefer, as Harsanyi claims, a rule of *equiprobability*: not knowing their position in the distribution, they would expect to have an equal chance to gain.[39]

It is true that Rawls is vulnerable to Harsanyi's charge when he writes in *A Theory of Justice* that "The two principles are those a person would choose for the design of a society in which his enemy is to assign him his place" (*TJ*: 132–3). Harsanyi is correct to say that, in a situation of full information or behind a thin veil of ignorance, the maximin would be irrational, but this does not apply in the OP. "Risk aversion of the parties in OP is a consequence, not an assumption of the veil of ignorance" (*CP*: 245–9). Rawls' answer to Harsanyi's criticism is complex and important for the success of the argument that the maximin transforms Pareto efficiency into a proper moral reasoning. Let us summarize it in the following way.[40]

First, Rawls claims that the maximin "leads to weight more heavily the advantages of the least fortunate" (*TJ*: 144). The rationale is that the *self-respect*, not simply the resources, of the least fortunate should be taken account of (J. Cohen, 1989).

Secondly, he claims that the maximin must satisfy the three conditions of finality, publicity and stability. In his later work (see below, Section 5), he insists that *reciprocity* is the rationale for taking the position of the least fortunate as a criterion when selecting conceptions of justice. Social cohesion needs much more than mutually advantageous arrangements to be stable and lasting. It needs a sense of reciprocity and civic friendship. Remember that the parties have access to a utility function where social cooperation has a great weight. They reason on principles of justice that are to regulate the basic structure of society, not individual positions, and they rank the alternative conceptions according to how well they contribute to social cohesion. The public knowledge that the more fortunate contribute to the improvement of the situation of the least fortunate and to their welfare, thanks to their more valuable talents or favoured circumstances, represents a major factor for social stability and lessens the strains of commitment. We know that Rawls is concerned with social unity and solidarity in a way that is untypical of contemporary liberals and more reminiscent of Mill. Such concerns are further developed in *Political Liberalism*, when Rawls addresses the problems of the second part of justice as fairness, and questions of stability come to the fore. The major difference between Rawls and utilitarians or libertarians lies in his holistic conception of justice, a conception that leads him to select principles of justice according to how well, as public conceptions, they contribute to social cohesion.

Thirdly, the maximin is not a principle and should be used under specific conditions. It is simply "a useful heuristic rule of thumb to identify the worst outcome of each available alternative and to adopt the alternative whose worst outcome is better than the worst outcomes of all the other alternatives" (*JAFR*: 97). "The maximin rule was never intended as a general principle of rational decision in all cases of risk and uncertainty" (*ibid.*: 97, n. 19). The maximin rule superficially resembles the difference principle in that it takes the situation of the least fortunate as the criterion for a just distribution. The difference principle states that a distribution is just if the inequalities it tolerates are to the greatest benefit of the least fortunate (*TJ*: 72; *JAFR*: 42–3). So much so that, for economists, this principle has been relabelled as "Rawls' maximin principle", a confusion of the criterion with the principle![41] The OP argument seems to be biased in favour of some of the principles it has to select at the end of the procedure. In *Justice as Fairness*, as we shall see, Rawls clarifies this point: a criterion is not a principle of justice, even if both refer to the position of the least fortunate as relevant for matters of justice, not simply to the positions of equality of income and of opportunity. The maximin rule allows the parties to rank the concurrent conceptions of justice according to their results, equality being the benchmark and the criterion being improving the prospects of the least fortunate against Pareto efficiency without harming the more fortunate.[42]

In his later formulation of the OP argument, as I show (Section 5), Rawls has strengthened the moral and political conditions present in the maximin in important ways.

Let us conclude this justification of the maximin by saying that it gives moral force to concerns for efficiency and connects them with the protection of the self-respect of the least fortunate. It satisfies the conditions of reciprocity, publicity and stability. Finally, it should be used only on certain conditions and not as a first principle.

Critics of the argument (G. A. Cohen)

One might object that this argument amounts to no more than a fairly crude defence of capitalism according to which some fairly extreme inequalities, in wealth and income in particular, are justified as incentives for the more fortunate in the name of efficiency, and that trickle-down effects may usually generate improvements and prosperity for the least fortunate, especially if close-knittedness is assumed (*TJ*: 71). Conversely, so the reasoning goes, equality is both irrational and inefficient if it leads to a worsening of the situation of the more fortunate without significantly improving that of the least fortunate. The argument seems at first sight not only to tolerate a high level of inequalities, but even to make them sound justified as well (*ibid.*: 136). It could easily lead to persuading the least fortunate that their lot would be even worse in any other situation or, more precisely, that "under any other feasible scheme, someone's prospects would be even worse than yours currently are".[43] We can see how controversial this notion is.

The relevance of an appeal to Pareto efficiency can thus be questioned within a theory of justice. It is seemingly more typical of contractarian reasoning, one that constantly balances economic benefits against equal rights and liberties and allows departure from strict equality in consequence. Why does Rawls introduce such a reference to welfare levels and to utility, given that he opposes the utility principle and that, for him, efficiency or increases in welfare cannot override fundamental equal rights?

Many critics have argued that the appeal to efficiency is typically a utilitarian argument and that the OP is biased in favour of utilitarianism or of capitalism, in a way that Rawls himself does not fully acknowledge. G. A. Cohen, for instance, writes: "the Pareto argument makes sense in contractarian terms, not in impartiality terms" (1995: 181). Does that mean that Rawls is an inauthentic egalitarian? I shall simply indicate the main following points in Cohen's argument.[44] Efficiency needs *incentives* for the more talented to work more and redistribute part of their benefits in the direction of the worse off. In the strict interpretation of Rawls' egalitarianism, incentives should not be permitted and selfish choices are not possible. This is obviously inconsistent with Rawls' appeal to Pareto efficiency. The argument turns on the question of motivation: are all talented producers ruthless and self-interested maximizers (*ibid.*: 184), or are they assumed to have a concern for justice, even to act for justice's sake? Rawls fails to properly exclude motivational psychology from the OP as his appeal to Pareto efficiency means that special psychologies, envy and egoism, that were banned from the motivational set-up of the parties reappear behind the veil of ignorance. Only a widespread ethos of solidarity would make it acceptable for the more talented to work more for less and such a motivational assumption makes the whole setting of the OP redundant, introducing a special psychology. Pareto efficiency and equality are thus incompatible and the OP cannot both start from equality as the benchmark for justice and then add Pareto efficiency, even corrected by the maximin. The OP is both contradictory and redundant.[45]

This is a very serious objection that would, if it were founded, undermine the whole demonstration. However, it stems from a misunderstanding of the nature of OP arguments and Rawls himself has answered the question whether justice as fairness is biased towards self-interested maximizers. An argument, such as Cohen's, based on questions of *motivation* is out of place at the stage of the selection of the principles. The OP clarifies that point in excluding considerations of motivation from the choice situation: the parties do not know what real people's motivations are beyond the general conception of justice, that all should benefit from the scheme and that persons have a sense of justice as well as a conception of the good. The question of motivation is addressed by Rawls in the third part of *A Theory of Justice*, where he explains at great length that, given human nature, the stability of a conception of justice requires that people should progressively recognize the good of justice, the *congruence* between justice and rationality, and shape their motivations so that in the end they adhere freely to a system of rules that might not maximize their own situation but lead to a stable and just or quasi-just cooperative scheme. However, at the level of the OP, ignoring the special psychologies of the citizens whose interests they have to promote, the parties select principles that are beneficial for the least fortunate against a background of equal rights and liberties, of fair equality of opportunities and the fair value of political liberties. People are possibly selfish maximizers, but they are also attached to certain fundamental values that are reflected in the choice of principles. At this stage, we know only that they will possibly reach agreement on the principles of justice as fairness; however, we do not know if they all possess the relevant psychology to enact them, beyond rationality and a concern for justice: this is a completely different matter. Cohen is confusing the information concerning the choice of principles with the motivations necessary to implement them. Rawls has a satisfactory answer in the distinction that I have indicated.

Another answer would appeal to "the fact of pluralism" in the following way. Remember that the parties do not know whether they are utilitarians, Rawlsians, Christians, perfectionists, or whatever. The OP argument should therefore provide as wide an umbrella as possible for different arguments about justice, including utilitarian ones, in view of human nature, no one knowing in advance what kind of argument will have more weight for them. For instance, "the parties use a utility function, but so constructed as to reflect the ideal normative conceptions of society as a fair system of cooperation and of citizens as free and equal and characterized by the two moral powers" (*JAFR*: 107). The benchmark for measuring justified inequalities is how close it brings the distribution to realizing these ideals. The efficiency argument may be used, as justice as mutual advantage (individual) cannot be separated from justice as impartiality (moral) and as reciprocity (societal). It is a prudential, a societal and an ethical concept. This is reflected in the way the reasoning is organized in the OP. The parties combine efficiency and fairness to reflect citizens' considered views. This does not prejudice their impartiality, but utilitarian arguments do certainly have their place in the OP and in a possible overlapping consensus on justice[46] (*PL*: 170; *JAFR*: 107). First, it shows how much Rawls tries to include utilitarianism in the whole argumentative process.[47] Utilitarians are familiar with the maximin principle, which "is compatible with the familiar principle of maximising the fulfilment of one's interests or (rational) good. The parties' use of the rule to organize their deliberations in no way violates this familiar principle of rationality" (*JAFR*: 98–9). They can, then, understand the difference principle: it resembles the justification of economic inequalities by reference to some notion of the general interest, as in the utilitarian tradition. The parties in the OP use a utility function, but as with any conception appearing in the OP, it is constructed to reflect both the ideal normative conception of citizens as free and equal and their rational interests (*ibid.*: 107). This means that the OP is not biased toward utilitarianism in using the maximin rule, as the latter simply represents one of the available tools of rationality. The only caveat, warns Rawls, is that expected utility should be understood as ordinal and as having no substantive content. It is a *formal* idea that helps in ranking the alternatives according to how well they meet "the agent's fundamental interests" (*ibid.*: 99). It appealingly tries to avoid "the outrageousness of maximising the aggregate no matter how distributed".[48] The difficulty is that, as we have seen in that case, the difference principle would not be selected for reasons of justice, but for selfish reasons of efficiency, for minimizing the risks if one's worst enemy were to assign one's place in society.[49] Rawls needs to show that both sets of reasons are plausible and that the OP selects principles on the basis of a variety of plausible arguments, such as rational choice criteria, ethical arguments, and that the convergence of the different arguments is more important than reaching a definitive proof as such. There is nothing in the OP banning the use of the maximin criterion as non-ethical. However, Rawls has to prove that the maximin rule is *also* an ethical criterion and that this is what makes it valuable: it encompasses the idea of equal and free citizens and the defence of their fundamental interests as moral interests, the interests they have as moral persons.

OP arguments are far from exhausting the list of plausible arguments. Indeed, Rawls refers to Part III arguments (those developed in Part III of *A Theory of Justice*, the least-read part, which deals with ends), or moral psychology arguments as being equally important (*JAFR*: §59). Part III arguments in particular select the various alternatives not only on the basis of reasons of justice, but also of stability. They constitute a different range of arguments that should work together with OP arguments to reinforce the position of justice as fairness and to defeat the various forms of utilitarianism that Rawls is examining. Finally, the last word belongs to the reader, to "you and me" with our capacity to place all these various arguments in reflective equilibrium, to use the device of the OP to gain a better understanding of the weight of the various conceptions and to agree on one preferred public conception of justice. The democratic impulse is reflected in the open-ended texture of OP arguments and their inclusion in a wider justification process.

4. The outcome of the OP: rejecting the principle of utility and selecting justice as fairness

I now turn to the conclusion of the process. The parties proceed to comparisons between the various principles on the list, applying the many requirements mentioned. I start with a brief summary of all the various constraints that apply in the OP and that the parties have to keep in mind. I then present the results of the comparisons. The reasons for selecting justice as fairness now become obvious. This is the simple argument from *A Theory of Justice*: §5–6 and §26–30. However, in view of the many criticisms and misunderstandings encountered, Rawls has worked out a second, more developed, argument from OP in "The Reply to Alexander and Musgrave" (1974) and in his second book, *Political Liberalism*: VIII. The final version is summarized in *Justice as Fairness: A Restatement*. Joshua Cohen (1989) presents a very interesting and useful sketch of such a developed argument.

In the next section, I summarize this new, more complex argument for the priority of basic liberties and for the second principle, mainly the difference principle, presented in terms of "a unified rationale" that embodies the ideals that are present in the democratic tradition: equal respect and, in particular, the protection of the self-respect of the least fortunate, stability and social cohesion, and not simply considerations of rationality and maximization (J. Cohen, 1989: 729).

155

Separate first-order interests

First, let us remember that the parties accept the "circumstances of justice" as the context for making sense of the demands of justice (*TJ*: §22 and above, Chapter 1, Section 1). This, in particular, means that they consider the persons as separate, that is, as having distinctive first-order interests. In the OP, "we have assumed that the parties have a determinate character and will, even though the specific nature of their system of ends is unknown to them. They are so to speak determinate persons" (*TJ*: 152). This is a very important detail. Conflicting interests give rise to the demands of distributive justice. Note that this is also a major constituent of moral individualism as understood by Rawls: persons have distinct interpretations of their first-order interests and comprehensive doctrines that may not be easily reconciled. Principles of justice should take account of both the separateness of persons and the plurality of their higher-order interests.

On that first count, obviously, being action-centred, utilitarianism in all its forms has no consideration for agents' distinctive interests. For average utilitarianism, in particular, "the individual is thought to choose as if he has no aims at all which he counts as his own" (*TJ*: 150). Persons are "bare-persons" (*ibid.*: 152), and utilitarianism does not recognize the separateness of persons. "It assumes that the parties and the persons they represent have no definite character or will, that they are not persons with determinate final interests or a particular conception of the good that they are concerned to protect" (*ibid.*). This is also striking when we look at the general principle and at the metaphor of the impartial spectator as a basis for estimating just arrangements. "The conflation of persons into one is at the root of the classical view" (*ibid.*: 167). "It fails to take seriously the distinction between persons" (*ibid.*: 163). "The fault of the utilitarian doctrine is that it mistakes impersonality for impartiality" (*ibid.*: 166). As a consequence, in the OP the parties will reject the general utility principle because "they are concerned to advance their *own* interests" (*ibid.*: 160, emphasis added). They will also reject the purely formal reasoning of average utilitarianism as it lacks an appropriate meaning. Justice as fairness, in contrast, takes seriously the plurality and distinctness of individuals and distributive, not allocative, justice. It is individualistic in the correct sense and assumes that persons have conflicting first-order desires (*ibid.*: 26). It takes seriously the separateness of persons.

Secondly, the veil of ignorance means that persons cannot be described as having "special psychologies". This means that the selection of the principles cannot be contingent on the persons having these special psychologies. For instance, we cannot assume a high degree of identification with other persons' interests. Neither can we assume a high degree of risk-aversion. General utilitarianism, in contrast, as a consequence of its method of the impartial spectator who conflates all first-order desires into one single utility function (*TJ*: 167), assumes that persons are not attached to their specific ends and are capable of a high degree of sympathy and benevolence so that some will accept sacrifices in the name of the maximization of welfare for all. "The classical doctrine is the ethic of perfect altruists" (*ibid.*: 165). In contrast, average utilitarianism assumes that persons are ready to take chances: "it is the ethic of a single rational individual with no aversion to risk, who tries to maximize his own prospects" (*ibid.*: 164–5). In both cases, appeals to special psychologies go beyond the choice conditions assumed in the OP.

The constraints of finality, publicity and stability (*TJ: §29*)

Remember now that another condition for meaningful reasoning on justice is the appeal to the formal conditions of right (see above, Section 2), in particular, the conditions of publicity and finality.

First, the condition of *finality* means that the parties must make sure that they can honour their agreement on a specific principle of justice as final and in perpetuity, under all relevant and foreseeable circumstances. There is no second chance. Once the veil on the information is removed, they must accept the consequences of their choice as final. In particular, the parties must take care that the strains of commitment (*TJ*: 153) are not too high. In other words, the selected principle must guarantee a satisfactory social minimum in order to avoid excessive strains for the people who have to abide by it, especially for the least fortunate. We saw that the maximin rule had a crucial role to play here in selecting the position of the least fortunate as relevant for measuring the outcomes in terms of "the strains of commitment".

From the point of view of the strains of commitment, justice as fairness fares much better. It protects fully and, most importantly, *directly* the basic liberties and rights as well as the fair value of political liberties. This will give the least fortunate enough weight in the public forum to protect and improve their lot. It shelters them against the worst eventualities. Their social minimum should again be the highest possible in view of the difference principle in order to meet the requirements of the maximin rule. I leave aside here the discussions on the exact assessment of the situation of the least fortunate following the various principles.[50] But note that they will never be asked to make sacrifices for the sake of a greater good enjoyed by others (*TJ*: 154). All in all, the outcome of justice as fairness is far better than that of the general utility principle. The other two variants, average and restricted, are better but still cannot compete with justice as fairness. The average principle is more egalitarian and thus closer to Rawls' justice as fairness. Average utility will provide a more satisfactory level in terms of primary goods, of both basic rights and liberties and a social minimum. Because utilitarianism is not interested in the distribution, but only in the efficient allocation of resources, it fails to secure equal rights and a satisfactory social minimum for the least advantaged.

The principle of utility may justify intolerable outcomes such as slavery or serfdom, or a worsening of the situation of anyone well below the minimum level in order to improve that of others. "The principle of utility may sometimes permit or else require the restriction or suppression of the rights and liberties of some for the sake of a greater aggregate of social well-being" (*TJ*: 29 and 155). Such outcomes are unacceptable and threaten the possibility of any commitment to abide by the principles of justice: the strains of commitment are too high (*ibid.*: 126), and they threaten the possibility of any stable well-ordered society.

Utilitarians could answer that the disutility of such disastrous outcomes is such that they would be banned. For instance, Rawls notes:

> Harsanyi excludes what he calls antisocial preferences ... Now this is a fundamental departure from the classical utilitarian view in which all pleasures regardless of their source are intrinsically good ... He owes us an explanation of the grounds for counting some pleasures for naught. (*JAFR*: 100, n. 22)

Even so, utilitarianism only indirectly guarantees the protection of citizens' basic rights and liberties and a satisfactory minimum. It fails when compared with the two principles of justice as fairness and puts our basic rights and liberties at risk.

What the OP and in particular the condition of finality singles out very clearly is the necessity to guarantee the two principles together and not to have a principle simply for economic justice. For Rawls, as I have shown many times, economic justice is inseparable from political safeguards, and he affirms the priority of politics over economics in that specific sense. The OP is a tool for assessing together both aspects of the social structure. Utilitarianism is myopic and does not appreciate the relevance of political factors. Rawls concludes that, judged in this light, the two principles seem distinctly better.

Secondly, from the point of view of *publicity*, again, justice as fairness fares better. When a conception of justice is publicly known to satisfy the agreed principles of justice, people develop a sense of justice that will sustain the relevant institutions and transform the political culture. Psychological and social stability will ensue from this public knowledge. "A conception of justice is stable when the public recognition of its social realization by the social system tends to bring about the corresponding sense of justice" (*TJ*: 154). From the point of view of stability, utilitarianism requires too much from the person, it requires more than a sense of justice: it "seems to require a greater identification with the interests of others than the two principles of justice" (*ibid.*). It even asks such identification from those who suffer most from the scheme and have to make greater sacrifices. Utility principles do not deliver a stable scheme of cooperation in the long run (*TJ*: 155). Neither are they credible from the point of view of the laws of moral psychology and the available human motives.

I summarize the various parameters and their results in Table 3.1.

Now, the condition of *stability* is only sketched in the OP argument, even if we understand that the fact that utilitarian principles ask too much from individuals is a threat to social justice and stability. This is the part of the OP argument that has been comprehensively reshaped in Rawls' later work. I present its new formulation in the following section.

5. The new argument from the OP in *Political Liberalism*

It is only at the end of *A Theory of Justice*, in Part III, §75–6, that Rawls discusses how the development of a sense of justice may provide the necessary stability for a just or quasi-just arrangement. However, as I have already indicated (see Introduction and Chapter 1), this account has proved deeply controversial not only according to Rawls' critics, but to Rawls himself. The main reason is that it assumed a shared

Table 3.1 Ranking the various alternatives in the OP

Selection criteria / Alternative conceptions	General utility	Average utility	Restricted utility	Justice as fairness
I.a. Separate and conflicting first-order interests	No: ignores separateness of persons. Wrong kind of individualism	No: "bare persons" with the "same deep utility function"	Yes: individualism and separateness of persons	Yes: separateness of persons
I.b. Determinate results behind veil of ignorance	No: relies on estimates of probabilities	Equiprobability (Harsanyi).	Yes: no use of probability	Yes
I.c. Special psychologies	Yes: "perfect altruism". Sympathy and identification	Yes: rational egoism. No aversion to risk	Yes	No: no egoism or altruism. No aversion to risk
II.a. Condition of finality: satisfactory social minimum and few strains of commitment	No: lowest social minimum and highest strains of commitment. Unacceptable sacrifices	No: low average of well-being, but higher than general utility	Yes: "Guaranteed social minimum" for persons as "human beings"	Yes: "Highly satisfactory social world" for citizens, not simply human beings. High level of protection
II.b. Condition of publicity	No: no public assurance that everyone benefits	No	Yes	Yes: persons develop a sense of justice

comprehensive conception of the good among the members of a well-ordered society that proves unrealistic, given the conditions of modern democratic societies, in particular the existence of deep and intractable cultural and moral conflicts. In view of this, Rawls has deeply transformed his account of the OP and of the defence of the two principles in *Political Liberalism* and it is this new argument that I want to present now.

I explain first the main criticisms encountered by Rawls' defence of justice as fairness in the OP and the reasons for the changes and the new argument. I then describe the main changes: how *stability* becomes part of the political conception of the person and of society available in the OP; how a new formulation of the basic liberties is needed and how the use of the maximin needs to be more clearly defined. I conclude with a case model for the defence of basic liberties in *Political Liberalism*: VIII and I sketch the corresponding argument for the difference principle.

Why a new formulation?

Rawls develops his new arguments in the Tanner Lectures of 1981, lectures that were a response to H. L. A. Hart's criticism (Hart, 1975) and that, once revised, make up Lecture VIII of *Political Liberalism*.

In his detailed 1975 review, Hart insisted on two inconsistencies. He noted first that Rawls was hesitating in his account of rationality in the OP (Hart, 1975: 252). A main error in *A Theory of Justice* was the justification of the basic liberties by reference to rational interests alone (*PL*: 290 and 299). This is a criticism that Rawls accepts. The task in *Political Liberalism* is thus to connect the list of basic liberties not with a social minimum, but with a conception of moral personality. The important point is to establish a correspondence, not to give an exhaustive account of all the grounds for the protection of basic rights and liberties. This would be out of reach for the parties in the OP. For instance, the right to private property is specified not as a basic liberty, but solely on the basis of what is needed for "a sense of personal independence and self-respect" (*PL*: 298). The first principle has nothing to say on, for instance, private versus public property of the means of production.

Hart also pointed to the lack of consistency within *A Theory of Justice* concerning the priority of liberties. Rawls was seemingly defending liberty for liberty's sake instead of examining it as a primary good for the parties to distribute. Using the example of free speech laws, he now shows how basic liberties are to be balanced against one another and how none of them has priority as such (*PL*: 294–5; also above, Chapter 2, Section 3). The main inconsistency concerns the clash between two formulations of equal liberty. One talks about liberty in general and claims that "each person participating in a practice, or affected by it has an equal right to the most extensive *liberty* compatible with a like liberty for all" (*TJ*: 302). Rawls adds: "liberty can be restricted only for the sake of liberty" (*ibid.*).[51] He seems to imply, as Hart remarks, that "no form of liberty may be narrowed or limited for the sake of economic benefits, but only for the sake of liberty itself" (Hart, 1975: 237). But, then, he admits elsewhere the possibility of restraining some basic liberties within the overall scheme, such as the right to private property of the means of production in the light of the demand for social and economic efficiency (*TJ*: 242). This contradicts the general conception and leaves one asking about the exact meaning of the principle.

Finally, another main idea that was not properly developed in *A Theory of Justice* is the idea of *stability*. The idea appears, as we have seen, as connected with the formal constraints of finality and publicity. It is then developed in Part III as the result of a common conception of the good, of goodness as rationality. However, this proved unsatisfactory. In the introduction to *Political Liberalism* (1999), Rawls writes: "a serious problem internal to justice as fairness is the fact that the account of stability in part III of *Theory* is not consistent with the view as a whole … it is therefore unrealistic and must be recast" (*PL*: xvii–xix). This serious problem is the *fact of pluralism* (see below, Chapter 4): not all citizens endorse the same doctrine as a basis of their sense of justice. Stability cannot be the result of a shared conception of the good, from which a sense of justice derives, as this would jeopardize the whole point of doctrinal autonomy that is the original ambition of Rawls' conception of justice. My interpretation suggests that "the fact of pluralism" expresses Rawls' conception of the priority of justice and of individual freedom that underpins the whole democratic ideal, pluralism being a consequence of the exercise of the basic liberties over time.

As a consequence, stability and the development of a sense of justice cannot be presented directly as arguments in the OP. They need a further addition that spells out more clearly the requirements of the democratic ideal: the twin ideas of the person and of society. The premises of the OP appear now to have been too sketchy and too weak. Even weak premises must include this ideal if they are to yield some result. Joshua Cohen takes the merit for this clarification in his 1989 paper that helped Rawls redraw a more satisfactory argument for his two principles.

The main changes

The political idea of the person (equal citizenship) and its moral content given by her two moral powers, and the political idea of society as a fair scheme of cooperation are the two new ideas that inform the reasoning of the parties in the OP behind the veil of ignorance. As they are such central ideas in conditioning the reasoning in the OP, it is worth analysing them.

First, the *political idea of the person* (*PL*: I, §5; *JAFR*: §7) develops the abstract conditions of freedom and equality in terms of the two moral powers that define moral personality.

> Persons are regarded as free and equal persons in virtue of their possessing to the requisite degree the two powers of moral personality, namely the capacity for a sense of justice and the capacity for a conception of the good. These powers we associate with the idea of cooperation, the idea of the fair terms of cooperation and the idea of each participant's rational advantage, or good.   (*PL*: 34)

The first moral power is the "capacity (1) to form, (2) to revise and (3) to rationally pursue a conception of what we regard for us as a worthwhile human life" (*ibid.*: 302). It also includes "a higher-order interest in advancing our determinate conception of the good" (*CP*: 365) and "the desire to conform the pursuit of one's good to public principles of justice" (*ibid.*: 367). In contrast with the first presentation of the OP argument, justice and reciprocity are built into the first moral power. In particular, this includes a sense of responsibility and of realism, the person's capacity "to assume responsibility for their ends and to moderate the claims they make on their institutions in accordance with the use of primary goods" (*ibid.*: 371). The first moral power also includes an acceptance of the finality of the agreement and of the strains of commitment. We agree to honour our agreement in good faith and to abide by principles that match our capacities. Such a moral power detaches "reasons of justice not only from the ebb and flow of fluctuating wants and desires, but even from long-standing sentiments and commitments" (*ibid.*: 372). The paradox of the liberal Paretian

(Sen, 1970) that, in the name of Pareto optimality, even a minimal level of individual rights may be rejected, does not arise within the OP in view of the notion of moral personality (*CP*: 372, n. 11).

The second moral power is "the capacity for a *sense of justice*, that is, to understand, apply, and to act from (and not merely in accordance with)[52] the principles of political justice" (*JAFR*: 18–19).

Freedom is defined as the capacity to form, revise and take responsibility for one's conception of the good and to regard oneself as "a self-authenticating source of valid claims" (*PL*: 32). *Equality* is defined in terms of a moral status or moral personality: an equal capacity to form a conception of the good and to develop a sense of justice that makes citizens equal cooperating members of a political society (*ibid.*: 19). This gives content to the idea of citizens as free and equal: it gives them a moral status that overrides economic considerations.

This is not, of course, a metaphysical conception, simply a normative view that is implicit in the basic institutions and practices of a functioning democracy. The conception of the person is a moral ideal, not an empirical fact as a conception of human nature would be (*ibid.*: 18 and II, §8). "It is not an ideal of personal life" but a political ideal (*ibid.*: 299). Citizens are seen and treated as having equal dignity based on their possession of a moral personality and two specific moral powers.

The *political idea of society* (*JAFR*: 20–21) as a fair scheme of cooperation is the second equally central idea in the experience of democracies: everyone should benefit from its basic structure, institutions and policies, and no one should be unjustly discriminated against, persecuted or sacrificed. The idea of *reciprocity* and of social cohesion as distinct from the idea of mutual advantage is deeply seated in Rawls' conception of democracy not only as a political regime, but also a social ideal of equality and fraternity. It gives weight to the democratic ideal of solidarity or fraternity: we should all benefit from cooperation on equal terms. I have already stressed that Rawls' doctrine is remarkable in view of its emphasis on the "social nature of human relationships" (*PL*: VII, §8; 278).[53] More importantly, the idea of society as a fair scheme of cooperation leads to arguments based on reciprocity and mutuality (different from altruism, egoism, justice as impartiality or as mutual advantage). It constrains arguments on public reasons (IPRR: 141). This crucial information was lacking in the first version of the OP and it is now made accessible to the parties. It clarifies Rawls' claim that the theory of justice is not a part of the theory of rational choice, but a normative conception anchored in democratic values.

In line with these two important clarifications, Rawls adds the following three conditions for the use of the maximin in the OP in *Justice as Fairness*: §§28–9 and 33.

(a) Behind the "thick" veil of ignorance, the parties have no means for computing probabilities and estimating risk. They choose under conditions of uncertainty (*TJ*: 145; *JAFR*: 98). They are neither risk-averse nor irrational; they simply do not have any reliable basis for estimating the probabilities of occupying any one position in the overall distribution, in contrast to Harsanyi's use of equiprobability. The maximin rule is thus the best criterion they can rely on, as they know that they only have to improve the lot of the persons they represent, especially the least fortunate. By how much: maximum or satisfactory improvement?

(b) The parties are not interested in maximization or in what might be gained above a "guaranteeable level" as that could jeopardize efficiency and be too costly for the better off. These may stop their cooperation and worsen the position of the least fortunate. No one needs further advantages once their main interests or their conception of the good are satisfied (*TJ*: 134; *JAFR*: 98). This guaranteeable level is not very different from what Rawls also calls a *social minimum* (*JAFR*: §38) and is present in various conceptions of justice when we apply the maximin rule. For instance, a socialist egalitarian regime would enforce a social dividend as an equal share of the social product (*ibid.*: 128). In the name of political prudence the average utility principle would ensure the lowest minimum necessary for a decent human life for all and that basic needs were met, whereas for Rawls' difference principle the social minimum is what is owed to persons as free and equal *citizens*, not solely as human beings (*ibid.*: 129). It is thus higher than in a capitalistic welfare state. It is what is needed (a) to protect fundamental interests, (b) to provide an adequate level of primary goods and (c) not to impose excessive strains of commitment on the persons concerned (*ibid.*: 103). These are extremely important points for comparing the various alternatives. Depending on how each conception answers these three conditions, we will rank them differently. Unfortunately, Rawls recognizes, "this important point about the guaranteeable level, while perhaps obvious, is never expressly stated in *TJ*" (*ibid.*: 100, n. 21). It is nevertheless crucial to rank all the alternatives according to how they fare for the least fortunate and how these alternatives compare with equality.

(c) The parties reject unacceptable outcomes that may fall below this guaranteeable level, such as slavery, serfdom, etc., even if the

Table 3.2 Justification of the list of primary goods

Primary goods	Person's highest-order interests
(a) Basic liberties	(a′) Development and exercise of the two powers of moral personality: conception of the good and sense of justice (which includes responsibility for our choices: *CP*: 369)
(b) Freedom of occupation	(b′) Pursuit of final ends and decision to revise and change them
(c) Powers and prerogatives of offices of responsibility	(c′) Development of various self-governing and social capacities of the self
(d) Income and wealth	(d′) All-purpose means for achieving a wide range of ends
(e) The social bases of self-respect	(e′) Ability to realize their highest-order interests and advance their ends with self-confidence

distribution is found efficient (*TJ*: 135; *JAFR*: 100). From that point of view, the protection of the basic equal liberties is crucial and it is from that point of view that the various alternatives should be ranked. The utility principle might allow a level that is below the guarantee-able level, especially for small and weak minorities, if the aggregate welfare is increased (*CP*: 67). "Utilitarianism cannot account for the fact that slavery is always unjust" (*ibid.*: 67; *TJ*: 218). It would allow the rights of some to be sacrificed in order to attain greater welfare for the majority.

The defence of the two principles

These ideas transform the OP argument in favour of justice as fairness. Note that in the 1981 Tanner Lectures and in *Political Liberalism*: VIII, Rawls presents the developed version of the argument in the OP only for the first principle. It is obviously easier to defend each principle separately. However, I think that Joshua Cohen is right to present a joint defence (J. Cohen, 1989: 729). Ideally, the parties would now reason in the OP by tightly connecting the list of primary goods with the two moral powers (see Table 3.2).

Let us first examine how the defence of basic liberties is transformed. These are the primary goods necessary for the development of the two moral powers. The good represented by a working conception of justice is part of the first moral power. Conversely, a conception of justice is only workable if it ensures good care for the person's religious, moral or philosophical beliefs. If not, it would never gain their allegiance.

There are three major grounds for *liberty of conscience* as a basic liberty needed for (a) the capacity for forming a conception of the good, (b) the capacity for changes and revisions according to our deliberative reason and thus making it our own, and (c) the exercise of a given and firmly rooted conception of justice.

First, liberty of conscience is crucial for forming a conception of the good and for developing our intellectual and moral capacities. This justifies its priority with respect to the constitutive needs of our moral personality, not simply with respect to the pursuit of our rational interests (*PL*: 314). It is also needed "to protect the integrity of the conception of the good" (*ibid.*: 311). Conceptions of the good are incommensurable and non-negotiable. They are a central part of personal identity, as well as giving meaning and worth to a human life.

Secondly, liberty of conscience guarantees the crucial possibility "that conversions and changes are not prompted by reasons of power and position, or of wealth and status, but are the result of conviction, reason and reflection" (*ibid.*: 312). This connects obviously with the importance of *self-respect* for Rawls and of treating ourselves as ends and not simply as means, but gives it a stronger backing (*TJ*: 155–7). Another aspect of liberty of conscience is "the liberty to fall into error and to make mistakes" and the role of "deliberative reason" (*PL*: 313).[54] Here *liberty of association* is essential to the exercise of liberty of conscience and has to be guaranteed too. "Those two basic liberties go in tandem" (*ibid.*).

Finally, the exercise of the first moral power needs liberty of conscience, even if our conception of the good has not been "fashioned for ourselves", but is part of a religious, philosophical or moral tradition in which we have been raised. Still, we need that freedom and the social conditions secured by it to express our moral personality.

The protection of the second moral power, the capacity for a sense of justice, provides the grounds for securing the political liberties and freedom of thought (*PL*: 332).

There are three criteria that allow one to check if a conception of justice does enough to protect the sense of justice and the political liberties. The first is based on the criterion of stability (*ibid.*: 316–17): only

167

a stable conception of justice is defensible in the name of the second moral power as it can generate its own support on the basis of citizens' sense of justice. The second is connected with the primary good of self-respect (*ibid.*: 318; *TJ*: §67, 178). The third is connected with the idea of the well-ordered society. In this way, the argument in favour of the first principle combines liberty and equality into one coherent notion (*PL*: 327).

Let us now turn to the defence of the difference principle (*JAFR*: §35–7) There is no similarly developed defence of the difference principle in *Political Liberalism*, but in *Justice as Fairness*, there is an example of what it should be like. Now, building a satisfactory defence of this principle is not easy. As Rawls admits it is a controversial principle. He thus develops stability as a ground for choosing the difference principle against its alternatives, mostly the principle of restricted utility (see above, Chapter 2, Section 5).

The first ground for the difference principle relates to publicity and is linked to psychological stability (*JAFR*: 120–21). The question is how well a conception of justice generates its own support and is publicly recognized in doing so.

The second ground for the difference principle is reciprocity. The restricted utility principle, in contrast, has no tendency towards either equality or reciprocity. If equal division of wealth and income is the starting point, then those who gain more are to do so on terms acceptable to those who gain less and in particular to those who gain the least (*ibid.*: 123). "Those who are better off at any point are not better off to the detriment of those who are worse off" (*ibid.*: 124). Reciprocity, in effect, is not only a societal and political value, but also a psychological fact of great importance to Rawls. The psychological law of reciprocity is developed in *A Theory of Justice*: 463, 470, 473–4. Human beings will respond in kind to benefits shown them by persons and associations, and will develop allegiance to institutions that operate for their good. The tendency to reciprocate is, for Rawls, a "deep psychological fact" (*TJ*: 494–5). It is the psychological basis for the sense of justice. It has an evolutionary basis: survival value for our species. Inspired by Rawls, Allan Gibbard (1990) has attempted to substantiate this hypothesis. Parties in the OP know enough about the principles of moral learning and psychology to have good reasons to adopt the two principles, especially the difference principle, on that ground: the likely stability of justice as fairness shows its superiority over average utility (*TJ*: 177).

The third ground is stability. This brings the cooperation of the more talented into the picture, of which we have heard little so far.

"Those most likely to be discontent are the more advantaged" (*JAFR*: 125). How can we guarantee their cooperation or their acceptance of the difference principle? How can we avoid continual renegotiations? Other reasons than further income and gain might persuade them to cooperate. The main reason described by Rawls is the value of a public political culture and of its values encouraged by the difference principle: "a culture that inhibits the wastes of endless self- and group-interests bargaining and offers some hope of realizing social concord and civic friendship" (*ibid.*: 126). However, psychological reasons are playing their part too: the stability argument is closely linked to the reciprocity argument based on the "good of justice".[55] As we shall see in Chapter 4, this argument for stability that is developed extensively in Part III of *A Theory of Justice* has been reworked in the light of the fact of pluralism: a stable society is not one that is unified by a shared conception of the good of justice, but one that reaches an overlapping consensus over a public political conception of justice. The revision of OP arguments leads Rawls to a version of liberalism that he now labels as political liberalism.

6. The OP as an educational device

I would like now to conclude by explaining why, in my view, the OP is neither redundant nor useless. It is not redundant as the strains of commitment and the condition of finality gain their full meaning from the consideration of the person's two moral powers in the OP. It is useful because in my view, the process has profound educative and transformative virtues: it transforms citizens' preferences through reflection and deliberation (*JAFR*: 122). Working together with the use of reflective equilibrium and of public reason as arguments for the principles of justice, the OP is part of a wider process and should not be assessed independently. I first examine the connection with reflective equilibrium, and then with public reason.

The OP and the practice of reflective equilibrium

I would like, first, to go back to the method of *reflective equilibrium* that Rawls uses as a complement to the OP argument.

> Moral philosophy is Socratic: we may want to change our present considered judgments once their regulative principles are brought

to light. And we may want to do this even though these principles are a perfect fit. A knowledge of these principles may suggest further reflections that lead us to revise our judgments. (*TJ*: 49)

In effect, reflective equilibrium also takes place in the OP when we have to adjust our contradictory intuitions concerning distribution with the regulative principles that we now more clearly identify. For instance, we might be persuaded to reject appeals to merit or entitlements, or to perfectionism, against our first judgement. As a consequence, *thinking* in the sense of placing one's own convictions in reflective equilibrium with the shared principles of justice is an essential part of citizenship. This is exemplified in the OP as a position of reflective thinking, distinct from both the position of the observer and of the participant that Hannah Arendt and Habermas famously opposed.[56] The OP is neither simply the position of the detached observer nor of the committed participant or actor, but is closer to an experiment in role-taking (G. Mead). It is neither partial nor impartial, but reciprocal and *omnilogical*. "It is you and I – and so all citizens over time, one by one and in associations here and there – who judge the merits of the original position as a device of representation and the principles it yields" (*PL*: 383, n. 14). In the OP, an imaginary construct represents the part of the self that is concerned with political autonomy and its consequences on both the others and the self. It allows an exercise of intrapersonal justification where the consequences of our private reasons are weighed against public reasons. Intrapersonal deliberation is never totally private for Rawls as Habermas mistakenly suggests (1999: 85) and the reasons supporting public agreement on justice are not simply preferences, but are transformed by the reflective process of the OP.

The OP with its veil of ignorance is a personal test and experiment where each citizen can visualize the consequences of her choices such as voting or supporting a candidate for office rather than another, etc. It may be expanded to cover not only the initial choice of principles, but also most of the difficult choices that are part and parcel of citizenship. Abstracting from one's personal position and accepting arguments and reasons that others can relate to is one crucial aspect of the OP. The value of abstraction is one clue to understanding its full potential, which shows how mistaken Michael Sandel's (1982) interpretation is.

It can thus be useful at this stage to complement Rawls' view with an enlarged definition of citizens' power for forming a conception of the good. This means that they are capable of *both* a personal conception of their own good and of a public conception of the common good. The divide between individuality and society, as Thomas Nagel strikingly explains, is "a question about each individual's relation to himself. Ethics, and the ethical basis of political theory, have to be understood as arising from a division in each individual between two standpoints, the personal and the impersonal" (Nagel, 1991: 3).

The educational consequences are such that the OP and the veil of ignorance can become part of educational games, teaching young people the values of civic engagement and responsibilities.

The OP and the use of public reason

I would like now to connect the OP with Rawls' conception of public reason, which he advances in *Political Liberalism*, and that I present in the following chapter. At this stage, let us simply define public reason as the reason that citizens use in the public political realm once they have access to full information, to advance their claims in public terms that the others cannot reject, even if they do not agree with these claims. Is the OP an example of the use of public reason and of public deliberation? Given its lack of informational content and its description in terms of a thought-experiment, it is difficult to answer positively. Still, the two types of reasoning are connected. Citizens using public reason are developing arguments for justice constrained by the condition of publicity that applies in the OP. I would suggest that the thought-experiment in the OP is a first step in the use of public reason, at the level of first principles, not policies.

Now public reason is distinct from personal reasons and shows a high degree of abstraction from one's own belief system and traditions. The OP is a good exercise in public reason from that angle. Remember that I have insisted that the OP is oecumenical and pluralist; it hosts many different arguments, not solely different conceptions of justice. It has often been said that the OP is a soliloquy, that it is "monological" (Habermas, 1999: 91). Nothing could be less true. The OP is a vast, crowded stage where many opinions are represented, examined and confronted. It is highly theatrical in essence. Rawls mentions deliberative rationality (*TJ*: §64) a number of times, and this is its proper location. For instance, the appeals to rational choice theory or to instrumental rationality represent very important arguments in the debate on justice that are not necessarily Rawls' own arguments, or represent his own voice. He is trying to represent them, perhaps not always successfully; but the main point is that they have a place in the overall debate. Less convincing are the arguments for egoism, and Rawls fails to give them space; they are only supporting characters in the play. Again, perfectionists are not very well served; they are mentioned only in passing. However, utilitarians being, so to speak, the main villains in this drama, a great deal of effort is directed towards making them credible, probably too credible. What needs to be kept in mind is that not only various conceptions of justice, but also other typical arguments in this area are represented on the stage and that the OP welcomes them as long as they abide by the rules of the game: the description of the parties, the circumstances of justice, the formal constraints of rights, the veil of ignorance, the maximin rule and its three conditions, considerations for feasibility and the strains of commitment, etc. The OP is not simply a thought-experiment; it is a "device of representation": it tries to give a vivid presence to most of our reasonable ideas on justice, to our considered convictions as well as to our familiar modes of reasoning.

I think that Susan Okin perfectly captured what Rawls meant when she writes:

> the combination of conditions he imposes on them forces each person in OP to take the good of others into account ... Those in OP cannot think from the position of nobody as suggested by those critics who conclude that Rawls' theory depends upon a disembodied concept of the self. They must rather think from the perspective of everybody, in the sense of each in turn. To do this requires, at the very least, both strong empathy and a preparedness to listen carefully to the very different points of view of others.
>
> (Okin, 1989: 100–101)

These are the very qualities that Rawls is demonstrating in the OP argument. The generosity of his approach, the fact that he tries to be all-encompassing and to play down his own arguments, to present as vast an array of plausible reasons as possible, have been on the whole overlooked. I argue that the development of justice as fairness into political liberalism clarifies these misunderstandings and correctly locates the problem of justice in the fact of pluralism. Justice is a collective effort, it can never be encapsulated once and for all in one formula, and it needs the overlapping consensus of all participants in a deliberative democratic forum. The idea of an overlapping consensus is already present in the OP argument. The OP argument should and must be properly understood as an exercise, however imperfect, in deliberative rationality. Now, of course, the main problem becomes: how can we reach a unanimous agreement as the outcome of the whole OP process? Rawls' suggested answer in *Political Liberalism*, as indeed in some parts of *A Theory of Justice*, is that we may, but only through a series of approximations, through a pragmatic approach typical of the exercise of practical reason.

Conclusion

There is no doubt that the OP argument is a complex and sometimes overwrought argument compared to its results. Is it worth the effort? A number of commentators have insisted that Rawls would be better off without it, since it imposes highly problematic choice conditions behind a veil of ignorance. A strong enough case in favour of justice as fairness could be mounted in its absence. I have instead tried to show that it is an important part of Rawls' doctrine that is not only effective, but that, in its transformed version, conveys Rawls' main ideas about democratic citizenship in a vivid and striking way. In that sense, OP plays a central part in expressing the doctrinal autonomy that is so crucial for the success of his ambitions.

Still, we may be disappointed with the outcome of the OP, in view of the cumbersome nature of the process. We do not reach definitive conclusions and we do not have a proper proof. However, we have a *transformative* process whereby our considered convictions as citizens of a modern constitutional democracy are strengthened and clarified, whereby some illusions are defeated and some myths are debunked (such as meritocracy), whereby certain *prima facie* attractive options are categorically dismissed (average utility) and we discover more resources to fight for what is non-negotiable, namely the equal basic rights and freedoms, fair equality of opportunity, the social conditions for self-respect and human dignity, and even more importantly, for a full exercise of citizenship. OP arguments may sustain reasonable hopes not of unanimous agreement, but of creating the conditions for a community of justification. There cannot exist a philosophical foundation for human rights because attempts to provide one would derive them from a specific cultural context or history and, in view of cultural pluralism, be counterproductive. But with OP arguments, we now have a multifaceted defence that borrows the language of as many moral languages as possible, that speaks with as many voices as possible, even decent but non-democratic ones, as Rawls claims in *The Law of Peoples*. This is probably the best we can hope for.

Chapter 4

Pluralism and political consensus: The argument for political liberalism

Introduction

In the *second stage* of the theory of justice, presented in Part III of *A Theory of Justice*, Rawls leaves the sphere of theoretical thinking and becomes concerned with the more political questions of *feasibility* and *stability*. Once the veil of ignorance is lifted and full information becomes available to citizens, the principles of justice and the rules of public reasoning are firmly settled (*PL*: 140–41). In order for the theory of justice to be complete, we now have to address the question of its stability, of the support it will get over time from all or from a majority of citizens. The test of the theory for Rawls, given his concern for "realism", is whether it has a fair prospect of being applicable and meeting public approval.

Rawls provides two distinct answers, which have in some ways been confused and misunderstood. The form of stability that he is trying to advance has to be "moral": it has to address people's autonomous judgement and capacities of moral reasoning. It has also to be political, but in what sense? The two answers correspond to the two requirements of morality and realism.

The first answer is centred on the motivational value of the "good of justice". Living with just institutions will transform citizens as they experience the value of their public conception of justice. They will develop over time a sense of justice, which will create the right conditions for stability. This is developed in Part III of *A Theory of Justice* as the "congruence argument", that is, the possibility of the congruence between the good and the right that unites a Kantian motivation for justice as fairness (*TJ*: §40) with a more Humean outlook on the rationality of justice.

The second one is based on the idea of *legitimacy* as a source of stability.[1] Legitimacy should not be confused with justice. It is connected with the origins of power, and of the authority of the law, not with its intrinsic justice. However, what characterizes liberal constitutional democracies is that legitimacy can no longer be the result of sheer force or authority. It is the result of discussion and the use of public reason.

> Political liberalism says that our exercise of political power is fully proper only when it is exercised in accordance with a constitution the essentials of which all citizens as free and equal may reasonably be expected to endorse in the light of principles and ideals acceptable to their common human reason. This is the liberal principle of legitimacy.
>
> (*PL*: 137)

An agreement on justice combined with a political consensus creates the conditions of lasting stability. Rawls draws a clear distinction between the agreement in the OP, which is both prudential and moral, and its translation into a proper political consensus, which is binding and which channels political power in ways that are generally understandable and acceptable for citizens.

In this chapter, I seek to explain why and how Rawls undertook to transform his conception of stability in *A Theory of Justice*, realizing that its source could not be solely a moral consensus on liberal shared values, as he assumed in that book, but a form of liberalism that answers the question:

> How is it possible for there to exist over time a just and stable society of free and equal citizens, who remain profoundly divided by reasonable religious, philosophical and moral doctrines?
>
> (*PL*: 4)

What are the conditions that will make the principles of justice legitimate for all or a majority of citizens? Such a conception cannot be legitimate on the same grounds for *all* citizens in view of their conflicting views of the good life, and only a form of *political* liberalism,[2] differing from classical liberalism as a comprehensive doctrine, can meet the requirement of the "liberal principle of legitimacy". Rawls now focuses on whether people will over time overcome their deep moral or religious disagreements and recognize as legitimate a shared public conception of justice, building in this way a lasting political consensus.

We should then read his second book, *Political Liberalism* (1993 and 1996), as developing themes that were already present in *A Theory of Justice*, but with a different set of assumptions. The new idea of stability is presented in a series of papers published between 1978 and 1989, which led to the publication of *Political Liberalism*, and in an important paper, "The Idea of Public Reason Revisited" (1999, IPPR hereafter). In particular, it is important to assess how compatible this idea is with justice as fairness as, after the publication of *Political Liberalism*, the idea of a major shift and of a "second Rawls" developed rapidly. As I have already indicated, I disagree with this interpretation and I argue in favour of the consistency of Rawls' approach.

In Section 1, I describe the reception of *A Theory of Justice* and the many debates and criticisms that led Rawls to revise it in 1975 and to answer his communitarian critics with his "political" turn of 1985. I then explain in Section 2 what he means by political liberalism in the light of "the fact of reasonable pluralism" characteristic of contemporary democratic and multicultural societies. In Section 3, I argue that his move is essentially determined by a concern for a form of political stability that would be compatible with citizens' autonomy, not solely with pluralism, and that this provides a strong continuity with the ambitions of *A Theory of Justice*. In Section 4, I analyse the possibility of a political "overlapping consensus" that would, according to Rawls, be distinct both from a mere *modus vivendi* and from the domination of a shared conception of the good. This should be a model of political consensus in democratic and culturally diverse societies. In Section 5, I show how Rawls' conception of public reason is the basis for an agreement on justice that reinforces and transforms the agreement in OP. In Section 6, I briefly present the debate with Habermas on the scope and the nature of the political consensus in a context of pluralism. In the final section, I conclude by listing some of the major difficulties encountered by Rawls' political liberalism: that he is not pluralist enough, the controversial consequences of his conception of the person for the unity of the self, the feminist critique of his divide between the "political" and the personal, the apparent abandon of the defence of social rights, and the uncertain structure of the new theory.

1. From *A Theory of Justice* to *Political Liberalism*

Let us now briefly describe the different stages in the reception of *A Theory of Justice* as well as Rawls' responses to his various critics. As a consequence, he engaged in rewriting and amending parts of the book, without renouncing its main distinctive features until, in the end, he published a new volume, *Political Liberalism,* which was a reworking of his papers published between 1978 and 1989.

The reception of A Theory of Justice

How was *A Theory of Justice* received after 1971? It rapidly became clear that Rawls' achievements were massive and, to his genuine surprise (see his interview with the *Harvard Philosophy Review*), numerous books and collections of articles began to be published, trying to understand and scrutinize the project and to advance original critical interpretations.[3] As a consequence of this growing interest, a new academic discipline, *normative political philosophy,*[4] was created, new courses were progressively offered by philosophy, economics and government departments, law schools, and so on. By the 1980s, for instance, nearly 50 per cent of PhDs in political philosophy were dedicated in one way or another to the study and the discussion of *A Theory of Justice,* and Rawls was regarded as the major contemporary political philosopher in the Anglo-American world, reclaiming a very important intellectual area that had been left to dry out, and producing work on a scale unseen since Rousseau, Kant, Hegel or Mill. Most reviews were positive and insisted on the scale of the ambition and on the "return to grand theory" (Skinner, 1985), which many had thought was dead. Alan Ryan, writes:

> Since *A Theory of Justice* was published in 1971, it has sparked off more argument among philosophers, and has been more widely cited by sociologists, economists, judges and politicians than any work of philosophy in the past hundred years ... Commentary on Rawls quickly attained the status of a "Rawls industry"; but not even the most hostile critics ventured to suggest that these initial estimates of Rawls' importance were exaggerated.
>
> (Ryan in Skinner, 1985: 103)

In view of the quality of the body of work that was inspired by *A Theory of Justice* from the 1970s onwards, and of commentators such as

Ronald Dworkin (1977), Robert Nozick (1974), Brian Barry (1973), Bruce Ackerman (1980), John Harsanyi (1975), Amartya Sen (1975), Will Kymlicka (1990) and David Gauthier (1986), it soon became clear that *A Theory of Justice* was now the one major work of political philosophy.

The most important debates that took place in the 1970s and 1980s focused on the following issues in *A Theory of Justice*: the meaning of the priority of liberty (Hart, 1975), the possibility of justified inequalities (Wolff, 1977), distributive justice as a threat to liberty (Nozick, 1974), and the limits of contractarianism (Gauthier, 1986). The debate with H. L. A. Hart on the priority of liberty, as I showed in Chapter 3, led Rawls to rework his presentation of the principle of equal liberty and of the priority of basic liberties in an important paper published in 1981 and reprinted in *Political Liberalism*: VIII, "The Basic Liberties and their Priority". Another major debate, as expected, raged around the controversial difference principle. For Marxist and socialist writers, Rawls' defence of justified inequalities seemed "to make the critique of egalitarianism respectable again".[5] Rawls took this criticism very seriously from the start and endlessly repeated in numerous papers and in *Political Liberalism* that the *fair* value of the political liberties as well as the principle of *fair* equality of opportunity were so constraining that the inequalities admitted by the difference principle would be much less important that those allowed by any other alternatives. Conversely, following libertarian liberals such as Friedrich Hayek or Milton Friedman, who claimed to be true followers of Locke's liberal conception of freedom, Robert Nozick's critique of Rawls (1974) and of the difference principle insisted on the dangers of interference with constitutional liberties in the name of redistributive justice. Libertarianism had a major influence on the formative ideas of both the British Conservative Party and Margaret Thatcher and the Republicans of the Reagan years and on the rejection of the welfare state and the defence of market economy. Rawls' answer to libertarianism[6] is to be found in his 1978 paper, "The Basic Structure as Subject", which is reprinted in *Political Liberalism*: VII. Less politically engaged, but still very influential, contractarians, in particular David Gauthier (1986), were criticizing Rawls for not sticking to the programme of a fully procedural and contractarian conception of justice in the third part of *A Theory of Justice*. Rawls replied in reaffirming his connection to Kant and the priority of the Reasonable over the Rational, in his 1980 Dewey Lectures, "Kantian Constructivism in Moral Theory", which constitute the better part of *Political Liberalism*: I–III, where he applies

179

himself to "overcoming the dualisms in Kant's doctrine" and to revising the ideas of the person and society operative in OP arguments in a more Kantian way. This was to become his "Kantian turn". He also contrasted his conception of the person and of primary goods with contractarian views in his 1982 paper, "Social Unity and Primary Goods".

The communitarian debate

However, a new and more lasting debate came to occupy the forefront of political philosophy from the 1980s onwards. So-called "communitarian" writers started rejecting the priority of the right over the good and the priority of liberty, as advocated by Rawls' liberal individualism, in the name of the value of community and membership, of the particular duties that they generate and that are not reducible to free choices. Their critique was the spearhead of a wider critique of liberalism, Rawls being its most prominent representative. They also were rejecting what they saw as Rawls' abstract universalism and rationalism in favour of new analysis more attuned to historical and social contexts. New social movements such as feminism, minority rights, gay rights, the politics of recognition, etc., were replacing the civil rights movement that had been the formative event for Rawls' political philosophy. They claimed that justice, contrary to Rawls' deontological and Kantian doctrine of the priority of the good, is dependent on people's conceptions of the good that are shaped by the communities they happen to live in, a notion that, so it is assumed, is rejected by Rawls in *A Theory of Justice*. Readers will find an extensive presentation of the debate in Mulhall & Swift (1992 and 2003). Let us briefly summarize the four main criticisms of Rawls that the authors describe.

First, Charles Taylor (1985 and 1989) presents a critique in the name of *personal identity*. Personal identity cannot be separated from moral and cultural identities, from membership in a community where persons are shaped by their allegiance to moral traditions, a view that directly contradicts Rawls' so-called asocial individualism and atomism. Then, the works of Michael Walzer on the "spheres of justice", which I mentioned in Chapter 1, and that of Alasdair MacIntyre on moral traditions, explicitly accuse Rawls of failing to attend to the various ways in which different cultures embody different values at different times. His ahistorical universalism and conception of rationality are alleged to be inadequate, given the diversity of *cultural backgrounds* that shape our understanding of contemporary democratic institutions. Again, the ideal of neutrality and anti-perfectionism, argued for in *A Theory of Justice*, is now seen as incompatible with the active role of the state in promoting and protecting valuable ways of life that would disappear otherwise, as numerous contemporary examples would show, and with the ideal of fairness to all, as affirmed by Rawls himself.

However, the most relevant criticism of Rawls, for our understanding of his move toward political liberalism, has been Michael Sandel's critique of the priority of justice and of the "unencumbered self". OP arguments, as we saw, are based on the fiction of representatives who have to choose first principles behind a veil of ignorance. This fiction actualizes the hidden assumptions in Rawls' liberalism that individuals can detach themselves from their ends and their own nature and that they are "unencumbered by previous moral ties". It is above all the conception of freedom advocated by Rawls that raises alarm. Freedom, for him, as we saw in the previous chapters, is defined as the capacity to choose one's ends, to modify them and to take full responsibility for them. Such a conception makes no room for people's allegiances to their cultural traditions or for history.

> Those who disputed the priority of the right ... argued that a conception of the self given prior to its aims and attachments could not make sense of certain important aspects of our moral and political experience. Certain moral and political obligations that we commonly recognize – such as obligations of solidarity, or religious duties – may claim us for reasons unrelated to a choice. Such obligations are difficult to dismiss as merely confused and yet difficult to account for if we understand ourselves as free and independent selves, unbound by moral ties we have not chosen.
>
> (Sandel, 1994: 1770)

It is true that a Kantian conception of the autonomous self is the basis not only of the argument in the OP, but also in Part III of *A Theory of Justice*. It is presented as a capacity to act voluntarily from a sense of justice alone, from a morality of principles, not solely one of association or authority. Cultural and moral ties are simply instrumental in the realization of our personal autonomy. Sandel and communitarians are arguing, in contrast, that they are *constitutive* of the self and that Rawls is mistaken in his understanding of social structures as voluntary associations. His use of the social contract is particularly revealing of this mistake. In the same way that the self cannot be detached from its ends, justice cannot be detached from a conception of the good. Communitarians return to the teleological conceptions rejected by Rawls in the name of the priority of justice and of autonomy. This criticism is obviously an echo of Hegel's critique of Kant's view of the moral self as pure abstraction in both the *Phenomenology of Spirit*, §613, and the *Philosophy of Right*, §141.

Is Rawls' political liberalism an answer to his communitarian critics? How much does he owe them and to what extent are the defining features of his new theory explained through a comparison? It goes beyond the scope of this chapter to present a comprehensive account of the complex discussions that have taken place under this label over the last twenty years among Rawls' most influential critics, some of whom now reject the label "communitarian" anyway.[7]

A first important remark is that Rawls never directly responded to the communitarian critique.[8] One main reason, besides a feeling that communitarians did not understand him properly, is that, in Part III of *A Theory of Justice*, he had already been trying to answer similar questions and to enrich his Kantian view of moral motivation and personality. There, in effect, he develops another quite different, more Aristotelian, conception of "the good of justice": persons cannot simply act on a sense of justice alone; they need to understand the good of justice to act upon it, a view much closer to the communitarian defence of duties and obligations to one's own community and cultural traditions. Obviously, the communitarian critique addressed a problem of moral motivation of which Rawls had been very much aware in *A Theory of Justice* and which he had tried to answer. In a sense, Rawls' communitarian shift was emerging *before* communitarianism came into existence. This is why the communitarian debate, important and interesting as it is in its own right, is not the main source for Rawls' shift which led to the publication of *Political Liberalism*. This shift has many sources, external and internal to the doctrine itself.[9] Among the *external* sources, besides the communitarian debate, the new social movements of the 1980s brought to his attention questions of identity and culture that influenced new rival conceptions of justice. For feminism, gay rights movements, and race awareness groups, a lack of recognition of the importance of identities and differences is probably as significant as exploitation and poverty as a source of injustice.[10]

A second remark is that the main reasons for change, as he himself explains in the preface to the revised edition of *A Theory of Justice*, were mostly *internal* to justice as fairness and to its failure to meet its double ambition: to provide a satisfactory political theory of justice and a public and successful justification for it. Having dealt with most criticisms in his papers of the 1980s, one major task was still awaiting him: to address the question of stability, which had been presented in an "unrealistic" way in *A Theory of Justice*. This is why, in 1993, he published a new book, *Political Liberalism*, which addressed the problem, building on previously published and revised papers with a new introduction.[11] A paperback edition with a new introduction and the 1995 "Reply to Habermas" was published in 1996.

From A Theory of Justice *to* Political Liberalism: *the "political" turn*

In the 1993 introduction to *Political Liberalism*, Rawls says that the changes that he wants to make now are

> arising from trying to resolve a serious problem *internal* to justice as fairness, namely from the fact that the account of stability in part III of *Theory* is not consistent with the view as a whole ... and concerns the *unrealistic* idea of a well-ordered society associated with justice as fairness ... that all its citizens endorse this conception on the basis of what I now call a comprehensive philosophical doctrine.　　　　　　(*PL*: xvii–xviii, emphasis added)

What Rawls is saying now is that unanimity as required by OP arguments is unrealistic in view of the character of modern societies and of their pluralism. This has been widely understood as a lowering of ambitions. If we cannot all endorse the public conception of justice on the basis of the same conception of the good, then we have to agree on a less demanding basis, on the recognition of our differences. We have to add a conception of *toleration*, which was missing in *A Theory of Justice* and to renounce universalism as the benchmark of ideal public justificatory processes at work in democratic societies. Such a move seems to signal that Rawls is renouncing the values of the Enlightenment that are so characteristic of *A Theory of Justice* and of the influence of Rousseau and Kant on its arguments. Rawls writes, for instance:

> Political liberalism is not a form of Enlightenment liberalism, a *secular* doctrine founded on reason and viewed as suitable for the modern age now that the religious authority of Christian ages is said to be no longer dominant.　　　　　　(*PL*: xl)

One apparently clear sign that Rawls had lost the impetus and drive of *A Theory of Justice* in the name of pragmatism was that writers such as Richard Rorty were now praising him for having finally shed his allegiance to the Enlightenment[12] and changed the scope of the book. This is the most widely shared view of the second Rawls. I would like to argue that there is a deeper and more philosophical interpretation. Rawls is not changing his view because society has changed, because immigration, post-colonialism, etc, have made our democratic societies more diverse and ask for a different conception of toleration and for a more cultural and historical understanding of justice. Rawls has changed his view because the third part of *A Theory of Justice*, on the good of justice and on moral motivation, contradicts his whole project of a conception that is *doctrinally autonomous*, and respects people's autonomy in its very method and arguments, rather than by simply advocating autonomy as a value. This ambition has been abandoned and the new move is a return to it: *Political Liberalism* should be understood as a correction of *A Theory of Justice*. Unfortunately, Rawls does not admit this in a clear and straightforward way. He prefers to present the change as the result of an awareness of the "political" dimension of justice as fairness. My interpretation is that we should from now on understand "political" as meaning "freestanding" or "autonomous" in contrast to a conception that depends on a comprehensive doctrine. The doctrinal autonomy of justice as fairness mirrors the political autonomy of free and equal citizens, not dependent upon one dominant conception of the good.

Now, what is meant here by political autonomy? Because an agreement on justice means an agreement on the use of coercive political power, it cannot be derived from a shared conception of the good that would destroy people's autonomy and may require the use of oppressive state power. I suggest that the main issue here is with *political power* and that if we understand Rawls' concept of the political as meaning that, as citizens, we have to recognize that we must share political power with other citizens who are equally autonomous and cannot be expected to endorse our personal conceptions of the good, then the purpose of his new book might appear more clearly, that people's autonomy should not be understood solely as a value, but as a standard for our public debates and arguments on justice. However, it is only in Lecture III of *Political Liberalism* that Rawls fully presents his reasons for "an autonomous political doctrine", and on the whole, he has not developed the idea in a fully satisfactory way.

> A view is autonomous then because in its represented order, the political values of justice and public reason are not simply presented as moral requirements *externally imposed*. Nor are they required of us by other citizens whose comprehensive doctrines we do not accept. (*PL*: 98, emphasis added)

In contrast to this requirement, Part III of *A Theory of Justice* imposed a conception of the good of justice, which seemed to be universally convincing and which contradicted the whole endeavour of OP arguments. This is the major mistake that Rawls made, confusing personal moral agreements and public political consensus. In the private sphere, it is obvious that we may accept duties and obligations in the name of beliefs, traditions and values we are attached to and we do not feel free to renounce. This is a matter of personal decision for us, especially, but not only, in religious matters. But in the political sphere, the main feature of democracies and free societies is that obligations and duties, the use of coercive political power, cannot be based on conceptions of the good characteristic of some sectors of society, for instance on religious doctrines, that we are not free to question and decide upon. The basis should be as much as possible independent of private beliefs and in that sense autonomous and "political". The important 1985 paper "Justice as Fairness: Political, not Metaphysical", which was to be the turning point and the foundation of "political liberalism", claims that this crucial distinction between the personal and the political was missed in *A Theory of Justice*, and led to major misunderstandings and confusions in the communitarian debate: the distinction between a public conception of justice that is derived from a comprehensive, religious, philosophical and "metaphysical" or moral doctrine, and one that is solely "political" or autonomous and independent. Such a crucial distinction is missing in communitarianism, which sees personal conceptions of the good as constitutive of political conceptions of justice.

2. What is political liberalism?

In this section I concentrate on Rawls' understanding of pluralism and I conclude with a presentation of the main features of the new political liberalism.

The "fact of reasonable pluralism"

One major new idea to be found in *Political Liberalism* is the recognition of the fact of reasonable pluralism that was overlooked in *A Theory of Justice* and which led to an unrealistic view of the well-ordered society.[13] *A Theory of Justice* was too optimistic about the homogeneity of a democratic society and the impact of the exercise of reason within the framework of free political institutions. In contrast, any view of the good, even the comprehensive liberalisms of Kant and Mill, would necessitate "the oppressive use of state power" to endure as main comprehensive doctrines (*PL*: 37; Dreben: 2003). In order properly to understand Rawls' purpose, we have to make two critical distinctions.

The first is between pluralism and *reasonable* pluralism (*PL*: 144). Pluralism as such may be undesirable as it allows for doctrines that are not only irrational, but also mad and aggressive to develop and prosper. Divergences and conflicts are mostly the results of selfish categorical interests or of the will to power, of irrationality, ignorance and false consciousness. However, the important claim is that another form of pluralism exists, which is "compatible with the reasonableness of those who disagree" (*ibid.*: 54–8). This claim is the foundation for toleration not as indifference but as respect for insurmountable but reasonable differences. *Reasonable* for Rawls means compatible with OP arguments: the capacity to listen to OP arguments and to place one's considered convictions and the public conception of justice in reflective equilibrium once access to full information is granted. Reasonable pluralism should then be understood as *reasonable disagreement* and to express a different reality from mere pluralism: the outcome of the work of human reason under free institutions may not be unanimity. A more modest conception of reasonableness may help to understand how reasonable disagreement is possible. Among the many views that develop, some are reasonable, in the sense that they accept the limits of reason and *the burdens of judgement* (Rawls also mentions the burdens of reason) even if we still disagree with them. The burdens of judgement are "the many hazards involved in the correct and conscientious exercise of our powers of reason and judgment in the ordinary course of political life". They apply to both theoretical and practical reason (*PL*: 55–7). A conception of rationality as finite and revisable, as deliberative and modest, underlies Rawls' conception of reasonable pluralism.[14]

The second distinction opposes *value-pluralism* and reasonable disagreement (*PL*: 36, n. 37; J. Cohen, 1993; Larmore, 2003 and 1996). Value-pluralism is a comprehensive view of the nature of the human good expressed, for instance, by Max Weber (1918) and Isaiah Berlin (1969, 1990).[15] For Weber and Berlin, value-pluralism is the result of values being generated by generally non-rational preferences. Value-multiplicity is the result of the proliferation of many different and incompatible, even incommensurable, ways of life, which correspond to the multiplication of individual and usually irrational non-reflective decisions, similar to the existentialist view of liberty. For Rawls, in contrast, a reasonable pluralism of doctrines may be typical of free societies – the doctrine of value-pluralism, or of the existence of deep and insurmountable disagreements about the nature of the human good, being one such conception (*PL*: 36–7).

Reasonable pluralism, then, is not a comprehensive view, but an aspect of contemporary public culture that is here to stay; it is not "the upshot of self- and class interests or … an unfortunate condition of human life" or the result of "perversity or ignorance" (*PL*: 37). It is not contingent on specific social conditions, but part of what a well-ordered society should be (*PL*: I, 6; *JAFR*: §3); not one where everybody should necessarily reach the same conclusions, but one where most people, respecting the diversity of their belief-systems, but still using the same guidelines for reasoning and deliberating, and for the exercise of their two moral powers, should be able to reach a reasonable agreement on their political norms or principles of cooperation. Even if critics are right to emphasize that Rawls does not always take seriously enough the full intensity of such moral and cultural conflicts and that the only form of fair adjudication between comprehensive doctrines as a consequence of the fact of reasonable pluralism may be only procedural, not substantive,[16] it is obvious that, for him, pluralism should not be understood as a disaster, but as a fact to be reckoned with in political theory. I leave aside the many criticisms that this concept has raised and I move on to show the nature of its contribution to the doctrine of political liberalism.

First, reasonable pluralism or disagreement helps to redefine the central concept of impartiality in OP (*JAFR*: 84). The public conception of justice is not derived from one single conception of the good, but may be interpreted on the basis of many different world-views: liberal, Kantian, Millian, utilitarian, Christian, and so on. Impartiality is a distinct independent point of view that can be reached from various starting points; it is not to be confused with neutrality in the sense of a neutralization of disagreements and differences. Secondly, at the stage of public justification and stability, it means that the principles of justice can and should be interpreted and discussed in many different cultural idioms and that their universality is defined by this process, not by transcending or abstracting from it – Rawls says they are "universal in reach" (*LOP*: 85–6). This is a crucial distinction. Finally, the "fact of pluralism" leads to a better understanding of what political society is. It is not a *community* united by shared beliefs and one single dominant good. Neither is it a voluntary *association* of free individuals, as the libertarians would have it (*PL*: 40–43; *JAFR*: 198–9). It is, says Rawls, "a social union of social unions" (*PL*: 320), a formula that in spite of its awkwardness seeks to convey the idea that cultural diversity does not destroy a sense of belonging, but leads to defining it in political, rather than cultural or moral terms.[17]

What is political liberalism?

Political liberalism,[18] then, is the new context for developing the public conception of justice as fairness, when considerations of stability, and not solely of justice, come to the fore. It is derived from a distinction between *comprehensive* and *political* conceptions (*PL*: 154–8). A comprehensive conception aims at answering a wide range of questions affecting the whole of human life and experience in the name of certain moral or religious ideals, such as autonomy, individuality, social cohesion, solidarity and so on. The liberalism of Mill, which sought to be a "complete art of the good life", is such a doctrine as is Rawls' doctrine in *A Theory of Justice*. In contrast, a political doctrine is limited in range and scope: it deals solely with political questions, questions of the common good and of basic justice debated in the public political arena and concerning the structure of society – its main political, economic and social institutions. More importantly, it is neutral towards the various views expressed in an open society and does not takes sides concerning their truth. It is a freestanding view with no special commitment to one doctrine rather than another and it exhibits what Rawls calls doctrinal autonomy or the desire for "applying the principle of toleration to philosophy itself" (*CP*: 388; *PL*: 10). As a form of liberalism, political liberalism is obviously implicit in the public political culture of a democratic society (*PL*: 11–13). However, it is not "political in the wrong way" as in consensus politics (*JAFR*: 188–9), that is, as a result of political compromises between conflicting interests. It does not take part in controversies on the dominant good, but makes room for any reasonable view. Being political means that Rawls' version of liberalism excludes any appeal to truth as we see it, as this would be divisive in the public sphere, and its language is the language of reasonableness in the name of "epistemic abstinence".

At this stage, we might ask: is Rawls not describing a *secular* state, which would be far from neutral towards conflicting comprehensive religions? It is quite common for neutrality towards religious views to be, in effect, a way of expressing strong anti-religious feelings and of limiting religion to the private sphere. *Secularism* is fairly often a form of comprehensive anti-religious doctrine aiming to replace religion with the authority of reason and science. This is not the case for Rawls. It goes beyond the limits of this chapter to examine the precise consequences of Rawls' political liberalism for citizens of faith, but, as he makes it clear in "The Idea of Public Reason Revisited" (*PL*: xl; IPRR: 143), he understands the neutrality of the political conception of justice in a very specific way. *Neutrality* may be defined in an extreme way as excluding any appeal to moral values. This is not the case for Rawls. Political liberalism is based on a strong moral commitment to equal respect and to protecting the person as an end in herself. In that sense, it is not neutral and it promotes certain political values; but these are the values of neutrality: impartiality, consistency and equal respect (*PL*: 191). It is neutral in a different way: it has no views, positive or negative, on religious *truth*; this however does not mean scepticism or agnosticism, solely that religious truths are not directly political matters even if they may become such issues. Instead he sees the political domain as shaped by a multiplicity of faiths, not by their exclusion and privatization. Political liberalism is tolerant of such doctrines as long as they are reasonable. It might happen that some religious traditions will disappear in the course of time and that secularism will be the end-result, but it cannot be the starting point; again, this would breach the demands of doctrinal autonomy as the main requirement of a public conception of justice, which is rather an umbrella organization of many different views, united by a similar concern for common principles of justice and capable of reaching a consensus but for very different reasons. Justice as fairness is but one of the many liberal views that make up political liberalism in Rawls' sense; for instance Habermas' discourse ethics would be one of them, as well as the Catholic view of the common good, the liberalisms of utilitarianism and of Kant and Mill (IPRR: 142, n. 27 and 28). Political liberalism encourages, in fact, the robust confrontation of various political discourses, grounded in a wide range of reasonable comprehensive doctrines (*ibid.*: 143, n. 30). Instead of value-neutrality, controversies and pluralism should figure as the main features of the public space of a free society. Political liberalism does not therefore wish to "privatize" religion.

Five basic ideas characterize political liberalism: (1) the political conception of the person, (2) the political conception of society, and (3) the political conception of justice as fairness, the three ideas that we have already seen at work in OP, as the minimalist interpretation or reconstruction of the basic moral ideals of a constitutional democratic regime. To those, Rawls adds (4) the idea of an *overlapping consensus* as the basis for lasting stability and (5) the idea of *public reason* as the exercise of reason by citizens. The political conception of the person is the *citizen*, seen as free and equal, as rational and reasonable, as exercising her two moral powers over a lifetime and as fully cooperating in society. The political conception of society is that of a fair scheme of *cooperation* where everyone is expected to benefit from the advantages of social life, notwithstanding natural and social contingencies, where the principle of reciprocity applies. The political conception of *justice* specifies certain basic rights, liberties and opportunities; it assigns them a special priority, and it initiates measures assuring all citizens of the all-purpose means to make effective use of them (*PL*: 223). The aims of political liberalism are to redefine tolerance and civic friendship in terms of pluralism, not of unanimous agreement, and to create the conditions of a lasting political consensus and of a new form of social unity, where diversity is no longer an obstacle to public communication and deliberation.

However, this conception of stability brings out the deeper features of political liberalism, in particular how it claims to overcome the failures of the congruence argument in *A Theory of Justice*, Part III.

3. Autonomy and the concern for stability[19]

Now, I would like to argue that the reason for Rawls' move towards political liberalism is more likely to be his concern with a form of stability compatible with autonomy than as a reply to his communitarian critics. We need to see, first, what Rawls means by stability "for the right reasons". Secondly, it is important to understand how the search for stability in *A Theory of Justice* runs into major difficulties. In particular, I insist on the paradox of stability as the result of autonomy, not of coercion or of ideological domination. Thirdly, I conclude that we should understand *Political Liberalism* as correcting the mistakes made in *A Theory of Justice*. Autonomy, not solely pluralism, is the problem: how to gain the allegiance of free and equal persons divided by their personal comprehensive doctrines and to reach a political consensus on justice in an *autonomous* way. The concern for doctrinal autonomy is, as I have maintained, the key to understanding *Political Liberalism*.

The problem of stability

Why is Rawls concerned with questions of stability? One could wonder why philosophers should be interested in such empirical questions.[20] As many critics have pointed out, stability is a matter of complex historical and social contingencies beyond the scope of philosophical analysis. The answer is in Rawls' ideal of political philosophy as aiming both at the *desirable* and the *feasible*, and his concern for realism, for a practically feasible conception of justice and for reconciling utopia with realism (*JAFR*: 4). The full problem of stability is much more complex than empirical concerns for social cohesion and Rawls makes a distinction between three different forms of stability.

(1) One is gained through submission to a common shared vision of the good and to the oppressive use of state power to impose "the truth".[21] Cultural, ethnic or religious unanimity may create the social conditions of stability. However, this is social order mistaken for justice in the sense of Plato's authoritarian Republic. "A continuing shared understanding on one comprehensive religious, philosophical moral doctrine can be maintained only by the oppressive use of state power" (*PL*: 37). It lasts as long as absolute power or brainwashing triumphs.

(2) Another type of stability results from practical and contingent political compromises between conflicting interests and parties, as in the case of representative government. This is what Rawls calls a *modus vivendi* type of stability. It results from an amoral balance of power and cannot last. Both types exclude autonomy.

(3) The liberal principle of legitimacy calls for an entirely different form of stability: one based on justice and compatible with individual autonomy such that it results only from *autonomous*

191

John Rawls

> decisions and commitments, what Rawls calls "stability for the right reasons" (*PL*: 143 and 388, n. 21).

> Autonomy, in Rawls' Kantian account, requires acting for the sake of principles that we accept, not because of our particular circumstances, talents or ends, or due to allegiance to tradition, authority, or the opinion of others, but because these principles give expression to our common nature as free and equal rational beings.
>
> (Freeman, 2003: 300)

Following Kant,[22] Rawls sees the stability of democratic regimes as deriving from *three* sources – cognitive, institutional and psychological: (i) a *public conception* of justice corresponding to the liberal principle of legitimacy and embodied in OP arguments and in the *Constitution*, with its interpretative tradition and prescriptive principles of justice; (ii) the democratic *institutions* that derive from it, i.e. the public financing of elections, a certain fair equality of opportunity, a decent distribution of income and wealth, society as employer of last resort, and basic health care for all citizens (*PL*: lviii–lix); and (iii) the *allegiance* of principled citizens to their political regime as a matter of moral conviction, not simply of prudential interest. What is remarkable, though, is the emphasis on moral psychology and on (iii). Contrary to Kant, Rawls does not believe that institutions are sufficient to guarantee stability. Contrary to Kant, too, he does not believe that moral and political motivations are far apart. He trusts moral psychology and education to give the right answers and bridge the gap between the three sources of stability. As he notes (*TJ*: §§80–81), destabilizing psychological tendencies such as envy, spite, the will to dominate and the tendency to submit are all typical of heteronomy. They are the psychological effects of servitude and dependence that should not exist in a free society. It is interesting to note how determinist he is: free societies should be able to produce free minds. The problem of stability is that of correcting these destructive tendencies with the help of the moral sentiments that free institutions normally generate. On this criterion, as we have already seen, utilitarianism, for instance, does not fare very well as it is too demanding of citizens in terms of the strains of commitment. It is not stable in the right way, as it is not based on a sense of justice, but on identification and sympathy. Does justice as fairness fare better and, if so, why? Part III of *A Theory of Justice*, the lesser-read part of his first book, discusses at length how a *moral* consensus on a public view of justice in the midst of various world-views could last over time.

Stability in A Theory of Justice

Stability "for the right reasons", for Rawls, is thus not an *empirical* concern, but a result of people developing *moral sentiments*, in particular a sense of justice, that support the two principles. It has a strong psychological source as noted in (iii). The conception generates its own support, so to speak, to create the well-ordered and lasting society of justice as fairness. Order and stability thus result from justice, not the other way round, as, for Rawls, justice can never be sacrificed to civil peace. This is what Rawls calls in *A Theory of Justice* the "congruence argument" for stability: justice and the good are congruent and "the good of justice" is the only source of stability compatible with liberal legitimacy (*TJ*: 450). Rational citizens will end up recognizing the benefits of free and just institutions and will progressively identify with them from within.[23] More precisely, the argument says that persons living in a free and just society will develop a sense of justice over time as part of their conception of the good.

Such an argument is surprising, as it seems to appeal, like utilitarianism, to a conception of the good as rationality, which contradicts Kant's view on the priority of the right over the good and Rawls' arguments in OP. The conception of the good of justice implies that the main motivation for the allegiance to the principles is not justice itself, but interest. It moves in the direction of psychology and motivational problems of the kind developed by Hume: sentiments or feelings, not reason, move us to act justly. In particular, the appeal to the psychological laws of reciprocity seems to omit any mention of people's autonomy (*TJ*: §76). Obviously, for Rawls, the sense of justice is not sufficient in itself to sustain a stable well-ordered society. Justice as fairness has to be compatible with our own good for us to go on acting consistently in accordance with its principles. To solve the problem of stability, Rawls must show how the individual point of view defined by individual principles, and the impartial public perspective defined by reasonable principles, are not fundamentally at odds (Freeman, 2003: 285). The congruence argument is a complement to OP arguments and, like them, suffers from the tension between rationality and morality. Rawls shows in Part III that it is rational to be just, whereas, if possessing a sense of justice is motivational, there is no need for that kind of reasoning.[24] Moral psychology and appeal to the good of justice seem incompatible with the overall aim of the theory of justice: equal respect for persons and their autonomy.

Correcting A Theory of Justice

What Rawls now realizes is that this argument is not working for two main reasons. First, free and equal citizens are divided by their own moral views. Secondly, imposing such a shared conception of the good of justice would contradict their autonomy. The assumption of a moral agreement on justice is thus controversial and fails to create the right conditions for political consensus. Stability needs consensus, but not in the form of a *moral* consensus, as argued for in Part III of *A Theory of Justice*. The idea of a political consensus is very different. Politics is about coercive power and it is only in sharing this power with their government that citizens can protect their autonomy. This involves a different type of stability "for the right reasons". We have to find a new form of consensus which would be both "moral", but not in the sense of a shared conception of the good of justice, and "political", but not in the sense of a *modus vivendi* or of an unstable balance of powers and interests. This is the new formulation of the problem of stability that Rawls addresses in *Political Liberalism*.

Rawls is acutely aware that democracies are not immune to the tyranny of ideologies, and that autonomy can become an alienating conception of the good. In a very interesting essay on Nietzsche and Socratic citizenship, Dana Villa (2001) explains that Nietzsche's criticism of democracies, with its warning that they may end up as nations of slaves in the very name of autonomy, is in part well founded. Autonomy should not degenerate into a comprehensive morality without deep internal contradiction. It should remain the regulative idea that allows us to criticize and reform our political institutions and practices as we consider them from OP. Such fears certainly underlie Rawls' main reasons for his move toward political liberalism. Far from seeking to accommodate communitarians, Rawls seeks to re-establish autonomy as the main source of stability for a public conception of justice, albeit not as a shared view of the good, even if this is paradoxical; his claim is that justice as equal respect for persons is not an external or "heteronomous" constraint, but is built into personal conceptions of the good in the democratic context by citizens themselves. Thus, political values have priority over personal non-public views "in the right way" and from within, from a "political" sense of justice, not as the result of coercion.

Such stability is rarely characteristic of electoral or majoritarian democracies where the political background culture does not support autonomy in all its aspects. It is no surprise that in *Political Liberalism* and in his later work, Rawls refers more and more frequently to the evils of the Third Reich and to the shortcomings of the Weimar Republic where allegiances to democratic principles were not built into the moral make-up of citizens and where stability was understood as the result of sharing a single totalitarian view of the good (*JAFR*: 101, n. 23). This is where Rawls, wrongly or rightly, locates the vulnerability of democracies and the reason why moral psychology comes to the fore: institutions and principles as such are simply not enough. The challenge is to formulate justice as fairness in terms that wholly protect autonomy, but which are also acceptable to all or at least a majority of reasonable citizens. It is out of the question to advocate autonomy as simply a liberal value, as citizens of faith, for instance, would reject it (*PL*: xliv–xlv). Such is the challenge of stability in democratic terms. The public conception of justice can only generate its own stable support as well as generating a stable democratic society if citizens' full autonomy is taken into account, if they do not have to submit to one single conception of the good. The challenge is to recast the comprehensive Kantian ideal of individual autonomy, explicit in *A Theory of Justice* and in OP arguments, in new, more acceptable terms in the context of pluralism and respect for citizens' autonomy.

Rawls' political liberalism explores this very different interpretation of stability. It calls for new resources such as those of public reason. Its aim too is redefined: not as a moral consensus, but more modestly as an overlapping political consensus between reasonable comprehensive doctrines and the public conception of justice (*JAFR*: 184). The consensus is not based on a comprehensive doctrine of the good of justice that would justify political values through metaphysical or religious ones. It is only overlapping, not unanimous, as was the case in the OP. The two stages of the theory, (1) the OP as a process of rational justification, and (2) the overlapping consensus as resulting from public justification, are now clearly distinct. However, the major transformation, in my view, and what makes the process more credible is that the appeal to the good of justice is left for people to decide; it is no longer a political matter, but a personal one.

I suggest that in *Political Liberalism*, Rawls comes to realize that autonomy means a more complex conception of the person than the Kantian ideal. It means that each of us is split between two sets of beliefs concerning justice, which we as citizens have to reconcile. This is the necessary result of the exercise of democratic rights and liberties over time. We have personal beliefs based on our own conceptions of the good, which we would like to impose on others; however, as citizens and members of a democratic well-ordered society, we also acquire proper political values resulting from OP arguments, for instance. Political autonomy is the autonomy of self-disciplined citizens reworking their own beliefs in order to comply with the *duty of civility* or the duty to express their reasons in publicly stated terms, respectful of others' divergent moral or religious views, no longer solely in terms of their own personal beliefs (*PL*: 217). The distinction between political conceptions and personal comprehensive doctrines is not conceptual and formal; it is instead constitutive of modern citizenship and central to the liberal concern that no one may use his or her personal views as a basis for collective public norms and that the public and the non-public realms should be kept distinct.

In that sense, *Political Liberalism* emphasises even more clearly than *A Theory of Justice* the empowering effect of a public conception of justice. How the public conception of justice fits in with personal belief-systems, the nature of motivations, the unity of the self and its relations to its culture, tradition, etc., are all left for everyone to articulate for himself or herself. They are not to be discussed at the political level. The main point is the congruence with the conception of justice as a *result*, not as a *motivation*. This major distinction avoids the difficulties of the congruence argument in *A Theory of Justice*. It also helps to regain full responsibility for the principles of justice and their regulative force. Citizens decide on the kind of connections they wish to establish, regaining the initiative and their full moral autonomy (*JAFR*: 190). Autonomy is not limited to acting solely for justice's sake, but also involves relying on the congruence between justice and the good established in an autonomous way. Citizens have at their disposal five "thin" ideas of the good that are discussed politically and are autonomous from specific conceptions of the good: (a) goodness as rationality as exemplified in economics; (b) a list of primary goods, already available in the OP; (c) the possibility to associate the conception of justice with a comprehensive doctrine; (d) the good of the political virtues; and (e) the good of political society as the social unions of social unions (*TJ*: 462–3; *PL*: 176).

The argument in *Political Liberalism* is stripped down in order to eliminate building a consensus on a single comprehensive and heteronomous doctrine of the good of justice and to leave citizens free to coordinate, as they may see fit, the public principles of justice with their own personal world-views.

4. The possibility of an overlapping consensus[25]

Having explained what Rawls means by stability, I turn now to the first new idea of political liberalism: how is a liberal political consensus possible in a context of reasonable pluralism? What would be its content? Following Kymlicka (1989: Ch. 8), I then show how it fits fairly well with contemporary concerns, in particular the demands of recognition and of cultural identity and the rejection of the "neutral" colour-blind state. I conclude with a presentation of the main objections to Rawls' view.

A liberal consensus

By the expression "overlapping consensus" (OC hereafter), Rawls means a lasting and stable principled agreement among reasonable comprehensive doctrines with each endorsing the political conception of justice from its own point of view. He rejects as destructive of the democratic ideal a consensus that would be a pure *modus vivendi*, a purely short-term political arrangement that can only last as long as the existing balance of power. He equally rejects a thick *illiberal* consensus, typical of totalitarian regimes and relying on the use of oppressive state power. Avoiding the scepticism of the former and the dogmatism of the latter is a very difficult task. An overlapping consensus is a state of equilibrium that is the result neither of mere compromise nor of full-blooded ideology-based domination, though it may revert to either of these two forms, as democracies are particularly vulnerable regimes. It is *moral* in the specific sense that it is based on people's autonomy and on their own interpretation and acceptance of political norms. It is *political* in the sense that it separates the realm of personal beliefs from that of public deliberation and decision. It tries to model an agreement that is respectful of irreducible differences: citizens all affirm the same political conception of justice, but not necessarily for the same reasons.

Obviously, the possibility that such an OC could ever take place and, moreover, be stable, sounds very utopian (*PL*: 158–68; *JAFR*: §58).[26] Moreover, it is obvious for many readers that stability does not necessarily need consensus, even in a democratic regime. Rawls himself gives few detailed indications as to how to implement the process, suggesting only that a constitutional consensus could constitute both a model and a first step in the right direction (*PL*: 158–68). But let us examine now in more detail the content of OC.

The content of OC

Rawls gives *three examples* of the way in which reasonable and comprehensive doctrines can lead to a consensus on justice (*PL*: 145 and 168–72). However, his examples may be confusing in that he mentions the emergence of OC among doctrines, whereas to be more consistent and rigorous, he should have been talking of *citizens* themselves negotiating the fit between political and non-political values in an autonomous way, as I argued earlier. Comprehensive doctrines can be more or less rigid, more or less comprehensive, and leave more or less room for people to manoeuvre (*CP*: 445), but in the end, for Rawls, it is up to individuals to develop an independent allegiance to the political conception of justice, once its reasons are appreciated. Thus we should not forget that these are simply examples of *processes initiated by citizens themselves*. It is a process not dissimilar to that of "reflective equilibrium"; it can take a variety of forms, balancing ideas of the good and personal convictions in the light of full information, against principles of justice agreed upon in the OP. The content of OC is limited to *reasonable* doctrines in a very specific sense: to doctrines that accept the two basic ideas of the person and of society and that are promoted by reasonable citizens, characterized by their willingness to listen to doctrines, arguments and reasons opposed to their own, even if they do not agree with them. Reasonable citizens are supposed to have accepted OP arguments, and to have been educated by them at this stage. This is the specific meaning of *reasonable*. It is rather unfortunate that Rawls tends to talk only in terms of "doctrines", not also of arguments and reasons, as that would even more strongly emphasize the active role that citizens are taking in the creation of an OC and would mark more clearly that we are not talking here of academic debates!

In the first case, Rawls says that reasonable *religious doctrines* can support the political conception of justice on the basis of their own interpretation of free faith and of tolerance.

As long as they accept that apostasy is not a crime and that individuals are free to change their faith, they show that they are reasonable and they can be included in OC. The important point is that OC is political, not comprehensive, and that the truth of religious doctrines is bracketed: no one should publicly question it. It is only the *free access to truth* that has to be guaranteed in the name of free faith by comprehensive religious doctrines. This, of course, is a very tall order and is probably mostly applicable to religions that tend towards individualism and some form of liberalism (*PL*: 144). It is very difficult to envisage how that could work for the various fundamentalisms that are increasingly emerging, as Rawls himself concedes (*ibid.*: 170). But it is difficult too to understand for liberal citizens of faith who take seriously their beliefs and refuse to bracket grave moral questions, such as slavery, abortion, gay rights, and so on, for political purposes.[27] We could object that OC goes too far in the direction of epistemic abstinence and sounds too agnostic to be able to satisfy traditional and liberal citizens of faith alike. Where should we locate its use? One suggestion is that it is *transitional*; it may be capable of easing the transition from a mere *modus vivendi* to a principled public order.[28] One has to expect that public education and a common civic curriculum will instil in the minds of citizens of faith the principles of constitutional democracy, transforming them into reasonable citizens. This is an empirical question and Rawls' remarks lack the necessary sociological and historical basis. They are in any case very sparse. Still, they are interesting because of the way in which they address questions of secularism and of neutrality toward religions.

The important point about OC is that the political conception of justice should not be misunderstood as *neutral* or *secular*, as we saw earlier. It does not demand that religions agree with each other in the name of reasonableness, solely that they fully endorse the public conception of justice. One could object, as Charles Larmore does, that at a deeper level, it is religious and assumes a certain Christian conception of human dignity.[29] Still, what is remarkable in Rawls' view is that, contrary to the dominant tendency in contemporary democracies, he sees religious doctrines as fully participating in the public debate as part of the background public culture and of OC, and does not accept the current view on the "privatization" of religions as a consequence of the separation of state and church. This is an extremely important point for citizens of faith. For many critics of secular political regimes, it is pluralism, not secularization, that best protects the basic liberties of all citizens, whether religious or not. "Political liberalism offers a way to defuse the war of absolutes. It seeks grounds shared by reasonable people and leaves it to citizens individually to connect political values with their beliefs about the truth as a whole".[30] What is striking in Rawls' view is that it is not agreement as such that is important, but the way in which it is achieved: in an autonomous and personal way.

> The idea of respect is what directs us in the first place to seek the principles of our political life in the area of reasonable agreement. Respect for persons lies at the heart of liberal thought, not because looking for common ground we find it there, but because it is what impels us to look for common ground at all. (Larmore, 2005: 74)

The second case of an OC among *liberal moral doctrines* is more straightforward.

In the case of Kant's moral philosophy, "the relation with the political conception is deductive, even though the argument can hardly be set out very rigorously" (*PL*: 169). The next view is utilitarianism, as in the classical doctrines of Bentham, Mill or Sidgwick, this being one of the main constituents of democratic thought. Here the relation is one of approximation (*ibid.*: 170). Liberal comprehensive doctrines may easily find grounds for supporting the political conception of justice, even if there is a tendency towards a certain form of intolerance in the requirement that critical thinking and individuality be the dominant values. One can note that liberal doctrines can disagree among themselves while still being part of a political consensus and still endorsing the public conception. Rawls' own critique of utilitarianism is a good example of such an OC among conflicting liberal views. The libertarian critique of Rawls' egalitarianism is another striking example. Finally, the debate between communitarians and liberals could probably be expressed in those terms too, even if some still reject the priority of the right over the good.[31]

The third case involves *mixed non-political doctrines* that are loosely compatible with the political conception of justice, but being incomplete and less comprehensive, they leave room for reinterpretation and for endorsing the public conception (*PL*: 146). A further example would be the kind of constitutional consensus that exists in America in spite of wide-ranging moral disagreements among religious and non-religious people, and between different faiths, and that is protected by the First Amendment (*ibid.*: 149, n. 15). Again, the transition from constitutional consensus to OC is seen by Rawls as a sign that political liberalism is a loose federation that admits of many shades and degrees in its make-up (*PL*: IV §§6–7).

Multiculturalism and the OC

I would now like to touch briefly upon the question of religious and cultural integration and the wider question of multiculturalism in the light of *Political Liberalism* and of the idea of the OC. As I have suggested, because OC does not necessarily imply neutrality, it is much more welcoming to various cultures and religions than comprehensive liberalism would be.

Multiculturalism as a social fact arises because numerous minority cultures have come to coexist with the host culture as a result of immigration and post-colonial migrations, as well as from the presence of national minorities. In order to move on from mere coexistence to full integration, multiculturalism as a policy recommends a set of fairly controversial measures, such as affirmative action or special minority rights, aimed at reducing the inequalities resulting from such a minority position. On the whole, *A Theory of Justice* has been interpreted as ignoring the weight of ethnicity, race, gender and culture in the development of social inequalities. The "ethnicization" of injustice, as well as its "feminization", seems to have been bypassed by its liberal colour-blind conception, and it is true that Rawls hardly mentions race or culture and only briefly alludes to the feminist critique of liberalism (*JAFR*: §50; Okin, 1989; Young, 1990; Fullinwinder, 1995; Nussbaum, 2003). Has *Political Liberalism* made some progress in the understanding of this new formulation of questions of justice? In a persuasive argument, Kymlicka shows why this is the case.

First, there is no reason why ethnic, cultural and gender differences are not one of the sites of "unchosen inequalities" that Rawls mentions. Like inequalities in wealth and social capital, they are "profound and pervasive and present from birth", and they too may constitute the relevant position from where to assess the justice of the basic structure in the OP, that of the least fortunate person (see above, Chapter 3). Thus there is no difficulty in adding these inequalities to the list examined by the parties and in seeing the principles of justice as addressing them. "Clearly Rawls should have included cultural membership as one of the positions used in assessing justice, at least in culturally plural countries" (Kymlicka, 1990: 202). I shall examine later the more complex case for feminism.

However, the problem with multiculturalism is not simply that inequalities generated by culture, race or ethnicity should be accounted for, but that cultural membership should have a public role in OC and be entitled to respect and *public recognition*. This is the main theme of Charles Taylor's well-known analysis of multiculturalism.[32] But here again, we may find an answer in Rawls. We saw that self-respect, for Rawls, is the most important primary good that a just democratic regime should deliver to its members. To ensure self-respect, we need the freedom to examine our beliefs and to confirm their worth. Freedom remains an empty concept if the options presented to us are not meaningful. For a choice to be valuable, we need to confront the "definite ideals and forms of life that have been developed and tested by innumerable individuals, sometimes for generations" (*TJ*: 494). It is at this point that cultural membership becomes a crucial issue for minorities. Members of dominant cultures have "natural" ownership of their past culture and history in a way that immigrant population or Aboriginal peoples, and so on, do not. In order to have like access to the set of values that makes their lives meaningful and underpins their self-respect, they need a rich and secure cultural context of choice.

> Rawls' own argument for the importance of liberty as a primary good is also an argument for the importance of cultural membership as a primary good. It is of sovereign importance to this argument that the cultural structure is being recognized *as a context of choice.* (Kymlicka, 1990: 166)

This is the basis for Kymlicka's liberal defence of multiculturalism. Rawls, like most postwar political theorists, still works within a very simplified model of the various components of OC as "doctrines". He should have made room for majority and minority cultures and for assessing their respective weight in the process leading to OC. However, such a lack is not a major flaw and can be remedied, as Kymlicka shows.

The last aspect is much more difficult. Do cultural minorities need *specific rights* to protect them or can the fair worth of their equal rights and liberties be guaranteed within the public conception of justice without additional cultural rights? At first, it seems feasible to include cultural membership among the conditions for the fair value of political liberties (see above, Chapter 2). The freedom to participate politically should include the possibility to use one's own language, to set the agenda on specific issues concerning the survival of one's given culture and group, etc. Again, the application of the difference principle should ensure that, notwithstanding their culture, all have access to the all-purpose means that make one a fully participating citizen. The objective of fair equality of opportunity would have to take into account such disadvantages as may be caused by cultural membership where access to education, jobs and housing is concerned. The consistent application of the conception of justice should ban such discrimination or exclusion as may derive from being a member of a minority culture.

However, without specific rights to protect their own traditions, languages, religion, etc., it may be the case that people cannot fully endorse the conception of justice on the basis of their own comprehensive doctrines, as Rawls asks them to do, in so far as these doctrines, religions, cultures, languages, etc., are bluntly ignored in the name of colour-blind equality or are devalued or have disappeared or, even worse, have become an object of contempt or incomprehension for the majority. Remember that, for Rawls, justice can never be the result of the intensity of majority feelings, as it is for utilitarianism (*TJ*: 27). The argument for minority rights is thus strengthened by the appeal in OC to a wide range of reasonable participating cultures, but on condition that "reasonable" loses any imperialist connotation and that ignored or devalued cultures can also be treated as reasonable. For instance, OC could be strengthened if the public discourse included a discussion of slavery, colonization, the history of immigration, commemorations of past genocides, etc., as a precondition for agreement. Robust debates and disagreements should take place to prepare the ground for OC. How far new cultural rights can achieve these confrontations and catharsis remains to be seen, as they could also be a source of deep and insurmountable divisions.[33]

Objections

To conclude, Rawls mentions *four objections* that he has sought to address: that OC is in reality a mere *modus vivendi* (*PL*: IV, §3); that OC implies indifference or scepticism as to whether a conception of justice can be true (*ibid.*: §4); that OC cannot avoid involving a general and comprehensive view of justice that goes beyond the political sphere (*ibid.*: §5); and, finally, that OC is utopian, to which Rawls replies that it can in effect be achieved, but as the last stage of a long process, starting for instance with the well-known procedure of constitutional consensus, familiar to Americans (*ibid.*: §6–7). All these objections have now been presented and I turn instead to three more difficulties.

Psychologically, the skills needed to reconcile personal beliefs and political principles are very complex and it is far from obvious that the least fortunate citizens will have access to them. There is no mention of that difficulty in Rawls' analysis. First, we need a capacity to connect and reflect upon sets of ideas that we never really take time to examine systematically.

> Many if not most citizens come to affirm their common political conception without seeing any particular connection, one way or the other, between it and their other views. Hence it is possible for them first to affirm the political conception and to appreciate the public good it accomplishes in a democratic society. Should an incompatibility later be recognized ... they might revise these doctrines rather than reject the political conception. (*CP*: 441)

We then need highly developed analytic as well as interpretative skills such that they might weaken our capacity to identify with our own traditions and cultures.[34] It is highly unlikely that a majority of citizens will be able to develop such skills at the level required for a lasting OC. Rawls places his hopes in institutions and education (*JAFR*: 56), in the public background culture, but as he can no longer use the argument of the good of justice and the appeal to instrumental rationality, he admits that the chances of success are slim. Citizenship and the moral psychology of public reason may prove to be the answers to this problem.

Politically, OC might prove impossible and utopian. Actual democratic societies achieve stability without achieving consensus. They are characterized by high levels of organized dissent and competition between rival views and party interests. Moreover, the kinds of discussions that would seem to be necessary to reach OC are more in line with academic debates than with real political conflicts. The idea of public reason might help to clarify this point too. I suggest later that Rawls needs to support a deliberative conception of democracy, the view that public deliberation, not solely elections, is the backbone of democratic politics, and some form of communicative ethics of the kind advocated by Habermas (1999), as possible answers to this question of feasibility.

Morally, OC might involve too many compromises with truth in the name of both efficiency and social reconciliation (*JAFR*: 3–4). Rawls here seems to confuse political theory with a very different task, that of reconciliation, of ensuring social unity through public justification.

As a consequence – and the charge is valid for *The Law of Peoples* too – he seems too ready to make too many concessions in order to include even non fully democratic or "not unreasonable" (*LOP*: 74) ways of thinking or acting. The fact that this inclusion might lead to the disappearance or the withering away of valuable forms of life is mentioned, but possibly not properly explored. It is thus very important to assess the moral consequences of Rawls' view and the strains of commitment from that perspective too. The debate with Habermas (1999) on the relation of public reason and truth has provided an occasion for Rawls (*PL*: 384–5) for clarifying why OC does not compromise truth.

5. Public reason and the duty of civility

The last "new" idea in political liberalism is the increasing import-ance of *public reason*. The term hardly figures in *A Theory of Justice*; however, it becomes very important in the later work. For Rawls, *reasonableness* is certainly the main feature of citizens in a democratic polity, and, as I have explained earlier, the basis for OC should be "a balance of reasons within citizens' comprehensive doctrines, and not a compromise compelled by circumstances" (*PL*: 169). Their free exercise of public reason is the best chance of reaching a stable OC. This is described in two texts: in the introduction to the paperback edition of *Political Liberalism*, §§3 and 5, and in his last published article, "The Idea of Public Reason Revisited" (IPPR).[35] The use of public reason transforms merely personal allegiances and negotiations between personal and public identities into a proper and lasting acceptance of the shared conception of justice. It is the most solid ground for stability as it generates reciprocity and trust, and strengthens what citizens share, in spite of the fact of reasonable pluralism. In his "Reply to Habermas" (*PL*: 388–94), Rawls shows at length how the main ground for introducing the idea of public reason is the principle of democratic *legitimacy* according to which "political power should be exercised in ways that all citizens can publicly endorse in the light of their own reason" (*JAFR*: 90–91). Thus it is only when OC is publicly affirmed that the political conception of justice is fully justified and becomes legitimate in spite of the fact of reasonable pluralism. Hence the role of public reason in justifying justice is crucial. "Justification is addressed to others who disagree with us, and therefore it must always proceed from some consensus, that is, from premises that we and the others *publicly* recognize as true" (*TJ*: 508; *CP*: 426–7, emphasis added).

Under the general title of public reason, Rawls means three things.

> Public reason is public in three ways: as the reason of citizens as such, it is the reason of the public; its subject is the good of the public and matters of fundamental justice; and its nature and content is public, being given by the ideals and principles expressed by society's conception of political justice.   (*PL*: 213 and 386–7)

In this section I start, first, with the distinction between public and non-public reason, and I examine public reason as the reason of citizens, not of non-public associations or of members of civil society, and of political institutions. I show how the use of reason is transformed when it is *public* and how its content is the public conception of justice, which gives legitimacy to political power. Secondly, I analyse public reason as leading to the duty of civility or the duty to express one's own point of view in terms acceptable for other citizens, and Rawls' wider view of public reason.

Public and non-public reasons

First, it is very important to establish a clear distinction between the political realm and the (non-public) various associations and institutions, universities, churches, unions, etc., that make up civil society and its culture (*PL*: 220). The "background public culture" is distinct from the political forum where citizens deliberate and vote, where political parties and candidates present their programmes, where the Supreme Court judges present their reasoned opinions and conclusions, and so on (*ibid.*: VI, §6). This is an unusual distinction as the public sphere, in its non-technical understanding, usually covers both the political and the associational realms. The borders, of course, are porous, but in terms of justification, the reasons invoked are utterly different: churches appeal to their various religious doctrines to impose "local" rules and principles (of justice) whereas political institutions, practices and decisions may only appeal to a political conception of justice, independent of religious or other comprehensive doctrines. This is derived from the distinction between the justice of the basic structure of society and the "local" justice of specific institutions (see *A Theory of Justice*: and above, Chapter 1, Section 4). Remember that one main feature of democratic regimes and societies, for Rawls, is that a public and independent conception of justice, which is absent or non-public in non-democratic societies, mediates direct confrontations between comprehensive doctrines and the exercise of power. Independence from the background culture and associations is constitutive of the ideal of citizenship in contemporary liberal democracies and embodies the commitment to *fairness* as public respect for persons (Larmore, 2003: 389). As a consequence, the political sphere is in a special relationship with the public conception of justice: it must apply and sustain it in a stable and principled way as a condition of its *legitimate* use of power. It is also regulated by it, as citizens establish a reflective equilibrium between their considered personal views and the principles of justice, and verify that they are compatible, that they satisfy the criterion of reciprocity. Democratic stability and the possibility of OC rely on the possibility of coordinating these different levels in a free and public way, not in suppressing them, as in authoritarian or totalitarian regimes. "The political conception of justice and the ideal of honouring public reason mutually support one another" (*PL*: 252).

Secondly, Rawls correspondingly establishes a clear but controversial distinction between the various modes of *reasoning*, public and non-public, that characterize the two realms, and emphasizes the kind of reasoning that is acceptable in and compatible with the political conception of justice. Public reason is restricted to the reason of *citizens*. Liberal democracy "can win support by addressing each citizen's reason" (*ibid.*: 143). The modes of reasoning permitted in the public sphere are determined by the OP's companion agreement on specific guidelines for public enquiry and for public ways of reasoning, closely reflecting the principles of justice (*ibid*: 89). They include usual principles of inference and rules of evidence, standards of correctness and criteria of truth, but also the virtues of reasonableness and fair-mindedness, of adherence to the criteria of common-sense knowledge and science. They should not depend on comprehensive doctrines, philosophical views or elaborate economic theories (*ibid.*: 91–2). As Rawls says, in this public justification, "we are concerned with reason, not discourse" (*ibid.*: 92). However, nonpublic reasons are very important in sustaining the move towards more democratic institutions and we should never see the distinction as if it were hard and fast. This would be a nonsense. As Rawls often says, without a democratic background culture, democratic institutions will wither and die, as the example of the German Weimar Republic has shown all too clearly. The question is not whether the one influences the others – it always does – but of how they should be kept distinct. In the "wide view of public reason", Rawls recognizes that in certain contexts comprehensive doctrines may be used.[36]

The people using public reason are likewise limited. There are three main categories of people concerned: judges in supreme courts; government officials when they address the public; and candidates for public office. Citizens who are not government officials can still see themselves as ideal legislators and engage with political issues in a critical way, participating in the stability of democratic institutions (*JAFR*: 135–6). This obviously calls for a more developed conception of citizenship, which is only suggested by Rawls.

> Citizens are to conduct their public political discussions of constitutional essentials and basic justice within the framework of what each sincerely regards as a reasonable political conception of justice, a conception that expresses political values that others as free and equal also might reasonably be expected to endorse.
>
> (*PL*: l)

Here a warning is necessary. The idea of "private reason" is a nonsense for Rawls, as reason always operates in a *dialogical* relation: it manifests itself as reasons that we present to others and express in a public, not a "private", language. The structural opposition is with non-public reasons, which are certainly not private, but are reasons used in the non-public realm of civil society and its background culture, in associations such as churches, universities, unions, etc. The reasons used for supporting our comprehensive religious, moral and philosophical doctrines are thus *non-public reasons*: they cannot be fully understood beyond the confines of our communities, universities, churches, etc. Moreover, they are not really political in that comprehensive conceptions generally concern the good and the right, but only indirectly justice (see Larmore, 2003: 380). Note also here that Rawls refers to reason as a faculty of reasoning and to reasons as the arguments, grounds and statements that are used by this faculty. Such ambiguity and vagueness is indeed rich and useful since we are dealing with political, not with philosophical, issues.

Public reason is not only citizens' reason; it is also the reason of political institutions, regulated through the political principles of justice. We saw that in *A Theory of Justice*, publicity was an important requirement for defining a well-ordered society: that everyone should accept and know that the others accept the same principles of justice, and that the basic institutions should be known to satisfy these principles

(*TJ*: 4). In particular, Rawls stressed the importance of people addressing each other publicly and declaring publicly their allegiance to the principles of justice. Publicity for Rawls, as for Kant, is a condition of legitimacy and validity. The contractarian metaphor in the OP conveys just that. However, in *A Theory of Justice*, the condition of publicity is generally not presented as constituting such a pre-eminent criterion, simply a formal constraint of the right. It is much further developed in *Political Liberalism* by way of contrast with non-public reason. "Free public reason" embodies the ideal of a society whose institutions can always be publicly and mutually justified to and by all of its members: it embodies an ideal of citizenship as the basis for political *legitimacy* and the source of *stability*. It has been a central feature of democratic culture, from the Ancient Greek *agora* onwards to Kant. For the Greeks, debates in the public space were a source of the polity's cohesion and of civic friendship as well as of the legitimacy of its decisions. For Kant,[37] "the *public* use of our reason should always be free" so that we could progressively create an intellectual community of *savants*, of free citizens of the Kingdom of Ends, exercising "the freedom of the pen". This ideal is not only good for our society, for us, but also for the strengthening of human reason, says Kant, because "reason depends on this freedom for its very existence. For reason has no dictatorial authority; its verdict is always simply the agreement of free citizens, of whom each one is permitted to express, without let or hindrance, his objections or even his veto". "This freedom will carry with it the right to submit openly for discussion the thoughts and doubts with which we find ourselves unable to deal, and to do so without being decried troublesome and dangerous citizens".[38] The public use of reason by political institutions conforms to the public principles of justice, in particular the first principle of equal liberty, and is the best sign of their legitimacy and justice.

Finally, the content of public reason is the political conception of justice as agreed upon in *A Theory of Justice*, the "coercive norms to be enacted in the form of legitimate law" (*PL*: 223). An OC shows how the public use of reason by citizens and by institutions supports the same public conception of justice and underwrites its legitimacy. This is the main feature of a society regulated not by a shared conception of the good, but by a consensus on justice, and that fully acknowledges its members' full autonomy.

It does not apply to all the substantive questions citizens have to debate. Its content is limited to fundamental political questions of "constitutional essentials" (*PL*: 227–30)[39] and to "questions of basic justice" (*ibid.*: 214). A better way to explain this point is to say that constitutional essentials are, for instance, all the questions that the *constituent* power of the people is concerned with, in the sense developed by Bruce Ackerman (1991), that is, the power of the people contrasted with ordinary political power.[40] Rawls describes it as "a forum of principles" or "a public political forum"[41] and the Supreme Court is the central exemplar of public reason (*PL*: 231–40). These essentials include all the fundamental principles specifying the general structure of government, the political process, the powers of the legislature, executive and the judiciary, the limits of majority rule, who has the right to vote, to hold property or what religions are to be tolerated, and so on. Basic matters of social and economic justice too are included such as a concern for securing a social minimum for all, but not the difference principle as it is too demanding and controversial to be discussed as a matter of principle. It is discussed at the legislative level, not in the forum of principles (*ibid.*: 229; *JAFR*: 162). On all other questions, citizens should feel free to appeal to their own views. It is therefore not true to say that Rawls rejects the claims of morality and religion in grave moral political controversies (Sandel, 1994: 1777). In fact, Rawls' wide view accepts appeals to faith and authority as sources of reasons as long as they can be corroborated by public reasons.

The duty of civility and the wide view of public reason

Now the difficulty, for Rawls, is to explain how the content of public reason is the good of the public, the *public good*. This is the most controversial part of public reason. If the public good is the good of all, it must certainly appeal to all or most of citizens' deepest preoccupations. How is Rawls to combine the self-restraint that he expects from his ideal citizens with the need to give answers to grave moral questions and to determine the public good as a common good? The answer is to be found in Rawls' conception of civic virtues, in the duty of civility, which I examine first before detailing its various difficulties and its consequences for the search of the public good.

I turn to what Onora O'Neill (2003: 360) has called Rawls' "civic constructivism" and to the duty of civility. "Civic constructivism" means that citizens as public persons have a duty to *construct* a certain form of public discourse, to develop new reasons that other reasonable citizens, even if they do not share them, would not want to dismiss, as well as new skills and political virtues. They cannot turn to any given or antecedent doctrine, such as natural law or God's law, or to their own personal views to advance a justification for collective norms or for matters of fundamental justice that lead to full compliance. Self-discipline and self-restraint are the key virtues here to create the favourable conditions for stability, instead of the comprehensive doctrine of the good of justice that was used in Part III of *A Theory of Justice*. The "criterion of reciprocity" means that citizens are prepared to limit themselves in their range of arguments and not to appeal to what they may see as the whole truth. "Our exercise of political power is proper when we sincerely believe that the reasons we offer for our political action may reasonably be accepted by other citizens as justification of those actions" (*PL*: xlvi; IPRR: 136).

> The ideal of citizenship imposes a moral, not a legal duty – the duty of civility – to be able to explain to one another on fundamental questions how the principles and policies they advocate and vote for can be supported by the political values of public reason … The union of the duty of civility with the great values of the political yields the ideal of citizens governing themselves in ways that each thinks the others might reasonably be expected to accept.
>
> (*PL*: 217–18)

This duty is not a legal duty. Therefore it cannot mean, as Sheila Benhabib has claimed, that public reason implies a legal restriction on free speech (Nussbaum, 2003: 508). It consists in publicly enacting the psychological process, which we described earlier as the source of OC, and in placing different personal views in reflective equilibrium with the political conception of justice. Because this process is public, it is based on a duty to use mostly public reasons in public debates when discussing questions of basic justice or questions of constitutional interpretation or amendment. Implementing this duty means that citizens now actively support OC and make it last. OC is not a theoretical matter, but a practical one that involves actual citizens. They may not be fully aware that in behaving in such a way, they create the right conditions for a lasting OC; however, this is exactly what they are doing. Rawls, says O'Neill, "identifies the reasonable with the public reason of fellow citizens in a given bounded, democratic society" (O'Neill, 2003: 362). The duty of civility is thus the decision to present to others reasons that they could not reasonably reject, that is, "public" reasons. Rawls prefers here to use Tim Scanlon's negative formulation rather than the positive one as it is less demanding: in a democracy, we do not necessarily expect citizens to agree, but simply to recognize and accept as valid other people's reasons even if they do not share them (*PL*: 124). "A basic form of motivation is the desire to arrange our common life on terms that others cannot reasonably reject" (*ibid.*: 49, n. 2).

A series of examples may illustrate the meaning of the duty of civility.

> Consider, says Rawls, the abolitionists who argued against the antebellum South that its institution of slavery was contrary to God's law ... basing their arguments on religious grounds. In this case, the non-public reason of certain Christian churches supported the clear conclusion of public reason. The same is true of the civil rights movement led by Martin Luther King, Jr., except that King could appeal – as the abolitionists could not – to the political values expressed in the Constitution correctly understood.
>
> (*PL*: 249–50)

In the two cases, the campaigners were using a religious language, as if they were addressing members of their own community, not the wider society at large. As citizens, not as members of certain churches or associations, they should have had the possibility, which the abolitionists did not have, to use public reason or to exercise their duty of civility. Another example would be the debates on such divisive issues as creationism, school prayers, gay rights or abortion (*JAFR*: 117; IPPR: 164–5). Again, even if non-public reasons overlap with political values and reinforce them, it is our duty as citizens to restrict our arguments to public reasons that override our personal views and to only appeal to political principles. As citizens, we inhabit a different sphere: the political sphere, and we should distance ourselves from our personal doctrines, culture or religion to address our fellow citizens and to show our respect for them.

One last point will shed even more light on the duty of civility. Voting, says Rawls, contrary to what modern attitudes often seem to suggest, is not an expression of our deep-seated personal views and convictions; it is a public act that has considerable consequences for others. "The idea of public reason rejects common views of voting as a private and even personal matter ... such views do not recognize the duty of civility or respect the limits of public reason" (*PL*: 219). This

sounds very close to the republican ideal of citizenship. More importantly, it directly connects the ideal of fairness and the ideal of public
reason without the mediation of the contract metaphor (Larmore,
2003: 375).

However, in IPRR, Rawls has corrected his view of the scope of public
reason and now advocates a wider view, which includes the following
proviso.

> I now believe and hereby revise *PL* VI: 8, that reasonable such doc-
> trines should be introduced in public reason at any time, provided
> that in due course public reasons, given by a reasonable political
> conception, are presented ... I refer to this as the *proviso* and it
> specifies what I now call the wide view of public reason.
>
> (IPRR: 144)

It is interesting to note two new points that help to address this
difficulty. First, the range of reasons might include comprehensive
doctrines.[42] In that sense, public reason might be more inclusive than
it seemed at first view, and possibly include reasonable citizens of faith.
Secondly, we saw that the duty of civility is not a legal, but a moral,
duty.[43] It is not derived from a specific comprehensive moral doctrine,
but solely from the main features that best describe citizens: that
they are free, equal, rational and reasonable, in the sense that they
have internalized the limits of reason and are prepared to accept other
people's reasons.

The illuminating example of the separation between state and
church is developed at length in IPRR §3, and leads to the following clarification. Religion should never be the source of political
values and of justice in a democratic society. The principle of separation is valid in that it guarantees the fundamental freedom of
faith for all. However, this does not mean that the state has to
be secular or "neutral", as this would be imposing another non-
religious or even anti-religious comprehensive doctrine on political
debates and law-making decisions.[44] "It is a grave error to think that
the separation of church and state is primarily for the protection
of secular culture; of course, it does protect that culture, but no
more so than it protects all religions" (IPRR: 166). The main idea
behind this distinction is that we cannot proceed *directly* from
non-public to public reasons, as that would mean not respecting
other people's views; however, comprehensive doctrines have their

place in the main political debates, especially in the "wide view of public reason", but indirectly and mediated by public reasons (IPRR: 146).

6. The debate with Habermas

> Citizens cannot re-ignite the *radical democratic embers of the original position* in the civic life of their society ... because they cannot conceive of the constitution as a *project*.
>
> (Habermas, 1999: 70–71)

On the occasion of his 1995 debate with Habermas, Rawls was able to clarify his views on political liberalism in a much more detailed fashion. Habermas' criticism of Rawls' political liberalism is presented in detail in an article of the *Journal of Philosophy*, "Reconciliation through the Public Use of Reason", reprinted with a second paper, written after Rawls' reply, "Reasonable versus True", as Chapters 2 and 3 of his 1999 book *The Inclusion of the Other*. Some additional elements are presented in another paper in the same volume, "Three Normative Models of Democracy", and were already present in his major book, *Between Facts and Norms* (1992). Rawls' "Reply to Habermas" (RH, reprinted in *PL*: IX) is a lengthy reply to Habermas' main arguments, where Rawls' more personal ideas and his closeness to a form of republican liberalism[45] are expressed. But this debate is fairly difficult to follow in view of the very different backgrounds of the two authors.[46]

Philosophically, their projects are very different. Habermas belongs to the tradition of the Frankfurt School, which, following Adorno's and Horkheimer's critique of the Enlightenment, aims at a wide-ranging critique of "monological rationality", that is, the abstract and universalistic Kantian view of reason as the faculty of principles, a view definitely shared by Rawls in some parts of *A Theory of Justice*. In Rawls' terms, Habermas' project is a neo-Hegelian programme of logic that has very little to do with his own normative theory of justice.[47] In particular, being a German and having suffered indirectly under the Nazi regime, the question of truth has a strong moral resonance for Habermas and one can easily understand therefore his strong reaction to Rawls' "strategy of avoidance" of truth in *Political Liberalism*.

Philosophically there is another distance between the "device of the Original Position" and the "ideal speech situation", which characterizes Habermas' discourse ethics.[48]

Still, they share a wide agreement and both reject "market democracy" and simple majority rule. They also share the belief that public justification is the only source of both the legitimacy and the stability of the political process in constitutional democracies. They both believe that political power should and can be framed by normative principles that are not derived from natural law but from public justification. They reject both moral scepticism and moral dogmatism.

Their disagreements within this general framework concern:

(1) The nature and limits of public reason and the role of "truth" in the overlapping consensus (RH: §2).
(2) The nature of constitutional regimes versus popular sovereignty and the balance between civil and political rights, which is the main republican concern: free agents need free states (RH: §3 and 4).
(3) The notion of procedural versus substantive justice (RH: §5).

I shall mostly concentrate here on the first two issues.

Rawls and Habermas on truth in the public domain and public reason (RH: §2)

In what sense is the political consensus based on a moral endorsement of the conception of justice? How are appeals to "truth" to be dealt with in the public domain? Rawls' understanding of the moral basis of political liberalism is much narrower than Habermas'. He offers a *limited* view of public reason, which he sees as distinct from his wider understanding of the public use of reason (*PL*: 1 and 382, n. 13; Habermas, 1999: §2).

Rawls is aware that "the public reason of liberalism may be confused with Habermas' public sphere, but they are not the same ... Habermas' public sphere is much the same as what I call the background culture (I: 2.3) and public reason with its duty of civility does not apply" (RH: 382, n. 13). "It is the culture of the social, not the publicly political" (*ibid.*: 383). He makes a distinction between the point of view of civil society, which includes all citizens, and that of public reason, which is limited to basic questions of justice and constitutional essentials. In contrast to Rawls, Habermas sees the principles of justice as being constantly renegotiated and discussed in the public sphere, this negotiating process creating a new sense of shared identity through the public use of reason. Any "hot" political issue, not only "constitutional essentials", should be a matter of debate for public reason, which is precisely the reason of all the citizens exercising of their political autonomy. "It leaves the task of finding common ground to political participants themselves."[49] Such a view of public reason is at the heart of "deliberative democracy" and Habermas claims that Rawls is much too timid in his approach to democratic exchanges and to the public forum. In the same way, public reason should aim not only at political justification, but also at *social criticism*, a point that is not emphasized in Rawls' views. Habermas writes that "the public use of reason does not actually have the significance of a present exercise of political autonomy by citizens, but merely promotes the non-violent preservation of political stability" (*IO*: 70). Rawls fails to provide a satisfactory conception of active citizenship and limits the conception of deliberative democracy to questions of justice.

This gives rise to Habermas' criticism: by doing this, does he not limit the scope of citizenship? Habermas' conception of communicative ethics means that citizens should have equal rights and access to political communication and that any political decision, institution and practice be open to public discussion. In that sense, his understanding of democracy is more *procedural* than Rawls'. By procedural democracy, Habermas here means the possibility for citizens to question the whole political process from start to finish, whereas Rawls has a different view, where agreement on substantive concepts is the starting point for procedural justice. "Justice as fairness is substantive rather than procedural" (RH: 421–33).

Finally, for Habermas, in contrast to Rawls, *truth* should not be excluded from public reason and from the democratic debate for fear of intractable conflicts. There should be no such separation between "the non-public doctrines and their strong claim to truth and the public conception of justice and its weak claim to reasonableness".[50] Democracies should not fear the search for truth and "remain philosophically superficial", as Rawls suggests. Truth is the result of the free exercise of public reason, not something that should be kept "non-public". In a sense, Rawls has a conception of truth and of "true" doctrines that is metaphysically very charged: truth as dangerous for democracies. In contrast, Habermas' "communicative" ethics has debunked the myth of truth and sees it as the result of fair discussions in an ideal-speech situation. No need, then, for the stringent separation between the "true" and the "reasonable", which is the basis for Rawls' defence of pluralism. Instead of a view of tolerance based on a fear of dissent,

Habermas has a more robust and optimistic conception, based on confrontation, mutual respect and recognition.[51] "Because the public use of reason is ineluctably open and reflexive, our understanding of the principles of justice must remain so as well."[52]

In contrast, in the "second Rawls" and in *Political Liberalism,* the existence of a "universally binding practical reason"[53] is, according to Habermas, played down because of unacceptable motives. He writes: "The idea of the overlapping consensus involves a decisive weakening of the rational claims of the Kantian conception of justice".[54] The empirical question of stability seems to have imposed on Rawls the sacrifice of theoretical or metaphysical issues such as those concerning the truth or validity of such religious, moral or philosophical doctrines as the citizens may advance. The public justification process is thus emptied of its relevance, if the truth-value of these belief-systems is set aside as an intractable problem. The criticism is probably too strong, given the advances that Rawls' political liberalism allows in matters of religious toleration. Rawls, like Habermas, certainly wishes to avoid moral relativism, but his strategy of avoidance of metaphysical issues may possibly lead to a weakening of his position as well as to making it impossible to criticize any unreasonable comprehensive doctrine. Such an objection is convincingly advanced by many feminists, who oppose Rawls on the grounds that he leaves too much to be decided by comprehensive religious doctrines, in particular the role of women in the family and in society (Okin, 1994: 23–43; Nussbaum, 2003: 508–11).

In reality, the two have much more in common than seems at first sight. In his response, Rawls rejects Habermas' criticism that everything should be open to public discussion, because if it were, the principles of justice would never gain the clarity and systematicity required for their scrutiny by citizens. He is also less universalistic than Habermas and quite rightly hesitates to draw a clear distinction between ethical comprehensive doctrines and moral conceptions of justice, because he wants citizens to be able to negotiate and to move freely between the two realms, whereas, for Habermas, "our moral intuitions are rooted into something deeper and more universal than particularities of our traditions" (McCarthy, 1994: 47). He is also less optimistic than Habermas and does not share his hope to "reconstruct the *moral* point of view from which questions of right can be fairly and impartially adjudicated" (*ibid*.: 46). The universal moral point of view within political debates is accessed obliquely, indirectly, through an overlapping consensus on justice, certainly not as a universal common ground. "For Rawls, the pursuit of a practical aim in the face of a practical impossibility dictates the strategy of *PL*" (*ibid.*: 59).

Civil and political liberties: liberals and republicans (RH: §§3–4)

These differences lead us to another major point. For the kind of Kantian republicanism advocated by Habermas, political liberties are constitutive of civil liberties and it is impossible to claim to be free in an un-free state.[55] Personal and political autonomy are thus inseparable for Habermas (*IO*: 69). They are both universal human rights and have the same origin. However, we saw that Rawls is critical of such a thesis and that, for him, the civil and political spheres are distinct: the realm of non-public (but not private) interests is specific and distinct from that of the political forum. It is the realm not simply of the market, as Habermas seems to imply, but of the moral life of citizens, of their personal comprehensive doctrines, of their voluntary associations, of what gives meaning and worth to their lives, and the political should stop there. The personal, for Rawls, is not political. "To make the good of civil society subordinate to that of public life is mistaken" (RH: 420). We all have a universal human right to our personal choices, unhindered by the demands of the body politic within the limits of justice. Is that claim compatible with the view that civil and political rights are co-original? This is the next point of debate between them and it helps to better define what political liberalism stands for.

One main difference between liberals and republicans is their understanding of political rights. Traditionally, republicans see political rights or the "liberties of the Ancients" – the right to political participation, association, demonstration and organization, to run for elections, etc. – as *constitutive* of and not simply as *instrumental* for their civil rights, or of their subjective human rights, to use Habermas' vocabulary,[56] that is of the "liberties of the Moderns" – freedom of thought, conscience and religion, the right to personal property, the rule of law, etc. Such a claim is the consequence of the republican belief that only free states and citizens' political participation can fully protect their rights. For liberals, in contrast, civil rights are seen as fundamental *moral* rights that cannot be compromised and have to be protected by a higher court of appeal that towers above political struggles and divisions. The constitution traditionally represents this higher moral ground, which regulates the excesses of electoral representative democracy and majority rule. Liberals have then a very different conception of political engagements and struggles. They see them not only as instrumental, but also as threatening for personal liberties. The political process needs checks and balances to avoid unacceptable interference such as the "tyranny of majorities" (Tocqueville and Mill). As long as political institutions and practices abide by these constitutional rules, ordinary citizens should feel safe to lead their personal lives without interference. From that claim, republicans conclude that all that matters for liberals seems to be "negative" freedom, or freedom from interference, a freedom compatible with the absence of full political rights and with benevolent tyranny, and that the importance of the political process is undervalued.

Both Habermas and Rawls are aware of the difficulties involved in the two theories, and they are eager to overcome the divide and to find satisfactory answers. One may even say that Rawls' theory of justice is a method of justifying constitutional rules so as to avoid any claim to a comprehensive moral or religious foundation. Both claim to reject the priority of one kind of rights over the other and to defend the "co-originarity" of both.

According to Habermas, Rawls claims "a priority of liberal rights that demotes the democratic process to an inferior status" (*IO*: 69). Even if Rawls writes that "ideally citizens think of themselves *as if* they were legislators and ask themselves what statutes … they would think it more reasonable to enact and to repudiate" (IPRR: 135), he still sees their political rights are instrumental to the protection of personal rights. Citizens are passive in the democratic process. "Basic liberal rights constrain democratic self-legislation" (*IO*: 70). "The role of political liberties is largely instrumental in preserving other liberties … This contradicts the republican intuition" (*ibid.*). "Citizens are politically autonomous only if they can view themselves as the joint authors of the laws to which they are subjected as individual addressees" (*ibid.*: 71). "Public and private autonomy mutually presuppose each other" (*ibid.*: 72).

Rawls' answers to this traditional republican criticism are very interesting in that they provide a new assessment of his doctrine that shows how far he has travelled away from classical liberalism. His arguments are the following (RH: 412–20). There are three ways in which political and private autonomy are equally well protected and co-original: through the first principle of justice and its priority, through the two moral powers of the citizens and, finally, through the structure of the theory. Rawls claims that his doctrine does as good a job as Habermas' Kantian republicanism, but at a lower cost in terms of metaphysical assumptions.

First, remember the emphasis on the *fair value* of political liberties in the first principle (see above, Chapter 2). This should clarify how "the liberties of both public and private autonomy are given side by side and unranked in the first principle of justice" (RH: 413). The list of basic liberties does not privilege the liberal liberties over the republican ones, but gives them the same weight. Rawls is thus able to unite the two types of rights that make up citizenship. There is no unresolved competition between these two types of liberties and rights: they are both basic liberties and are correspondingly secure.

Secondly, they are rooted in the two moral powers of citizens. "These liberties are co-original for the further reason that both kinds of liberty are rooted in one or both of the two moral powers, respectively in the capacity for a sense of justice and in the capacity for a conception of the good ... both are essential aspects of the political conception of the person" (*ibid.*). Rawls' description of the political person is congruent with republicanism, but distances itself from classical liberalism.

Thirdly, the structure of the theory gives the best guarantee that political rights are not devalued.

> I believe that for Habermas the internal connection between the two forms of autonomy lies in the way that the discourse theory reconstructs the legitimacy of democratic law. In justice as fairness, the two forms of autonomy are also internally connected, in the sense that their connection lies in the way that conception is put together as an ideal.   (*Ibid.*: 417)

The structure of the theory itself and its two main ideas: that of the person and that of society, reflects the unity of the two kinds of rights.

Finally, Rawls is even clearer when he concludes with a reference to citizens' political liberties as an expression of their *constituent power*. Fundamental rights arise from the constitutional public debate itself, from democracy in action, hence the traditional expression, "We, the People".[57] The only priority that matters to Rawls is that of the basic liberties, of the whole system of liberties, over economic or perfectionist considerations. This is indeed the definition of a deontological conception of justice and rights and of the priority of the first principle of justice over the second. Economic efficiency or the intensity of citizens' needs, desires and preferences can never be taken as a benchmark for justice and take priority over the protection of basic liberties, as provided by the constitution. Rawls' conception of legitimacy is thus firmly centred on the participation and political autonomy of the citizens, but he feels no need to provide a philosophical theory to explain this. His principal concern is elsewhere. It is to oppose utilitarianism, which, he says, would accept a lesser degree of protection for rights and therefore for justice if, as a consequence, the general well-being of the population could be increased.

Liberalism and democracy

As a consequence of such an understanding of citizenship, Rawls and Habermas should not be seen as too far apart in their views on liberalism and democracy. The problem is how to incorporate a moral constraint on political processes through the control of the constitution, without hampering citizens' responsibilities and participation. How is their constituent power compatible with the very controls of constitutional democracies? What is the meaning for both of procedural democracy?

The way in which Rawls constructs his normative conception of citizenship is still far too liberal for Habermas. Citizens should reclaim this construction as part of their political rights; it should not be left to philosophers. In the division of labour between philosophers and citizens, in Rawls' "rational construction" of citizenship, not enough is left to people's power and to their public discussions. In that sense, the theory of justice is not *procedural* enough because it is not fully open to public discussion.[58] "The theory as a whole must be subjected to criticisms by citizens in the public forum of reason" (*IO*: 62). More precisely, citizens cannot accept as valid the choice of components of the public conceptions of justice if they are not submitted to their criticism. The validity seems to be pronounced by the philosopher and the theory, not by citizens and their public use of reason, which has then only an empirical use. The way Rawls borrows from both the liberal and the republican traditions seems thus arbitrary to Habermas. This choice should be the responsibility of public reason, not that of philosophers. "Rawls should have developed his substantive concepts out of the procedure of the public use of reason" (*ibid.*: 68). Substantive normative concepts such as those used by Rawls – the political conception of the person and the conception of society – should be the results of a public use of reason. Validity belongs to those procedures and their outcomes where citizens exercise their communicative rights and powers, not to what is pronounced as such by philosophers. All seems to be settled from the start of the democratic process: the constitution and the principles of justice that permit its interpretation. Political paternalism is a danger.

As a consequence, "the moral validity of conceptions of justice is no longer grounded in a universally binding practical reason, but in the lucky convergence of reasonable worldviews" (*IO*: 83). Rawls' construction of citizenship remains embedded in liberal preferences and fails to acquire universality and public support in a pluralist and conflictual social world such as ours. "Reasonable citizens cannot develop the original position as a device of representation so long as they are prevented of adopting an independent moral point of view" (*ibid.*: 77). Habermas, however, claims that in his Kantian republicanism, "the correct restrictions are the result of a process of self-legislation conducted jointly" (*ibid.*: 101). He thus succeeds in keeping the balance thanks to his own conception of the relation between the moral and the political dimensions of citizenship.

Rawls gives a response that is a defence of constitutional democracy in a most striking way. What must be set against the "ordinary" exercise of popular sovereignty is not the protective barrier of a constitution, which would be justified by pre-political natural law and remain external and superior to the political process, but the public debate on the constitution and the respect and protection that it gives for their fundamental rights.[59] Far from remaining passive and moved only by the defence of personal interests, citizens intervene actively in constitutional politics. Their political autonomy and their moral autonomy are inseparable because they do not act solely on the basis of their personal ethical convictions or their private interests, but on that of their political moral judgement: the representation of themselves as moral persons and of society as a fair system of cooperation.[60] Constitutional politics is what is missing from Habermas' analysis and what would properly answer his claim that, for Rawls, "citizens cannot re-ignite the *radical democratic embers of the original position* in the civic life of their society ... because they cannot conceive of the constitution as a *project*" (*IO*: 70–71). Here Rawls borrows from the political philosopher Bruce Ackerman the distinction between "ordinary" politics and "constituent" politics (RH: 405, n. 40). The "superior" politics of citizens, or of constituent politics, is Rawls' answer to the radical civic involvement described by Habermas as defining active citizenship. In the end, both agree that political autonomy is the fullest expression of moral autonomy and that political autonomy is constitutive: the very claim of neo-roman republicans!

In Chapter 1, "The primacy of justice", I have suggested that one of Rawls' most important contributions to both contemporary political theory and practice is possibly his insistence on the relevance of a public conception of justice for citizens.[61] A public establishment of clear principles of justice can *empower* them and make them capable of assessing their political institutions and practices and of initiating changes on the basis of these shared principles. "It is part", he writes, "of citizens' sense of themselves not only collectively, but also individually, to recognize political authority as deriving from them and that they are responsible for what it does in their name" (RH: 431). In "The Idea of Public Reason Revisited", he writes in terms not dissimilar to Habermas:

> Ideally, citizens are to think of themselves as if they were legislators and ask themselves what statutes, supported by what reasons satisfying the criterion of reciprocity, they would think it most reasonable to enact. When firm and widespread, the disposition of citizens to view themselves as ideal legislators, and to repudiate government officials and candidates for public office who violate public reason, is one of the political and social roots of democracy, and is vital for its enduring strength and vigour.   (IPRR: 136)

This leads to a new understanding of Rawls as going beyond liberalism, and to new rapprochements, in particular with republicanism.

Conclusion: questioning political liberalism

Along with Habermas' criticisms, there has been a rich crop of heated discussions and reasoned arguments around the meaning of *Political Liberalism* and the existence of a "second" Rawls. As I have already said, the continuity thesis seems to me to be the more convincing. Still, many questions remain open and some analyses are not really conclusive. To conclude, I would simply like to indicate a few important points that are still open to debate: mostly the apparent abandon of the defence of social rights, but also the question of pluralism, the conception of the self, the feminist critique, and the uncertain structure of the new theory.

The defence of social rights

In *Political Liberalism*: VI, §5 and in *Justice as Fairness*: 13, §6, Rawls says that the difference principle is not part of *constitutional essentials*, that is, of matters to be decided at the constitutional level and concerning the structure of government and the political process, the powers of the legislature, executive and the judiciary, the scope of majority rule, and so on, as well as the basic political rights and liberties that need to be respected and secured. In contrast, if a principle of equal opportunity and the provision of a decent social minimum, allowing all citizens to fully exercise their civil and political rights, are part of the constitutional essentials in that sense, "fair equality of opportunity" (the first part of the second principle) and the "difference principle" are not. The reason has to do with legitimacy. These are definitely principles of justice, as the OP argument has shown; however, proving to all or to a majority of citizens that they are legitimate and can regulate the exercise of political power and legislation is proving more controversial. It is obvious that "it is far more difficult to ascertain. These matters are nearly always open to wide differences of reasonable opinion ... This is not a difference about what are the correct principles, but simply a difference in the difficulty of seeing whether the principles are achieved" (*PL*: 229–30).

Unfortunately, this fairly vague and unsatisfactory statement has meant that, for many critics, Rawls has been seen as failing in *Political Liberalism* to guarantee the proper status for egalitarian justice that he had argued for so effectively in *A Theory of Justice*.[62] If proven, this would be a serious difficulty and a real retreat from *A Theory of Justice*. It would mean that because the difference principle is controversial and too demanding to gain general acceptance, it cannot be part of the constitution and of public reason, and must be left to mere political discussion to be decided. Its case is thus exemplary. It shows that, as many critics, from Benhabib (1992: 101–3) to Sandel (1994), have noticed, the use of public reason is constrained in such a way that controversial issues never come to the fore. It is a far cry from real political debates in the public forum. The absence of a discussion on economic and social rights from the deliberations of public reason is certainly problematic. It would deprive them of their legitimacy. Does that mean that *Political Liberalism* is a reduced version of justice as fairness, trimmed to be acceptable to a wide variety of comprehensive doctrines? Is Rawls bowing to popular votes and majorities? Does egalitarian justice survive in *Political Liberalism*? Is, as Brian Barry claims

(1995b), the difference principle abandoned at the stage of the overlapping consensus? This is a very important question, which would demand careful argument and more space. However, I would like to sketch a brief answer.

Why is the difference principle not part of constitutional essentials? The simple answer is that it is a question of *basic justice*: "political discussions of the reasons for and against fair opportunity and the difference principle, though they are not constitutional essentials, fall under questions of basic justice and so are to be decided by the political values of public reason" (*PL*: 229, n. 10). Basic justice is concerned with the second part of the basic structure that deals with economic and social inequalities. This is a field that is much more complex and which is best left to legislative bodies to decide, "so long as there is firm agreement on the constitutional essentials and established political procedures are reasonably regarded as fair, willing political and social cooperation between free and equal citizens can normally be maintained" (*PL*: 230). Such a result is probably too optimistic and based on wishful thinking. Still, in *Political Liberalism*, we have seen that Rawls is concerned with questions of political legitimacy and acceptance, no longer solely with social justice. Political legitimacy, of course, does not need justice; however, the application of justice and its authority require legitimacy and a stable consensus. Rawls examines the relation of the two principles with the various stages of the legitimating process: the constitutional, legislative and executive.

> Owing to greater controversy about what would be an appropriate principle of social and economic inequality, these matters are allowed to vary more within the bounds of legitimacy. The constitutional essentials on the other hand are relatively rigid requirements of legitimacy. (Estlund, 1996: 77)

We may conclude that Rawls does not want to weaken the defence of democratic equality; however, he is now more aware of the obstacles to its realization in the real world of party politics and thus makes a new distinction between constitutional essentials and matters of basic justice that are not decided at the level of the constitution. It is clear that social and economic liberties do not get the kind of full constitutional guarantees that apply to basic civil and political liberties. Is the balance between equality and liberty not compromised?

Pluralism

I have made it fairly clear that *Political Liberalism* acknowledges the role of controversies and takes pluralism seriously. But is it pluralistic enough? For many critics (Galston, 1995), Rawls does not take religious pluralism seriously. In particular, he excludes from the question of toleration the brute fact of difference, of cruel and bloody strife. He also assumes that only unreasonable people can be adversaries of democracies. He packs too much into his definition of the reasonable. He does not give enough thought to citizens of faith, who refuse to accept the companion agreement on modes of reasoning, in particular the methods and conclusions of science. The violent current debate on creationism could certainly not be accommodated by an appeal to public modes of reasoning. Rawls also misrecognizes the appeal to transcendence which characterizes monotheism and makes it much more difficult to integrate politically than Indian polytheism or the civic religion of the Ancients. Finally, is Rawls not one-sided when he sees religions as threatening for civil peace? The state can also submit religious communities to unfair coercion. It is a two-way relationship. Most of these criticisms have been answered by Rawls in IPRR, in particular those concerning the relation between faith and science. Remember that he sees the political domain as shaped by a multiplicity of faiths, not by their exclusion and privatization. Still, a point remains: has Rawls seriously integrated the politics of confrontation and conflicts or is he still thinking in terms of academic debates? Religious conflicts have developed since the publication of *Political Liberalism* in such a way as to make the idea of an overlapping consensus somewhat obsolete.

The fragmented self

One consequence of Rawls' distinction between comprehensive and political doctrines is the division of the self between a private and a public identity. This leads to a twin objection, that public reason leads us to adopt an artificial public identity and to renounce our deepest commitments in the name of the duty of civility when we enter the political realm. Is it not too demanding? What psychology does it need? Is there not some kind of schizophrenia involved in functioning in one world as a democratic citizen and in another such as the family or the church or the university, for instance, as a dogmatic religious fundamentalist? This point is one of the most interesting questions and I will come back to it in my conclusion. In reality, Rawls' answer is that it is up to the person to negotiate between these different identities, and this is arguably the best way to give autonomy its real position within the theory: a *theory* that is not "theoretical" but practical, that invites people to search themselves for answers in a very Socratic manner. Citizens, not philosophers, are the experts here!

Feminism[63]

This leads to the feminist critique that Rawls has not sufficiently explored the non-public question of family justice. I leave aside here the radical feminist critique of Rawls and concentrate solely on the kind of liberal feminism that has found in the OP a great potential for thinking about justice in the family.[64] However, in *Political Liberalism*: xxi, he recognizes that he omitted justice in the family from his concerns, but sees no reason why his principles should not ultimately handle the issue of gender inequality in the same way that they see race and ethnicity as markers of the least fortunate relevant position. More worrying is the distinction between the personal and the political, even if Rawls tries to address it in *Political Liberalism*: 137 and in "The Idea of Public Reason Revisited". It leads to leaving aside too many cases of injustice because the public citizens are so idealized. They are fully functioning human beings over a whole life whereas, for women, their intellectual and physical powers may experience huge variations due to pregnancy, lactation, child rearing, creating unacceptable inequalities, as does their unequal ability to convert resources into actual human functioning. Rawls will have to make serious changes to his view of citizens and of cooperation to account for these harsh realities. Reciprocity, where women are concerned, is a very positive ideal of justice but it clashes with the inequalities in access to public reason that they constantly encounter, with the way in which religions and ideologies tend to contain and resent women's potential for development, and the absence of recognition of the family as a public and political institution, not simply a voluntary one. Still, it is very difficult to maintain that *Political Liberalism* represents a retreat on *A Theory of Justice*, in terms of women's rights. It is obvious that Rawls is as aware of the shortcomings of his theory for feminism as he is concerned with race and ethnicity, and sketches ways to remedy these failures.

Structure of political liberalism

I conclude with an open-ended question. What is the structure of political liberalism? What is the new position of justice as fairness in it? If political liberalism is not Rawls' own view, why does he claim to be one of the first to have discovered it (*PL*: xix; Laden, 2006)? And how does it stand in respect of the specific conception of justice that he advances? There are at least two answers to that. The first is that political liberalism is Rawls' own interpretation of liberalism, which is at the basis of justice as fairness as a political conception of justice. It includes the two principles and their rules of priority, the device of OP, but also the fundamental ideas of society as a system of fair cooperation, of the political conception of the person, of the fact of pluralism, of the overlapping consensus and of public reason. The second answer is more vague and less satisfactory. It is the idea that contemporary forms of liberalism could all congregate and form a loose confederation of reasonable doctrines fit for democratic peoples. In that confederation, justice as fairness would be a "module", one among many competing conceptions, but it would be the best placed as the source of an overlapping consensus because of its metaphysical abstinence and its compatibility with a wide range of views, religious, moral or philosophical. It has been suggested,[65] and I agree, that what Rawls means by political liberalism would have been better formulated in terms of liberal republicanism, given the important roles he accords to the political forum, the ideal of citizenship and its civic virtues, and to social cohesion. Even more importantly, Rawls reiterates his defence of the priority of the right over the good in terms not only of the content of his doctrine, but of its structure. His conception of political liberalism includes a number of "political" conceptions of justice that are freestanding and doctrinally autonomous. It is not "applied moral philosophy". This means that, in contrast with most comprehensive doctrines, it does not need any form of metaphysical truth or dogma to provide a firm grounding of political principles of justice (*PL*: 98–9).

Chapter 5

A reasonable law of peoples for a real world

> The greatest problem for the human species, the solution of which nature compels him to seek, is that of attaining a civil society which can administer justice universally.
>
> (Kant, *Idea for an Universal History*, 1784: 45)

Introduction

Could the main ideas of the theory of justice be adapted and extended to provide a theory of *international* justice? Can the conception of "justice as fairness" be unanimously adopted as a guideline for foreign policies, for international public law and for international redistributive justice? Could it help to establish the rule of law at the international level and, as a consequence, a lasting peace? These are the questions that Rawls will try to address in the later part of his work.

We need, to start with, a clear definition of the term "international justice", which is very confusing and refers both to positive law and to normative rules or principles. As we have already seen, justice for Rawls does not mean institutional justice, or here, international law, but the normative guidelines that could regulate international relations at the legal, economic and political levels. It is important to make it clear that the "law of peoples" in Rawls' sense is not a reinterpretation of the classical *jus gentium* or law of nations, that is to say, of the existing body of international public law that applies to *all* nations.[1] Again, Rawls' Society of Peoples is not another version of the United

Nations, as it excludes two types of states: poor or "burdened societies" that do not have the means to cooperate; and "rogue" or "outlaw states" that do not want to cooperate and to abide by a common set of political and legal rules. Whereas at the domestic level, being united by a common citizenship means that people are willing to cooperate and to enter a beneficial social contract, the "state of nature" or "the war of all against all" (Hobbes) has long been seen as the best description of international relations. We should add that "international" justice is not "global" justice for it implies the durable existence of states or national structures. It is also different from "transnational" justice, which involves cooperative institutions and common legislations among nations within specific geographical areas such as the European Union.

Rawls' aim is specific and more restricted than what we usually have in mind when we mention international justice. The law of peoples is certainly less realistic than the *jus gentium*. However, it is less idealistic than the cosmopolitan dream of a world government. Its idea of a loose society or confederation of like-minded decent peoples is not far from the post-World War II dream that presided over the birth of the European Union. Such a society is not governed by a common legal or moral conception of justice, but rather by the guiding political principles recognized by all liberal and decent societies in their search for peace with non-liberal peoples, in their conduct in case of war and when faced with a duty of assistance to poorer countries. It follows Kant's essay on *Perpetual Peace* (1795) and his rejection of a world government as well as his sketch of a "pacific federation" of republican states. The word "global" is hardly used by Rawls as his thinking remains within the boundaries of existing states and peoples. Still, from within these constraints, he is searching for an alternative to two prominent albeit disappointing normative theories of global relations: so-called "realism" and "cosmopolitan" liberalism. One should add that *The Law of Peoples* is valuable too as an element of internal exegesis of Rawls' whole project. It sheds important new light on the meaning of the principle of reciprocity and fairness. It also shows more dramatically the tensions between Rawls' social holism[2] and his moral individualism, in particular on the question of the universal protection of human rights.

One important point is that Rawls' sensitivity to the social structure and to the idiosyncratic nature of peoples leads him to reject universal protection for the full list of human rights in favour of a limited list, more compatible with national cultures and conceptions of justice (see below, p. 252). Such a consequence is extremely problematic and it is difficult to see it as part of a theory of justice. Both the respect for the fact of pluralism and for peoples' autonomy and self-respect lead him to adopt such a controversial position. This confirms a point that I have made in various earlier discussions, that Rawls' use of social structures may lead him into deep difficulties as it is never fully justified in terms of the priority of moral individualism. It supports my interpretation that respect for autonomy, here the autonomy of peoples, as the "deeper doctrine" of the theory of justice, is phrased in terms that are not clearly compatible with moral individualism. This is a major drawback of the Rawlsian project.

In this chapter, I seek first to establish the continuities between the domestic theory of justice and the law of peoples and the reasons for the move from one to the other (Section 1). I then, concentrate on Rawls' original albeit controversial notions of peoples, of patriotism and of nationalism and how they connect with the contemporary rise of globalization (Section 2). Is Rawls not still locked into a "vanished Westphalian world" (Buchanan, 2000)? In particular I focus on the notion of *reciprocity* among decent peoples, hoping to shed some light on the difficult issue of his societal concept of justice as fairness, a concept that we examined in Chapter 1, in contrast with justice as mutual advantage and justice as impartiality. In the following sections, I address four main problems that face decent societies in their interactions at international level. The first is the question of defining the guidelines of a fair foreign policy for liberal states in their dealings with non-liberal but decent peoples and the threshold for admission to the Society of Peoples (Section 3). The second is the difficult question of Rawls' conception of human rights and the many criticisms he has received (Section 4). I insist here that the "realistic" view adopted by Rawls is deeply damaging. The third deals with the imperatives of peace and justice (Section 5). I examine, in particular,  the cosmopolitan criticism that Rawls, in the end, is more interested in peace than in justice in international relations. In that sense, he is much closer to the realist theory of international relations than he would wish. The last question concerns international aid to poor countries and the duty of assistance that, for Rawls, should replace any attempt at global economic justice (Section 6). I conclude with an assessment of the balance between realism and utopia in Rawls' project.[3]

1. Extending justice beyond borders

Moving from domestic institutions to international ones seems a natural if challenging move, which Rawls has attempted three times: in *A Theory of Justice* (§58), in his 1993 Amnesty Lecture and in his last work, *The Law of Peoples* (1999).

Three difficulties

The first point to note is that both *justice* and *normative* theory are "new" ideas in international relations theory, which has so far been dominated by "realists".[4] It is only recently that a normative discourse on international relations has been elaborated. The reasons for this change are historical. Under pressure from moral claims, especially the concern for human rights after World War II, the *Westphalian*[5] system of sovereign states has been transformed. Limitations to state sovereignty as well as a moral right to intervene in internal affairs in case of gross violations of basic human rights were deemed inevitable after the horrors of the Holocaust, even if the international community has since failed to act and to prevent new genocides in Cambodia, Bosnia, Kosovo and Rwanda. States' capacity to mistreat their populations, especially their minorities, as badly as they wanted had to be limited. It is, of course, difficult to appreciate how extensive these changes have been, and many, among them Rawls, doubt whether the Westphalian system will ever disappear, given in particular the proliferation of new states due to the decolonization process and to the break-up of the Soviet Union. These ideological changes are still the basis for what Rawls presents as a "realist utopia". They mean that the demands of justice, far from being unrealistic, are now seen as central to the establishment of lasting peace and security between nations.

However, behind the self-righteous humanitarian concern, there lies a major difficulty. One has to remember that the 1948 Universal Declaration of Human Rights was dictated by both moral and political imperatives. It affirmed one dominant view on justice, which was unashamedly liberal and democratic. Inspired by his sensitivity to the "fact of pluralism", Rawls insists that it should not simply be based on democratic and liberal terms, but include different views on justice. This is why the notion of *"decent"* peoples is so important in his extension of justice beyond borders. (Extension does not simply mean internationalization.) It plays the same role as the notion of *reasonableness* at the domestic level of the plurality of comprehensive conceptions of the good. "I think of decency as a normative idea of the same kind as reasonableness, though weaker" (*LOP*: 67). There is an immense difference between lawless states that have no respect whatsoever for human rights and justice, and societies which are not aggressive, which respect basic human rights, which possess a common-good conception of justice, a "decent consultation hierarchy", a respected and regularly enforced legal system, even if the values that they assume are neither liberal nor democratic, but hierarchical and communitarian (*ibid.*: 62–7). We should insist on pluralism and include other conceptions, those of "decent" peoples who are non-democratic and do not treat all their members as free and equal, but still respect basic human rights. It is thus crucial to go beyond comprehensive liberalism and work out how "peace and justice would be achieved between liberal and decent peoples both at home and abroad" (*ibid.*: 6).

The second reason which leads Rawls to examine international justice is his concern for democratic stability that, as we have seen, takes a central place in *Political Liberalism*. Liberal democratic societies cannot survive in isolation, sheltered from the global threats of terror, famines and widespread injustices. They live in a dangerous and violent world, and have to protect themselves. But, according to Rawls, the basis for peace and stability in liberal societies cannot simply be the balance of power and *Realpolitik*. The main condition for peace is the existence of legitimate international rules and institutions that can impartially regulate international relations among members of a Society of Peoples and limit state sovereignty. International law needs a theory of political justice that provides it with moral legitimacy and publicly agreed and enforceable guiding rules as much as it needs powers of enforcement and military intervention. The subject-matter of *The Law of Peoples* is, then, the establishment of a new normative framework for international relations, of a law of peoples based on moral principles that will regulate exchanges and arbitrate conflicts between peoples at all levels: economic, political and territorial, legal, cultural. As we have seen in *A Theory of Justice*, such a theory relies on a "holistic" or institutional view of justice. This means, in particular, leaving aside "many of the immediate problems of contemporary foreign policy that trouble citizens and politicians" (*LOP*: 8) and concentrating on "the *foreign policy* of a reasonably just *liberal* people" (*ibid.*: 10). The aim is to build "a *political* [my emphasis] conception of justice that applies to the norms and principles of international law and practice" (*ibid.*: 3). Such a project is at odds with more traditional views of international relations and this partly explains the dismal reception of *The Law of Peoples*.

The third point to note is that this extension of justice as fairness does not include a theory of global distributive justice, contrary to what could have been expected from the author of *A Theory of Justice*. It is ironic that the best-known theoretician of distributive justice should not regard distributive justice as appropriate to international relations. In the name of realism, Rawls, in fact, opposes a cosmopolitan view of a just world order, where the principles that apply at the domestic level are extended worldwide and where all individuals, their cultural background notwithstanding, are to be granted the same liberal constitutional rights. This is incompatible both with respect for cultural and political diversity and with the very notion of what a people is and of its autonomy. Distributive justice, for Rawls, is a matter of peoples' internal autonomy and cannot be imposed by international law. (In contrast, the difference principle has been applied to international justice by two Rawlsians, Charles Beitz and Thomas Pogge, whom Rawls discusses at length.[6]) The main reason for this is Rawls' "holism", that is, his view that the main agents, in international relations, are not individuals, but "peoples", if such a stark distinction can be made, this in spite of the fact that "peoples" are made up of individual persons. It is up to each people to adopt the most suitable conception of justice with appropriate choice procedures, and to individuals, within their society, to express their views. It would be "arrogant" to claim that "only a liberal democratic society can be acceptable … we cannot know that non-liberal societies cannot be acceptable" (*LOP*: 83). In that sense, Rawls sees himself as advocating a more realistic and less ethnocentric view of international relations than his liberal cosmopolitan critics. Hence his claims to be "realistically utopian" (*ibid.*: 4 and 11) and that liberal institutions could progressively be established *within* non-liberal societies and *among* all decent nations, leading to peace and stability, while respecting the autonomy and self-determination of "real" peoples.

But this midstream position has been attacked and submitted to three distinctive series of criticisms. For cosmopolitan writers such as Brian Barry, Charles Beitz, Thomas Pogge or Kok-Chor Tan,[7] on the one hand, its scope is too limited. In *The Law of Peoples*, Rawls is concerned mostly with justice *between* societies, not with justice *within* societies, whereas for most people the two are deeply connected. As a consequence, his criteria for toleration of non-liberal societies are too relaxed and provide justifications for too many limitations of the scope of full human rights. *The Law of Peoples* retreats from the ambitions of *A Theory of Justice*. A more nuanced criticism is that one may agree with Rawls' "target and cut-off point" principles for distributive justice, while still thinking that his list of human rights is too meagre, and that the target for decency and admission to the Society of Peoples is set too low.[8]

For cultural relativists and anti-universalists such as John Gray, Barry Hindess or Glen Newey,[9] on the other hand, its scope is dangerously universalistic and ignores the values and belief-systems of traditional non-liberal societies, as if the liberal paradigm should apply to the whole world. Because the law of peoples advocated by Rawls is an extension of a liberal conception of justice, it cannot escape its origins and may be unacceptable to non-Western cultures. It is nothing more, in the end, than an expression of cultural imperialism.

Finally, for "realists", Rawls' theory of limited state sovereignty and of a peaceful society of nations is still utopian or, even worse, ideological. It shows no sense of real-world political struggles and of the growth of the new economic order. Any agreement on democratic principles is a pawn in the power games that define international relations. The role of human rights, of "good governance" or of political justice is mainly to make self-interest look more acceptable. Rawls' project is in line with the liberal illusion that if all regimes were constitutional and liberal-democratic, there would be no war, that, following Kant's scheme, the populations of "republics" are committed to peace, and that domestic justice leads to global peace. The claim that peace is a moral concept, that it needs a degree of domestic political and social justice such as the protection of equal citizenship, representative government, the rule of law and equality of opportunities, is condemned by realists, who see peace as "political", that is as a result of diplomacy, negotiations, compromises, alliances and the balance of power. Rawls' law of peoples is just not relevant for the "real world".

The Law of Nations *(1971)*

Rawls has modified his initial views from *A Theory of Justice* where he claimed only a limited scope for a theory of justice.

> I am concerned with a special case of justice. I shall not consider the justice of institutions and social practices generally, nor except

235

> in passing the justice of the law of nations and of relations between states (§58) … The conditions for the law of nations may require different principles arrived at in a somewhat different way. I shall be satisfied if it is possible to formulate a reasonable conception of justice for the basic structure of society conceived for the time being as a closed system isolated from other societies.   (*TJ*: 7)

In *A Theory of Justice*, Rawls had been concerned with the problems of unjust laws and the right way to deal with them: civil disobedience and conscientious refusal. In a brief section of *A Theory of Justice*, he examines the justification of conscientious refusal for political reasons and its appeal to "the conception of justice underlying the constitution" in order to object to engaging in an unjust war. This leads to reflections, inspired by the Vietnam war, on what makes a war justified and on the necessity "to extend the theory of justice to the law of nations" (*TJ*: 331). "Our problem, then, is to relate the just political principles regulating the conduct of states to the contract doctrine and to explain the moral basis of the law of nations from this point of view" (*ibid.*). Note that, here, his thinking takes place within the traditional context of the law of nations or *jus gentium*, that is to say, a law that applies to *all* nations, well ordered or not.

Applying justice as fairness to international relations means "repeating" in the new international context the process of the Original Position (OP hereafter) in the case of domestic "closed" or "bounded" societies,[10] that is, the process of choosing principles and of verifying their fairness. These principles of the law of nations are to be determined by a second social contract forged in a second OP, in which the representatives are not individual persons, but societies or nations. They meet under a "veil of ignorance", which denies them particular information about themselves, in order to "choose together the fundamental principles to adjudicate conflicting claims among states" (*TJ*: 331). The information that they have about their particular situation is limited to "enough knowledge to make a rational choice to protect their interests" (*ibid.*: 332). This means that, as in the domestic case, there is no superior authority to arbitrate the conflicts, but that adjudication is through free choice and deliberation. Still, the difference is important: whereas the parties in OP select a public criterion of justice, at the international level, they directly choose particular binding rules in a two-tiered system. As Thomas Pogge (2006: 213–16) shows, this difference has serious implication at the economic level as it allows free bargaining among the members: rich and poor states.

At this primary stage, Rawls seems to accept that inter-state conflicts and competitions constitute the whole context of international
justice. He does not make a distinction between states and their eth-
nically and socially diverse populations. He does not mention the
fact that intra-state conflicts and the abuse of minority groups and
"ethnic cleansing" are now major causes of international conflicts
and foreign intervention in a global world. Neither does he mention
immigration, political asylum or world trade and global distributive
justice as major issues at stake. Thus his description of the agents of
international relations seems extremely narrow and conventional, not
taking in the major events that have shaped post-Cold War political
developments.

As a result, the political principles that would be chosen in the second
OP are the conventional principles of international law and diplomacy,
but acknowledged as *morally* binding, not simply *politically* imposed.
They will be recognized as fair and just among nations as the "original position nullifies the contingencies and biases of historical fate"
(*TJ:* 332). Their scope is the foreign policy of the just societies taking
part in the scheme and they are limited to "governing public policies
toward other nations" (*ibid.*). These principles correspond to the first
principle of justice, but there is no equivalent for the second principle of distributive justice. Within this very limited framework, these
principles are (1) a principle of equality among peoples analogous to
the first principle of equal rights for all citizens, (2) a principle of
self-determination, (3) the right of a people to settle its own affairs
without the intervention of foreign powers, (4) the right of self-defence
against attack, including the right to form defensive alliances to protect this right. A further principle (5) is that "treaties are to be kept,
provided they are consistent with the other principles governing the
relations of states" (*ibid.*). Besides these principles, which help define
the right to war or *jus ad bellum*, and stipulate that "it is unjust and
contrary to the law of nations to attack the liberty of other societies
for economic advantage or national power" (*ibid.*: 334), (6) "additional
principles regulate the conduct of war, *jus in bello*, which is determined
by the national interest of a just state to maintain and preserve its just
institutions" (*ibid.*: 333).

What is remarkable in this list of principles is how uncritical Rawls
remains of the "vanished Westphalian world"[11] where states were the
main actors on the world scene and no account was taken of the
basic human rights and freedoms of the populations involved, as
the emphasis remained on their governments. The many critics of

Rawls' first attempt to apply justice as fairness to the relations between nations have therefore reacted strongly to his views.

But it is important at this stage to keep in mind two aspects of Rawls' argument in favour of conscientious refusal, which will be emphasized in his later work and in his rejection of cosmopolitanism.

First, Rawls offers a *discriminating* view of any right to conscientious refusal in time of war. He is not an indiscriminate advocate of pacifism and he does not favour "a general pacifism, but a discriminating conscientious refusal to engage in war in certain circumstances ... based upon the principles of justice between peoples" (*TJ*: 335). This anticipates one main feature of his view on distributive justice and the duty of assistance as a "target and cut-off point" procedure, not as an indefinite and unrealistic commitment.

Secondly, as a consequence, this right cannot stand on its own. It has to be related to a general conception of justice agreed upon by the other members of society. "It is based on the same theory of justice that underlies the constitution and guides its interpretation" (*ibid.*: 333). "It can be justified in cases of unjust wars (*jus ad bellum*) or of violations of the moral law of war (*jus in bello*)" (*ibid.*: 334). "One may have a duty, and not only a right to refuse" (*ibid.*: 335).

The same remarks apply to the justification of conscription.

> Since conscription is a drastic interference with the basic liberties of citizenship, it cannot be justified by any needs less compelling than those of national security: the end of preserving just institutions ... for the defence of liberty itself, not only the liberties of the citizens of the society in question, but also those of persons of other societies. (*Ibid.*: 333–5)

The critics of the Law of Nations

Rawls' first attempt was so badly received that he felt compelled to rework his first treatment of the question. The first and most important group of criticisms came from writers close to or influenced by Rawls, who refuse the limitations of the "closed society" approach, which makes it very difficult to envisage justice at a global level (O'Neill, 2000: 133). Instead they adopt a cosmopolitan perspective: justice should be impartial beyond one's own society and treat everyone worldwide in the same way. Rawls does not sufficiently acknowledge the fact of so-called "globalization", the development of global economic and cultural exchanges across the globe and the subsequent transformations of social and political systems as well as of their relations. Ignoring this historical fact is a serious flaw and creates limitations. Societies are no longer closed systems and principles of domestic justice have to be developed in a global perspective, especially economic justice. Immigration, world trade, de-localization as well as the emergence of a "world culture" cannot be ignored when thinking about justice, as one of Rawls' critics, Allen Buchanan, remarked: "There is a global basic structure which, like the domestic basic structure, is an important subject of justice because it has profound and enduring effects on the prospects of individuals and groups".[12]

As a consequence, members of the international community, individuals as well as peoples, cannot realistically enter into reciprocally beneficial arrangements. Both abilities and resources are so far apart that levels of contribution cannot be compared. This shows even more vividly how limited Rawls' conception of *justice as reciprocity* is. Brian Barry, one of Rawls' major critics, shows how impossible it is to implement in view of the extreme inequalities that exist between nations. Justice demands that the basic needs of all should be met before the non-basic needs of anyone in the world can be considered. Thus justice as reciprocity is not the right model for international justice and should be replaced by a conception of *justice as impartiality*. A system of "progressive" global taxation to transfer resources to the poorer nations should be envisaged.[13] If one adds to this argument the contemporary fact of globalization where poor states are made more unequal by global economic exchanges and institutions, then it is obvious that justice requires more than reciprocity, even if we do not confuse it with mere humanitarian assistance. One crucial fact missed by Rawls is that economic inequalities *within* poor states, for instance ex-colonies, are made worse by the global exchange system and that inequalities *between* rich and poor states make their poorest members even poorer. They have consequences for their individual members' levels of opportunities. The new conceptual framework for thinking in global terms is strikingly absent in Rawls. Among Rawls' followers, there have been convincing attempts – which we shall examine later – at applying the difference principle to global distributive justice, and cosmopolitan liberalism has developed from this Rawlsian starting point, contrary to Rawls' own view, and has become the most prominent alternative view on international justice.[14]

A second group of critics at the other end of the spectrum, the "realists", claim that Rawls' "realist utopia" is in fact an idealized theory divorced from real politics. It is based on an idealistic portrait of liberal societies with not much historical authenticity.

A last group of critics that moved Rawls to change his views is the communitarians who, in the name of cultural diversity, oppose universalism and the search for universally abstract principles of justice. In spite of not mentioning them, Rawls is still aware of their criticisms and of the danger of cultural imperialism, which he addresses in *Political Liberalism* and which leads him to abandon any comprehensive liberalism as Western and ethnocentric in favour of "political liberalism". The communitarian approach will also inspire him to treat hierarchical, communitarian societies in *The Law of Peoples* with more sympathy so much so that some critics have mentioned a communitarian shift in his thinking (Tan, 2004: 75).

We shall examine Rawls' answers to his opponents at length, but let us first summarize the main reasons why his views were so badly received and generally understood as a retreat from, even a rejection of, *A Theory of Justice*. For moral cosmopolitans, Rawls' theory is morally mistaken, as it does not fully protect vulnerable individuals and their basic human rights wherever they are. Why should the contingencies of the place of birth not be as important as domestic circumstances for justice's purposes? For realists and cosmopolitans alike, because it still respects the Westphalian context of sovereign states and ignores globalization and the new complex political entities that have appeared in international relations, it ignores contemporary history. It provides too thin a doctrine of global economic justice, as it ignores the new global "basic structure" and the specific inequalities between nations that it generates. Thus it is inconsistent with Rawls' own conception of domestic distributive justice. Finally, the method employed, which consists in repeating the OP at the international level, is too simplistic. It amounts to no more than the provision of a "laundry list".[15]

2. From nations to "peoples": *The Law of Peoples* (1999)

In his 1999 *The Law of Peoples,* Rawls acknowledges all these major criticisms. If he admits that the realists' criticisms were well founded and that he should have specified who the legitimate subjects of the new law of nations are, if he is aware also of the communitarian's criticism that the law of peoples should not be Western and liberal and should include non-liberal peoples, he still resists the cosmopolitans' view that anyone anywhere in the world should benefit from the protection of liberal constitutional rights in the name of the autonomy and self-respect of actual "peoples".

The new book is on a larger scale than are both §58 in *A Theory of Justice* and the 1993 Amnesty Lecture. It deals with most issues of international relations, such as cooperation, assistance and aid, the notions of a just war and of democratic peace, the protection of human rights and the justification of an international tribunal for human rights and for criminal justice, etc. More specifically, it seeks to give a systematic basis to Rawls' arguments against cosmopolitanism. In Part I (§1–6), called "the first part of ideal theory", it explains why peoples, not states or nations or individuals, should be the members of the society of peoples (§2). Rawls examines the international relations of liberal peoples associated in a "society of liberal peoples" (§6) that should lead to democratic peace (§5), their principles (§4), the use of the OP to justify them (§3), and of public reason to guarantee their stability (§6), following the arguments for the theory of domestic justice. In Part II, which covers "the second part of ideal theory" (§7–12), Rawls presents guidelines for a liberal foreign policy, for the dealings of liberal peoples with decent, but non-liberal, peoples. He explains the arguments in favour of toleration (§7) and establishes a threshold for admission to the society of peoples (§8–9). It is in that section that Rawls argues for his minimalist conception of human rights (§10), which remains extremely controversial: probably too high a price to pay for the cooperation of non-liberal peoples! He repeats his opposition to a cosmopolitan view of international justice (§12), which would be too similar to a form of "liberal imperialism". In Part III, Rawls develops what he calls "the non-ideal theory", that is, the principles and guidelines that are necessary for the dealings of decent peoples, liberal or not, with aggressive societies and for waging just wars (§13–14), and with "burdened societies" that need assistance (§15). He concludes by arguing for a rejection of distributive justice among peoples (§16), another extremely controversial and unpopular view! On nationalism, human rights and international distributive justice, we see that Rawls adopts views that are not part of the usual liberal package. Why?

Why "peoples" and not states?

The first major change in the new version of *The Law of Peoples* is that *peoples*, not states, are the primary and legitimate members of the Society of Peoples. "I first chose the name 'peoples' rather than 'nations' or 'states' because I wanted to conceive of peoples as having different features from those of states, since the idea of states, as traditionally conceived with their two powers of sovereignty was unsuitable" (*LOP*: v). This answers the first criticism and provides a reply to both communitarians and realists while allowing a better criticism of cosmopolitanism. Defining peoples in contrast to states should help build his case against individualism and moral cosmopolitanism. Another useful aspect of the term is that Rawls can exploit the ambiguities of the two meanings of "peoples": (1) as *political* societies and (2) as *historical* entities.

First, as political societies, peoples are not only self-interested, they also have a higher-order concern for their own institutions and respect the fact that other peoples too cherish their institutions. "The interests which move peoples are reasonable interests congruent with fair equality and a due respect for all peoples ... What distinguishes peoples from states is that just peoples are fully prepared to grant the very same proper respect and recognition to other peoples as equals" (*LOP*: 35). In that sense, they are *reasonable*, using a distinction by now familiar to any reader of Rawls; they possess a sense of justice, and "offer fair terms of cooperation to other peoples" (*ibid.*: 25). In contrast, states are only rational, moved exclusively by their basic interests. "States are rational, anxiously concerned with their power and always guided by their basic interests ... if *rationality* excludes the *reasonable* ... then the difference between states and peoples is enormous" (*ibid.*: 28).

Peoples, then, as historical entities, have a collective identity, which is ignored by cosmopolitans who, like utilitarians, are individualistic in the "wrong way" and address the well-being of individual persons, rather than the justice of societies. "The contrast between the Law of Peoples and a cosmopolitan view is that the ultimate end of a cosmopolitan view is the well-being of individuals, not the justice of societies" (*ibid.*: 119–20). Exactly as utilitarians do not respect the "separateness of persons", cosmopolitans do not respect the separateness and distinct identities of peoples. What is important to understand here, even if this is not always emphasized, is that for Rawls, the moral status or character of a people is primarily based on its collective identity as a people, not solely on its democratic or decent political institutions. This is where he mainly differs from moral cosmopolitanism. What defines a people is a degree of self-determination and autonomy gained through history. A people is a people when it possesses a sense of being the author of its own history and of its government's powers. Rawls' argument draws on a distinction between *self-determination* and *sovereignty*. Peoples are characterized by self-determination as exemplified through historical struggles, which is completely different from the sovereignty of states that can "legally" treat their members as they wish without being threatened by any external control or punishments. As sovereign members of the system of international relations, no external or superior power, no world government can legitimately and effectively threaten them.[16] Peoples are more than collections of individuals. In common with individuals, peoples are autonomous, but in contrast to them, they have structural features that allow them to be fairly self-standing over time, even if they are not sovereign, as in the case of national identities surviving the absence of a state. As David Reidy (2004: 298) notes, "Unlike individual human persons, peoples are self-sufficient or independent, or at least always potentially so, in a way that individual human persons can never be. Grasping this difference is crucial to seeing the force of Rawls' position on international justice". The notion of a "people", then, is useful because it combines the *moral* features of the individual citizens who constitute it and the *social* features of a group that is more than the sum of its parties, as is the case for states. Thus "peoples" are said to have both the moral status that is lacking in the case of states and the collective dimension and autonomy that is lacking in the case of individuals.

Still, the notion of a "people" is so ill defined and problematic that we have no clarification concerning the relation between states and peoples, in particular the distribution of power between minority peoples and majority governments in non-liberal but decent societies. This is a major flaw, which is responsible for Rawls' failure to secure enough protection for vulnerable individuals and minority peoples. At the same time, being the "master argument", it plays such a central role and has to contribute so much in Rawls' theory that we might begin worrying about the soundness of the whole project. This is the first major problem that we encounter at this stage.

What peoples?

Now, who are the "peoples" that may be admitted to the Society of Peoples or excluded if they threaten it? While extending the use of the term "peoples", Rawls makes the following distinctions between five different categories.

First, "reasonable liberal peoples" as members of the Society of Peoples are similar to citizens in domestic liberal societies and have three basic features: institutional, cultural and psychological. They possess "a reasonably just constitutional democratic government", together with the relevant institutions that guarantee fair equality of opportunity, a decent distribution of income, long-term social security, basic health care for all and the social conditions of political participation (*LOP*: 50). Their citizens are united by a common political culture, what Mill called "common sympathies", and they have a sense of their corporate identity based not on one single comprehensive doctrine, but on political values. Finally, "they have a moral nature" (*ibid.*: 23) because of their firm attachment to a moral conception of right and justice (*ibid.*: 24), or to a common good conception of justice.

Next, Rawls mentions "non-liberal but decent hierarchical peoples" who do not treat their members as free and equal and do not respect the full list of institutional features of liberal societies, but still possess their cultural and psychological characteristics and satisfy essential conditions such as respect for basic human rights, a decent consultation hierarchy, recognition of a right to dissent, etc. "I use the term 'decent' to describe non-liberal societies whose basic institutions meet certain specified conditions of political right and justice (including the right of citizens to play a substantial role, say through associations and groups, in making political decisions) and lead their citizens to honour a reasonably just law for the Society of Peoples" (*ibid.*: 3, n. 2).

Finally, in contrast, "outlaw states" are banned from the Society of Peoples because of their obvious territorial appetites and non-respect for international law. Interestingly, Rawls moves back to "states" to contrast them with well-ordered peoples, liberal or not. This shifts the balance from a descriptive point of view towards a normative conception of "peoples" and may create some confusion. Unfortunately, Rawls does not mention the fate of their repressed members, an omission that obviously creates difficulties for his overall argument.

For very different reasons, "societies burdened by unfavourable conditions" cannot be part of the Society of Peoples and access the status of "peoples", because they are unable to meet certain conditions of economic development necessary for the political institutions and culture needed for "decency". In their case, well-ordered peoples have a duty to assist them and to help them build the just institutions needed for peaceful participation. Again, one should note a shift in the vocabulary between "peoples" and "societies" which does not help the overall discussion.

Finally, when "benevolent absolutism" reigns, governments can honour human rights, but because there is no political participation, we cannot talk of peoples as corporate moral agents with a decent level of self-determination and consultation.

Is the change introduced by Rawls an answer to his problems in *A Theory of Justice*? I shall examine the various criticisms later. But it seems obvious that the notion of a "people" is extremely ill defined and controversial. In particular, it leaves the fate of vulnerable individuals completely unresolved if the autonomy and self-respect of a people is more important than the well-being of its members! Stanley Hoffmann, in a critical essay, mentions three major difficulties.[17] Rawls does not provide a satisfactory description of who the legitimate political units concerned by the law of peoples are: states, peoples, nations or individual persons. The theory of justice is silent on numerous issues, which are the results of complex new realities such as immigration, right to secession, rights of minorities, etc. The modern states are much more porous and ill defined, at least in developing countries, than Rawls assumes them to be. Nor is Rawls able to clarify the institutions, methods and instruments that would be used by states to promote their interests in accordance with the law of peoples. Finally, the principles that result from the choice situation in the OP are too meagre and old-fashioned to address the new international realities of the post-Soviet era and of the end of nuclear deterrence.

The principles of the law of peoples and their justification

Having specified the subject-matter of justice and the agents concerned, Rawls can now present the way in which the principles of international law and justice could be justified to all well-ordered and peaceful peoples. The familiar "Original Position" procedure used for domestic justice is used again as a device of representation for the kind of thinking that will lead to adopting the principles as fair. "OP with a veil of ignorance is a model of representation for liberal societies" (*LOP*: 30). The argument is modelled in exactly the same way as it is in the case of the first (domestic) level and is based on the same features. But, because the international context is fundamentally different, the procedure has to be adapted and we now have a two-fold argument.

In the case of liberal societies, the process of legitimization is represented by a double OP procedure at the domestic and international levels. At the domestic level, we can identify five features of the domestic OP. The parties represent citizens *fairly*: symmetry and equality are required. They are modelled as *rational*, that is, concerned with citizens' basic interests in terms of primary goods. They choose principles for the basic structure and not for individual situations or preferences. The selection is based on appropriate reasons and, thanks to the "veil of ignorance", it bypasses people's comprehensive doctrines. Finally, the representatives care for the fundamental interests of citizens as reasonable. At the international level, there are three differences. A first difference is that liberal peoples do not have a comprehensive doctrine that supports their political conception of justice, whereas individuals in a liberal society may rely on comprehensive doctrines. Thus we are faced here with different problems of consensus and agreement on international principles of justice. The role of public reason is crucial to convince liberal peoples of the value of the principles and of their role in bringing about peace. The second difference is that a people's interests are specified politically whereas citizens' interests are defined by their comprehensive doctrines. As we have seen, peoples possess features *qua* peoples. This is the argument of "explanatory nationalism" (Pogge, 2002: 139–44; Tan, 2004: 70–72). In particular, *amour propre* is a fundamental interest of peoples *qua* peoples. The OP argument recognizes these interests and treats liberal peoples as rational in that sense. It will protect "the fundamental interests of democratic societies" in surviving a dangerous and threatening global context and chooses adequate principles. But it does so while remaining fair to the diversity of peoples involved. Fairness is guaranteed by the veil of ignorance. The representatives of the peoples concerned do not know the size of their territory or of the population or the extent of their natural resources, etc. The third difference is that they only consider choosing from a list of alternative interpretations of the eight principles of the law of peoples (§4.1), not from a list of alternative principles of domestic justice (§4.4). There is no room here for the principle of utility as it is excluded by the insistence on *equality among peoples* and the principle of reciprocity, which utilitarians do not recognize. Thus "the benefits for another people cannot outweigh the hardships imposed on itself" (*LOP*: 40).

The second, and more confused, part of the argument shows how non-liberal but decent peoples can come to see an OP procedure and the principles of justice as justified, even if there is no OP argument, of course, at the domestic level. This is an amazing claim, as these peoples do not treat their own members as free and equal persons, which is the criterion in the OP. "Although full equality may be lacking within a society, equality may be reasonably put forward in making claims against other societies" (*LOP*: 70). The main reason why, says Rawls, is that the OP treats them as equals and respects them as peoples even if they are not fully democratic. This makes the OP acceptable and even attractive to them. "The members of decent hierarchical societies would accept OP as fair among peoples" (*ibid.*: 69). Here again the "explanatory nationalism" argument is at work. Peoples want to be treated and respected as equal within the framework of a Society of Peoples and the OP gives substance to this claim. Secondly, the OP procedure, which they can then recognize as fair, acknowledges their interest for peace and security. This argument insists on the rationality of decent peoples and on peace being in their interest, even if it differs from the liberal argument, for it is based on notions of the common good and on comprehensive religious doctrines. The defence of the human rights and of the good of the people in question is rational, as it is in agreement with its own search for peace. The people will thus develop attachments and allegiances to the law of peoples, as human rights can be seen as compatible with its self-respect, not as foreign ethical demands. But we can already note that this argument in favour of "democratic peace" is not very satisfactory and will need careful examination.

All peaceful well-ordered liberal and decent peoples will agree upon the following first principles, which form a basis on which they can cooperate in spite of their opposing values and belief systems, given the fact of "reasonable pluralism". They represent the basic charter of the Society of "well-ordered" Peoples as a "pacific federation of republican states". The law of peoples consists of the following eight principles.

(1) Peoples are free and independent within limits, and should be treated as such. Sovereignty is replaced by self-determination and is restricted by precise conditions. The law of peoples limits permissible domestic and international policies, that is, the right to war and the right to non-interference with the treatment of its own people (§2.2). This article departs from the previous list in *A Theory of Justice*.

(2) Treaties are to be observed.

(3) Peoples are equal and are parties to the agreements that bind them.

(4) Peoples respect a duty of non-intervention in other peoples' domestic affairs, but this duty is qualified in certain circum-

stances. No toleration for outlaw states is possible as a consequence of both liberalism and decency.

(5) The right to self-defence is the only legitimate basis for the right to war. But, in extreme cases, defence of human rights might be a justifiable reason for war. "Liberal peoples have a right to war in self-defence, but not, as in the traditional account of sovereignty, a right to war in the rational pursuit of a state's rational interests; these alone are not a sufficient reason" (*LOP*: 90). The aim of war, in that case, should be "to protect and preserve the basic freedoms of its citizens and its constitutionally democratic political institutions ... To trespass on citizens' liberty may only be done for the sake of liberty itself" (*ibid.*: 91). "Decent peoples also have a right to war in self-defence ... Any society that is non-aggressive and that honours human rights has the right to self-defence" (*ibid.*: 92).

(6) Human rights (in the restricted sense that we have examined earlier) are to be honoured by all the members of the Society of Peoples, but the list of rights is different and more limited than in most internationally recognised human rights declarations. Again, this is the other main departure from *A Theory of Justice*.

(7) Specific restrictions in the conduct of war are to be respected. In particular, principles restricting the conduct of war (§14) should allow for a distinction between governments of outlaw states and their populations. (Rawls takes the examples of Japan and Nazi Germany, and criticizes the view expressed by Daniel Goldhagen that peoples and governments were equally criminal in the case of Nazi Germany: *LOP*: 95, n. 9 and 100, n. 22.) "Two nihilist doctrines of war should be repudiated absolutely: war is hell and anything goes, and we are all guilty" (*ibid.*: 8).

(8) Finally, there exists a duty of assistance to "burdened societies" that should help them build just institutions and become members in good standing of the Society of Peoples. As in *A Theory of Justice*, the difference principle cannot be a principle of the law of peoples.

After this presentation of Rawls' doctrine, I now turn to four main debates that help assess more clearly the weaknesses and strengths of Rawls' conception and its relationship to both realism and cosmopolitanism. *The Law of Peoples* presents itself as an alternative to both and claims to yield similarly good results but from more acceptable premises. This is expressed in the claim that the law of peoples is a

"realist utopia", more realistic than cosmopolitanism, and its affirmation that liberal human rights should be universally imposed, but
still more "utopian" than realistic in that justice, not only the actual
balance of power, should be the source of lasting peace and for solving
conflicts between nations. This latter claim is, in effect, less convincing
than expected and Rawls may be seen as supporting the realists' view.
The four debates concern (1) the charge of cultural imperialism and
the role played by the fact of pluralism; (2) the holistic dimension of
Rawls' conception and his neglect of moral individualism in his defence
of human rights; (3) the way he tends to sacrifice justice in the name
of realism and peace in matters of foreign intervention and war; and
(4) his rejection of global distributive justice in the name of a limited
duty of assistance to "burdened societies".

3. Liberal foreign policy and the "fact of reasonable pluralism": cooperating with non-democratic, but "decent" peoples

The first problem that Rawls addresses in the second part of the
ideal theory (the theory of relations between liberal and decent
peoples) is the question of the toleration of decent peoples and of
the scope of a liberal foreign policy. Should liberal peoples deal with
non-liberal and decent peoples, how far and for what purposes?

Admission to the Society of Peoples

There are many answers to that question. It is clear for Rawls that the
law of peoples should not be limited to liberal peoples while not admit-
ting all nations, as it requires a minimal list of shared conceptions of
justice. Its aims are peace, stability and cooperation. It should thus
in the name of realism include non-liberal, but decent, peoples (this
constitutes the ideal case where the ideal theory applies), while not
applicable to either "burdened societies" or "outlaw states" (where the
non-ideal theory applies). In that, it differs from the classical *jus gentium*, which applies to *all* nations, well ordered or not. Consequently
for Rawls, there exists no global forum for all nations to negotiate
their conflicts, no Society of Nations or United Nations. In that sense,
Rawls is clearly not a "realist" and one could say that the real chances
of preventing wars seem to be slim. The reason is that he sees the

Society of Peoples as united by a minimal conception of the right and justice, by what he terms *"decency"*, that will progressively create the conditions for peace and stability. Therefore it cannot be all-inclusive and can only wish for a general agreement on its principles of decency. But conversely, it includes peoples who should *not* be included in a liberal Society of Peoples because they do not treat their members as free and equal. Including them is a controversial point of view, especially for moral cosmopolitans and universal human rights advocates, as it means too large a constituency and risks compromising on moral values such as freedom and equal dignity for all. It is obviously a second major difficulty in the theory – perhaps even an insurmountable flaw next to the problematic conception of what a people is – that the threshold for decency be so loosely defined. We shall now examine the many arguments presented by Rawls to support his position.

Respect for peoples' self-determination

The first argument for pluralism and cooperation with decent, but non-liberal, peoples is linked to the very nature of what a people is and to Rawls' own holistic social ontology. It is important to recognize a people's relative autonomy and self-sufficiency as a major factor for international justice, even if we do not go as far as the full-blown notion of state sovereignty. Because of its specific corporate identity, self-respect and equality of status are very important for a people and should not be limited to democratic states. In effect, whether and how "democratic" a people is requires a *dynamic* criterion, not a final judgement: it is the trajectory, the historical processes and struggles, that make a people what it is and that are important for its identity, not abstract definitions. Respect is certainly good in itself, but it is also crucial for this trajectory, for the development of reciprocal relationships on which to base peace and democratization. Thus respect for autonomous decisions cannot be denied to non-liberal but "decent" peoples without serious consequences. "Self-determination, duly constrained, is an important good for a people" (*LOP*: 84) in the same way that "it is a good for individuals and associations to be attached to their particular culture" (*ibid.*: 61; compare with Chapter 4, above). Self-determination should thus be preserved as much as possible, which is Rawls' main argument against cosmopolitanism and the downplaying of national ties. As a consequence, patriotism should not be rejected. "Peoples (as opposed to states) have a definite moral nature. This nature includes a certain proper pride and sense of honour; peoples may take pride in their histories and achievements as what I call a 'proper patriotism' allows" (*ibid.*: 62). This self-respect does not rely exclusively on the moral beliefs of individual members or on democratic traditions. Thus a capacity for showing equal respect and consideration to other peoples' institutions and traditions, within the framework of the law of peoples, is present in decent peoples, even if they are not fully liberal and democratic and do not recognize all their members as free and equal persons. This is not contradictory to admission to the Society of Peoples and might even prove central to it. Moreover, treating peoples as equals within the Society of Peoples might initiate domestic changes in the long run and help internal transformations towards more democracy and freedom. Rawls' original contribution to the problem of a tolerant foreign policy should be connected to his holistic conception of justice.[18] The Society of Peoples respects boundaries and excludes any idea of a world state. Here Rawls finds himself in agreement with Michael Walzer and his critique of cosmopolitanism, of "a world of deracinated men and women" (*ibid.*: 39, n. 48).

The fact of reasonable pluralism among peoples

The second argument is derived from the "fact of reasonable pluralism", which was central for the move to political liberalism. The plurality of regimes is comparable to the plurality of comprehensive doctrines that conflict within contemporary domestic societies. Not including non-liberal but decent peoples would be as arrogant and ill advised as hoping for a consensus based on a shared idea of the good within domestic societies. Non-liberal, but decent, peoples are not unreasonable and we have to accept their views and beliefs as long as they respect certain fundamental or "core" values and rights. If we punish societies because they are not as democratic as we are, then we will be guilty of arrogance. "The danger of error, miscalculation and also arrogance on the part of those who propose sanctions must, of course, be taken into account … decent societies … deserve respect, even if their institutions as a whole are not sufficiently reasonable" (*LOP*: 84). It would be illiberal to treat decent non-liberal peoples as unequal and an expression of ethnocentrism to believe that non-democratic people should be penalized. This could lead to imperialism. "Decent non-liberal peoples will be denied a due measure of respect by liberal peoples" (*ibid.*: 61).

A major objection is that we have no clue as to what decent peoples expect in terms of respect for autonomy and consideration for their self-determination. How far should they extend? What should the threshold be?

A *"target and cut-off point" conception of decency*

This leads Rawls to a third argument, the "target and cut-off point" conception of decency, which is the most interesting of the three, and which we will find again in other aspects of Rawlsian international justice. It claims that in order to strike the right balance between respect for autonomy and protection of the basic human rights of the populations concerned, only "target and cut-off point" discriminating answers can overcome the mistakes of both realists and cosmopolitans. The specificity of international relations means that it is possible to treat peoples as equals within some precise limits even if internally they do not fully treat their own members as equals. "The Law of Peoples applies to how peoples treat each other as *peoples*. How peoples treat each other and how they treat their own members are, it is important to recognize, two different things. A decent society honours a reasonable and just Law of Peoples even though it does not treat its own members reasonably or justly as free and equal citizens, since it lacks the liberal idea of citizenship" (*LOP*: 83). But not recognizing full citizenship does not necessarily mean not respecting basic human rights. The main question is how to define this threshold of "decency" as rigorously as possible.

There are two criteria for "decent hierarchical societies" which specify a threshold of reasonableness necessary for admission to the Society of Peoples. The first is that these societies be reasonable in the sense of peaceful and non-aggressive. The second is that there should exist some equivalent to the rule of law, that is, "that a decent hierarchical people's system of law secures for all members what have come to be called *human rights*" (*LOP*: 65). The list is limited to core human rights, "a special class of urgent rights" (*ibid.*: 79), which differs from the full list of internationally recognized rights.[19] They include the right to life (to the means of subsistence and security), "security of ethnic groups from mass murder and genocide", the right to liberty (to freedom from slavery, serfdom and forced occupation, and to a sufficient measure of liberty of conscience to ensure freedom of religion and thought), (see *LOP*: 65, n. 2 and §9.2, §10, p. 79), to property (personal property) and to formal equality (that is, that like cases be treated alike). In particular, minority religions should not be persecuted even if religious freedom is limited. "This is the difference between fully unreasonable doctrines and doctrines which are not fully unreasonable, but not fully reasonable" (*ibid.*: 74). Representation of women should follow respect for basic human rights, even if these are not fully democratic and liberal rights (*ibid.*: 75, n. 16). Then, there should exist "a decent scheme of political and social cooperation" (*ibid.*: 66) and "a decent consultation hierarchy" (*ibid.*: 71) based on a "common good conception of justice". There should exist either a common aim in a hierarchical society or special priorities. "The pursuit of the common aim should be encouraged, but not maximised in and of itself, it should be consistent with the restrictions specified by the consultation procedure ... according to the common good idea of justice" (*ibid.*). Even if the nature of these societies is "associationist in form" (*ibid.*: 64) and not individualistic, the representation of groups, not individuals, by bodies in the consultation hierarchy does not exclude individual members, as each person belongs to a group and different voices can be heard. The right to some form of dissent is thus recognized.

These are very sketchy remarks that will need careful examination, in particular Rawls' worryingly "thin" doctrine of human rights. Still, within these limits, cooperation is possible and should generate enough trust to create the basis for peace and stability, for the general acceptance of the minimal principles of the law of peoples.

4. A limited defence of human rights

We must turn now to Rawls' controversial view of human rights and of their defence, of the moral right of intervention and of the limits of the Westphalian context of sovereign states.

Rawls' "holistic" view of peoples

One striking feature of Rawls' conception, as we have seen, is his emphasis on peoples as the main players in international relations and the fact that he objects to using the term "global justice". He does not believe in the decline of the nation-state, of peoples at any rate, and in the power of justice to address individual situations across the globe. The first feature of his theory is that he does not consider individual persons as the subject of justice, only members of a people or citizens of a state that can give them the protection of rights and liberties. Why is that? We saw that a crucial transformation of his conception of justice has been the move from traditional methodological individualism, in *A Theory of Justice*, where the agents considered are individual persons, towards a political conception of the person as citizen in *Political Liberalism*. The consequence of this evolution is that he now rejects as mistaken any form of what he calls "individualism in the wrong way", such as utilitarianism or cosmopolitanism, which ignores national, cultural and political memberships. One could label this his "communitarian" shift. Still, this social ontology is strong enough to cut his ties with a traditional liberal way of thinking. In that sense, he is deeply opposed to the cosmopolitan view of international justice that has become the alternative normative theory in that area. The reason is Rawls' *holistic* conception of justice, which is consistent with his domestic theory, something that commentators have sometimes failed to appreciate.[20] This conception takes him a long way from the traditional liberal and cosmopolitan view of international justice.

The second feature of his view is, of course, the particular attention that he pays to the collective dimensions of what makes a people a people and that echoes his emphasis on the institutional nature of domestic justice. This is why it is misguided to interpret his views as still Westphalian and attached to the traditional prerogatives of sovereign states (Buchanan, 2000). The reason goes much deeper and may bring Rawls to abandon liberal moral individualism altogether. One question is whether Rawls' critique of cosmopolitanism is not counterproductive as it threatens his own advocacy of moral individualism, of the inviolability of the human person, which seems to be played down at the international level. The difficulty is that Rawls is trying to open up a third way between the cosmopolitan view that the actors who count in international relations are individual moral persons, and the realist view that the states pursuing power games are the "real" actors. As we have seen earlier, he hopes that by introducing the notion of "peoples" as a halfway solution, he will answer the difficulty. Like individual persons, peoples share a moral status. But unlike individuals, peoples possess a collective identity that is more than the sum of its parts, as well as a specific form of autonomy and a capacity for self-determination. Taking this holistic view may, nevertheless, be more dangerous and controversial than it seems.

Opposing cosmopolitanism

But first, what is the cosmopolitanism that Rawls opposes so strongly? Its origins date back to Kant and his affirmation that "the distress produced by the constant wars in which the states try to subjugate or engulf each other must finally lead them to enter a *cosmopolitan* constitution".[21] To that Kant adds a word of caution: if such a cosmopolitan constitution leads to world government and the despotism inherent in it, then the best way to peace might be a "lawful federation under a commonly accepted *international* right".[22] However, cosmopolitanism is a doctrine that can also be derived from Rawls' own theory of justice as fairness. This is the paradox! For cosmopolitans, "all persons are to have the equal liberal rights of citizens in a constitutional democracy". Like Rawls' own justice as fairness, cosmopolitanism is a *moral individualism* which states that individual persons, not states, are to be recognized as the primary objects for concern in international relations. Only individual persons have a moral status that is the basis for any normative theory. It is because realists have ignored this moral status that they have been unable to account for the current changes in international relations, especially for the new role played by the implementation of human rights, good governance and the rise of liberal democratic values against unwilling states still attached to their prerogatives. Cosmopolitanism is *universalistic* in the Kantian sense: human rights should apply to anyone anywhere in the world and neither historical contingencies nor natural circumstances should play any role in their application. As Rawls himself wrote in *A Theory of Justice*: "Each person possesses an inviolability founded on justice that even the welfare of society as a whole cannot override" (*TJ*: 3). Cosmopolitanism takes seriously this inviolability and the priority of justice over state powers and prerogatives, economic welfare or religious traditions. It wants the full list of human rights, civil, political, social and economic, to be implemented. Universal human rights represent the moral basis for international law and foreign intervention. They override the autonomy of states, the rules of trade and commerce as well as domestic policies, which they should have the power to reshape as in the case of the European Union and the Human Rights Act.

It is this ambition to which Rawls objects in the name of respect for the autonomy of peoples as distinct from their individual members, and as capable of choosing their own path to just institutions, economic development and prosperity.

> It amounts to saying that all persons are to have the equal liberal
> rights of citizens in a constitutional democracy. On this account,
> the foreign policy of a liberal people will be to act gradually to
> shape all not yet liberal societies in a liberal direction until even-
> tually (in the ideal case) all societies are liberal. But this foreign
> policy simply assumes that only a liberal democratic society can
> be acceptable. (*LOP*: 82–3)

To that Rawls opposes six main objections, which I briefly detail.

Cosmopolitanism is *unrealistic*. The system of peoples and collective identities is here to stay even if global networks, sympathies and
institutions tend to control, even, sometimes, to override it. Short of
leaving nations completely out of the equation, one answer we saw that
Rawls proposes is to replace nations by "peoples". This gives a measure of "reasonable realism" to his view (*ibid.*: 83) without diminishing
its normative force.

Cosmopolitanism is *universalistic* in the wrong way. The pluralism
of peoples and cultures makes it impossible to envisage that they could
all eventually become democratic and liberal and implement the same
list of human rights. Globalization underestimates the sense of the
plurality and uniqueness of social and historical entities or "peoples" in
some form of abstract universalism. A "holistic" conception of justice
opposes it and should be "universalistic in reach", paying attention
instead to historical specificities (*ibid.*: 85–6 and 121).

But even more importantly, cosmopolitanism is *arrogant* as it ima-
gines that the liberal regime of human rights can be applied anywhere
to anyone. It ignores the self-determination and autonomy of peoples.
It may even become *imperialist*, and Rawls is aware of the danger. In
contrast, Rawls emphasizes that states or peoples ask for justice and
respect, not simply as collections of moral persons, but as having a
corporate moral status.

Cosmopolitanism, in contrast, is *individualistic* in the wrong way, for
Rawls, like utilitarianism (*ibid.*: 119–20). It does not give enough attention to the structural and historical conditions under which individual
persons actually live and which generate unjust inequalities. Among
these conditions is their membership of states, nations or "peoples".
Rawls now seemingly adopts a "communitarian" view, a fact that has
been noticed by a number of critics.[23]

It is not interested in social justice, but in the *welfare* of individuals, as it ignores the importance of the basic social structure of international relations, of a Society of Peoples. Interestingly, the expression "social liberalism" has been suggested to contrast Rawls' theory with cosmopolitan liberalism (Beitz, 2000: 677).

What makes Rawls abandon his philosophical ideals at the international level is now fairly clear. Still, the consequences for a proper protection of human rights might be very damaging.

Rawls' thin conception of human rights

Rawls' objective in *The Law of Peoples* is to disconnect the defence of human rights from liberalism as well as from any comprehensive doctrine in order to strengthen their case at the international level. How does he proceed?

First, human rights for Rawls are not simply vague and abstract ethical demands. They are the necessary, but not sufficient, conditions for international *cooperation* among peoples. "What have come to be called human rights are recognized as necessary conditions of any system of social cooperation ... These rights do not depend on any particular comprehensive religious or philosophical doctrine of human nature" (*LOP*: 68). "They set a necessary, though not sufficient standard for the decency of domestic political and social institutions" (*ibid.*: 80). These conditions, according to Rawls, are necessary for securing peace and stability between nations. "Human rights in a reasonable Law of Peoples restrict the justifying reasons for war and its conduct and they specify limits to a regime's internal autonomy" (*ibid.*: 79). "They reflect the two basic historical changes since World War II: war is no longer admissible as a means of government and a government's internal autonomy is now limited" (*ibid.*). "They set a limit to the pluralism among peoples" and "they are binding on all peoples and societies, including outlaw states" (*ibid.*: 80).

Rawls advances a controversial, restricted "target and cut-off point" view of human rights and suggests that contrary to mainstream views, they are not necessarily liberal and democratic, but set universal conditions of *cooperation*. They play a special role as a basis for restricting the reasons presented in the Society of Peoples for justified war and intervention. We must, still, specify that universal here means "universal in reach", not *de facto*, of course. It is a regulative idea for peaceful cooperation. Because the aim is cooperation between liberal and decent, but non-liberal, peoples, human rights must lose their connection with liberal democratic regimes. "They are distinct from constitutional rights or from the rights of liberal democratic citizenship" (*LOP*: 79). For instance, if "human rights proper" (*ibid.*: 80, n. 23) are covered by the 1948 Declaration, in particular, art. 3, 5–18 and the conventions on genocide (1948) and on apartheid (1973), other articles are more liberal, such as art. 1, or socialist, as the right to social security, art. 22, or the right to equal pay, art. 23, and do not have a place in the law of peoples. Such are the arguments for Rawls' limited or thin view of human rights in international relations. They mean that a threshold, not a full list, serves as a basis for discussion of cases of justified war and intervention. Once the target has been attained and the thin list has been restored, there is no longer a justification for intervention, even if the full list of human rights is far from implemented.

Rawls' efforts to disconnect human rights from liberalism (*LOP*: 79) and to show how decent, but non-liberal, peoples can enforce and support them in part are certainly laudable, but may have gone too far. He exhibits a mixture of realism and moral concerns that can be upsetting and does not sit easily with his main thesis of the priority of justice and the inviolability of persons. On the occasion of his discussion of human rights, one might question the role played by his appeals to realism.

Rawls' failure to defend human rights

For many critics, the main flaw in Rawls' argument is the appeal to peoples' autonomy against individual claims. Thomas Pogge has called such a claim "the myth of explanatory nationalism", a myth that should be debunked (Pogge, 1998: 497–502; Tan, 2004: 70–72). Has Rawls gone too far in his rejection of moral individualism at the global level, a rejection that contradicts his liberal view of justice? Letting peoples have a moral status and adding nationalism to the equation create a situation where one set of moral values is pitched against another, where individuals have hardly any claim against their governments in the name of national solidarity. Is that the best way to deal with moral issues such as the defence of vulnerable individuals, ethnic or religious minorities and dissidents in non-liberal countries, or with poverty and powerlessness in developing countries? The primacy of peoples leads Rawls to show less concern for individual persons than we can accept. This raises the question of the status of individuals in the wider international context. What if non-liberal societies "fail to treat persons who possess all the powers of reason, intellect and moral feeling as truly free and equal" (*LOP*: 60)? What about individuals who do not possess these powers, as Nussbaum (2006) rightly insists, and who are left unprotected in non-liberal societies? How should liberal peoples react? How far should respect for a people's autonomy go?

At the level of principle, it is certainly not helpful not to have a firm principle that reminds us of the inviolability of persons, such as the first principle of justice and the priority of liberties in the domestic case. What is needed here is more emphasis on the first principle and on the core human rights that go with it. This is assumed by Rawls in the case of "decent" societies, but the distinction is too crude. Many societies or peoples stand or fluctuate between the two extremes and the threshold is extremely difficult to fix. Why not say that the first principle has universal validity? This is probably one major failure of the law of peoples: it tries too hard to be accepted as "realist" and it does not emphasize the normative force of the first principle of justice strongly enough.

Another flaw that I have already considered is Rawls' use of the term "people". It is true that political concepts are "essentially contestable" concepts (Freeden, 2005). However, in the case of "peoples" we need more in terms of the definition of their moral status. It should be firmly rooted in the guarantees they offer for basic human rights as individual rights. For instance, the analysis of "burdened societies" and of their right to assistance is confused as we never know exactly where the threshold is, when a poor burdened society can make its own decisions, and show a degree of political autonomy and responsibility, or cannot (*LOP*: 117–18). Sometimes it is clear that democratic institutions are the key and that, following Rousseau's famous analysis, we should talk of peoples only as "republics" or free self-governing entities.[24] Sometimes, as I explained earlier, self-development and autonomy are enough, short of full self-government. In the latter case the threshold of decency is lower. But there are numerous ambiguities here. Rawls certainly agrees that the nature of its government and of the distribution of power has a clear impact on how "decent" a people is. However, he notes that "a government as the political organization of its people is not, as it were, the author of all of its own powers" and that the population, not only the government, should have a say (*LOP*: 26). Unfortunately, this is only true in cases of democratic institutions. We cannot disconnect the protection of vulnerable people from democratic institutions!

Even more importantly, Rawls fails to provide the anthropological clarifications that would distinguish peoples from nations and societies, or even from tribes and ethnic groups. He does not allow, for instance, for a distinction between a people and the many sub-groups that constitute it, which may react aggressively against each other in certain circumstances such as scarcity of resources, loss of political power, etc. (Buchanan, 2000: 701). There is more than sheer confrontation between states and individuals in the dialectics of international relations, and the notion of a "people" does not cover this complexity. Not all internal violence is state sponsored, even if this is usually the case. As a consequence of this superficial view of the relevant actors, it is not clear why peoples should have a moral status when states do not. If it is because of the way in which they are governed, then giving state apparatuses or governments the first role as actors in international relations is becoming very dangerous and contradictory. Decent citizens of outlaw states are not allowed to play a significant role and may individually struggle for better institutions without success, and their "people" still be seen as lacking a moral status. The complexity of what is at stake in according a "moral status" to a given people is definitely overlooked by Rawls.

Finally, Rawls' argument seems to ignore or discount the reality of a "global basic structure" and of its political and economic constraints on peoples and then on individuals. Since he starts with a notion of society as "a closed system", as a consequence of his "holistic" vision, it makes it very difficult to envisage justice at an international level. For many commentators (O'Neill, 2003), one of the many weaknesses of Rawls' extension of justice as fairness to global justice is his concept of a closed or "bounded" society, which is the starting point of his analysis of justice in *A Theory of Justice*. He does not sufficiently acknowledge the facts of so-called "globalization".[25]

Does Rawls really ignore globalization? In reality, he is well aware of the historical economic and cultural conditions that make contemporary societies highly dependent on each other in a way they never were before. But, for methodological reasons, he relies on a model of society as a closed system or structure. Working on the "ideal" or "strict compliance theory" (*TJ*: 8), he constructs an "ideal type" in the Weberian sense, concentrating on the central features that are relevant for questions of justice. This "closed structure" is the minimal entity that cannot be reduced to interpersonal relations, but forms a system of which we cannot imagine not being a part.[26] We are always part of *a* society, whichever it might be, in this minimal structural sense. "Persons enter only by birth and exit only by death" (*LOP*: 26). In *The Law of Peoples*, the emphasis is on "peoples", not on societies or states, and as we have seen, the distinction between peoples and societies in Rawls' terminology needs to be clarified. Because Rawls has a holistic view of justice, he tends to concentrate on the systematic features that a society possesses, and that allow the functioning of its institutions as a whole. But, as I have said, it would be a misunderstanding to see this holistic conception as evidence of his being unaware of the post-Westphalian transformation of states-relations. Historically, even if peoples and nations are increasingly interconnected, the specificity of each people is still very much in place and raises new questions of justice. Conceptually, Rawls' holism protects him against the illusions of cosmopolitan writers who tend to see globalization as the end of states or national structures. Boundaries are there to stay and make specific principles of justice necessary to deal with the inequalities they create (*LOP*: 39).[27] Still, it also prevents him from properly addressing the question of the protection of vulnerable individuals in non-liberal, decent or not, societies.

Concerning the first debate on "holism" and social ontology, their consequences for moral individualism and the protection of individual human rights, it is obvious that we have here a version of liberalism that is less individualistic and more realistic than cosmopolitanism. However, it is only with difficulty that it can be normatively critical of the status quo and of the sovereignty of states and that it addresses the vulnerability of persons and of religious or ethnic minorities in post-colonial situations in the modern nation states (see Hindess, 2005).

5. Peace or justice?

The second controversy concerns Rawls' unresolved notion of peace and stability and the role played in peace by justice.[28] Rawls' theory addresses peace at three levels. First, we have the first part of the "ideal" theory, which deals with relations among democratic peoples within a Society of Peoples. There, peace and justice are tightly connected as one major feature of democratic societies. Secondly, we have the other two levels where liberal democratic peoples have to deal with non-democratic societies, either "decent" peoples, or "outlaw" states and "burdened" societies. There, the connection between peace and justice is unresolved. Peace can be either the result of generalized democratic institutions *within* peoples – a very idealistic view – or of compliance with international principles by peoples who remain undemocratic domestically – the *modus vivendi* realistic solution. How does Rawls navigate between these two answers?

Domestic peace

Peace and stability *within* peoples require, for Rawls, two series of conditions. On the one hand, we have *psychological* conditions such as the understanding and internalizing of core liberal democratic values such as good governance, the rule of law, human rights, etc., and thus the existence of a widespread "overlapping consensus" based on a shared conception of justice (see above, Chapter 4). On the other hand, *institutional* conditions are crucial: the existence to some degree of fair equality of opportunity, a decent distribution of income, long-term security at work, the provision of basic health care and the public financing of elections, etc.[29] In *A Theory of Justice,* the balance between the two is examined, but Rawls typically tends to emphasize psychological conditions. Psychological processes that lead to allegiance to democracy and what Rawls has described elsewhere as the superior and more complex "morality of principles" (*TJ:* 406–14) are to replace the more primitive "morality of authority", external coercion and fear of authority, as a basis for peace and stability. Again in *The Law of Peoples*, Rawls interestingly mentions "moral learning" (*LOP*: 44), which relies on personal attachments, belief-systems and identifications, and should replace coercion or group pressure as the basis for peace and stability.

Now, how does that analysis translate to peace *between* peoples, at least between liberal and non-liberal but decent peoples? In that case, we do not have a consensus or shared democratic values that can cement the union. The answer again stresses the importance of psychological processes and how some kind of democratic "mimesis" can occur. "Citizens develop a sense of justice as they grow up and take part in their just social world ... Similarly, peoples, including both liberal and decent societies, will accept willingly and act upon the legal norms embodied in a just Law of Peoples" (*LOP*: 44). This is the assumption that I would like now to criticize, as some form of cultural imperialism seems to be at work in Rawls' conception of "democratic peace".

Cultural imperialism in The Law of Peoples

First, we can sketch a series of *external* criticisms, based on the idea that peace among peoples requires more than the internalization of a common sense of justice that Rawls assumes. Not only is that not effective, but it conveys an ideology that is not acceptable for many different cultures.

For instance, the idea that non-democratic peoples could act "willingly", as individuals may do in liberal societies, is problematic. This does not make much sense if the relevant checks and balances are not in place for this process to develop. In effect, and as recent history has shown, it is more likely that political and economic pressures, the need for assistance and cultural domination, will lead non-democratic peoples to a not very "willing" adoption of democratic institutions. Non-liberal peoples will have to bow in some ways to the moral superiority of the West. Moreover, it is obvious that stability and peace between peoples can often be reached on different basis, without developing a democratic or liberal sense of justice, without agreement on first principles, but thanks simply to political compromises, negotiations, treatises, promise keeping, respect and trust, which are very different, psychologically, from free agreements.[30] Indeed, the value of compromise and negotiation, even of incentives (*LOP*: 84–5), is very high in many cultures where bargaining processes have the force of social recognition and communication. This is an essential point, which is missed in Rawls' fictional example of a people that would be acceptable for membership in a liberal Society of Peoples: *Kazanistan* (§9.3). This example concentrates on one single aspect of non-liberal Muslim societies, that these are traditional communitarian and hierarchical societies. It misunderstands the role played in them by the value of negotiation and bargaining for reaching agreements. When agreement on regulative principles is reached through political bargaining and compromises, without asking for personal allegiance, then it can possibly preserve the honour and self-respect of the parties involved, and avoid intimidation, domination and imperialism.

It is equally worrying that Rawls' rejection of the very idea of compromise or *modus vivendi* in favour of principled agreements "for good reasons" is never questioned at the domestic and at the international levels as it opens the way to possible accusations of intolerance. The stress on the value of principles misrepresents the nature of authority at work in non-liberal societies, a morality which, according to Rawls, is "the morality of authority" or "that of a child" (*TJ*: 405) and should be abandoned in favour of the more mature "morality of principles". Unfortunately for Rawls' conception, the morality of authority is not necessarily "primitive", but dominates cultures alien to the liberal outlook, which do not rely on the psychological mechanism of norms internalization, but on their expressivity. In effect, the morality of principles, which involves a certain psychological transformation, is even worse for certain cultures than open external domination, as it challenges traditional forms of authority that are an important part of a people's identity. This may explain the level of resentment and frustration in some contemporary Muslim societies. The problem is that the "stability for good reasons"[31] that is "brought about by citizens acting correctly according to the appropriate principles of their sense of justice" (*LOP*: 13, n. 2) is not sustainable unless there is some kind of domination, even imperialism, at work. If international stability requires the personal allegiances of non-liberal, but decent, peoples to the core values of liberal democracies whereas these values are alien to their culture and tradition, these peoples are placed in a situation of deep inequality and we are faced with cultural imperialism. What Rawls calls "stability for good reasons" may in some ways be understood as the result of the kind of mental coercion that is typical of a Protestant culture, where citizens internalize social and political norms on the basis of their moral and political autonomy. I cannot develop this point here, but I would like to mention that, for instance, in non-Protestant Western democratic cultures, internalized obedience to the law is not the main source of stability, and rules are more often than not infringed rather than abided by as a matter of principle and of rebellion against central authorities. This is even truer in Muslim societies where legal norms have no authority if they are not deeply embedded in religious texts and traditions. This fact is not taken into account by Rawls.

One last illustration of this cultural misunderstanding would be Rawls' use of the old argument of "peace by satisfaction", an argument that is only too obviously culturally situated and inapplicable beyond the Western cultural world because of its appeal to rational self-interest.

> Satisfied peoples do not want to expand their territories or to rule over other populations or to convert other peoples. They are at peace. Democracies are not swayed by the passion for power and glory. They have nothing to go to war about. (*LOP*: 47)

The appeal to self-interest has little impact in cultures where the values of the community, or the duties of the individual to that community or honour and self-respect are more important than how well he fares individually in this world. The analysis of these arguments shows clearly how insensitive Rawls can be to different approaches to stability and peace, for instance, those established through compromise and negotiations, because these are possibly alien to his own Protestant sensibility.

Last, but again I cannot develop this point here, we know that, for many cultures, democracy encompasses a sense of disruption and potential conflict, because it exacerbates what is different and not what is common. Thus, it may be a factor of division in social contexts of deep ethnic and religious hatred. For Islam, in particular, but also in many other non-liberal contexts, democracy and the stress on conflict and diversity may be seen as disruptive and dangerous.

No overlapping consensus at the international level

A second series of *internal* criticisms indicating difficulties within the theory and tensions between imperialism and respect for diversity has probably even more weight.

First, Rawls' conception of stability may be criticized in that he does not distinguish between stability in a domestic context of opposing comprehensive doctrines and stability in an international context of conflicting peoples. He applies to the law of peoples the conceptual analysis already present in *Political Liberalism* in relation to a pluralist domestic context. As Kok-Chor Tan notes:

> the main flaw in Rawls's global thesis is his belief that the global overlapping consensus between different political societies is morally equivalent to a domestic overlapping consensus between different comprehensive doctrines ... the consensus Rawls presents in *LOP* is more a political compromise than a consensus around genuine liberal values.[32]

It is impossible at the global level to treat political liberalism as a neutral doctrine in relation to non-democratic peoples and practices. At some stage, assertion of its liberal content, especially of its commitment to individual liberty, has to be expressed, creating a tension and ruining the balance that Rawls wants to preserve.

An added difficulty is that, because the basis for stability is presented as psychological and very narrow, it is open to an objection that is also valid for Rawls' treatment of pluralism in a domestic context. How is it psychologically possible that non-liberal, but decent, peoples might be ready to switch allegiances and to accept liberal principles, whereas at the domestic level they would find them repulsive? Here we have a situation not entirely dissimilar to the problem of the "divided self" in *Political Liberalism* (see above, Chapter 4, Conclusion), where a member of a liberal society is said to be capable of being devoted to liberalism as a citizen, even while, as a private person, he or she is opposed to it.[33] To ask peoples to give their allegiance to values that are alien to them can sound fairly imperialistic. It can also lead to contradictions for the dominant side too. In the present context of development policies, for instance, the contemporary international regime of aid is fairly coercive. But it combines this powerful disciplinary focus with an emphasis on empowerment and self-development even for poor countries, which is paradoxical: it asks for compulsory measures to introduce more freedom and responsibility in the developing countries; this can be unsettling and destructive both for rich donors and poor recipients. The flaw in the argument is the supposed psychological basis for peace when it is obvious that many more objective and non-individual factors must play their part. There is clearly a deep tension in Rawls between the *psychological* nature of his conception of peace and stability, and his *holistic* and institutional conception of justice. The consequence is that too high a price has to be paid – the inclusion of non-democratic countries and their moral transformation – to establish a principled lasting peace in place of a more realistic *modus vivendi*.

6. Rejecting global distributive justice: the duty of assistance

The last controversy concerns the principles of international economic justice and redistribution. Taking seriously Rawls' two principles of justice, cosmopolitanism claims that a *global difference principle* that allows not only redistribution between richer and poorer members, but a correction of an unjust global structure, should be applied beyond borders to counteract the arbitrariness of the territorial distribution of natural resources and to fight poverty (Barry, 1991; Pogge, 1989; Beitz, 1999, etc.). As a matter of principle, all unjust inequalities among persons as well as nations should be fought against through, for instance, global taxation.

The cosmopolitan view on economic justice

Cosmopolitan thinkers such as Charles Beitz[34] accept Rawls' approach to justice. But their first objection is that Rawls' full account of justice, including the difference principle should be applied worldwide, given that the primary subject of justice is the well-being and dignity of individuals anywhere in the world. As Tan (2004: 67) says, "a fundamental cause of global poverty lies with our global arrangements and institutions, and so to seriously tackle global poverty would require reforming these institutions and arrangements". *Contra* Rawls, they claim that the existing distribution of natural resources between nations is as morally arbitrary as the distribution of natural abilities among members of a given society. To be consistent with the difference principle at the domestic level, Charles Beitz suggests a "resource distribution principle" that should be devised to give poor societies a starting point and a chance to establish just institutions and to satisfy their population's basic needs at the domestic level. A second principle, then, would take into account the global flow of investments and economic exchanges and interdependence between states, and permanently correct the imbalance between rich and poor countries through a global wealth tax. The "global distribution principle" treats the world as a single society and would redistribute the world's resources more equally to resource-poor countries, thus applying Rawls' difference principle globally.

Thomas Pogge's work (2006) is equally inspired by Rawls' difference principle, but argues that the existence of separate societies is not justified.

> It makes no sense to try to assess the justice of social institutions one by one ... for both the formation and the effects of such national basic structures are heavily influenced by foreign and supranational institutions ... We must aspire to a single, universal criterion of justice which all persons and peoples can accept.[35]

Like Barry and Beitz, he favours a scheme of global taxation, "a Global Resource Dividend", based on the value of natural resources actually used. The formulation of what has come to be labelled as the cosmopolitan conception of global justice could not be clearer.

Rawls' defence of the duty of assistance

Rawls vigorously rejects any such attempt at global redistributive justice. In the name of "realism", he proposes a "target and cut-off point conception" of assistance that rejects indefinite international redistribution and stops when the target of just institutions is met. "Well-ordered peoples have a *duty* to assist burdened societies ... It does not follow, however, that the only way is by following a principle of distributive justice to regulate economic and social inequalities among societies. Most such principles do not have a definite aim or cut-off point" (*LOP*: 106). Instead, the Rawlsian principle includes the following three guidelines.

(1) Assistance has a target: establishing the conditions for just institutions. Based on the argument for the principle of just savings for future generations that savings may stop once just (or decent) institutions have been established (*TJ*: §44), the argument claims that it is no longer a duty of justice to continue to save for future generations. "Great wealth is not necessary to establish just institutions" (*LOP*: 106–7). There is no need for indefinite growth.

(2) The aim of the duty of assistance is to provide the necessary conditions for respecting the core human rights and it is compatible with Amartya Sen's notion of capabilities (*LOP*: 109).[36]

(3) The cut-off point for assistance should be when just institutions are in place and functioning, even if there is still relative poverty (*LOP*: 111).

Examining Rawls' various objections to a global distributive principle will help shed light on the nature of his theory of justice. His first objection is connected with the structure of the theory of justice, its division into two parts: an ideal and a non-ideal theory. There are two principles valid for the foreign policy of liberal and decent peoples in a non-ideal situation: the right to just war when threatened by "outlaw states" and the duty of assistance when confronted by "burdened societies". The duty of assistance falls on more prosperous peoples and aims at helping poorer nations to reach a certain level of development. When that level is reached, assistance should stop and no global distributive principle should apply. In contrast, a difference principle belongs to the ideal theory of how well-ordered peoples regulate their relations with each other. A principle similar to the domestic principle of difference can thus only apply between well-ordered peoples that satisfy some conditions of political and economic development. Its application to burdened societies would require indefinite assistance without precise targets and cut-off points as in the domestic case, which is highly unrealistic. Realism demands, on the contrary, that we switch to transitional measures to assist them, measures that will stop when they are able to establish reasonably just institutions in the sense described earlier. Global distributive justice has no meaning in the context of non-ideal theory, that is of exchanges between societies that are not well ordered, liberal or decent, and that cannot share common principles of international justice. "The duty of assistance applies only to the duty that liberal and decent peoples have to assist *burdened* societies" (*LOP*: 106). "As I explain there, such societies are neither liberal nor decent" (*ibid.*: 43, n. 53).

But this argument can be defeated if, following our criticism of Rawls' definition of peoples, we stress that members of burdened societies can share in liberal and decent conceptions of justice even if their governments do not, and that the fact that such members of undemocratic societies are not part of the decision-making procedure jeopardizes the whole distinction between burdened societies and decent peoples. It is highly probable that, through global communication and information, the demands for Western-style developments and for changes in the global structure would be supported by most members if they were given a voice. There is no satisfactory reason, at the level of the structure of the theory of justice, to reject the principle of difference, once democratic liberties are guaranteed to citizens. The limitation of Rawls' theory, in particular the stark distinctions he establishes between different kinds of peoples, is based on his underestimating the role of globalization and the complexity of the make-up of peoples' identities. His social ontology, that is, his conception of societies as closed entities and his lack of concern for individual members' fate, makes it difficult to understand globalization as the primacy of new individual exchanges over the traditional national structures.

The second argument is that such a limitless application would have bad results for peoples' autonomy and self-respect. "If it is meant to apply continuously without end, without a target ... the second global principle gives what we would, I think, regard as unacceptable results" (*LOP*: 117). It would infringe on peoples' autonomy to decide collectively on their future and not to be forced to accept a model of development dictated by foreign powers. Global distributive principles have unacceptable consequences as they do not respect the autonomous choices made by peoples, in particular, and this is very important, it does not take into account their political culture. "The crucial element in how a country fares is its political culture – its members' political and civic virtues – and not the level of its resources" (*LOP*: 117). Rawls here gives two examples.

(i) Two liberal or decent countries at the same level of wealth make different decisions for their future. One decides to industrialize, whereas the other does not, and as a consequence becomes twice as wealthy as the other. "Should the industrialized country be taxed to give funds to the second? According to the duty of assistance there would be no tax; whereas with a global egalitarian principle without target, there would always be a flow of taxes as long as the wealth of one people is less than the other. This seems unacceptable" (*LOP*: 117). Here free *choice* and self-determination are central elements in the justice of international relations and Rawls' argument is appealing, as it seems to avoid cultural and political imperialism in aid policies. But such an example is fraught with problems. Rawls neglects the role of *un-chosen* global factors and limits the question of justice to the outcome of self-determination. This, for one, is highly unrealistic. As Tan (2005: 71–2) says:

> The distributive goal is to offset the effects of *un-chosen* global factors, not the effects of *chosen* national policies on a people's well-being ... There is space under a global distributive scheme for diversity and choices in national policies. Global distributive justice and national self-determination are not incompatible ... What is unjust and what distributive justice aims to mitigate is the background condition within which self-determination is exercised, not the outcome as such of self-determination.

(ii) The second example deals with population growth in two equally liberal or decent societies. The first does not reduce the rate of population growth and, some decades later, the second one is twice as wealthy as the first. The duty of assistance and a global distributive principle will give equally good results in assisting the poorer society to become a full member of the Society of Peoples, but the former avoids unacceptable infringement on peoples' autonomy. "The duty of assistance does not require taxes from the first, now wealthier society, while the global egalitarian principle without target would" (*LOP*: 118). Again, this example is not convincing because the starting point is neither a really burdened society nor the vulnerable poor individuals that make up its population, but an imaginary poor, though decent, society that freely decides, for religious reasons, not to regulate its population growth.

What Rawls does not seem to notice, here, is that such free or autonomous choices, at the level of countries, are impossible if some political institutions as well as economic conditions are not in place. Here he is not discussing the case of truly burdened societies, but that of poor, but decent peoples, which puts his whole distinction into question. It would have been more convincing to distinguish between truly burdened societies that will need major changes of the global economic structure, possibly a global distributive principle, to truly prosper one day, and poor, but decent countries that simply need some transitional principle of assistance to reach a satisfactory level. The duty of assistance does not replace global distributive justice, but complements it.

The third and perhaps more powerful of Rawls' arguments is that international "society" does not constitute a cooperative scheme for mutual advantage, as its members do not contribute to any collective output. For redistribution to be justified and meaningful, we need cooperation and reciprocity within boundaries. If not, the whole scheme is unjust according to Rawls' "societal" conception of justice as reciprocity (see above, Chapter 1). Rawls here is very much in agreement with Mill on nationality. Without the "special" sympathies that bind the members of a given people or "nation", distributive justice has no meaning.[37] There is no possibility of using the difference principle because peoples want to preserve the equality and independence of their own society. But as cosmopolitans have noted, the new global structure creates such sympathies and solidarities, especially in matters of sustainable development and protection of the environment, issues that are not taken up by Rawls.

The main claim is that inequalities between poor and rich countries are, then, not necessarily unjust. As we mentioned earlier, for Rawls, "great wealth is not necessary to establish just institutions" (*LOP*: 107). "There are two views about equality: one holds that equality is just or a good in itself, the law of peoples on the other hand holds that inequalities are not always unjust" (*LOP*: 113). Fighting poverty and reducing inequalities in domestic and international society is a justifiable aim so long as the criterion of reciprocity is not satisfied. In a liberal domestic society, the gap between rich and poor "cannot be wider than the criterion of reciprocity allows ... Similarly, once the duty of assistance is satisfied and all peoples have a liberal or decent government, there is no reason to narrow the gap" (*ibid.*: 114). This obviously contradicts the present international policy of the United Nations of reducing poverty globally without a target and cut-off point. This excludes the so-called "right to development", which is presently discussed by economists and development agencies. For Rawls, it is more important to preserve the self-respect of the poorer members or countries and fairness and equal representation for all peoples than to indiscriminately assist low- and medium-income peoples. The "Malibu surfer" argument is relevant here: once opportunities are created, it is up to peoples to decide to become wealthier or not. However, this shows a fairly unrealistic view of political and economic development for autonomy to cease being mere utopia.

Let us conclude now. Rawls' forceful advocacy of a duty of assistance is controversial in the following ways. It is based on an unsustainable confusion between burdened societies and poor, but decent, societies, which, contrary to Rawls' view, need different forms of assistance from wealthier members, because of their very different political and economic situations. In reality, the latter need a duty of assistance whereas the former obviously need a complete overhaul of the global structure and the application of a global distributive principle. In the second case, simple redistribution is sufficient. In the first case, this is not enough. A duty of assistance is a humanitarian duty that accepts the existing baseline resource and wealth distribution as a starting point and wishes to correct the imbalances and to change the flow of wealth. The global distributive principle goes much further and means reconceiving this present global structure because of the injustices it generates. Rawls ignores the effects of the global basic structure. Justice as reciprocity does not work in the global environment because the distribution of natural resources is too unequal. This is recognized by Rawls at the domestic level, not however at the international one. Again, Rawls ignores the plight of individual members of burdened societies when he insists on the value of choice. Either he is too ethnocentric to fully understand the different models of power distribution and decision-making procedures that characterize truly burdened societies, or he has become too "communitarian", as some critics have stressed. Still, it is unacceptable to treat these deprived societies as capable of autonomy and free choices when their institutions are far from democratic and liberal. The main flaw of Rawls' conception is in the confusions of the notion of "peoples" that undermine his argument in favour of abandoning the difference principle at the international level. Still, Rawls' target and cut-off point conceptions of both human rights and assistance sound convincing against global redistribution principles for more extreme cases.

Conclusion: a "critical" theory of international justice

I have insisted on three controversies where Rawls has attracted major criticisms: his holistic conception of international justice at the cost, possibly, of moral individualism and a failure to protect universal human rights; his emphasis that the aim of the law of peoples is peace and stability among peoples on the basis of a shared sense of justice, not a just world order; and his rejection of global distributive justice in the name of "explanatory nationalism" and respect for peoples' autonomy, at the cost of possibly ignoring the disastrous effects of the global economic and political structure. These criticisms explain the poor reception of the book and some, as I have shown, are fully justified. I would like to conclude with what I think are the weaknesses and strengths of Rawls' position.

The weaknesses are certainly the lack of attention to detail in the definition of a "people" and the consequences for the situation of vulnerable individuals and minorities. Rawls also obviously underestimates the role of the global basic structure as a source of deep and pervasive inequalities between peoples. He equally underestimates the dangers of cultural imperialism while being aware of the arrogance of cosmopolitanism.

The strengths are that he offers a truly "critical" theory of international justice, in the Kantian sense, that is, he seeks to avoid both the dogmatism of cosmopolitans and the scepticism of both "realists" and cultural relativism. This is a difficult and courageous position and Rawls could not possibly overcome all the difficulties. Still, he is moving in the right direction, trying to define a conception of international justice from the point of view of peace and stability, not from that of the creation of a just world order. Philosophers cannot determine what universal justice may be without violating the fact of reasonable pluralism, but they can examine what the conditions for peace and stability are, justice being one of them. Rawls quite rightly emphasizes that a people is a political entity with a corporate moral status of its own. Thus, the demands of peace are paramount and a lesser ambition in terms of domestic justice and full human rights can be justified in the name of respect for peoples' self-determination.

To that, I would like to add that, in spite of its limitations, *The Law of Peoples* is a good example of how political philosophy should work. It should aim at offering distinctions and discriminating analyses whereas, in the field of international relations, we are more accustomed to grand generalizations. As he said in 1971, and repeats in 1999:

> Just and decent civilized societies depend always on making significant moral and political distinctions ... there is never a time when we are excused from the fine-grained distinctions of moral and political principles and graduated restraints.   (*LOP*: 103)

Conclusion: Beyond liberalism

To conclude, I wish to focus on the main challenges that Rawls has set himself and to assess his success in meeting them.

The first challenge was to build a convincing argument for both social justice and the protection of basic rights and liberties, which would avoid direct appeals to moral motivation, as *homo oeconomicus* only connects with instrumental rationality, but which would be an alternative to utilitarianism and its indirect and usually weak defence of justice.

The second challenge was to construct a conception of justice that would overcome the traditional conflicts between freedom and equality which have characterized democratic thought. How is it possible to reconcile liberalism with social democracy and economic and social rights without appealing to oppressive state power and threatening basic liberties?

The third challenge was to take proper account of the new pluralism of contemporary democratic societies, which results from the freedom of choice and the basic rights enjoyed by most members for over two hundred years. How is it possible to base a reasoned justification of justice on such a diversity of creeds and cultures? However, pluralism is also a problem at the international level and a just Society of Peoples presents the challenge of defining new forms of admission, regulation and cooperation among peoples that would respect their cultural and religious diversity. Has Rawls properly addressed the challenges of cultural and moral pluralism, which are so crucial for peace within and among nations?

Finding a new method of justification for such a context was therefore, as I have insisted, going to be the most difficult challenge for Rawls at the meta-ethical level. In my Introduction and in Chapter 4, I have argued that "doctrinal autonomy", that is the requirement that the doctrine itself should be defended in an autonomous way, is his answer to the crucial questions of pluralism and the defence of autonomy. Such a method has left many commentators puzzling over Rawls' deeper doctrine and his reasons for not presenting it at the start of the demonstration (Larmore, 1999). Has Rawls been consistent enough and successful in meeting his own goal?

Finally, in his far-reaching transformation of liberalism and in his insistence on empowerment, has Rawls not come very close to the classical doctrine of republicanism and to its conception of civic virtues and duties, in contrast with liberal rights-based conceptions of justice? Creating citizens seems now to play a major part in the quest for stability and in the strengthening of the public conception of justice. Without good citizens, just institutions cannot survive.

Arguing for justice

It is, obviously, the first challenge and the solutions proposed by Rawls that have attracted the most interest. Using vocabularies and modes of reasoning familiar in welfare economics, he has opened up new lines of communication between philosophers and economists. His aim was at first to provide an alternative to utilitarian solutions. However, not only has he succeeded in replacing them with new principles, but in so doing he has started a whole new debate about the nature and content of distributive justice.

First, he has shown that distributive justice should not be limited to allocative justice, but should take into account the specific distributions of goods rather than their overall aggregate. He has replaced maximization with equality as the benchmark for fair distribution. Secondly, he has argued that persons have first-order interests that are not exchangeable. In the economic calculus, the gains of some cannot compensate for the losses of others. Thirdly, he has shown how a social minimum can be guaranteed without harming economic efficiency by using the Pareto argument for justified inequalities. Social justice and economic efficiency are compatible. Finally, he has replaced the reference to rational individuals in *A Theory of Justice* with the "political idea of the person", that is, with the idea of citizenship, and this has been one of the great clarifications provided by his later work, as has been his insistence on a conception of justice as reciprocity, not solely as mutual advantage or impartiality (see Chapters 1 and 2). This has led him to define the social minimum in terms not simply of basic human needs, as in the case of the capitalistic welfare state, but of what is needed to properly exercise one's rights and duties as a citizen, and is of great consequence for the notion of the *stakeholder society* (Ackerman & Alstott, 1999) or of a "property-owning democracy", which he now advocates as the just or quasi-just society.

Still, his contractarian argument, as we have seen, has attracted many controversies and criticisms. Based on the method of the social contract, it defines the people concerned as equal and free parties to a reciprocal contract and as symmetrically represented in what he calls the Original Position (Chapter 3). Members of society all expect to gain from the arrangements resulting from the original contract, even if the price to pay, the demands of justice and redistribution, seems at first difficult to accept. The argument appeals *directly* to rational self-interest (understood as interests *of* the self rather than as selfish interests) and to justice as mutual advantage, and *indirectly* to moral concerns such as impartiality and fairness, requirements that are built into the situation itself (the veil of ignorance and the primary goods), rather than into motivational dispositions.

For some authors (Gauthier, 1986), on the one hand, Rawls fails to meet the challenge of defending redistribution on the basis of instrumental and amoral rationality, and his use of the social contract is not consistent. His later distinction between the Reasonable (the demands of justice) and the Rational (the demands of interest), and his claim that the Rational is subordinated to the Reasonable, weaken the whole argument (see Chapter 3). He does not succeed in deriving morality from rationality and in showing that redistribution of resources and outcomes is rational. For libertarians (Nozick, 1974), on the other hand, any redistribution is a potential violation of individual basic rights and interferes with legitimate transactions among self-interested individuals. Finally, for some others (Barry, 1995a), defining justice as reciprocity is too limiting. It excludes from access to justice and redistribution people who cannot contribute or cooperate on an equal basis over a whole life, such as handicapped persons, children, etc.

A good example of the latter criticisms would be those of Martha

Nussbaum (2006) in her recent book, *Frontiers of Justice*. She takes great care to salvage the Rawlsian principles of justice as much as possible, showing how they could be expanded in order to deal with grave unresolved questions of justice, while rejecting his use of the social contract and of the Original Position and situating herself firmly on the more Aristotelian ground of the "capability approach" that treats human dignity no longer in terms of rationality or productivity, but "of an acknowledgement that we are needy temporal animal beings ... rationality and sociability being themselves temporal, having growth, maturity and decline" (Nussbaum, 2006: 160).

She notices three areas where the theory of justice is wanting, and most critics would agree that these certainly constitute major limitations of Rawls' theory.

First, there is no room for dealing with people afflicted by temporary or severe mental and physical disabilities. His principles of justice envisage persons as "normal", fully functioning and fairly equal cooperating members of society over a whole life. They exclude less productive people from the arrangements of justice: the physically and mentally ill, babies and adolescent children, pregnant and child-rearing women, elderly and vulnerable people, etc. Rawls himself is certainly aware of this limitation and doubts whether his own theory is capable of providing satisfactory answers (*PL*: 20–21). His answer lies in the distinction between questions of justice and questions of care, charity and humanity, a distinction that is grounded in the meaning of the concept of justice itself and in the description of the circumstances that make justice a necessity (Chapter 1) – mental and physical illnesses, old age and temporary or durable dependence not being part of them. Assuming rough equality of powers, capacities and needs of contractants has a severely limiting effect and requires us to put some issues of justice on hold. In that sense, many readers of Rawls may share a similar feeling that he is not addressing some of what they see as the most urgent issues of justice in our societies. Such a limitation hangs on the conception of the person as free, equal and independent, and as entering a social contract that is meant to apply to her and her likes only. What happens to those members who do not possess the required abilities to enter contracts and to accept their terms as fully cooperating citizens? Are they excluded from justice? For Nussbaum, the contractarian method is a severe limitation.

Secondly, we saw in Chapter 5 that one of the main flaws in Rawls' conception of international justice was the failure to consider the place of birth or nationality as an accident that is on a par with the natural and social circumstances that justice must correct (see Chapters 2 and 5). Why, we asked, is the fact of being born into a poor nation structurally different, for matters of justice, from being born into a poor family? Do the staggering differences between poor and rich nations in a globalized world not multiply the differences in wealth and resources within a domestic society? For Nussbaum, nationality should not be an obstacle preventing access to justice.

Thirdly, and this is a point that I did not make, but that Nussbaum strongly emphasizes, the theory of justice as fairness fails to be fair and just to non-human animals. In that sense, it is in retreat from utilitarianism. Both Bentham and Sidgwick took as their benchmark for happiness "sentient beings", capable of pain and pleasure, be they human or animal.

For Nussbaum, these failures find their origin in the conception of justice as contractarian. The fact that such theories conflate the question "Who frames the principles of justice?" with the question "For whom are these principles framed?" means that they cannot include animals, physically/mentally impaired persons and members of non-democratic illiberal poor countries as none could ever be equal, free and independent parties to a contract on justice.

This assessment of Rawls' conception, of its difficulties, limitations and shortcomings, would receive, I think, a great deal of support. Moreover, in the way it is expressed, it has the advantage of sounding extremely fair to Rawls too. My main disagreement with Nussbaum would be that, for all its fairness, it does not account for Rawls' specific limited ambition: to provide a political conception of justice, not of care and compassion, fit for democratic societies. He is arguing in favour of an empowering *political* conception of justice for citizens, not of a moral conception of our duties to our fellow human and living beings. If the objective had been the latter, I think that such an assessment would have been correct. However, at the heart of my interpretation has been an effort to insist on the relevance of Rawls' theory for present-day functioning democracies, not for the world at large. Moreover, one should not forget that the contractarian argument is part of a wider justification process, which includes the appeal to reflective equilibrium (Chapter 1) and to the use of public reason (Chapter 4).

Within these constraints, the social contract approach is justified because it is a political approach that deals with issues of power, bargaining and partiality. Its aim is to eliminate unfair biases, and to insist on fair terms of cooperation, not to bring "justice" to all corners of the world and to nature. It is to tame power and to localize injustices at the level of social and political institutions. As I have shown (Chapter 4), there is no obstacle in Rawls' theory to the feminization or ethnicization of injustices and to his principles tackling institutional discriminations and inequalities. In contrast, the case of illnesses and of conditions that make it impossible, durably or for a limited period, to fully exercise one's rights and liberties as citizen is a separate issue and should not invalidate the general design. Within the general principles of justice, there is ample room for fighting institutional injustices, in mental institutions, hospitals, the police, the courts, the education system and the family.

Reconciling liberty and equality

The next challenge concerns the tensions between the demands of liberty and of equality within democratic thought and politics. Traditionally, the demands of equality, especially in a socialist context, have posed a threat to basic liberties, and illiberal states do not hesitate to interfere with private property and basic civil rights in the name of the fight for equality and redistribution. In contrast, liberalism has too often been seen as concerned only with what Rawls describes as "liberal equality", that is, formal equality of opportunities that does not take into account the social conditions that interfere with individual decisions and give them a real content. Liberals see the inequalities that occur in spite of equality of opportunity as the result of personal deficiencies and individual mistakes, not as injustices. They put a major emphasis on individual circumstances and responsibility, and not enough weight on the role of social institutions. In contrast, we have seen that, for Rawls, the subject of justice is the basic structure of society (Chapter 1). This leads him to go much further than simply reconciling liberty and equality. His principles of justice (Chapter 2) transform liberal conceptions beyond recognition.

First, he takes the Marxist critique of formal liberties very seriously in an unprecedented way. He insists that equality of opportunity is not enough for justice, but that it should be *fair*, that is, it should correct natural and not only social circumstances. In particular, we saw how he treats talents as not only a personal, but also a social and collective asset (Chapter 2). Secondly, he is deeply concerned with the fact that, without political expression, these equal opportunities will remain meaningless, with people having no access to political rights or with their rights being distorted by extreme inequalities of wealth. Citizens should have an equal chance of influencing policies, irrespective of their economic and social class. Placing the *fair* value of political liberties on a special standing is one of the major innovations of justice as fairness. Thirdly, it is clear for him that political and civil rights should not be dissociated from the defence of social and economic rights. One of the most controversial aspects of his conception is the way in which he combines a defence of all aspects of justice. This was not absolutely clear in *A Theory of Justice*, but we saw how, in his later work and in Joshua Cohen's important 1989 paper, this is made clear (Chapter 3). *Democratic equality* includes three inseparable components: a principle of equal basic liberties, with the emphasis on the fair value of political liberties; a principle of fair equality of opportunity; and the difference principle or the requirement that to be justified, inequalities of outcomes should benefit the worse off.

Such a deep transformation of liberal values has been met with stark criticisms on all sides. For the left, as we saw, Rawls is not egalitarian enough as he relies on a Pareto argument for inequality that is seen as inconsistent with his claim that equal distribution is the benchmark for a just distribution (G. A. Cohen, 1995). For the right, he is too egalitarian as he allows excessive transfers of outcomes, which may weaken the incentives for more talented and productive persons to work and to produce more for the benefit of all.

However, leaving aside these deep political debates, it is worth noting that Rawls has succeeded in reconciling liberty and equality in a very specific and structural way; it is the very *structure* of the conception and the way in which its various principles are connected that establishes such a tight connection between these values (Chapter 2). This is made possible by the two following features. First, the first principle of justice as fairness is a principle of equal basic liberties. This means that, in it, civil, political and social rights are connected and are claimed to be co-original and to have the same source in the two moral powers of the person (Chapter 4). Secondly, the lexical *priority rules* between the various principles exclude the possibility that the principle of equal liberty could be sacrificed in the name of social justice. The rule of priority is parallel to the affirmation of the priority of justice over the good and is the central moral claim in *A Theory of Justice*: that economic advantages or redistribution cannot justify infringements of the absolute claims of equal liberty (Chapter 1).

This transformation of liberalism has had deep and pervasive effects on contemporary democratic thought. It has strengthened the defence of constitutional democracy in detaching it from purely liberal concerns for individual freedom. It has introduced an awareness of the weight of unequal basic social structures and of the threat that they pose to liberty and security. It has also given a new urgency to the combined defence of political, civil and social rights, and to opposing governments who still argue that the fight for economic growth can justify the sacrifice of basic rights. In that sense, one can conclude that Rawls has successfully met the challenges of reconciling liberty and equality and of defending a convincing conception of democratic equality.

Facing pluralism

The next major challenge that has occupied Rawls is that of pluralism as the new context within which the pursuit of redistribution and democratic equality now takes place. How is it possible to provide stability in a pluralistic context through a growing *inclusiveness* without weakening the primacy of justice? His answer, and this has proved to be very controversial, is that such an inclusiveness will need to gain the support of a wide range of conceptions of the good, not all of them liberal. It will also, at the international level, need to be supported by various peoples, not all of them liberal and democratic. In the name of peace and stability, justice should be defined in various non-liberal and non-democratic terms. We cannot follow Kant's motto when he writes: "*Fiat justitia, pereat mundus* (i.e. let justice reign, even if all the rogues in the world must perish) may sound somewhat inflated, but it is nonetheless true" (Kant, *Perpetual Peace*, 1795 in Kant, 1991: 122). We cannot, for Rawls, simply apply the liberal paradigm to the whole of society and to the whole world.

The way in which Rawls meets the challenges of pluralism is thus crucial, but, unfortunately, it has been on the whole misunderstood. As I have shown, it is useful to clarify it in the light of his last work: *The Law of Peoples*, as it gives an excellent insight into his way of thinking (Chapter 5). Rawls reasons in terms of "target and cut-off points" conceptions. This means that we should have a precise target: a political consensus on just institutions, and precise cut-off points or criteria: *reasonableness* in the case of domestic justice, and *decency* in the case of international justice. In this way, we should be able to combine the primacy of justice with respect for pluralism within very precise limits.

Pluralism within society should be limited in the name of *reasonableness*. Among the many non-liberal religious or moral views that may develop within a free society, some are unreasonable and dangerous and should be excluded because they represent an obstacle to an agreement on common principles of justice. However, some others are non-liberal but reasonable, in the sense that they accept the limits of reason and the burdens of judgement, which we must acknowledge even if we disagree with them. They offer reasons that we do not share, but still understand and cannot reject as unreasonable. Their advocates accept the duty of civility: the moral duty to use public reasons along with their comprehensive doctrines in their dealings with their fellow citizens at the level of questions of basic justice and constitutional essentials. A conception of rationality as finite and revisable, as deliberative and modest, underlies Rawls' conception of reasonable pluralism and of the possibility of an overlapping political consensus.

Pluralism among peoples should be limited in the name of *decency*. Admission to the Society of Peoples and inclusion that leads to a consensus on international principles of justice is based on a precise cut-off point: decency. Non-liberal but decent peoples do not treat their members as free and equal, and do not respect the full list of institutional features of liberal societies, but they still satisfy essential conditions such as non-aggression, respect for basic human rights, a decent consultation hierarchy, recognition of the right to dissent, the right of citizens to play a substantial role in making political decisions, say, through associations and groups, etc. In that sense, one can hope that they can join liberal and democratic peoples in an effort to guarantee peace and stability based on common principles of international justice, not simply on a *modus vivendi* or on the present balance of power.

Still, as I have said, such a treatment of pluralism has been of great concern to those who are convinced that a theory of justice should have a firm universalistic basis and should not make too many concessions in the name of inclusiveness and stability. As we saw at the end of Chapters 4 and 5, it is not clear that Rawls has fully succeeded in meeting the challenge not so much of pluralism as that of finding the right balance between realism and normative imperatives.

Defending autonomy and equal respect for persons

I now turn to the methodological challenge faced by Rawls: that his justification of justice should proceed in a way compatible with autonomy and equal respect for persons. This is the challenge of *doctrinal autonomy* (Chapters 1 and 4). It means that autonomy, for him, is not a *value* among others, like utility, happiness or individuality, which may be defended by a comprehensive doctrine of the good. It is rather a *practice*, a way of treating persons and presenting arguments within the framework of an autonomous or freestanding doctrine, which does not advocate a dominant end or *telos*, but can be reconstructed in ways compatible with a variety of such ends.

Many authors have emphasized the fact that there is something highly puzzling and unusual in Rawls' method that the device of the social contract tends to hide, that at its heart there is a unformulated "deeper doctrine" of autonomy and equal respect for persons that relies either on a doctrine of natural rights (Dworkin, 1977) or of Kantian ethics (Larmore, 1999) that is never fully explicit. Is this a failure on Rawls' part or is it deliberate?

The answer that I have advanced, based on Rawls' own admission, is that this "deep doctrine" should be seen as the *result* of the various justification processes, such as the Original Position, the appeal to reflective equilibrium or the use of public reason, not as a *foundation* for the whole argument. A theory of justice is not applied moral philosophy. Such a procedure is the only way in which a public conception of justice can appear to fully respect persons' autonomy. We should always remember that justice is about power and coercion. In order to be implemented and respected, it has to exact a price even from those who benefit from it: it represents a loss in terms of potential gains and benefits. Still, democratic regimes claim that such loss may be understood as a legitimate outcome if it is the result of freely *agreed* constraints on our pursuit of the good. It is thus extremely important that autonomy should be part of the process of justification itself, not simply of the content of the conception or, in other words, that autonomy should be autonomously endorsed. In that way, a public conception of justice may become the moral basis for an overlapping consensus and a source of unity and belonging in a way in which a comprehensive doctrine cannot. A Kantian interpretation of Rawls such as the one I have argued for is not a way of deriving its content from a Kantian moral doctrine or of applying moral philosophy to politics. That would be destructive of such a respect for the autonomy of the citizens concerned. A truly Kantian interpretation leads to seeing public justification and the "construction of justice" (O'Neill, 1989) by citizens themselves as the main aim of practical reason and of a theory of justice that is not theoretical, but practical (Chapter 1).

This also has very important consequences for the understanding of the *political* role of a public conception of justice. In my introductory chapter, "The primacy of justice", I have suggested that one of Rawls' most important contributions to both contemporary political theory and practice is his insistence on the relevance of a public conception of justice for *empowering* citizens. "It is part", he writes, "of citizens' sense of themselves not only collectively, but also individually, to recognize political authority as deriving from them and that they are responsible for what it does in their name" (*PL*: 431). The most important part of this responsibility is the public justification and legitimization process of our own principles in front of one another, a process that requires the context of deliberative democracy. We have seen how Rawls has indeed situated deliberative democracy at the heart of his method of doctrinal autonomy (Chapter 4).

Creating citizens

This leads me to emphasize what is possibly the richest legacy of Rawls: an understanding of citizenship that goes beyond traditional liberalism and possibly points towards a "strong" or republican conception. I concentrate on two issues. First, we may ask whether and in what sense it is a republican conception of citizenship, as some authors have argued (Laden, 2006). Secondly, how does it articulate the public and personal dimensions of the self and how "unencumbered" (Sandel, 1982) is the political self for Rawls?

The first claim, that Rawls is becoming more republican, is supported by Habermas (1999: 69) when he describes, in his debate with Rawls, "the radical democratic embers of the original position", meaning by that that there is a radical republican dimension in Rawls' theory that we should recognize. Many authors too claim that republicanism is due for revival as an alternative to rights-based liberalism. Michael Sandel has recently declared that he is a republican, not a communitarian. Jürgen Habermas claims to represent a form of Kantian republicanism.[1]

Traditionally, republicanism is characterized by an understanding of citizenship based on an agreement on a shared conception of the good and on the priority of public values over private interests.[2] The first aspect would make it unacceptable for Rawls' political liberalism. Rousseau, for instance, advocated a sort of "civic religion" as a means of creating citizens and the republic. Rawls rejects that kind of "civic humanism" as being too tyrannical[3] (*PL*: 206). So, would the second aspect of republicanism be compatible with his views? In what sense do political values override private interests?

He shares with republicanism a major concern with stability and social cohesion, and he recognizes that the latter is more effective than liberalism in producing the kind of stability and consensus that modern democracies require, especially in view of their cultural diversity. In contrast, liberalism's emphasis on individual rights impoverishes the meaning of citizenship as it creates a culture of grievances, demands and claims, not of solidarity and reciprocity. It is not concerned with the bonds of citizenship, but with the needs of individuals. The societal aspect of citizenship is played down. It is clear that Rawls does not remain as indifferent as most liberals to the question of the fair value of political liberties. As I mentioned in the Introduction, it is the erosion of these very liberties in a "market democracy" that started his enquiry into political and social justice in the first place. He shows great concern for what we could call the "privatization of politics" or the politics of lobbies and private interests, and he calls for a renewal of citizens' participation as an answer. In "The Idea of Public Reason Revisited", he gives his most explicit statement of how he understands citizenship, a statement that sounds fairly republican in view of its emphasis on citizens' responsibilities and on public reason!

> Ideally, citizens are to think of themselves as if they were legislators and ask themselves what statutes, supported by what reasons satisfying the criterion of reciprocity, they would think it most reasonable to enact. When firm and widespread, the disposition of citizens to view themselves as ideal legislators, and to repudiate government officials and candidates for public office who violate public reason, is one of the political and social roots of democracy, and is vital for its enduring strength and vigour.   (IPRR: 136)

Obviously, empowering citizens and treating them as responsible for the justice of their institutions and for putting forward social and political criticism is an important part of Rawls' project, as I have shown. Let us now quote Rawls' own description of republicanism.

> Classical republicanism I take to be the view that if the citizens of a democratic society are to preserve their basic rights and liberties, including the civil liberties which secure the freedoms of private life, they must also have to a sufficient degree the

"political virtues" (as I have called them) and be willing to take part in public life. The idea is that without a widespread participation in democratic politics by a vigorous and informed citizen body, and certainly with a general retreat in private life, even the most well-designed political institutions will fall into the hands of those who seek to dominate and impose their will through the state apparatus ... The safety of democratic liberties require the active participation of citizens who possess the political virtues needed to maintain a constitutional regime.   (*PL*: 205)

The central tenets of republicanism, which Rawls obviously shares, can be briefly summarized as follows: civil liberty needs political rights and participation; liberty is always at the mercy of domination; and citizens' engagement and participation are the conditions for stability. We can certainly find corresponding ideas in Rawls' theory. It is clear, for instance, that Rawls' fight against "market democracy" and the "privatization of politics" echoes classical republican concerns. We saw how his conception of voting as a public duty, not as a matter of personal preferences, is unusual within liberal thought (Chapter 4). His insistence on the basic structure echoes the social ontology of most republican authors such as Rousseau. The idea of the duty of civility as crucial for the stability of democratic institutions is a reference to the list of civic virtues characteristic of republicanism. The whole idea of justification as an ongoing effort that involves public reason is fairly characteristic of republican politics. What is distinctive in Rawls' theory are the two new ideas of the OP and of placing intuitions and principles in reflective equilibrium, for which there are no obvious republican equivalents. Finally, giving the fair value of political liberties a special priority (Chapter 2) was also a meaningful innovation in the principles of justice as fairness. Recall too that the needs of *citizens*, not of individual persons, dictate the guaranteed social minimum (Chapter 4).

However, what appears to be specific of Rawls' view of citizenship and to lead to a distinctive form of liberal republicanism is that, for him, (1) civil and political rights have the same importance and origin in popular sovereignty or in "constituent politics" (Ackerman, 1991), but that (2) the sphere of the personal and of the political are kept separate, contrary to classical republicanism.

(1) Whereas in classical liberalism, civil rights have priority over political rights, which are instrumental to the protection of personal autonomy, for Rawls, they are constitutive of it. This implies that he

adds a republican sense of political responsibility to the list of liberal rights that define citizenship and that he thus tries to reconcile the "liberties of the Ancients" (political participation) with the "liberty of the Moderns" (personal autonomy and non-interference). For instance, freedom for Rawls is not simply freedom from interference, as this may still leave you at the mercy of a benevolent but all powerful ruler. Equality matters, and emphasizing the link between individual freedom and an equal structure of power is characteristic of Rawls' theory (Chapter 2). This is why "the liberties of both public and private autonomy are given side by side and unranked in the first principle of justice" (RH: 413). The list of basic liberties does not privilege the liberal liberties over the republican ones, but gives them the same weight.

> These liberties are co-original for the further reason that both kinds of liberty are rooted in one or both of the two moral powers, respectively in the capacity for a sense of justice and in the capacity for a conception of the good ... both are essential aspects of the political conception of the person.　　　　　　　　　　　　(RH: 413)

Rawls is thus able to unite the two types of rights that make up citizenship. The first corresponds to the "liberty of the Moderns" and the rational concern for one's own good, the second to the political liberties of the Ancients and the concern for justice and the common good. Here we have the first elements of a new conception of citizenship, which is neither liberal nor republican. Rawls' description of the political person is congruent with republicanism, but a long way from classical liberalism.

(2) Where Rawls differs from classical republicanism, and could thus renew it in terms more at one with modern political life, is that for him the value of political liberties does not mean that the "personal is political" in the way that it is for republicans. We saw in his debate with Habermas that he is critical of such a thesis and that, for him, the civil and political spheres are distinct: the realm of non-public (but not private) concerns and associations is specific and distinct from the political forum. It is the realm not simply of the market, as Habermas seems to imply, but of the moral life of citizens, of their personal comprehensive doctrines, of what gives meaning and worth to their lives – and the political should stop there. The distinction between civil society and politics is crucial for Rawls. Not everything is "political". "To make the good of civil society subordinate to that of public life is

mistaken" (*PL*: 420). Within the limits of justice, we all have a universal human right to our personal choices, unhindered by the demands of the body politic. This liberal claim is compatible with the view that political rights are as important as civil rights and have the same origin. It simply notes that *republican moments*, where the political invades personal life, such times like that of the 1989 fall of the Berlin Wall or the 1989 student demonstrations in China, are on the whole exceptional in the life of citizens and that we cannot define citizenship solely through these exalted circumstances that correspond to the "constituent will of the people" or to their "constitutional power", the capacity to give themselves a new political constitution, in contrast to ordinary politics. Rawls' adoption of Ackerman's dualist conception of constitutional democracy does not mean that citizenship is exclusively about "re-igniting the radical democratic embers in a just society", but that political and civil rights are separate while having the same origin in popular sovereignty (Chapter 4). This would be Rawls' own brand of liberal republicanism.

I now turn to the second aspect of citizenship, to the way in which the political self is reassessed by Rawls and how rich and complex his view has become as a consequence. The acquisition of political rights has transformed modern identity, and Rawls is particularly attentive to the consequences of this revolution, not simply in terms of the "fact of reasonable pluralism", as we saw (Chapter 4), but also in terms of "pluralism within the self", of the divided self and the new tensions between private and public identities. It is thus clear, for Rawls, that conflicts taking place within contemporary societies also take place *within* the citizens' own selves. As a consequence of their political rights, they have to address and combine two sets of values: personal and political. Some, of course, might not have a comprehensive doctrine at all, or have a null doctrine, such as agnosticism or scepticism (RH: 386, n. 18). Some might not be fully aware of the tensions between the two sets and only eventually acknowledge the ensuing internal conflicts and inconsistencies. It is all part of the modern fragmented identity. The "fact of pluralism" leads to a debate taking place within the self too. Human good is heterogeneous because the aims of the self are heterogeneous. The self is fragmented, divided in the same way as contemporary societies are, for there exists no given unifying belief or norm beyond intersubjective justifications and negotiations. This fact is characteristic of modern identity as analysed, for instance, by Charles Taylor in his book *Sources of the Self*. But the paradox of modern reflexive identity is that it needs a constant dialogue with norms and values to define it. Personal identity is an ongoing process where moral identifications are necessary. This is the main argument of the communitarians against the "unencumbered self" in Rawls (Sandel, 1982), but far from being a criticism, it could help us to understand Rawls' own conception of moral individuality.

The result of political liberalism has been, as we saw, to tend to separate appeals to non-public and public reasons in the political debate (Chapter 4). This leads to unsettling consequences, which reflect the tensions of conflicting identities in contemporary democracies. As Thomas McCarthy writes: "Can individuals reasonably be expected to divorce their private and public beliefs and values to the extent required by an ideal of citizenship which, according to Rawls, demands that we not even vote our conscience on fundamental political issues?" (McCarthy, 1994: 52).

To answer McCarthy's objection, let us go back to the political conception of the person and to how Rawls sees the transformations induced by political autonomy and political rights and the split between the non-public and the public person or citizen. If, as private persons or members of associations or churches, etc., individuals may be defined by their cultural or religious membership, "as citizens, they view themselves as capable of revising and changing (their) conception of the good on reasonable and rational grounds and they may do this if they so desire" (*PL:* 30). This leads to intense conflicts. Two things need to be clarified. First, citizens have a power to distance themselves from their beliefs if they wish to, a power that they do not necessarily have as members of communities, churches or associations. This is a moral and intellectual power: the power of reasoning and of making new decisions on that basis; it is not simply the freedom to choose arbitrarily. This inevitably creates deep contradictions. Secondly, personal and political autonomy are tightly connected and exist together within the self and this, of course, generates major tensions. Rawls is careful not to eliminate these tensions, but also to stress their richness. The conflict between, for instance, personal desires and the freedom or the right to express them is at the heart of the modern condition and of the self-creation of moral individuality in a non-authoritarian democratic context. For Rawls, liberal freedom does not mean permissiveness or the reign of arbitrary desires and the absence of controls, but rather that citizens, being well protected by their rights and wishing to alter their most important ends, see themselves as "self-authenticating sources of valid claims" (*PL:* 32).

Now, what would be his answer to the split between the public and the personal, to McCarthy's objection? In his "Reply to Habermas", Rawls writes that:

> It is left to each citizen, individually or in association with others, to say how the claims of political justice are to be ordered, or weighed, against non-political values. The political conception gives no guidance in such questions, since it does not say how non-political values are to be counted. This guidance belongs to citizens' comprehensive doctrines.   (*RH*: 378–9 and 386–7)

Fragmentation, conflicts and divisions are thus at the centre of democratic individuality. The political conception of the person both acknowledges these conflicts and exacerbates them. Political rights are not simply external to and instrumental in the development of personal ends and commitments. They obviously play a *constitutive* role. Rawls' political conception of the person as citizen describes a moral individuality divided, on the one hand, between valuable inherited historical and personal commitments and, on the other hand, the power that modern political rights have yielded to critically distance oneself and even to rebel against those very crucial commitments. Either emancipation from or acceptance of traditions increasingly becomes a matter of personal responsibility. Far from being an "unencumbered self", the liberal self in Rawls' sense carries too much baggage and is in essence divided. Rawls in reality is very attentive to the divided nature of the self that goes with new rights and possibilities.

These internal conflicts and divisions lead citizens to "think" in a way that traditional communitarian contexts do not favour, and to advance public justifications and reasons for their preferences, as these are not obvious for the rest of society. I would like to suggest that this is why Rawls' central concern is rightly with public justification and citizenship, since these internal conflicts and the necessary validation processes that they call for are precisely the reason why citizens have to "think" reflectively and to search for public justification. There is an organic link between the emergence of political rights and the split nature of the democratic self. Political rights may both create and heal these divisions. It is thus wrong to look at the self of political liberalism as possessing a unity independently of public commitments and citizenship. It does not possess a moral identity anterior to and independent of its political and civil rights and its commitments to other citizens as spelt out in the principles of justice. It is wrong to see it as uncommitted and available for anything or as indifferent and amoral. On the contrary, the self learns to recognize that the weight of its preferences has nothing to do with their psychological intensity, but with their compliance with the principles of justice. This is the deep moral meaning of the demands of the duty of civility.

Rawls has tried first to reconcile liberalism with the demands of justice, beyond the narrow confines of rights-based demands, and then to reconcile civil with political liberties in a conception of citizenship. This is an extremely important move that has brought him closer to a form of liberal republicanism and to a richer conception of the political self, which both reflect his central commitment to autonomy and equal respect for persons.

Notes

Introduction

1. Ben Rogers, Obituary of John Rawls, *The Guardian*, London, 27 November, 2002. See also Thomas Pogge's excellent essay, "A Brief Sketch of Rawls' Life", in Richardson & Weithman (1999) vol. I: 1–15.

2. An exception is a rare interview for *The Harvard Review of Philosophy*, spring 1991, in which he appears in a lovely photograph wearing a Stetson hat, describing in a very personal manner the effects that the Vietnam war and the civil rights movement had on his thinking and on the reception of *A Theory of Justice*. Another characteristic example of his conception of political philosophy is to be found in the Preface to the French translation of 1987. When, asked to indicate for a French audience where he would stand on the political spectrum, he first wrote, in the manuscript version, "Like any political conception, we are likely to see [the conception of justice presented in *A Theory of Justice*] as having a location on the political spectrum. In the United States this conception might be referred to as liberal, or possibly as left liberal; in England more likely as social democrat or perhaps in some ways as Labour. My unfamiliarity with French politics makes me hesitate to suggest how it might be described in France." He then refused to have his personal political views made public as "too pompous" and the original French version was never fully translated in English (*CP*: 415–20). This shows how far he stood from the contemporary ideal of the public intellectual.

3. Interestingly, the 2006 World Bank Report on World Development is entitled "Why does Equity matter?" and dedicates Chapter 4 of Part II to, among others, Rawls' contribution to social justice.

4. On Rawls' increasing influence in Europe, see *The European Journal of Political Theory*, **1**(2), October 2002.

5. On this experience, see "Fifty Years after Hiroshima" in Rawls' *Collected Papers*: 565–72, and the rare interview of Rawls for *The Harvard Review of Philosophy*, spring 1991, vol. 1, no. 1: 38–47, which I mention in note 2.

6. Rawls mentions only once the famous dilemma: is moral philosophy still relevant after Auschwitz and, with typical resilience, writes: "The fact of the

293

Holocaust and our knowledge that human society admits this demonic possibility, however, should not affect our hopes ... for the future of our society ... Otherwise, the wrongful evil, and demonic conduct of others destroys us too and seals their victory. Rather, we must support and strengthen our hope by developing a reasonable and workable conception of political right and justice" (*LOP:* 21–2).

7. Charles Larmore suggests that the American abolitionists along with the more recent civil rights movement have also inspired Rawls (Larmore, 2003: 385).

8. This should be understood as a statement of fact, not a devaluation of politics. See Amy Gutmann's essay, which corrects the misconception according to which Rawls denigrates democracy (Gutmann, 2003: 168) and Joshua Cohen's convincing argument that Rawls' conception of "justice as fairness is a conception for a democratic society" (J. Cohen, 1989: 87).

9. *TJ*: 24. On the critique of the economic theory of democracy, see *TJ*: 316–18 and 431–2.

10. Dworkin in Audard (1988: 40).

11. References to Marx are more abundant in *Justice as Fairness: A Restatement*, where a whole section is dedicated to Marx's critique of liberalism (§52).

12. On the discussion of "formal" equality in the Marxist sense and on the "worth" of basic liberties, see *TJ*: 5 and *JAFR*: 148, where Rawls explicitly asks: "how shall we meet the familiar objection, often made by radical democrats and socialists (and by Marx) that the equal liberties in a modern democratic state are in practice merely formal?" See also *TJ*: 179 and Norman Daniels (1975: 259).

13. The main contemporary debate with Marxism is presented in G. A. Cohen's critique of Rawls (G. A. Cohen, 1995), which I examine at length in Chapter 3, Section 6.

14. The libertarian and free-market critique of distributive justice and of Rawls represented mostly by Robert Nozick (1974), is examined at length in Chapter 3, Section 6.

15. To gain an overall view of the way Rawls' ideas on the welfare state have affected social policies in Europe, see the essays in *The European Journal of Political Theory* 2002, vol. 1(2): Rawls in Europe.

16. My thanks to Stephen Mulhall for insisting that, contrary to what I seem to suggest, Rawls castigates himself for not having made his reasons clearer in *A Theory of Justice*. I agree that this is the case; however, this does not weaken my unifying interpretation, as the last remarks from *TJ*: 513 show.

17. In that, Rawls follows Aristotle's conception of equity in *Nicomachean Ethics*, V, 10, 1137b, and Sidgwick's principle of fairness or equity, as a corrective to mere impartiality and to formal justice (*Methods of Ethics*, III, v, §6). Fairness takes into account specific conditions, either aggravating or attenuating, that bear upon the application of the general law and the search for the common good. Justice as fairness recognizes persons as both equal and different.

18. Intuitionism is the doctrine that rational intuitions, not arguments, offer the only access to independent moral truths. These intuitions cannot be ordered and questions of priority remain. Constructivism is the opposite view, which claims that moral truths are constructed and not derived from independent intuitions. On intuitionism and constructivism in Rawls, see Barry (1989:

274) for whom, clearly, Rawls remains an intuitionist as "considered judgments or considered convictions are in my terms intuitions". It might be helpful to describe Rawls as a "weak" constructivist, given his appeal to considered intuitions.

19. Rorty (1991: 179–84).
20. Freeden (2005: 113); see also Barber (1988); Wolin (1996). A fairly extreme statement of that critique is found in Mouffe (1990: 226): "Rawls' well-ordered society rests on the elimination of the very idea of the political." Finally, John Gray has launched a fierce critique of "the epistemological route to the justification of liberalism" of which Rawls is one of the major figures, a view that echoes the continental criticism of Rawls' failure to understand the political (Gray, 1989: 248).
21. Habermas (1999: chs 2 and 3).
22. See Amy Gutmann (1999) in Richardson & Weithman, vol. 1: 341.
23. See for instance, *JAFR*: 3–4: "Political philosophy has mainly four aims: *practical*; *orientation* or helping people to think of their political and social institutions as a whole; *reconciliation* through rationalisation of our frustration or rage against our society; and *realistically utopian* in probing the limits of political feasibility."
24. Laden (2003: 388).
25. "The theory of justice tries to present a natural procedural rendering of Kant's conception of the kingdom of ends, and of the notions of autonomy and the categorical imperative (§40). In this way, the underlying structure of Kant's doctrine is detached from its metaphysical surroundings so that it can be seen more clearly and presented relatively free from objection" (*TJ*: 233).
26. Ronald Dworkin signals the presence of "a deeper theory" in Rawls' conception and "that the principles of that deeper theory are constitutive of our moral capacity" (1977: 158). See also Larmore (2003 and 1999), for a similar interpretation. Rawls' response is in *TJ*: 513. My own comments on the connection between the "deeper theory" and the public conception of justice are in Chapter 1, Section 3.
27. On the accusation of "philosophical incoherence", see Wenar (2004: 265–7). My answer to such an accusation and the "continuity thesis" that I advocate are developed in Chapter 4, Section 2.
28. See Kant, *On Perpetual Peace*, in Kant (1991: 93–130), and on Kant and Rawls, Höffe (1984).
29. *JAFR*: 4–5 and 13: "justice as fairness is realistically utopian: it probes the limits of the realistically practicable, that is, how far in our world (given its laws and tendencies) a democratic regime can attain complete realization ... democratic perfection, if you like". See also *LOP*: 6–7 and 13: "Here I follow Rousseau's opening thought in *The Social Contract*: "My purpose is to consider if, in political society, there can be any legitimate and sure principle of government, taking men as they are and laws as they might be."
30. The reader will benefit from S. Freeman (ed.): *Cambridge Companion to Rawls* as a precious tool for navigating the way through this literature.
31. "Rawls' writings subsequent to *A Theory of Justice* have helped us realize that we were misinterpreting his book, that we had overemphasized the Kantian and underemphasized the Hegelian and Deweyan elements ... it no longer seems committed to a philosophical account of the human self, but only to a historico-sociological description of the way we live now" (Rorty, 1991: 185).

32. See Bohman & Rehg eds (1997), for a selection of the main views, including Rawls', in that new field.
33. Nussbaum (1999: 424–5). See, as an illustration of this interest, Rawls' *Lectures on the History of Moral Philosophy*, which cover classical texts from Hume, Leibniz, Kant and Hegel. See also his "Themes in Kant's Moral Philosophy" (*CP*: 497–528), and his introduction to the new edition of Sidgwick's *Methods of Ethics*, 1981.
34. R. G. Collingwood, *An Autobiography,* quoted by Jonathan Glover in his book *Humanity* (London: Jonathan Cape, 1999) on the moral history of the twentieth century.

Chapter 1: The primacy of justice

1. "The principles followed by associations and institutions within the basic structure are principles of local justice" (*JAFR*: 11).
2. On the indeterminacy of political concepts, see Freeden (2005).
3. This idea originates in Hobbes and Hume, but is also developed in H. L. A. Hart (1961: 189–95). See Rawls, *TJ*: §22 and *JAFR*: §24.
4. Onora O'Neill (1993: 309) defines Rawls' view as a practical conception of the circumstances of justice when a plurality of persons shares a world. But Rawls, according to her, overestimates the importance of sovereignty and self-sufficiency.
5. Martha Nussbaum bases her criticism of Rawls' limitations on his use of the circumstances of justice. For her, "such an equality assumption requires us to put some important issues of justice on hold. In particular, justice for people with severe mental impairments and justice for nonhuman animals cannot plausibly be handled within a social contract so structured" (2006: 31–2).
6. The "burdens of judgment" weigh on conscientious and sincere attempts to reason with one another as we encounter (a) conflicting and complex evidence; (b) disagreements on the weight of considerations; (c) vagueness of our concepts; (d) differences in personal experiences; (e) difficulty of making overall assessments; (f) nature of political judgements. One could compare these limitations with Michael Freeden's analysis of political concepts and judgements (2005: 123).
7. See Martha Nussbaum (2003: 490–91) and Brian Barry (1995a: §41). I present in more detail the feminist critique of Rawls and its difficulties in Chapter 4.
8. Marx, 1875, *Critique of the Gotha Programme*, I §3. Note that Rawls misquotes him and simply says "from each according to his needs" instead (*TJ*: 268 and n. 32).
9. Henry Sidgwick, *Methods of Ethics* (*ME* hereafter), III, xiii, 3. Note Sidgwick's influence on Rawls.
10. Rawls does not always clearly distinguish criteria and principles. However, as the discussion of the maximin criterion shows (see Chapter 3), this is important for the argument in favour of equality. Examples of criteria that specify the general principle of democratic equality are, for instance, the criterion of maximizing happiness (utilitarian maximax) or of maximizing the worst-off position in society (Rawls' own maximin) or Gauthiers' minimax relative concession (Gauthier, 1986). For a very good presentation, see Joshua Cohen (1989: 280–81).
11. Rawls mentions that his theory could be described as "a theory of moral sentiments" in the sense of the eighteenth century (*TJ*: 44).

12. Marx is critical of the concept of justice itself as a "bourgeois" mystification and, says Rawls, aims at a "society beyond justice" (*TJ*: 249, n. 18).
13. Plato, *Republic*, Book I, 315c, translated by Benjamin Jowett.
14. Barry (1989: 7).
15. Hart (1961: 155). Hart is explicitly quoted by Rawls as his mentor here.
16. "One of the central questions to be asked is whether there is any way in which Rawls' two apparently quite different ideas about justice can be fitted together" (Barry, 1989: 141). See also *ibid*.: 145–52.
17. Scanlon (1982: 116).
18. Another major influence on Rawls has been W. D. Ross's 1930 book: *The Right and the Good*. Interestingly, a similar distinction can be found in Hegel between conceptions of the good or *Sittlichkeit*, and a universal conception of the right or of moral duty as *Moralität*. Habermas (1999: 66) also bases his analysis on a similar distinction between what he calls *ethics*: the conceptions of the good that define communities, and *morality*: the universal conception of justice and rights that regulates any well-ordered society.
19. Rawls, *CP*: 384: "We may view the subjective nature of the utilitarian conception of the good as a way of adapting the notion of the one rational good to the institutional requirements of a modern secular and pluralistic democratic society ... In a democratic society, then, the one good must be conceived as subjective, as the satisfaction of desire or preferences."
20. For Kant, "moral personality" means the status of rational and accountable human beings as moral persons who possess "respect for the moral law as in itself a sufficient incentive of the will" (*Religion within the Limits of Reason Alone*: 27 and 23). Such a person should be treated as an end in herself, not solely as a means. In that sense, a moral person is an *autonomous* being: "A person is subject to no other laws than those he gives to himself " (*Metaphysics of Morals* in Kant, 1991: 223). "Freedom is the basis of our dignity and of right ... the moral law is a law of freedom and our having the capacity to act from that law is the basis of our dignity and makes us a member of the kingdom of ends" (Rawls, *LHMP*: 340).
21. See Sandel (1982) and Mulhall & Swift (1992 and 2003).
22. On Rawls and utilitarianism, see the comprehensive presentation by Samuel Scheffler (2003).
23. First-order desires are directed toward objects of desire, whereas second-order or higher-order desires are directed toward the first ones. See Frankfurt (1971). See Rawls, *TJ:* 163–7 on the absence of first-order desires in classical utilitarianism's conception of the person and *PL*: 74 on citizens' higher-order or fundamental interests.
24. Sidgwick himself confirms Rawls' insight here, when he writes that the higher executive echelon of society should be utilitarian, but that the rest of the population should ignore it (*ME*, IV, v).
25. In *TJ*: §14, Rawls draws useful distinctions between imperfect, perfect and pure procedural justice.
26. The traditional meaning of fairness or equity is exposed in Aristotle, *Nicomachean Ethics*, V, 10, 1137b, and in Sidgwick, *ME*, III, xiii, §3, as a corrective to mere impartiality and to formal justice. Fairness takes into account specific conditions, either aggravating or attenuating, that bear upon the application of the general law.
27. Autonomy is the conception of liberty that insists not only on freedom of choice but also on responsibility for these choices and on the duties that derive from

them. It constitutes the basis for moral dignity and status. To be free is both to be the author and the subject of the moral law, to be bound only by it. Rousseau and Kant are the main philosophers associated with this new view on freedom. Heteronomy is the opposite of autonomy. It means that one's will is subjected to an authority based not on reason, but external to it.

28. Hume, *Treatise*: 477.

29. Rawls quotes Rousseau very often and is obviously inspired by his conception of equality and by his republicanism. See for instance, *JAFR*: 131–2. On Rousseau and Rawls, see Jean Hampton (1980) and Onora O'Neill (2003) among others.

30. Kant (1991: 139).

31. Rational agents have a conception of their own good. Reasonable persons have also a sense of justice, understanding that their pursuit of the good has consequences for fellow citizens and should be constrained (*PL*: II, 1: 48–54).

32. This is made explicit when Rawls asks us to distinguish three points of view: "the point of view of the parties in the original position, the point of view of citizens in a well-ordered society, and the point of view of you and me who are setting up justice as fairness as a political conception and trying to use it" (*JAFR*: 45, n. 8; *PL*: 28). This means that the separation from reality is the most useful aspect of the theory that allows us to use it as a tool or a method for understanding ourselves and assessing our institutions from a distance.

33. Dworkin (1977: 157–8).

34. On Rawls' constructivism, see Barry (1989: 264–82), O'Neill (1989 and 2003), Brink (1987), Hill Jr (1989) and McCarthy (1994).

35. "Tho' the rules of justice be artificial, they are not arbitrary." Hume, *Treatise*: III ii 1: 484.

36. Note, for instance, the reference to Marx in the choice of the basic structure as the subject of justice (*TJ*: 229).

37. *LOP*: 3, n. 2: "Decent societies or peoples are well ordered but non-democratic and non-liberal. They still satisfy essential conditions such as respect for basic human rights, a decent consultation hierarchy, recognition of a right to dissent, etc."

38. On "common good ideas of justice" and on their role in decent societies, see *LOP*: 71 and n. 10.

39. Barry (1995a: 214). Amy Gutmann too insists that "the most specific change that Rawls has brought is the integration of social criticism into liberal theory … his liberalism pays tribute to the socialist critique". See Gutmann in Richardson & Weithman (1999, vol. I: 16–20). In *LHMP*, Rawls writes that "*A Theory of Justice* follows Hegel in this respect when it takes the basic structure of society as the *first* subject of justice" (*LHMP*: 366).

40. This shift toward institutions is attributed to the influence on Rawls of Hart's lectures in Oxford in 1952–3.

41. Rawls often quotes Rousseau's formula: "Men as they are, and institutions as they might be" (*Social Contract*, 1968: 49) to mean that human laws, not human nature can be changed (*LOP*: 7 and 13). Thus attention should focus on the social conditions that can be transformed: "the social system is not an unchangeable order beyond human control but a pattern of human action" (*TJ*: 88).

42. Bernard Williams (1985) mounts a fierce but interesting attack against Rawls and moral philosophers' intrusion into ethics and public culture.

43. But note that in *JAFR*: 8, "the socialist critique of liberal constitutional democracy" is mentioned among the different political conceptions at stake.
44. See Tan (2004: 75) on the communitarian shift in Rawls.
45. *JAFR*: 1: "the practical role of political philosophy arises from divisive political conflict and the need to settle the problem of order".
46. On the Rational and the Reasonable and Rawls' critique of David Gauthier's contractarianism, see *PL*: 51–3 and *JAFR*: 82, n. 2: "Here I correct a remark in *TJ*: §3, where it is said that the theory of justice is a part of the theory of rational choice [decision]. This is simply a mistake and would imply that justice as fairness is at bottom Hobbesian rather than Kantian ... The theory of rational choice is itself part of a political conception of justice, one that tries to give an account of reasonable principles of justice. There is no thought of deriving these principles from the concept of rationality as the sole normative concept."
47. This debate on the relation between personal and institutional ethics is crucial for the credibility of Rawls' conception of justice as, without the corresponding motivations, there is very little chance that the principles of justice will ever be put in practice. See Barry (1989: ch. 6), Van Parijs (1993: 311) and G. A. Cohen (1995: 180–85).
48. Gauthier (1986).
49. This is a very controversial point well picked up by Schopenhauer in his critique of Kant's dualism.
50. The mediation of law between politics and morality is the major theme of Habermas' book, *Between Facts and Norms* (1996), which addresses Rawls' failure to satisfactorily connect the two in *A Theory of Justice*.
51. On Rawls' philosophy of history, see Müller (2006).

Chapter 2: Constructing the principles of justice

1. Note that in *Political Liberalism*, he changes his view and says that "the main principles are present in the leading traditional theories ... from the tradition of moral and *political* philosophy" (*PL*: 294, emphasis added). It is important to remember that Rawls comes from a tradition where political philosophy was nearly extinct and where the distance between moral principles and the violence of political life as the competitive struggle for power was underestimated, except by realists such as Joseph Schumpeter. He has to re-create the whole new concept of *normative* political philosophy, which now seems so familiar to us because of his pioneering work.
2. This is the question asked persuasively and in a very sympathetic way by Joshua Cohen (2003: 102–3 and 130–31). The answer he suggests is that, for Rawls, political theory cannot ultimately replace political judgement (2003: 128); it can aim solely at enhancing the self-esteem and competence of the average citizen (2003: 110). This is a view I share when I suggest that citizens' empowerment is the main aim of political philosophy for Rawls.
3. A similar doubt was raised by H. L. A. Hart (1975: 252) when he said that "the apparent dogmatic course of Rawls' argument for the priority of liberty may be explained by the fact that ... he does harbour a latent ideal of his own ... of a public-spirited citizen who prizes political activity and service to others as among the chief goods of life".
4. Analysing Rawls' method of reflective equilibrium, T. M. Scanlon notes the tension between a descriptive and a deliberative interpretation of the method

and claims that "in the descriptive interpretation, the method of reflective equilibrium does not seem to be a method of justification" (Scanlon, 2003: 143). This duality is obvious too in the method of the Original Position. Rawls himself advances a conception of the moral theorist as both an observer and someone who practises a self-analysis of her own particular moral conception (*CP*: 288).

5. See *A Theory of Justice*: §43 on socialism. The discussion of Rawls' egalitarianism has been characteristic of the Marxist and socialist critiques as well as of libertarianism. I present the debate in Chapter 3 when I examine Rawls' Pareto argument for inequality. Equally, Rawls' liberal egalitarianism has been influential for European socialism. See the special issue on Rawls in Europe of the *European Journal of Political Theory* (2002: vol. 1, no. 2).

6. By social values, here, Rawls means the primary goods that are the *distribuandum* in his conception of distributive justice. I introduce the full analysis of the primary goods in Chapter 3, Section 2. On the definition of primary goods see *TJ*: §15 and *PL*: V.

7. Among the many critics of the hypothetical contract, see Dworkin (1977: ch. 6).

8. In particular, Brian Barry's insistence that Rawls' conception of justice as reciprocity and of society as a cooperative venture excludes individuals who are not in a situation to cooperate or reciprocate is misplaced (Barry, 1989: 244 and Kymlicka, 1990: 91–2 n. 5). We should underline that this is a general conception of justice and that special cases need different principles and conceptions.

9. Note that Rawls, like many authors, does not distinguish between freedom and liberty. See Q. Skinner on Hobbes in Skinner (1998: 17, n. 53).

10. Other formulations have included the following: *TJ*: 266 and *CP*: 227. "Each person has an equal right to the most extensive scheme of equal basic liberties compatible with a similar scheme for all" (*CP*: 392; *PL*: 291 and VIII: §8). "Each person has an equal right to a fully adequate scheme of equal basic rights and liberties, which scheme is compatible with a similar scheme for all" (*JAFR*: 42). The quantitative criterion is no longer satisfactory following Hart's criticism (*PL*: 331).

11. On basic needs, see *JAFR*: 47, n. 7 and Peffer (1990: 14).

12. Ackerman & Alstott (1999); Ackerman & Fishkin (2004).

13. *PL*: lviiif.

14. On human rights, Rawls says that there are two ways of drawing up their list, historical and analytical, and that "justice as fairness follows this traditional view" (*JAFR*: 45).

15. See *PL*: 300 for a distinction between the conceptions of the good expressed in the Declaration of the Rights of Man, and a political conception of justice. "This conception is not to be mistaken for an ideal of personal life or ... an ideal for members of some association, much less as a moral ideal such as the Stoic idea of a wise man."

16. For Philip Pettit: "John Rawls manifests a concern for liberty as non-interference, for example, when he writes, 'liberty can be restricted only for the sake of liberty'. Rawls' assumption is that law always represents a restriction of liberty, and reveals a conception of liberty that is directly continuous with that of Hobbes and Bentham" (1997: 50). I take the view that this interpretation is wrong, and that Rawls' concern for equality is not instrumental for liberty, but a moral concern for equal respect for persons more characteristic of the republicanisms of Rousseau and Kant.

17. See Laden (2003) for an excellent account of the standard view of Rawls and of its shortcomings.
18. See Van Parijs (2003: 224–6).
19. Rawls here is influenced by Bruce Ackerman's dualist conception of political power as the constituent power of We, the People, on the one hand, and the ordinary political power of governments, officials, etc., on the other hand (Ackerman: 1991). For further developments, see Rawls' "Reply to Habermas" in *PL*: 405–6.
20. See Amy Gutmann: "Basic to the ideal of democracy is equal political liberty... the question is whether Rawls's political liberalism devalues equal political liberty by subordinating it to equal personal liberty" (2003: 169). For an extensive presentation of the debate on democracy and liberalism, see below, Chapter 4. For a general introduction to the contemporary debate, see Zacharia (2003).
21. On the impossibility of the liberal Paretian, see Sen & Williams (1982: 7), who note the incompatibility between the Pareto principle and even a minimal assignment of individual rights. See also Van Parijs (2003: 224–6), Rawls (*CP*: 372, n. 1), and Nozick (1974: 164–6).
22. On the difference principle, see Van Parijs' illuminating essay in Freeman (2003: 200–40). The meaning of this rather puzzling expression is given by Rawls (*CP*: 163), in the following way: "All differences in wealth and income, all social and economic equalities, should work for the good of the least favoured. For this reason, I call it the difference principle." One could also connect it with the traditional meaning of fairness or equity as exposed in Aristotle, *Nicomachean Ethics*, V, 10, 1137b, and Sidgwick, *ME*, Bk III, xiii, §3, as a corrective to mere impartiality.
23. See G. A. Cohen for a formulation of the socialist principle that requires that the surplus generated by the more talented should be equally redistributed, not simply improve the situation of the worse off (G. A. Cohen, 1995: 172–5 and n. 37).
24. See Kymlicka (1990: 70–6) for a criticism of Rawls' justification of the inequalities generated by natural abilities. I develop Kymlicka's views as well as Nozick's and G. A. Cohen's critiques of Rawls' egalitarianism in Chapter 3, Section 6.
25. "A rational person does not suffer from envy. He is not ready to accept a loss for himself if only others have less as well" (*TJ*: 124). Irrational envy blurs the distinction between unjustified inequalities that raise legitimate feelings of envy and resentment, and justified inequalities that should not be a cause for envy in a rational person. It is thus extremely important to define justified inequalities and have them publicly recognized as such. This is the condition for social stability and for avoiding alienation.
26. For the debate with Nozick and with libertarians see, *JAFR*: §15, 53, n. 19, and 83, where Rawls recognizes that the libertarian principles could possibly be added to the list, but does not explain why.
27. Note, however, that this makes it more difficult to understand why, in *PL*: 229, social and economic rights are not treated by Rawls as constitutional essentials. On that see, Fabre (2000).
28. Daniels (2003: 250–51).
29. *Ibid.*
30. On complex equality, see *ibid.*: 251–2.
31. For a stimulating presentation of the debate between "luck-egalitarians" who concentrate mostly on justice as compensation for natural disadvantages and

undeserved bad luck, and democratic equality in the sense of Rawls, see Anderson (1999: 289) and Baynes (2006).

32. On the distinction between self-respect and self-esteem, see Sachs (1981). On self-respect as the most important social primary good, see *TJ*: §67 and my comments below in Chapter 3.

33. See, on the politics of recognition, Taylor (1994), Honneth (1995), and Fraser & Honneth (2003).

34. Margalit (1996).

- 35. Scheffler (2003: 449): "to accept a holistic account of justice is to acquiesce in an erosion of the status of the individual which is one of the most striking features of modern life".

36. "Justice as Fairness" (*CP*: 47–72) is a very important paper for understanding the meaning of fairness and why this is missing in utilitarianism. "Fairness is the elimination of arbitrary distinctions and the establishment, within a practice, of a proper balance of claims … It is the concept which relates to right dealing between persons who are cooperating with or competing against one another as when one speaks of fair games" (*CP*: 48 and 59). There, he presents his difference principle as a modification of the utility principle with the added condition that "every party must gain from the inequality" (*CP*: 50).

37. In contrast, Rawls seems to recognize that justice as fairness might be seen as a natural rights doctrine: "Justice as fairness is more deeply embedded in the first principles of the ethical theory. This is characteristic of natural rights views (the contractarian tradition) in comparison with the theory of utility" (*TJ*: 28 and n. 16). But, in *JAFR*: 9, he claims that the two are distinct and to share utilitarianism's critique of natural rights doctrines.

38. See *CP*: 33, n. 21: "The utilitarian principle was quite naturally thought of, and used, as a criterion for judging social institutions (practices) and as a basis for urging reforms."

39. Hare (1973: 82).

40. Singer (1975).

41. This *experientialist* and cardinal conception of utility has famously been criticized by Nozick (1974: 42–5) in his experience machine, which shows that virtual satisfaction could replace actual satisfaction without any consequences for the principle! The most common form of utilitarianism, in contrast, is *preferentialist* and ordinal: utility is not a measure of subjective satisfaction, but is represented by the way preferences or choices are ranked by individuals (*TJ*: 143).

42. Harsanyi (1982: 47): "Each individual has two very different sets of preferences… personal preferences which are expressed in his utility function Ui … and moral preferences … expressed in his social-welfare function Wi."

43. Sidgwick, *ME*, Bk III, ch. xiii, §3.

44. See Sen's similar example: "if person A as a cripple gets half the utility that the pleasure-wizard person B does from any given level of income, then in the pure distribution problem between A and B the utilitarian would end up giving the pleasure-wizard B more income than the cripple B. The cripple would then be doubly worse off: both since he gets less utility from the same level of income and since he will also get less income" (Sen, 1987: 145).

45. Two extreme examples of this sacrificial aspects are: Helvetius' *De l'Esprit*, 1758, Discours II, ch. 6: 83–4, and William Goodwin on Fénelon and his valet, in *Enquiry Concerning Political Justice*, 1793, II, ii.

46. Rawls' position is to be found in *PL*: 16–17 and n. 18: "Brian Barry thinks that justice as fairness hovers uneasily between impartiality and mutual advantage." See Gibbard (1991) and Barry (1995a: ch. 3).

47. For a full discussion of constructivism as opposed to intuitionism, see *PL*: Lecture III, "Political Constructivism", O'Neill (2003), and below, Chapters 3 and 4.

48. Habermas (1996: ch. 2).

49. Bentham in Parekh, 1973: 151. On sanctions, see Bentham (1948:147): "There are four distinguishable sources from which pleasure and pain are in use to flow: the physical, the political, the moral and the religious ... they may all of them be termed sanctions ... a sanction is a source of obligatory powers or motives." On Bentham's use of sanctions and "interest-and-duty-junction-principle", see Harrison (1983: 111).

Chapter 3: Defending democratic equality: The argument from the Original Position

1. See, for instance, Dworkin (1977), in particular ch. 6; Larmore (2003: 383). Rawls' answer to Dworkin's objections is in "Justice as Fairness, Political not Metaphysical", *CP*: 400–401.

2. See Gauthier (1986).

3. I disagree here with interpretations that see OP as dead and redundant for various reasons. Another common criticism that I examine is that OP is contradictory with the principles it defends. See G. A. Cohen (1995), and K. Baynes' answer (2006).

4. On these distinctions, see above, Chapter 1, Section 1, Rawls, *CP*: 190–224 and *PL*: 16–17 and 50, Barry (1995a: ch. 3), and Gibbard (1991).

5. For a formulation, among others, of this widespread worry, see Sen (1987: 143): "I find the lure of the original position distinctly resistible since it seems very unclear what precisely would be chosen in such a situation. It is also far from obvious that prudential choice under *as if* uncertainty provides an adequate basis for moral judgment."

6. On the difference between practical and theoretical reason, see Rawls' *LHMP*: Lectures on Kant: 217–19. "The procedure of construction is based essentially on practical and not on theoretical reason. Following Kant's way of making the distinction, we say that practical reason is concerned with the production of objects according to a conception of these objects – for instance the production of a just constitutional regime taken as the aim of political endeavour – while theoretical reason is concerned with the knowledge of given objects" (*PL*: 93 and 117).

7. This point clearly shows practical, not simply theoretical reason at work here. The confusion entertained by Rawls in *A Theory of Justice* between them is eventually lifted, showing that the aim of *A Theory of Justice* is not theoretical, in spite of its title, but practical. See my Introduction. See also *Political Liberalism*: 53, n. 7.

8. *Ibid.*: 306, n. 21: "I hope that this will prevent several misinterpretations of this position, that it is intended to be morally neutral, or that it models only the notion of rationality ... that justice as fairness attempts to select principles of justice purely on the basis of a conception of rational choice as understood in economics or decision theory. For a Kantian view, such an attempt is out of the question and is incompatible with its conception of the person." In *A*

Theory of Justice, Rawls gives some indications of what he means by the kind of Cartesian justification that he rejects, but on the whole, he was not clear enough (*TJ*: 506–7).

9. See Rawls on Kant's categorical imperatives in *LHMP*: 162–216.

10. On the distinction, see *CP*: 250; *TJ*: 126, 153–4, and *JAFR*: 103.

11. *TJ*: §4. Reflective equilibrium complements the OP procedure that is not sufficient on its own. See below, Section 6.

12. On the three ideas of justification in Rawls: OP, reflective equilibrium and public reason, see Scanlon (2003) and below, Section 6 and Chapter 4, Section 4.

13. On Rawls' OP and deliberative democracy, see J. Cohen (2003: 100–103), and below, Section 6.

14. Onora O'Neill: "The principles of justice are constructed using OP, but OP itself only receives a coherentist justification ... whereas in *PL* we have a more narrow scope of justification" (2003: 349 and 357). On justification see also, Scanlon (2003).

15. *TJ*: 105: "We should strive for a kind of moral geometry"; *JAFR*: 133–4 and 82–3: "We should like the argument from OP to be a deductive one ... But the principles of justice agreed to are not deduced from the conditions of OP."

16. The perfect example of theoretical reason applied to normative choice is Gauthier (1986). See Rawls' discussion of Gauthier in *PL*: 52–3.

17. *PL*: 15–22, where the two normative ideas are introduced.

18. On comprehensive doctrines, see *PL*: 11–14. On pluralism as part of the circumstances of justice, see *JAFR*: 84: "We take pluralism to be a permanent feature of a democratic society and view it as characterising what we may call the subjective circumstances of justice."

19. The best advocate of the impartial spectator as a method for defining the moral point of view in a rational manner is Harsanyi (1982: 39–40).

20. Braithwaite (1955), criticized by Rawls in *TJ*: 116, n. 10.

21. Public reason first appears in *PL:* VI and is developed in IPRR (1997). See below, Chapters 4 and 5. See also the debate with Habermas on the public use of reason (Habermas, 1999: ch. 2).

22. Sidgwick, *ME*: IV, v.

23. Note that Rawls here follows Rousseau, who was equally concerned with neutralizing contingencies and bargaining advantages during the process leading to agreement on the social contract and included a equivalent of the veil of ignorance: "From the deliberations of a people properly informed, and provided its members *do not have any communication among themselves*, the great number of small differences will always produce a general will and the decision will always be good" (*Social Contract*, Bk II, ch. 3, emphasis added).

24. Harsanyi (1982) suggests a "thin" veil of ignorance as a condition for moral choices.

25. See in particular Habermas (1999: 57).

26. *PL*: 383, n. 14.

27. See *TJ*: §44: "the difference principle does not hold for the question of justice between generations" (*TJ*: 254), and *JAFR*: 159–60 and n. 39. See also Van Parijs (2003: 209–10).

28. See Sen (1993: 40, n. 30), on the pitfalls of "commodity fetishism" in the concern for basic needs.

29. Compare *TJ*: 79, *PL*: 308–9 and *JAFR*: 58.

30. Sen's criticism insists that Rawls should have considered human diversity more closely and has not avoided the "fetishism of commodities", not paying

enough attention to the relationship between persons and goods (Sen, 1987: 155–8). Similar criticisms that rights cannot be possessed like *things* can be found in Young (1990: 25) and Habermas (1999: 54–6).

31. Sachs (1981) raised an important point, that Rawls confuses self-respect and self-esteem, the latter being more dependent on social validation and less compatible with personal autonomy, to which Rawls responds in *PL*: 404, n. 39.

32. On gender, see *TJ*: §16: 85 and *JAFR*: 64–6. Inequalities related to gender belong to the partial (or non-ideal) theory of justice as civil disobedience and conscientious refusal to serve in an unjust war. So it is not a fault, but a deliberate omission from the agenda of the theory. See also below, Chapter 4 on *Political Liberalism* and the feminist critique. On race, see the discussion of Barry's example in *JAFR*: 69–72: "the difference principle does not appeal to the self-interest of those particular persons or groups identifiable by their proper names." Again, it is not what you are, Indians or British, women or men, whites or blacks, that counts, that is decisive for the second principle, but what you do. One could object to Rawls a form of abstraction and universalism that is totally unacceptable in view of historic injustices and the politics of recognition and identities. See below, Chapter 4, on citizenship and identities.

33. Note that the least fortunate cannot be defined as a particular individual and that proper names cannot be used.

34. See Laden (2003) for a good presentation of the mainstream interpretation of OP.

35. On the various primary goods and their measurement, see Van Parijs (2003: 213).

36. Rawls applies Pareto optimality to social choices, not to individual decisions and calls it a principle of allocative efficiency (*TJ*: 58). He insists that the concept has no normative force: not all efficient distributions are just or fair and they need normative conditions to qualify them (*TJ*: 104). See Van Parijs (2003: 207).

37. For a vindication of the maximin as a proper moral argument fit for a democratic context, see J. Cohen (1989).

38. In a zero-sum game, the maximin is the best strategy that leads to the least worst scenario. But in a non-zero-sum game and with n players, it loses its meaning.

39. Harsanyi advances an *equiprobability* model of moral judgement, in which persons make moral judgements behind a "thin" veil of ignorance: they ignore their position in society and make their choice assuming that they have an equal probability of occupying any place in the distribution. This compares with Rawls' "thick" veil of ignorance where the parties also ignore their specific conception of the good and their particular interests, but, in contrast, they assume that their worst enemy might assign their place to them (Harsanyi, 1982: 45–7).

40. The detailed answer to Harsanyi is in *JAFR*: §31.

41. On the confusion between DP and the maximin rule, see *TJ*: 72–3 and *JAFR*: 94–5. "The widespread idea that the argument for DP depends on extreme aversion to uncertainty is a mistake" (*JAFR*: 43, n. 3).

42. For a detailed analysis, see Van Parijs' ranking (2003: 203–6), which takes into account the positions of both the least fortunate and of the more fortunate.

43. *Ibid.*: 207

44. G. A. Cohen (1995 and 2000), Anderson (1999), and Baynes (2006), for a robust treatment of Cohen's criticisms.
45. Note that the criticism is directed at Brian Barry and his notion of two conceptions of justice, mutual advantage and impartiality, whereas Rawls never makes such a contrast and works with a complex concept of justice as mutual advantage (prudential), reciprocity (societal) and impartiality (moral). See above, Chapter 1, Section 1.
46. On the place of utilitarianism in an overlapping consensus over justice, see Scheffler (2003: 451).
47. See *JAFR*: 107: "we would be cheered if utilitarians can find from within their point of view, a way to endorse the ideas and principles of justice as fairness ... they can join an overlapping consensus on that conception".
48. Van Parijs (2003: 200).
49. This is Hart's criticism in Daniels (1975). It is based on the confusion between criterion and principle, and on a misunderstanding of OP.
50. See Van Parijs (2003) for a complete assessment of the difference principle.
51. Rawls has corrected this earlier formulation, which no longer appears in the revised edition of *A Theory of Justice* in 1999.
52. This is the Kantian conception of autonomy which colours Rawls' analysis of moral personality. It is clear that in Rawls' highly idealistic view of democracy, fundamental rights and liberties allow citizens a life of dignity where they are fully autonomous, in contrast to any other political regime. This is the liberal principle of legitimacy, that citizens should be recognized not only as free to choose, but also as autonomous and responsible for themselves and their choices.
53. On Rawls and Hegel's conception of civil society, see *PL*: §10: 285.
54. Rawls refers to Mill: "As Mill would say, we may seek to make our conception of the good our own; we are not content to accept it ready-made from our society or social peers" (*PL*: 313).
55. However, a defence of the difference principle based on the stability argument, but with no appeal to the OP, is possible, according to writers worried that choices under such conditions of extreme uncertainty as those created by the veil of ignorance are impossible to make.
56. Habermas (1999: 83–6).

Chapter 4: Pluralism and political consensus: The argument for political liberalism

1. On the principle of legitimacy, see RH: 393, and on legitimacy and justice, RH: 427–33.
2. In *PL*: 374, n. 1, Rawls notes that political liberalism seems to be a new doctrine without predecessors. He mentions as his closest contemporaries Charles Larmore (1990), Judith Shklar (1989), Bruce Ackerman (1980) and Joshua Cohen (1989/1997). Anthony Laden (2006) suggests that republicanism is, in reality, the antecedent of political liberalism.
3. See, among others, Daniels (1975), Wolff (1977). The main revisions from 1975 are listed in the preface for the revised edition of *A Theory of Justice*. They are the new accounts of liberty in ch. 2 and of its priority in ch. 9, of primary goods in chs 2 and 7, and of the idea of the person and of OP in ch. 3, of the just savings principle in ch. 5, of property-owning democracy and the capitalist welfare state in ch. 5.

4. See, among others, Hamlin & Pettit (1991): "The rediscovery of normative political analysis is one of the intellectual events of the last quarter-century ... a growing interdisciplinary concern ... with all questions concerning the nature of the good polity ... associated particularly with the work of John Rawls" (1991: vii).

5. As we saw in Chapter 3 with G. A. Cohen's critique of the Pareto argument for inequality. But note that the criticism was raised immediately in Wolff (1977).

6. But not to Nozick (1974), who is never mentioned!

7. See Mulhall & Swift (2003: 485, n. 7).

8. Rawls mentions the main protagonists: Sandel, Taylor and Walzer only once each in *Political Liberalism* and in *The Law of People*. It is obvious for him that Sandel's interpretation is based on a serious confusion between the parties in OP, who can be described as "unencumbered selves", and the moral conception of the person, which is built into the choice conditions of OP (see above, Chapter 3). In that sense, it was not worth a serious debate.

9. This shift has been labelled by some a "communitarian shift". It concerns not only the conception of domestic, but also of international justice. See for instance Tan (1998 and 2004: 75): "Rawls's rejection of cosmopolitanism to my mind reveals a fundamental shift in his political philosophy."

10. See Taylor (1994), Honneth (1995) and Fraser & Honneth (2003) on the politics of recognition.

11. *Political Liberalism* includes a revised version of the 1980 Dewey Lectures (Lectures I–III), the 1978 paper, "The Basic Structure as Subject" (Lecture VII), which in part answers the libertarian critique, the 1981 response to Hart, "The Basic Liberties and their Priority" (Lecture VIII). The important 1985 paper, "Justice as Fairness: Political not Metaphysical", constitutes Lecture I. The 1987 paper, "The Overlapping Consensus", is Lecture IV, followed by the 1988 paper, "Priority of Right and Ideas of the Good", which makes up Lecture V. Only Lecture VI on the idea of public reason is new in *Political Liberalism*. All the papers of that period (1978–89) find their place in *Political Liberalism*, except for the 1982 paper, "Social Unity and Primary Goods", which finds its way into the 1999 revised edition of *A Theory of Justice*. Due to that origin in a series of papers, the book probably lacks clarity and the argument is weakened, which explains why it was not so well received. The best presentation of the new ideas in *Political Liberalism* is to be found in the 1996 introduction for the paperback edition. I hope that the new interpretation that I advance concerning the consistency of the theory in *A Theory of Justice* and *Political Liberalism*, will help overcome some of these difficulties.

12. Rorty writes: "Rawls' writings subsequent to *A Theory of Justice* have helped us realize that we were misinterpreting his book, that we had overemphasized the Kantian and underemphasized the Hegelian and the Deweyan elements ... Rawls is not interested in conditions for the identity of the self, but only in conditions for citizenship in a liberal society" (Rorty, 1991: 185, 189). Habermas (1999: 60) expresses the opposite view that "Rawls has not become a contextualist".

13. For a clear and concise account of the fact of reasonable pluralism, see *Political Liberalism*: introduction to the paperback edition: §3–4.

14. Compare with Habermas on replacing universal with discursive/deliberative reason (1999: ch. 1).

15. *JAFR*: 154, n. 29. See also Larmore (1996: ch. 7, "Pluralism and Reasonable Disagreement").

16. See, for instance, Stuart Hampshire (1978, 1983 and 1999); on "agonistic liberalism", John Gray (1989: ch. 10; and 1995: 111–35). Rawls' answer is in IPRR: 141, n. 26, and in his "Reply to Habermas", *PL*: 425. See also J. Cohen (1994).

17. This is a very important point that has far-reaching consequences, for instance, for our understanding of the concept of the nation, in terms of political, not cultural, membership. Compare with Habermas' conception of "constitutional patriotism". See also Tamir (1993).

18. For a list of predecessors, see *PL*: 374, n. 1. For the relationship between political liberalism and republicanism, see Laden (2006).

19. Freeman (2003: 281–3; *JAFR*: §55; *PL*: IV, 2).

20. See Thomas McCarthy (1994), for a useful distinction inspired by Habermas, between acceptance of the principles of justice as fairness, which is an *empirical* concern, and acceptability, which is a *moral* one. Rawls is obviously concerned with making justice as fairness acceptable to a majority of citizens, not with its empirical acceptance. He is criticized for not having sufficiently clarified this point.

21. See Dreben (2003: 318).

22. See Kant, "The Idea for a Universal History", in Kant (1991).

23. *TJ*: 15. For an excellent presentation of the congruence argument in *A Theory of Justice*, chs 8 and 9, see Freeman (2003: 277–315).

24. See *ibid.*: 281–3.

25. *TJ*: 340; *CP*: 1985, 1987, 1989; *PL*: IV; *JAFR*: §§11 and 58.

26. For Barry, for instance, "the idea of overlapping consensus is thoroughly misconceived" (Barry, 1995b: 914).

27. See Sandel (1994: 1777).

28. See Macedo (1995: 494).

29. Larmore (2005: 75–6). See also Habermas (2006).

30. See Macedo (1995: 481).

31. For a recent addition to this debate, see Thomas Nagel's review article of Michael Sandel's latest book, *Public Philosophy*, in *The New York Review of Books*, 25 May 2006.

32. Taylor (1994).

33. Compare with Greenawalt (1995) and Fullinwinder (1995). See Larmore (2003: 381 and n. 11), on Québec and multiculturalism as not incompatible with Rawls' *Political Liberalism*. OC does not lead to the avoidance of all controversial political debates such as slavery as Sandel claims: 1996: 21–3. See Rawls' reply in IPRR: 609–10. Basic justice takes precedence over civil peace.

34. See Villa (2001) on Arendt and Socratic examination.

35. For a thorough analysis of Rawls' and Habermas' different conceptions of public reason, see McCarthy (1994). For an illuminating analysis of public reason and of the role of fairness in it, see Larmore (2003).

36. Note the difference between the restricted view of PR and the wider or inclusive view in IPRR: 584, 591–2 and in *PL*: Preface, 1996. See also Larmore (2003: 387). For Larmore, Rawls confuses two forms of public debate: open discussion and decision-making (Larmore, 2003: 382).

37. Kant, "An Answer to the Question: What is Enlightenment?" (1784) in Kant (1991). See also O'Neill (1989: 48–50) and Rawls (*PL*: 213, n. 2 and 296, n. 13).

38. *Critique of Pure Reason*, N. Kemp Smith trans., A738/B766: 593 and A752/B/780: 603.

39. For a thorough review of Rawls' constitutional essentials, see Michelman (2003).
40. See Ackerman (1991) and *PL*: 405, n. 40.
41. IPRR: 132–3.
42. See also *PL*: li–lii, and n. 25: "This is more permissive than *PL* VI: 8 ... and what it refers to is the inclusive view."
43. IPRR: 144.
44. If following Tocqueville, Rawls praises the way the American people have so far sustained religious peace thanks to the First Amendment, we know that the balance is fragile. For a good contrast, see the French situation where the 1905 law on the separation of church and state has meant the imposition of secular values in the political realm, exactly what *Political Liberalism* rejects! Pluralism, not secularization, is the true democratic form of tolerance.
45. Rawls never uses the term for his own political liberalism; however, he sees no incompatibility between them.
46. On Rawls' reception in Germany and Habermas' role, see Müller (2002). He notes an interesting rapprochement from both sides: "whereas Habermas has become more Kantian, Rawls has become more Hegelian." (2002: 170).
47. "Habermas' own doctrine, I believe, is one of logic in the broad Hegelian sense: a philosophical analysis of the presupposition of rational discourse (of theoretical and practical reason) which ... is metaphysical" (*PL*: 378–79).
48. See *IO*: ch. 1, for a short presentation of discourse ethics as a normative ground for the authority of the law, morality and justice.
49. McCarthy (1994: 61).
50. *IO*: 86.
51. On recognition, see for instance Honneth (1995).
52. MacCarthy (1994: 49).
53. *IO*: 83.
54. *Ibid*.
55. On republicanism, see Pettit (1997) and Skinner (1998).
56. There is a different political and legal tradition in Germany where civil rights and liberties are treated as *subjective* rights in the sense of personal as opposed to political liberties. For liberals, in contrast, these liberties are the liberties of the Moderns, that is the result of modernity, of the Scottish Enlightenment and of the Industrial Revolution of the eighteenth century, of the creation of a personal sphere that was unknown to the early-modern republican tradition. Hence the disconcerting vocabulary, for liberals, that is used by Habermas in his discussion. The canonical text in the liberal tradition on the historical and conceptual distinctions between civil liberties and political rights is Marshall (1950, 1977).
57. See Ackerman (1991).
58. By procedural, Habermas here does not mean not pure procedural justice in Rawls' sense, but the general processes of public deliberations that characterizes a deliberative democracy. He tends to oppose procedural and substantive in a way that is criticized by Rawls.
59. See also Michelman's formulation, cited by Rawls, *PL*: 407, n. 44.
60. It is thus that, even if on a personal ethical level, one disapproves of abortion, one may consent to it as one of the rights derived from the human right to determine what affects one's own body. A citizen is someone who is capable of reasoning as follows: can the right, which I myself refuse to exercise, become a protected constitutional right? Does this right go against not simply my own

convictions or interests, but the representation of myself as a responsible member of a fair society?

61. Amy Gutmann notes that "remarkably little has been written on the relationship between liberalism and democracy in the theory ... whereas it has a lot to say about the ideal of free and equal citizens" (Gutmann, 2003: 168–9). I follow slightly different lines of argument here, but insist too that democratic citizenship figures high in Rawls' preoccupations.

62. See Baynes (2006) and Lehning (1994); Williams (1985); Barry (1995b) and Estlund (1996).

63. See the excellent review by Martha Nussbaum in Freeman (2003), and Okin (1989) for a presentation of the potential of Rawls' theory for liberal feminism.

64. Okin (1989) and Nussbaum (2000 and 2006).

65. Laden (2006).

Chapter 5: A reasonable law of peoples for a real world

1. See Charles Beitz: "The Law of Peoples is not to be confused with the *jus gentium*: it is not a body of principles universally accepted by states, nor is it intended necessarily to constitute a reasonable basis for the cooperation of all existing states" (2000, n. 3 and 676–7).

2. On Rawls' social holism, see Pettit (2005 and 2006).

3. An excellent guide to reading Rawls' *The Law of Peoples* is Reidy & Martin (2006). Martha Nussbaum's *Frontiers of Justice* is also essential reading (chs 4 and 5) as is Pogge (1989 and 2002).

4. For a presentation of current trends in international relations theory and of the influential role of Rawls' theory of justice, see Brown (2002: 167–8).

5. The *Westphalian* system of states is the international legal system that grew out of the Peace of Westphalia of 1648. It is based on the economic and political autonomy of equal sovereign states within their borders in contrast to the empires that had dominated in Europe. There is widespread consensus that this system ended after World War II with the establishment of international institutions that control economic fluxes and prevent intra-state conflicts and wars by restricting states' sovereignty. The creation of the European Union and the proliferation of transnational institutions are other factors of the apparent demise of the Westphalian system. See, among others, Buchanan (2000: 701).

6. The main point of contention, as we shall see, is that a global principle is not respectful of peoples' autonomy and own choices concerning their development.

7. Barry (1991), Beitz (1979 and 2000), Buchanan (2000), Pogge (1989 and 2002) and Tan (2004).

8. See Taylor (1996).

9. See Audard (2006) for an analysis of the ethnocentric dimensions of *The Law of Peoples* and of Rawls' reply to this charge.

10. On the "closed" or "bounded" society in Rawls, see O'Neill (1994).

11. Buchanan (2000: 697).

12. *Ibid.*: 700–1.

13. Barry (1989: 193, and 1995a: chs 2 and 3).

14. See Pogge (1989 and 2002) and Beitz (1979 and 2000).

15. See Reidy's summary of the exception of the Law of Nations (2004: 292–3).

16. See Max Weber's definition of the state as having the monopoly of legitimate violence over its territory. Even a state that uses this violence in a reasonable and measured manner is still not a moral agent whereas a people that exercises self-determination has necessarily a moral obligation not to harm or destroy itself.

17. Hoffmann (1995: 54). "This overlapping consensus is really just a *modus vivendi* among quite different models of society."

18. On Rawls' holistic conception of justice, see Scheffler (2003: 449); see also references to Hegel in *LOP*: §9.2, 73, n. 13.

19. See Beitz (2000: 684).

20. See Pettit (2006).

21. Kant (1991: 90 and 49).

22. Kant refers to the peaceful federation of states as *foedus amphyctionum* (*ibid.*: 47), and also as *foedus pacificum* (*ibid.*: 104). The latter expression is mentioned by Rawls, *LOP*: 10. The discussion of cosmopolitan justice and Rawls' objections to it is in §11.1 and §16.3.

23. Tan (1998 and 2004: 75).

24. Rousseau, *Social Contract* (1762: ch. 5, 10–11). "There will always be a great difference between subduing a multitude and ruling a society. Even if scattered individuals were successively enslaved by one man, however numerous they might be, I still see no more than a master and his slaves, and certainly not a people and its ruler." The problem is that "people" has at least two meanings: political and sociological. It does not denote any kind of human grouping but essentially one where the value of autonomy is affirmed. For Rousseau, peoples and republics were the same. Rawls seems to share this view, which excludes any kind of "nationalism" in the usual sense. But, at the same time, he includes non-democratic peoples in the category and this is where the difficulty starts.

25. Buchanan (2000: 700–1).

26. See Barry (1995a: 214).

27. On boundaries and transnational justice in Rawls, see O'Neill (1994).

28. For a more detailed discussion, see Audard (2006).

29. In *LOP*: 50, Rawls gives a detailed account of both conditions in a domestic liberal situation. But how might this apply to a non-liberal situation where these institutional conditions do not obtain? We are left with only subjective conditions, beliefs and allegiances, and this is where the argument is failing. Only moral domination can make up for the missing democratic institutions. This gives strength to the cosmopolitan view that only democratic regimes can be the basis for real stability and peace in international relations.

30. On these alternatives to Rawls' overlapping consensus, see Arnsperger & Picavet (2004: 167–204).

31. On the question of stability, see also *PL*: 142–3 and *LOP*: 44–5. *PL*: xix: "the problem of stability has played very little role in the history of moral philosophy". It is surprising that Rawls does not seem aware that, as stability is a political/social problem, involving analysis of historical forces at work, and not simply a theoretical problem, it cannot be solved at the level of moral first principles. What is even more confusing is that stability seems to be a property not only of political societies, but also of the conceptions of justice at work themselves. This is why the nature of the question of stability, and peace at the international level, is still unresolved in *The Law of Peoples*. Rawls looks at the question of stability only from the subjective point of view, that of the

allegiances or beliefs that sustain a conception of justice. He does not take into account the objective social and historical forces at work.

32. Tan (1998: 289).

33. On the "divided self", see Galston (2001: 153), and his critique of Rawls, especially of his conception of individuality: "Persons must be emotionally, intellectually and ontologically capable of drawing an effective line between their public and non-public identities … but this excludes individuals and groups that do not place a high value on personal autonomy." The same must be assumed of non-liberal peoples in their exchanges with the liberal Society of Peoples, and this is highly problematic as basic human rights allowing these choices and critical reflections are non-existent in non-democratic societies.

34. Beitz (1999: 137). This is commented upon by Rawls in *LOP*: 116–20.

35. Pogge (2002: 32–3).

36. On the "capabilities approach", see above, Chapter 3 on primary goods and capabilities, and on its application to international redistribution, see Nussbaum (2006).

37. "In liberal peoples … citizens are united by what Mill called 'common sympathies'" (*LOP:* 23 and n. 17).

Conclusion: Beyond liberalism

1. Habermas (1999: 101) and ch. 9: "Three Normative Models of Democracy".

2. On classical or neo-roman republicanism, see Pettit (1997) and Skinner (1998).

3. Dagger (1997: 187) finds Rawls' distinction questionable as it is not clear that classical republicanism is no less a teleological comprehensive doctrine than civic humanism and is thus equally incompatible with political liberalism. Pettit also claims that republicanism is mostly a teleological conception that considers freedom from domination as the dominant end that both the state and the body politic have to implement (Pettit, 1997: 97–102). In that sense, Rawls could not be republican.

Bibliography

An excellent comprehensive bibliography can be found in S. Freeman (ed.), *The Cambridge Companion to Rawls*, Cambridge: Cambridge University Press, 2003.

Rawls' main works

A Theory of Justice, revised edition with a new preface of the 1975 revised text which has been used for all translations, Oxford: Oxford University Press, 1971 and 1999.

Political Liberalism, revised paperback edition with a new preface and "The Reply to Habermas", New York: Columbia University Press, 1993 and 1996.

The Law of Peoples, with "The Idea of Public Reason Revisited", Cambridge, MA: Harvard University Press, 1999.

Collected Papers, edited by Samuel Freeman, Cambridge, MA: Harvard University Press, 1999.

Lectures on the History of Moral Philosophy, edited by Barbara Harman, Cambridge, MA: Harvard University Press, 2000.

Justice as Fairness: A Restatement, edited by Erin Kelley, Cambridge, MA: Harvard University Press, 2001.

Books and collections of articles on Rawls

Audard, C. (ed.). 1988. *Individu et justice sociale: Autour de John Rawls*. Paris: Le Seuil.

Audard, C. (ed.). 2005. *John Rawls*. Paris: Presses Universitaires de France.

Barry, B. 1973. *The Liberal Theory of Justice*. Oxford: Oxford University Press.

Baynes, K. 1992. *The Normative Grounds of Social Criticism: Kant, Rawls and Habermas*. Albany, NY: SUNY Press.

Blocker, H. G. & Smith, E. H. (eds). 1980. *John Rawls's Theory of Social Justice*. Athens, OH: Ohio University Press.

Daniels, N. (ed.). 1975. *Reading Rawls*. Oxford: Blackwell.

Freeman, S. (ed.). 2003. *The Cambridge Companion to Rawls*. Cambridge: Cambridge University Press.

Kukatas, C. & Pettit, P. 1990. *Rawls: An Interpretation and Defence of Justice as Fairness*. Stanford, CA: Stanford University Press.

Kymlicka, W. 1990. *Contemporary Political Philosophy*. Oxford: Clarendon Press.

Pogge, T. 1989. *Realizing Rawls*. Ithaca, NY: Cornell University Press.

Reidy, D. A. & Martin, R. (eds) 2006. *Rawls's Law of Peoples: A Realistic Utopia*. Oxford: Blackwell.

Richardson, H. S. & Weithman, P. J. (eds). 1999. *The Philosophy of John Rawls: A Collection of Essays* in 5 volumes. New York: Garland:
    Volume I: *Developments and Main Outlines of Rawls's Theory of Justice*
    Volume II: *The Two Principles and Their Justification*
    Volume III: *Opponents and implications of A Theory of Justice*
    Volume IV: *Moral Psychology and Community*
    Volume V: *Reasonable Pluralism*

Wolff, R. P. 1977. *Understanding Rawls*. Princeton, NJ: Princeton University Press.

Ethics, 1989, **99**(4): Symposium on Rawlsian Theory of Justice: Recent Developments: 699–944.

Ethics, 1994, **105**(1): Symposium on John Rawls.

Ratio Juris, 1995, **8**(1): Consensus and Democracy, A Debate on John Rawls.

European Journal of Political Theory, 2002, **1**(2): Rawls in Europe.

The Harvard Review of Philosophy, 2003, **XI**: John Rawls Remembered.

La Revue Internationale de Philosophie, 2006, **60**(237): John Rawls.

References

Ackerman, B. 1980. *Social Justice in the Liberal State*. New Haven, CT: Yale University Press.

Ackerman, B. 1991. *We, the People, I: The Foundations of American Democracy*, and 1998, *II: Transformations*. Cambridge, MA: Harvard University Press.

Ackerman, B. & Alstott, A. 1999. *The Stakeholder Society*. New Haven, CT: Yale University Press.

Ackerman, B. & Fishkin, J. S. 2004. *Deliberation Day*. New Haven, CT: Yale University Press.

Anderson, E. 1999. "What is the Point of Equality?", *Ethics* **109**(2): 287–337.

Arnsperger, C. & Picavet, E. 2004. "More than modus vivendi, less than overlapping consensus", *Social Science Information* **32**(2): 167–204.

Audard, C. 1995. "The Idea of Public Reason", *Ratio Juris* **8**(1): 15–29.

Audard, C. 2002. "Rawls in France", *European Journal of Political Theory* **1**(2): 215–27.

Audard, C. 2006. "Cultural Imperialism and 'Democratic Peace' ". In *Rawls's Law of Peoples*, D. Reidy & R. Martin (eds). Oxford: Blackwell, 59–75.

Barber, B. 1988. *The Conquest of Politics*. Princeton, NJ: Princeton University Press.

Barry, B. 1989. *Theories of Justice*. Brighton: Harvester Wheatsheaf.

Barry, B. 1995a. *Justice as Impartiality*. Oxford: Oxford University Press.

Barry, B. 1995b. "John Rawls and the Search for Stability", *Ethics* **105**(4): 874–915.

Barry, B. 2001. *Culture and Equality*. Cambridge: Polity.

Baynes, K. 1992. *The Normative Grounds of Social Criticism*. Albany, NY: SUNY Press.

Baynes, K. 2006. "Ethos and Institution: On the Site of Distributive Justice", *Journal of Social Philosophy* **37**: 184–98.

Beitz, C. 1979 and 1999. *Political Theory and International Relations*. Princeton, NJ, Princeton University Press.

Beitz, C. 2000. "Rawls' Law of Peoples", *Ethics* **110**(4): 669–96.

Benhabib, S. 1992. *Situating the Self*. Cambridge: Polity.

Bentham, J. 1948. *A Fragment on Government* [1776] with *An Introduction to the Principles of Morals and Legislation* [1789], W. Harrison (ed.). Oxford: Blackwell.

Berlin, I. 1969. *Four Essays on Liberty*. Oxford: Oxford University Press.

Berlin, I. 1990. *The Crooked Timber of Humanity*. London: John Murray.

Bohrman, J. & Rehg, W. (eds). 1997. *Deliberative Democracy*. Cambridge, MA: MIT Press.

Braithwaite, R. 1955. *Theory of Games as a Tool for the Moral Philosopher*. Cambridge: Cambridge University Press.

Brink, D. O. 1987. "Rawlsian Constructivism in Moral Theory", *Canadian Journal of Philosophy* **17**(1): 71–90.

Brown, C. 2002. *Sovereignty, Rights and Justice*. Cambridge: Polity.

Buchanan, A. 2000. "Rawls's Law of Peoples: Rules for a Vanished Westphalian World", *Ethics* **110**(4): 697–721.

Cohen, G. A. 1995. "The Pareto Argument for Inequality", *Social Philosophy and Policy* **12**(1): 160–85.

Cohen, G. A. 1997. "Where the Action Is: On the Site of Distributive Justice", *Philosophy and Public Affairs* **26**(1): 3–30.

Cohen, G. A. 2000. *If You're an Egalitarian, How Come You're So Rich?* Cambridge, MA: Harvard University Press.

Cohen, J. 1989. "Democratic Equality", *Ethics* **99**: 727–51.

Cohen, J. 1993. "Moral Pluralism and Political Consensus". In *The Idea of Democracy*, D. Copp, J. Hampton & J. Roemer (eds). Cambridge: Cambridge University Press.

Cohen, J. 1997. "Deliberation and Democratic Legitimacy". In *Deliberative Democracy*, J. Bohrman & W. Rehg (eds). Cambridge, MA: MIT Press.

Cohen, J. 2003. "For a Democratic Society". In Freeman (ed.) (2003): 86–138.

Dagger, R. 1997. *Civic Virtues*. Oxford: Oxford University Press.

Daniels, N. 1975. "Equal Liberty and Unequal Worth of Liberty". In Daniels (ed.) (1975): 253–81.

Daniels, N. 2003. "Rawls' Complex Egalitarianism". In Freeman (ed.) (2003): 241–76.

Darwall, S. 1976. "A Defense of the Kantian Interpretation", *Ethics* **86**: 164–70.

Dreben, B. 2003. "On Rawls and Political Liberalism". In Freeman (ed.) (2003): 316–46.

Dworkin, R. 1977. *Taking Rights Seriously*. London: Duckworth.

Dworkin, R. 1988. "L'impact de la théorie de Rawls sur la pratique et la philosophie du droit". In Audard (ed.) (1988): 37–53.

Estlund, D. 1996. "The Survival of Egalitarian Justice in John Rawls's *Political Liberalism*", *Journal of Political Philosophy* **4**(1): 68–78.

Estlund, D. 1998. "Liberalism, Equality and Fraternity in Cohen's Critique of Rawls", *Journal of Political Philosophy* **6**(1): 99–112.

Fabre, C. 2000. *Social Rights under the Constitution: Government and the Decent Life*. Oxford: Oxford University Press.

Frankfurt, H. 1971. "Freedom of the Will and the Concept of a Person", *Journal of Philosophy* **68**(1): 5–20.

Fraser, N. & Honneth, A. 2003. *Redistribution or Recognition?* London: Verso.

Freeden, M. 2005. "What Should the 'Political' in Political Theory Explore?", *Journal of Political Philosophy* **13**(2): 113–34.

Fullinwinder, R. K. 1995. "Citizenship, Individualism and Democratic Politics", *Ethics* **105**(3): 497–515.

Galston, W. 1995. "Two Concepts of Liberalism", *Ethics* **105**(3): 516–34.

Galston, W. 2001. *Liberal Purposes*. Cambridge: Cambridge University Press.

Gauthier, D. 1986. *Morals by Agreement*. Oxford: Oxford University Press.

Gibbard, A. 1990. *Wise Choices, Apt Feelings*. Oxford: Clarendon Press.

Gray, J. 1989. *Liberalisms*. London: Routledge.

Gray, J. 1995. "Agonistic Liberalism", *Social Philosophy and Policy* **12**(1): 111–35.

Greenawalt, K. 1995. *Private Conscience and Public Reasons*. Oxford: Oxford University Press.

Gutmann, A. 1989. "The Central Role of Rawls' Theory", *Dissent*: 338–42; reproduced in Richardson & Weithman (1999), vol. I: 16–20.

Gutmann, A. 2003. "Rawls on the Relationship between Liberalism and Democracy". In Freeman (ed.) (2003): 168–99.

Habermas, J. 1996. *Between Facts and Norms: Contributions to a Discourse Theory of Law and Democracy*, W. Rehg (trans.). Cambridge, MA: MIT Press (*Faktizität und Geltung*, Frankfurt: Suhrkamp, 1992).

Habermas, J. 1999. *The Inclusion of the Other*, C. Cronin (trans.). Cambridge: Polity (*Die Einbeziehung des Anderen*, Frankfurt: Suhrkamp, 1996).

Habermas, J. 2006. "Religion in the Public Sphere", *European Journal of Philosophy* **14**(1): 1–25.

Halévy, É. 1955. *The Growth of Philosophical Radicalism* [1901]. Boston, MA: Beacon Press.

Hamlin, A. & Pettit, P. (eds). 1991. *The Good Polity*. Oxford: Blackwell.

Hampton, J. 1980. "Contracts and Choices: Does Rawls have a Social Contract Theory?", *Journal of Philosophy* **77**(6): 315–38.

Hampshire, S. (ed.). 1978. *Public and Private Morality*. Cambridge: Cambridge University Press.

Hampshire, S. 1983. *Morality and Conflict*. Oxford: Blackwell.

Hampshire, S. 1999. *Justice is Conflict*. London: Duckworth.

Hare, R. 1975. "Rawls' Theory of Justice". In Daniels (ed.) (1975): 81–107.

Harrison, R. 1983. *Bentham*. London: Routledge.

Harsanyi, J. 1976. "Can the Maximin Principle Serve as a Basis for Morality?". In *Essays on Ethics, Social Behavior and Scientific Explanation*. Dordrecht: Reidel.

Harsanyi, J. 1982. "Morality and the Theory of Rational Behaviour". In Sen & Williams (eds) (1982): 39–62.

Hart, H. 1961. *The Concept of Law*. Oxford: Clarendon Press.

Hart, H. 1975. "Rawls on Liberty and its Priority". In Daniels (ed.) (1975): 230–52.

Hill, T. Jr 1989. "Kantian Constructivism in Ethics", *Ethics* **99**: 752–70.

Hindess, B. 2005. "The Globalization of Citizenship". In *Challenging Citizenship*, Sor-hoon Tan (ed.). Aldershot: Ashgate, 63–74.

Höffe, O. 1984. "Is Rawls's Theory of Justice Really Kantian?", *Ratio* **26**: 104–24.

Hoffman, S. 1995. "Dreams of a Just World", *New York Review of Books* **42**: 52–7.

Honneth, A. 1995. *The Struggle for Recognition*, J. Anderson (trans.). Cambridge: Polity (*Kampf zur Anerkennung*, Frankfurt: Suhrkamp, 1992).

Hume, D. 1978. *Treatise of Human Nature* [1740]. Oxford: Oxford University Press.

Kant, I. 1960. *Religion within the Limits of Reason Alone* [1793], T. M. Greene & H. Hudson (trans.). New York: Harper & Row.

Kant, I. 1976. *Critique of Practical Reason* [1788], L. W. Beck (trans.). Indianapolis, IN: Bobbs-Merrill.

Kant, I. 1978. *Critique of Pure Reason* [1781], N. Kemp Smith (trans.). London: Macmillan.

Kant, I. 1991. *Political Writings*, H. Reiss (ed.). Cambridge: Cambridge University Press.

Laden, A. S. 2003. "The House that Jack Built", *Ethics* **113**(2): 367–90.

Laden, A. S. 2006. "Republican Moments in Political Liberalism", *Revue Internationale de Philosophie*, forthcoming.

Larmore, C. 1990. "Political Liberalism", *Political Theory* **18**(3): 339–60.

Larmore, C. 1996. *The Morals of Modernity*. Cambridge: Cambridge University Press.

Larmore, C. 1999. "The Moral Basis of Political Liberalism", *Journal of Philosophy* **96**(12): 599–625.

Larmore, C. 2003. "Public Reason". In Freeman (ed.) (2003): 368–93.

Larmore, C. 2005. "Respect for Persons", *The Hedgehog Review*. Charlottesville, VA: University of Virginia Press.

Lehning, P. 1994. "The Idea of Public Reason", *Ratio Juris* **8**(1): 30–39.

Macedo, S. 1995. "Liberal Civic Education and Religious Fundamentalism: The Case of God v. John Rawls?", *Ethics* **105**(3): 468–96.

McCarthy, T. 1994. "Kantian Constructivism and Reconstructivism: Rawls and Habermas in Dialogue", *Ethics* **105**(1): 44–63.

Margalit, A. 1996. *The Decent Society*. Cambridge, MA: Harvard University Press.

Marshall, T. H. 1950. *Citizenship and Social Classes*. Cambridge: Cambridge University Press.

Marshall, T. H. 1977. *Class, Citizenship and Social Development*. Chicago, IL: University of Chicago Press.

Michelman, F. 2003. "Rawls on Constitutionalism and Constitutional Law". In Freeman (ed.) (2003): 394–425.

Mill, J. S. 1969. *Utilitarianism* [1861]. In *The Collected Works of J. S. Mill*, vol. X, J. M. Robson (ed.). London: Routledge.

Mill, J. S. 1973. *System of Logic, Book VI* [1843]. In *The Collected Works of J. S. Mill*, vol. VIII, J. M. Robson (ed.). London: Routledge.

Miller, D. 1996. "Two Cheers for Meritocracy", *Journal of Political Philosophy* **4**(4): 277–301.

Mouffe, C. 1990. "Rawls: Political Philosophy without Politics". In *Universalism vs. Communitarianism*, D. Rasmussen (ed.). Cambridge, MA: MIT Press (217–35).

Mulhall, S. & Swift, A. 1992. *Communitarians and Liberals*. Oxford: Blackwell.

Mulhall, S. & Swift, A. 2003. "Rawls and Communitarianism". In Freeman (ed.) (2003): 460–87.

Müller, J.-W. 2002. "Rawls in Germany", *European Journal of Political Theory* **1**(2): 163–79.

Müller, J.-W. 2006. "Rawls, Historian: Remarks on Political Liberalism's 'Historicism' ", *Revue Internationale de Philosophie* **60**: 327–38.

Nagel, T. 1991. *Equality and Partiality*. Oxford: Oxford University Press.

Nozick, R. 1974. *Anarchy, State and Utopia*. Oxford: Blackwell.

Nussbaum, M. 1999. "Conversing with the Tradition: John Rawls and the History of Ethics", *Ethics* **109**(2): 424–30.

Nussbaum, M. 2000. *Women and Human Development*. Cambridge: Cambridge University Press.

Nussbaum, M. 2003. "Rawls and Feminism". In Freeman (ed.) (2003): 488–520.

Nussbaum, M. 2006. *Frontiers of Justice*. Cambridge, MA: Harvard University Press.

Okin, M. S. 1989. *Justice, Gender and the Family*. New York: Basic Books.

Okin, M. S. 1994. "Political Liberalism, Justice and Gender", *Ethics* **105**: 23–43.

O'Neill, O. 1989. *Constructions of Reason*. Cambridge: Cambridge University Press.

O'Neill, O. 1993. "Justice, Gender and International Boundaries". In *The Quality of Life*, M. Nussbaum & A. Sen (eds). Oxford: Oxford University Press.

O'Neill, O. 1994. "Justice and Boundaries". In *Political Restructuring in Europe: Ethical Perspectives*, C. Brown (ed.). London: Routledge, 69–88.

O'Neill, O. 2000. *Bounds of Justice*. Cambridge: Cambridge University Press.

O'Neill, O. 2003. "Constructivism in Kant and Rawls". In Freeman (ed.) (2003): 347–67.

Parekh, B. (ed.). 1973. *Bentham's Political Thought*. London: Croom Helm.

Peffer, R. G. 1990. *Marxism, Morality and Social Justice*. Princeton, NJ: Princeton University Press.

Pettit, P. 1997. *Republicanism*. Oxford: Oxford University Press.

Pettit, P. 2005. "Rawls's Political Ontology", *Politics, Philosophy and Economics* **4**: 157–74.

Pettit, P. 2006. "Rawls's Peoples". In *Rawls's Law of Peoples*, D. Reidy & R. Martin (eds). Oxford: Blackwell, 38–55.

Pogge, T. 2002. *World Poverty and Human Rights*. Cambridge: Polity.

Pogge, T. 2006. "Do Rawls's Two Theories of Justice Fit Together?". In *Rawls's Law of Peoples*, D. Reidy & R. Martin (eds). Oxford: Blackwell, 206–25.

Raz, J. 1986. *The Morality of Freedom*. Oxford: Clarendon Press.

Reidy, D. 2004. "Rawls on International Justice: A Defence", *Political Theory* **32**(3): 291–319.

Rorty, R. 1991. *Objectivity, Relativism and Truth*. Cambridge: Cambridge University Press.

Ross, W. D. 1930. *The Right and the Good*. Oxford: Clarendon Press.

Rousseau, J.-J. 1968. *Social Contract* [1762], M. Cranston (trans.). Harmondsworth: Penguin.

Sachs, D. 1981. "How to Distinguish Self-Respect from Self-Esteem", *Philosophy and Public Affairs* **10**(4): 22–36.

Sandel, M. 1982. *Liberalism and the Limits of Justice*. Cambridge: Cambridge University Press.

Sandel, M. 1994. "Political Liberalism: A Review of Rawls's Political Liberalism", *Harvard Law Review* **107**(7): 1765–94.

Sandel, M. 1998. "Religious Liberty: Freedom of Choice or Freedom of Conscience". In *Secularism and its Critics*, R. Bhargava (ed.). Oxford: Oxford University Press, 73–93.

Sandel, M. 2006. *Public Philosophy: Essays on Morality and Politics*. Cambridge, MA: Harvard University Press.

Scanlon, T. 1982. "Contractualism and Utilitarianism". In Sen & Williams (eds) (1982): 103–28.

Scanlon, T. 2003. *What We Owe to Each Other*. Cambridge, MA: Harvard University Press.

Scanlon, T. 2006. "Rawls on Justification". In Freeman (ed.) (2003):139–67.

Scheffler, S. 2003. "Rawls and Utilitarianism". In Freeman (ed.) (2003): 426–59.

Sen, A. 1970. "The Impossibility of a Paretian Liberal", *Journal of Political Economy* **78**: 152–7.

Sen, A. 1975. "Rawls versus Bentham". In Daniels (ed.) (2003): 283.

Sen, A. 1987. "Equality of What?" (1979 Tanner Lecture). In *Liberty, Equality and Law*, S. McMurrin (ed.). Cambridge: Cambridge University Press, 137–62.

Sen, A. 1993. "Capability and Well-being". In *The Quality of Life*, M. Nussbaum & A. Sen (eds). Oxford: Clarendon Press, 30–54.

Sen, A. & Williams, B. (eds). 1982. *Utilitarianism and Beyond*. Cambridge: Cambridge University Press.

Shklar, J. 1989. "The Liberalism of Fear". In *Liberalism and the Moral Life*, N. Rosenblum (ed.). Cambridge, MA: Harvard University Press.

Sidgwick, H. 1981. *Methods of Ethics* [1874], 7th edition with a preface by John Rawls. Indianapolis, IN: Hackett.

Singer, P. 1975. *Animal Liberation*. New York: Avon Books.

Skinner, Q. 1985. *The Return of Grand Theory in the Human Sciences*. Cambridge: Cambridge University Press.

Skinner, Q. 1998. *Liberty before Liberalism*. Cambridge: Cambridge University Press.

Tamir, Y. 1993. *Liberal Nationalism*. Oxford: Oxford University Press.

Tan, K.-C. 1998. "Liberal Toleration in Rawls's Law of Peoples", *Ethics* **108**(2): 276–95.

Tan, K.-C. 2004. *Justice without Borders*. Cambridge: Cambridge University Press.

Taylor, C. 1985. *Philosophical Papers*, vol. 2. Cambridge: Cambridge University Press.

Taylor, C. 1989. *Sources of the Self*. Cambridge, MA: Harvard University Press.

Taylor, C. 1994. "The Politics of Recognition". In *Multiculturalism*, A. Gutmann (ed.). Princeton, NJ: Princeton University Press.

Taylor, C. 1996. "Modes of Secularism". In *Secularism and its Critics*, R. Bhargava (ed.). Oxford: Oxford University Press, 31–53.

Van Parijs, P. 1993. "Rawlsians, Christians and Patriots: Maximin Justice and Individual Ethics", *European Journal of Philosophy* **1**(3): 309–42.

Van Parijs, P. 2003. "Difference Principles". In Freeman (ed.) (2003): 200–40.

Villa, D. 2001. *Socratic Citizenship*. Princeton, NJ: Princeton University Press.

Walzer, M. 1983. *Spheres of Justice*. Oxford: Martin Robertson.

Weber, M. 1946. *Politics as Vocation: From Max Weber, Essays in Sociology* [1918], H. H. Gerth & C. W. Mills (trans.). New York: Oxford University Press.

Wenar, L. 2004. "The Unity of Rawls's Work", *Journal of Moral Philosophy* **1**(3): 265–75.

Williams, B. 1985. *Ethics and the Limits of Philosophy*. London: Fontana.

Wolin, S. 1996. "The Liberal/Democratic Divide: On Rawls' Political Liberalism", *Political Theory* **24**(1): 97–119.

Young, I. M. 1990. *Justice and the Politics of Difference*. Princeton, NJ: Princeton University Press.

Zacharia, F. 2003. *The Future of Freedom*. New York: Norton.

Index